GRENADIER グレネーダー

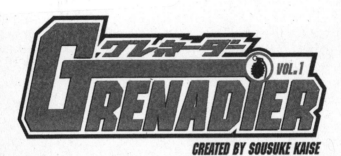

VOL. 1

CREATED BY SOUSUKE KAISE

TOKYOPOP®

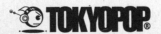

HAMBURG // LONDON // LOS ANGELES // TOKYO

Grenadier Vol.1
Created by Sousuke Kaise

Translation - Nan Rymer
English Adaptation - Terry Atkins
Associate Editor - Peter Ahlstrom
Retouch and Lettering - Ethan Russell
Production Artist - Erika Terriquez
Graphic Designer - Kyle Plummer

Editor - Alexis Kirsch
Digital Imaging Manager - Chris Buford
Production Manager - Elisabeth Brizzi
Managing Editor - Sheldon Drzck
VP of Production - Ron Klamert
Editor in Chief - Rob Tokar
Publisher - Mike Kiley
President and C.O.O. - John Parker
C.E.O. and Chief Creative Officer - Stuart Levy

A  Manga

TOKYOPOP Inc.
5900 Wilshire Blvd. Suite 2000
Los Angeles, CA 90036

E-mail: info@TOKYOPOP.com
Come visit us online at www.TOKYOPOP.com

GRENADIER Vol 1© SOUSUKE KAISE 2003
First published in Japan in 2003
by KADOKAWA SHOTEN PUBLISHING CO., LTD., Tokyo.
English translation rights arranged with
KADOKAWA SHOTEN PUBLISHING CO., LTD., Tokyo
through TUTTLE-MORI AGENCY, INC., Tokyo.
English text copyright © 2006 TOKYOPOP Inc.

ISBN: 1-59816-623-9

First TOKYOPOP printing: August 2006
10 9 8 7 6 5 4 3 2 1
Printed in the USA

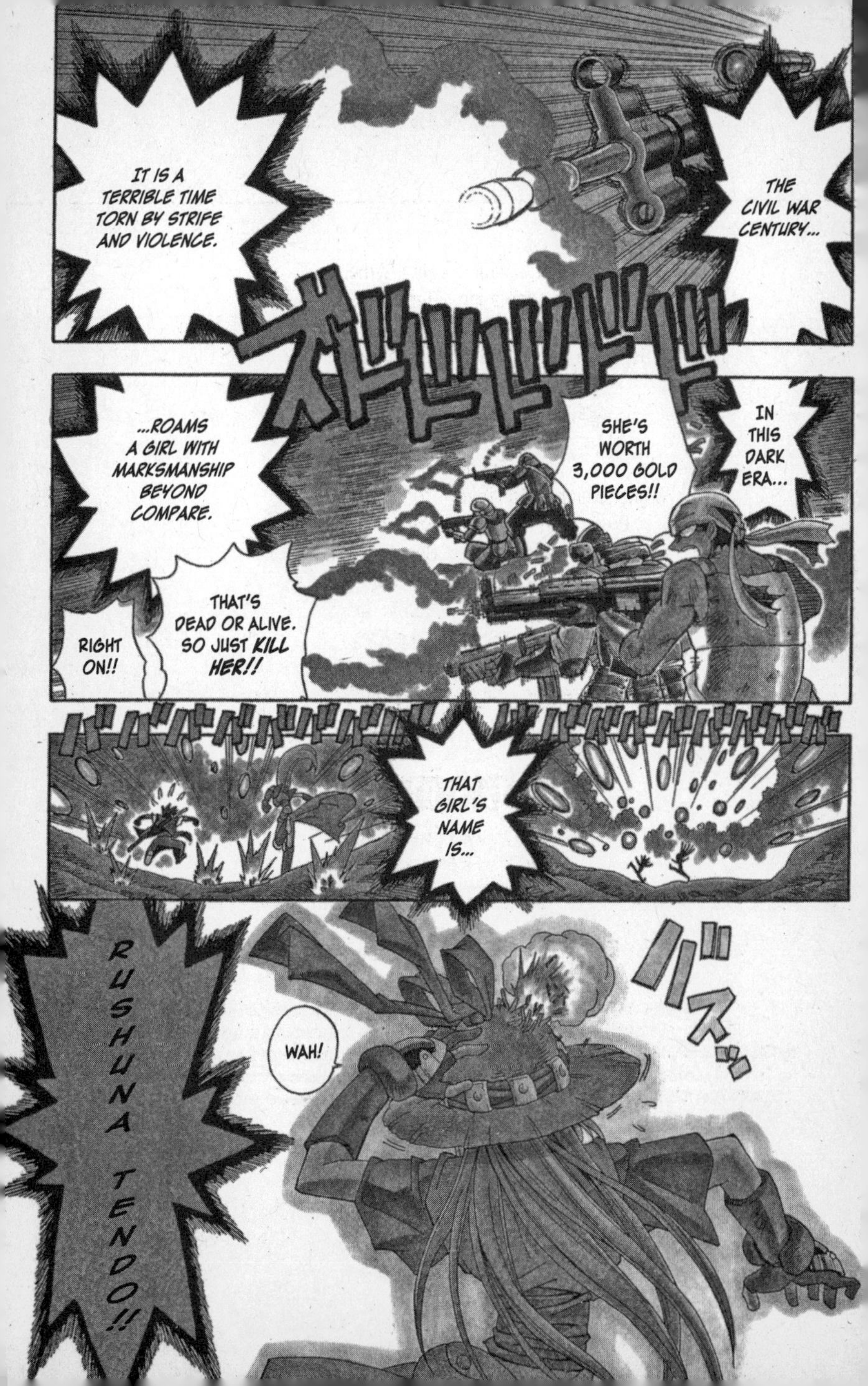
THE CIVIL WAR CENTURY...
IT IS A TERRIBLE TIME TORN BY STRIFE AND VIOLENCE.
IN THIS DARK ERA...
...ROAMS A GIRL WITH MARKSMANSHIP BEYOND COMPARE.
SHE'S WORTH 3,000 GOLD PIECES!!
THAT'S DEAD OR ALIVE. SO JUST KILL HER!!
RIGHT ON!!
THAT GIRL'S NAME IS...
RUSHUNA TENDOU!!
WAH!

GRENADIER

THE GOLDEN-HAIRED SENSHI #1

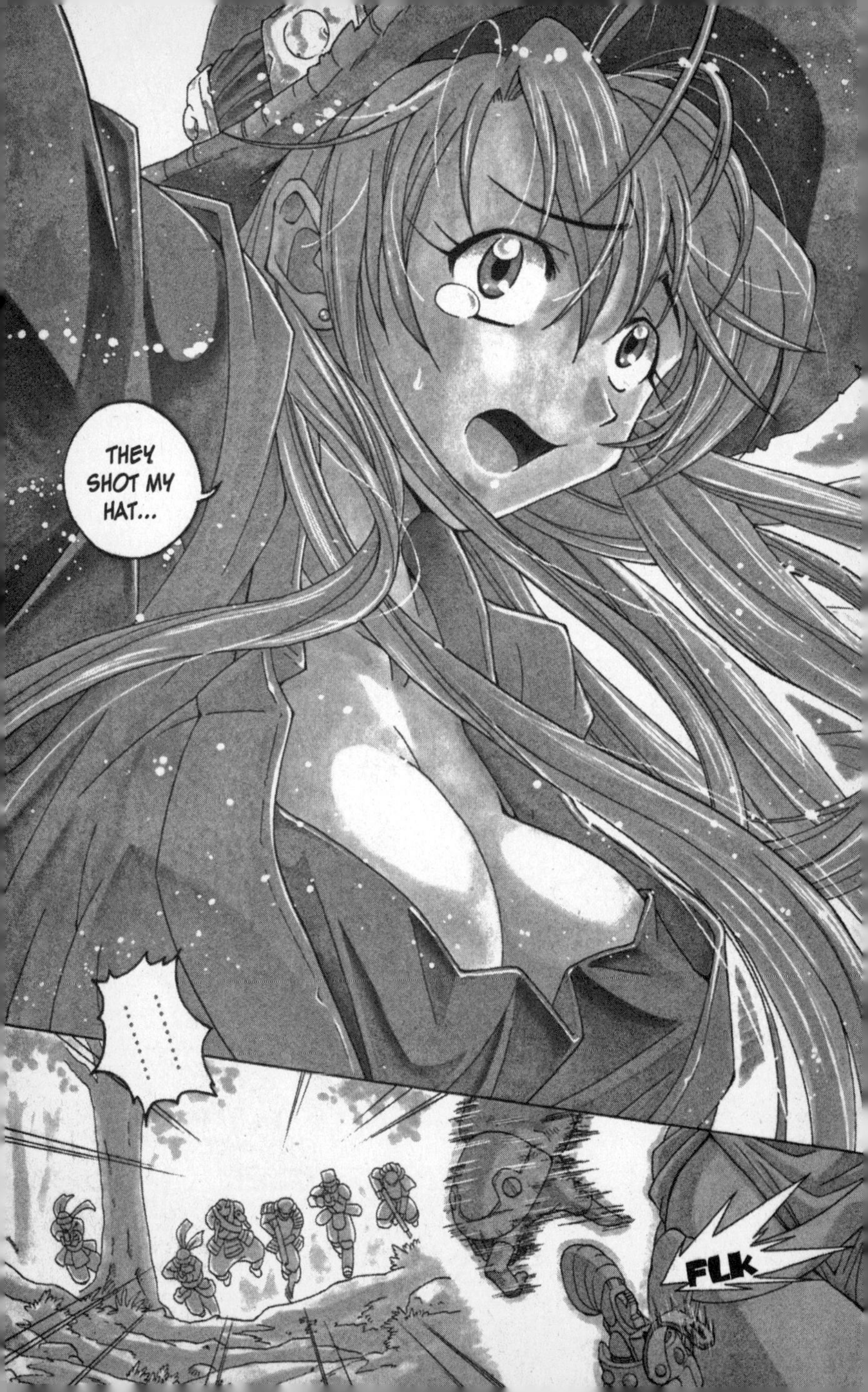
THEY SHOT MY HAT...
......
FLK

VOL. 1
CONTENTS

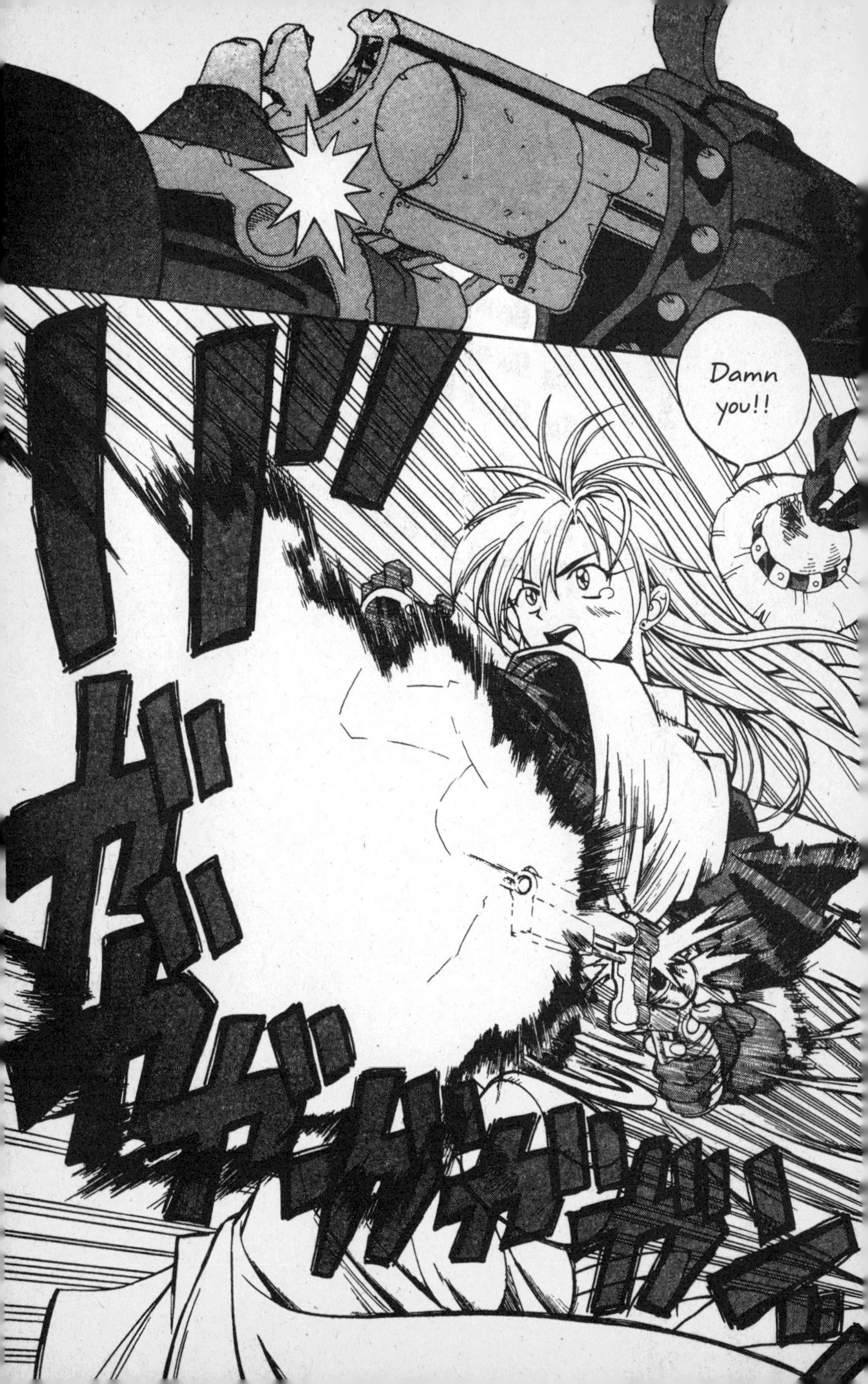
Damn you!!

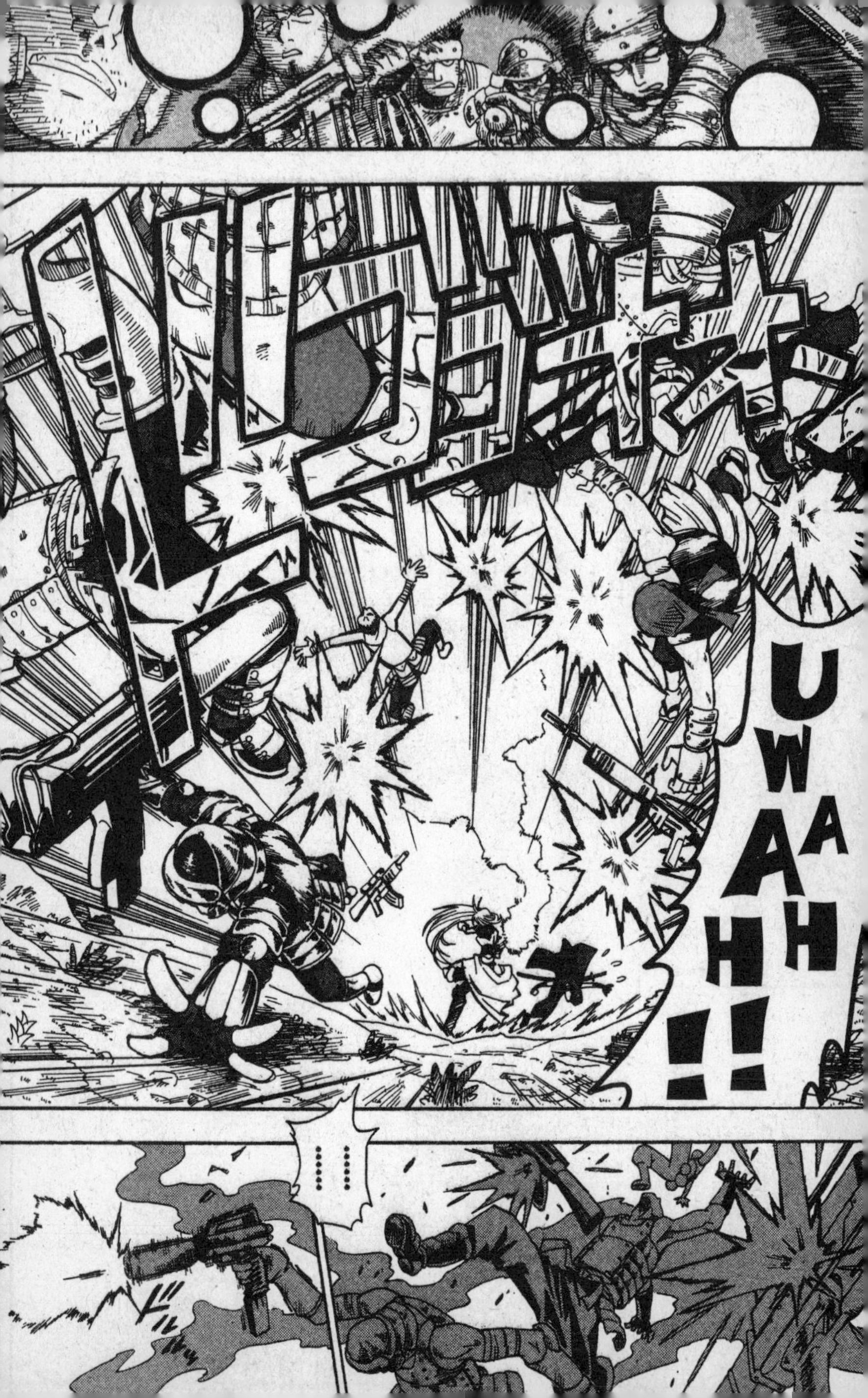
UWAAAHH!!

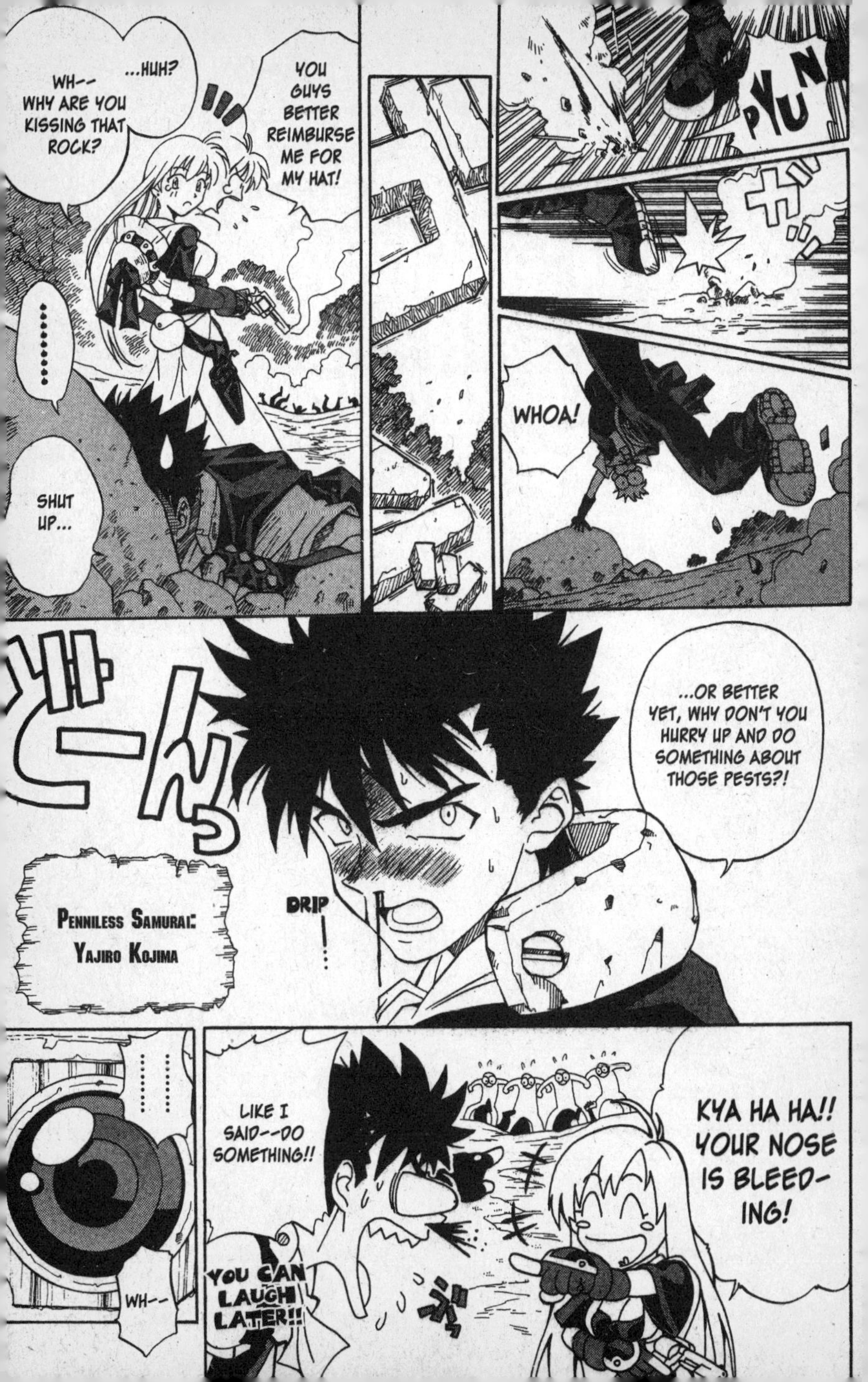
PYUN
WHOA!
YOU GUYS BETTER REIMBURSE ME FOR MY HAT!
...HUH?
WH-- WHY ARE YOU KISSING THAT ROCK?
....
SHUT UP...
...OR BETTER YET, WHY DON'T YOU HURRY UP AND DO SOMETHING ABOUT THOSE PESTS?!
DRIP
Penniless Samurai: Yajiro Kojima
KYA HA HA!! YOUR NOSE IS BLEED-ING!
LIKE I SAID--DO SOMETHING!!
YOU CAN LAUGH LATER!!
......
WH--

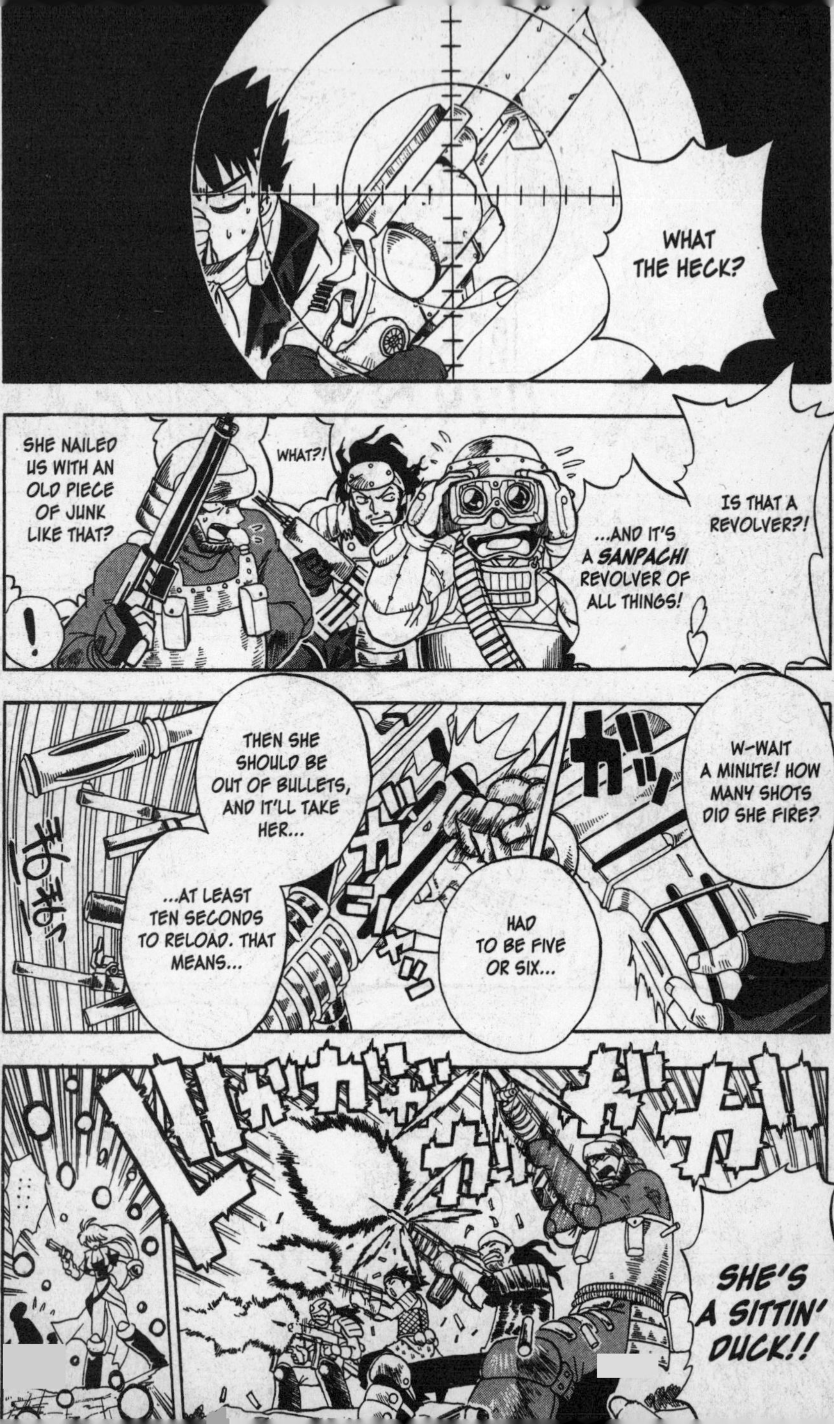
WHAT THE HECK?
IS THAT A REVOLVER?!
...AND IT'S A *SANPACHI* REVOLVER OF ALL THINGS!
WHAT?!
SHE NAILED US WITH AN OLD PIECE OF JUNK LIKE THAT?
!
W-WAIT A MINUTE! HOW MANY SHOTS DID SHE FIRE?
HAD TO BE FIVE OR SIX...
THEN SHE SHOULD BE OUT OF BULLETS, AND IT'LL TAKE HER...
...AT LEAST TEN SECONDS TO RELOAD. THAT MEANS...
SHE'S A SITTIN' DUCK!!

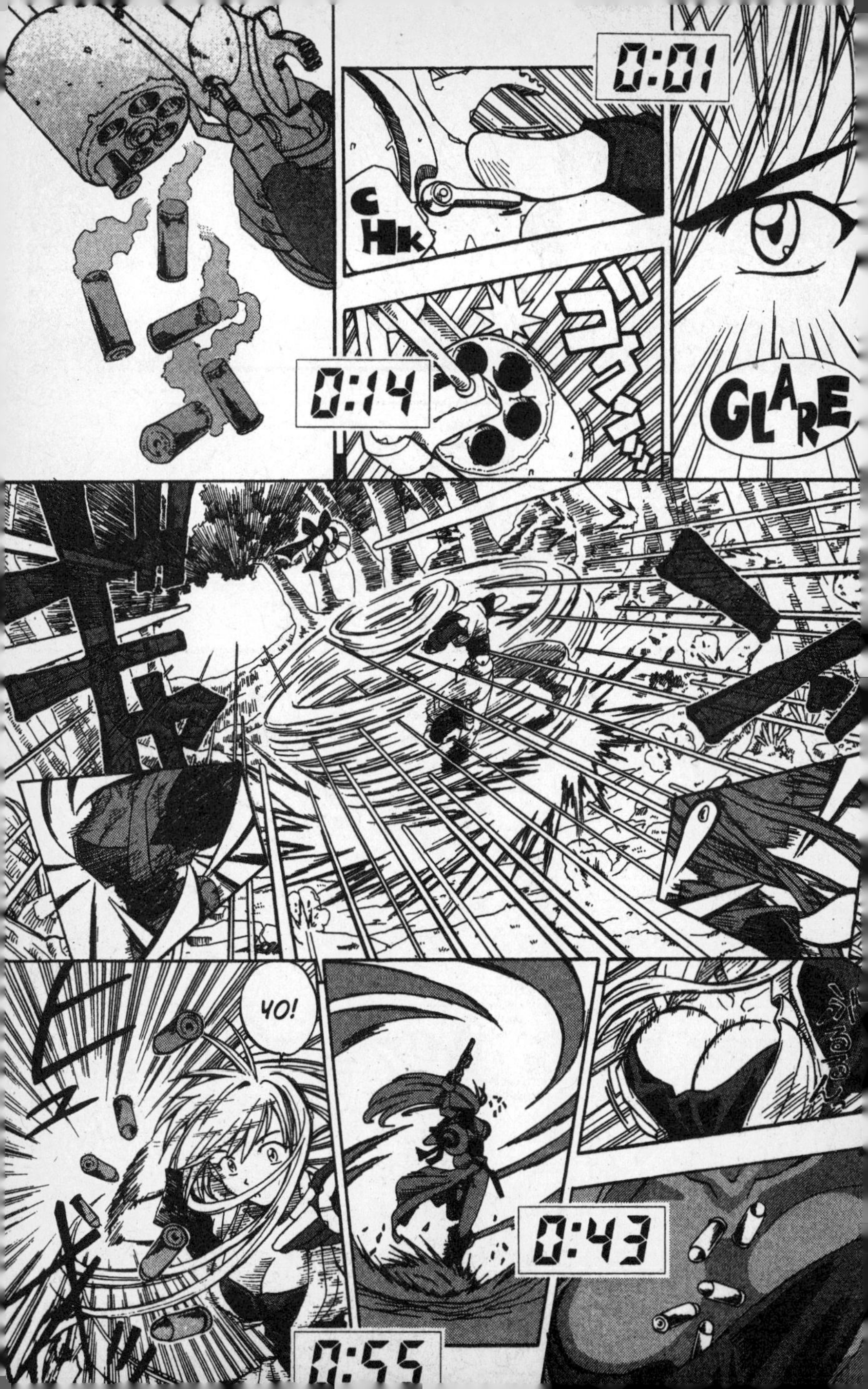

GLARE
0:01
CHK
0:14
0:43
YO!
0:55

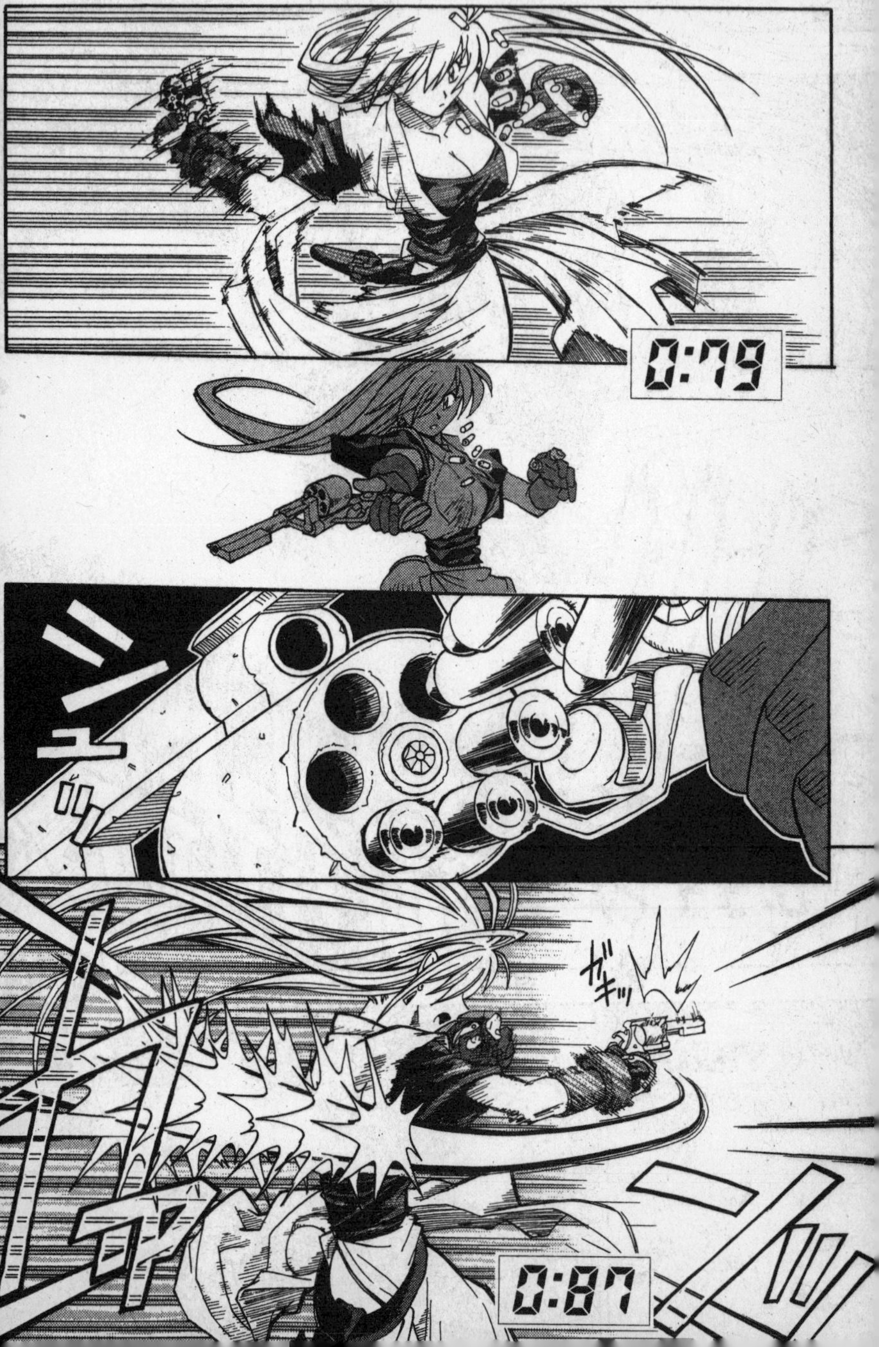
0:79
シュッ
ガギッ
0:87

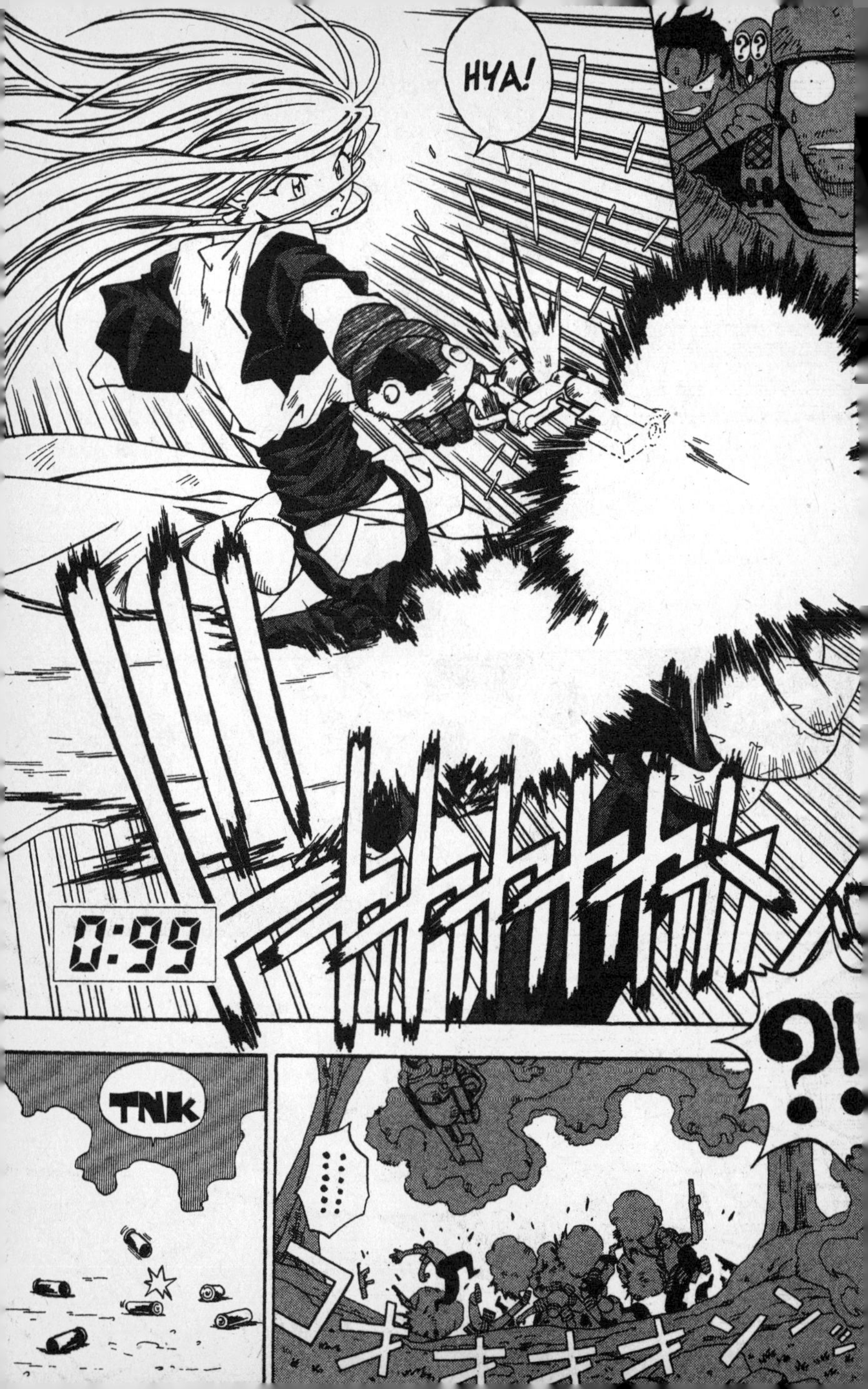
??
HYA!
0:99
?!
......
TNK

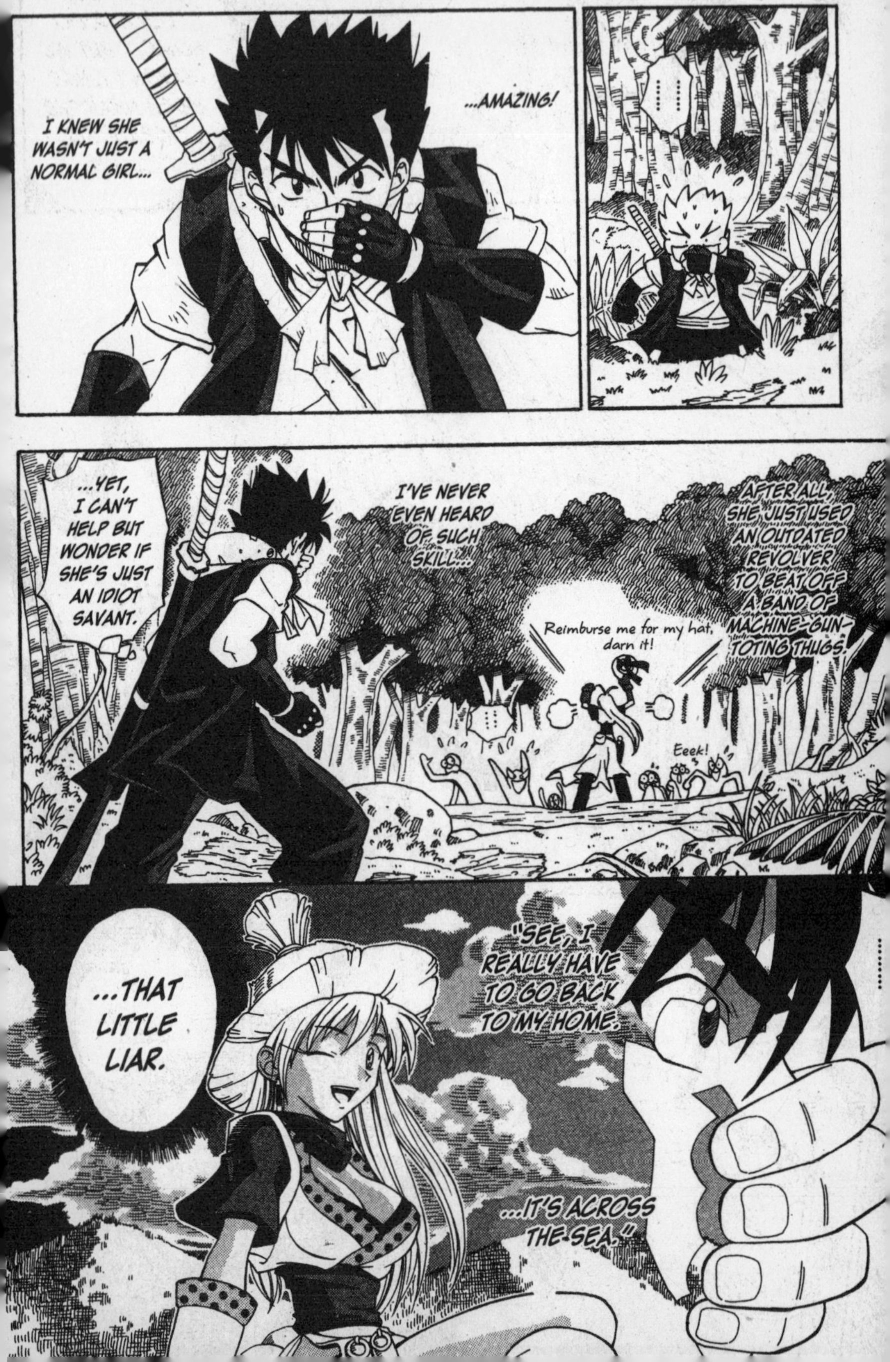
......
...AMAZING!
I KNEW SHE WASN'T JUST A NORMAL GIRL...
AFTER ALL, SHE JUST USED AN OUTDATED REVOLVER TO BEAT OFF A BAND OF MACHINE-GUN-TOTING THUGS.
I'VE NEVER EVEN HEARD OF SUCH SKILL...
...YET, I CAN'T HELP BUT WONDER IF SHE'S JUST AN IDIOT SAVANT.
Reimburse me for my hat, darn it!
Eeek!
"SEE, I REALLY HAVE TO GO BACK TO MY HOME.
...THAT LITTLE LIAR.
...IT'S ACROSS THE SEA."

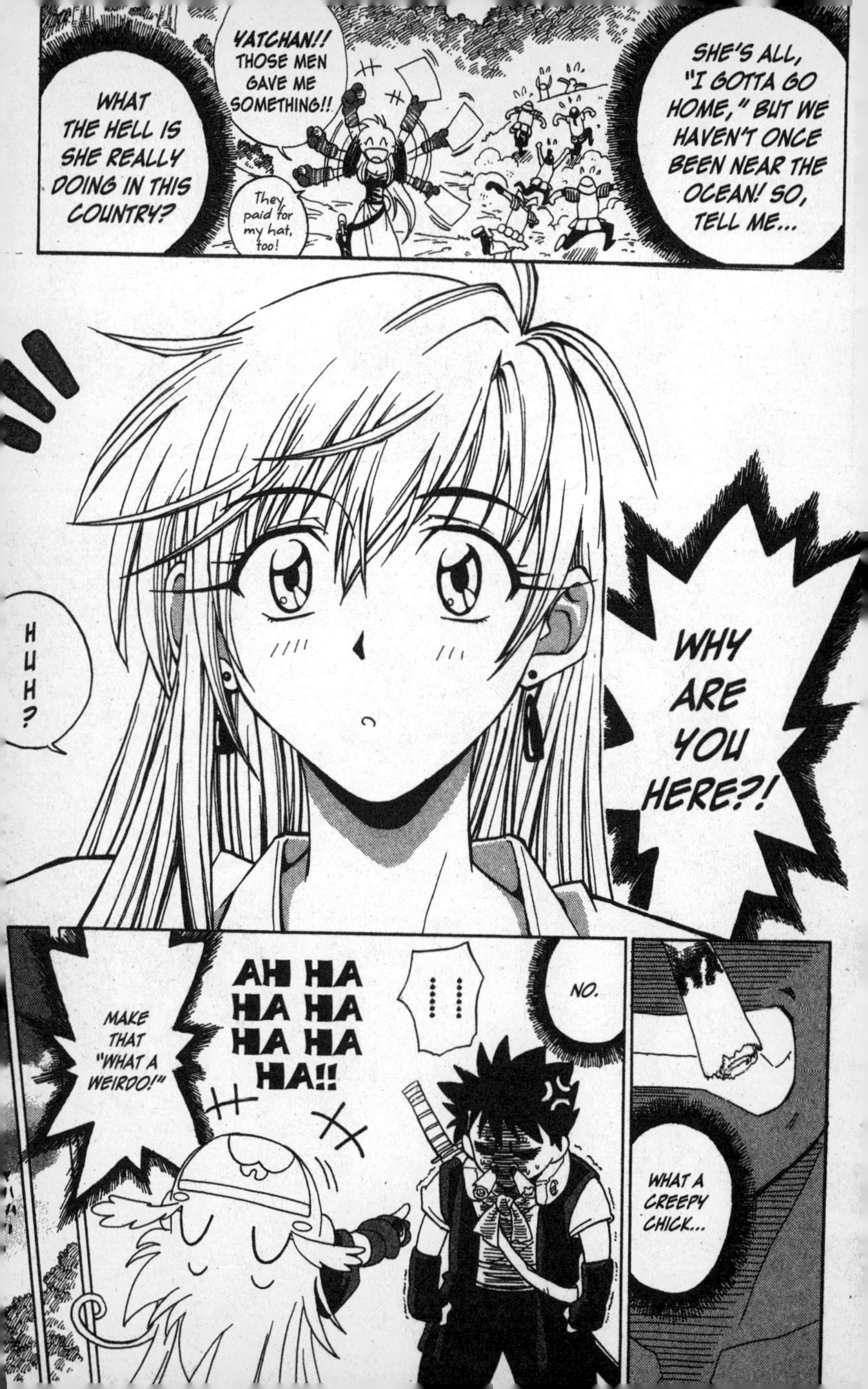

SHE'S ALL, "I GOTTA GO HOME," BUT WE HAVEN'T ONCE BEEN NEAR THE OCEAN! SO, TELL ME...
YATCHAN!! THOSE MEN GAVE ME SOMETHING!!
WHAT THE HELL IS SHE REALLY DOING IN THIS COUNTRY?
They paid for my hat, too!
WHY ARE YOU HERE?!
HUH?
WHAT A CREEPY CHICK...
NO.
......
AH HA HA HA HA HA HA HA HA!!
MAKE THAT "WHAT A WEIRDO!"

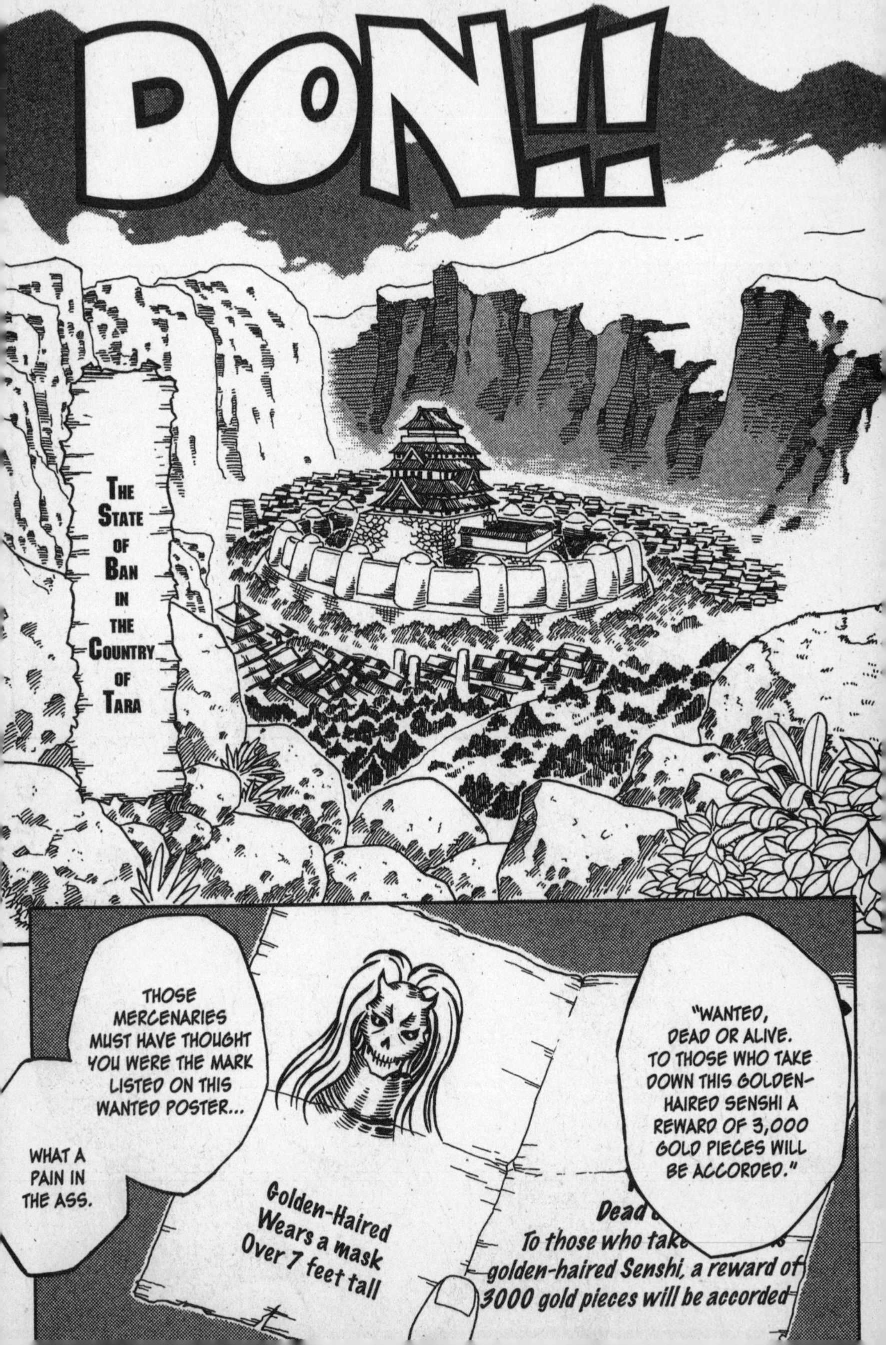
DON!!
THE STATE OF BAN IN THE COUNTRY OF TARA
"WANTED, DEAD OR ALIVE. TO THOSE WHO TAKE DOWN THIS GOLDEN-HAIRED SENSHI A REWARD OF 3,000 GOLD PIECES WILL BE ACCORDED."
Dead
To those who take
golden-haired Senshi, a reward of
3000 gold pieces will be accorded
Golden-Haired
Wears a mask
Over 7 feet tall
THOSE MERCENARIES MUST HAVE THOUGHT YOU WERE THE MARK LISTED ON THIS WANTED POSTER...
WHAT A PAIN IN THE ASS.

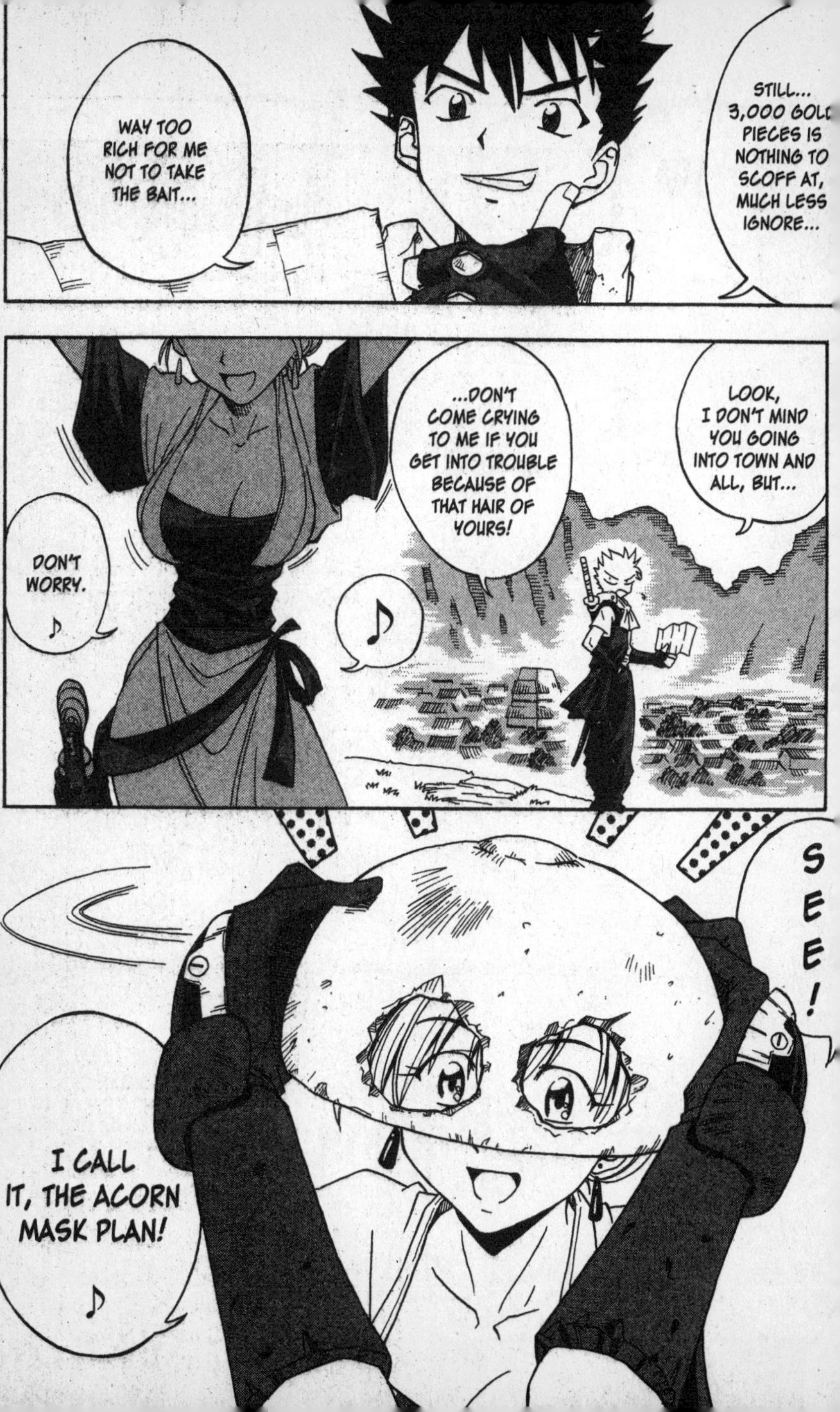
STILL... 3,000 GOLD PIECES IS NOTHING TO SCOFF AT, MUCH LESS IGNORE...
WAY TOO RICH FOR ME NOT TO TAKE THE BAIT...
LOOK, I DON'T MIND YOU GOING INTO TOWN AND ALL, BUT...
...DON'T COME CRYING TO ME IF YOU GET INTO TROUBLE BECAUSE OF THAT HAIR OF YOURS!
♪
DON'T WORRY. ♪
SEE!
I CALL IT, THE ACORN MASK PLAN! ♪

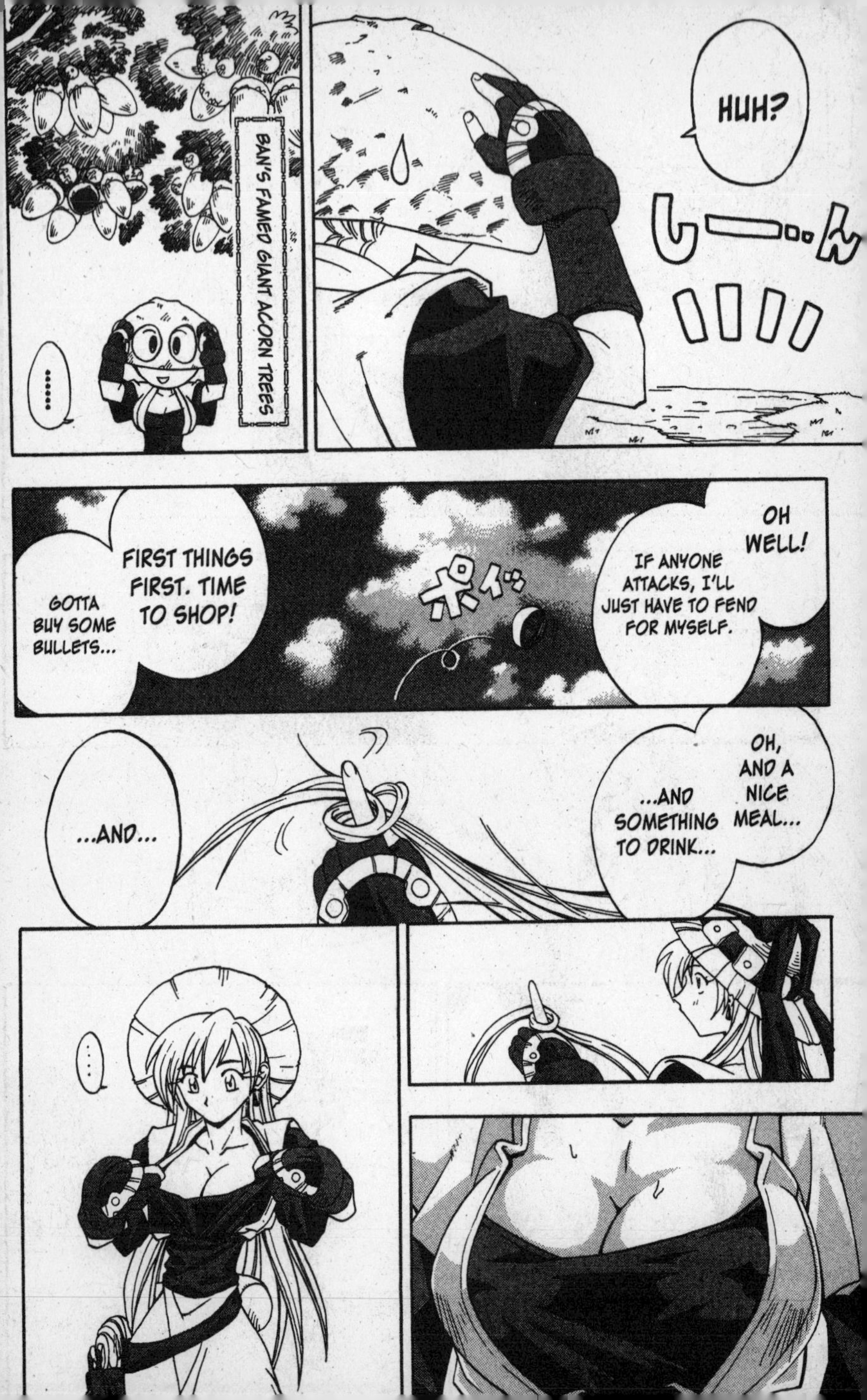
HUH?
しーー…ん
BAN'S FAMED GIANT ACORN TREES
......
OH WELL!
IF ANYONE ATTACKS, I'LL JUST HAVE TO FEND FOR MYSELF.
ポイッ
FIRST THINGS FIRST. TIME TO SHOP!
GOTTA BUY SOME BULLETS...
OH, AND A NICE MEAL...
...AND SOMETHING TO DRINK...
...AND...
....

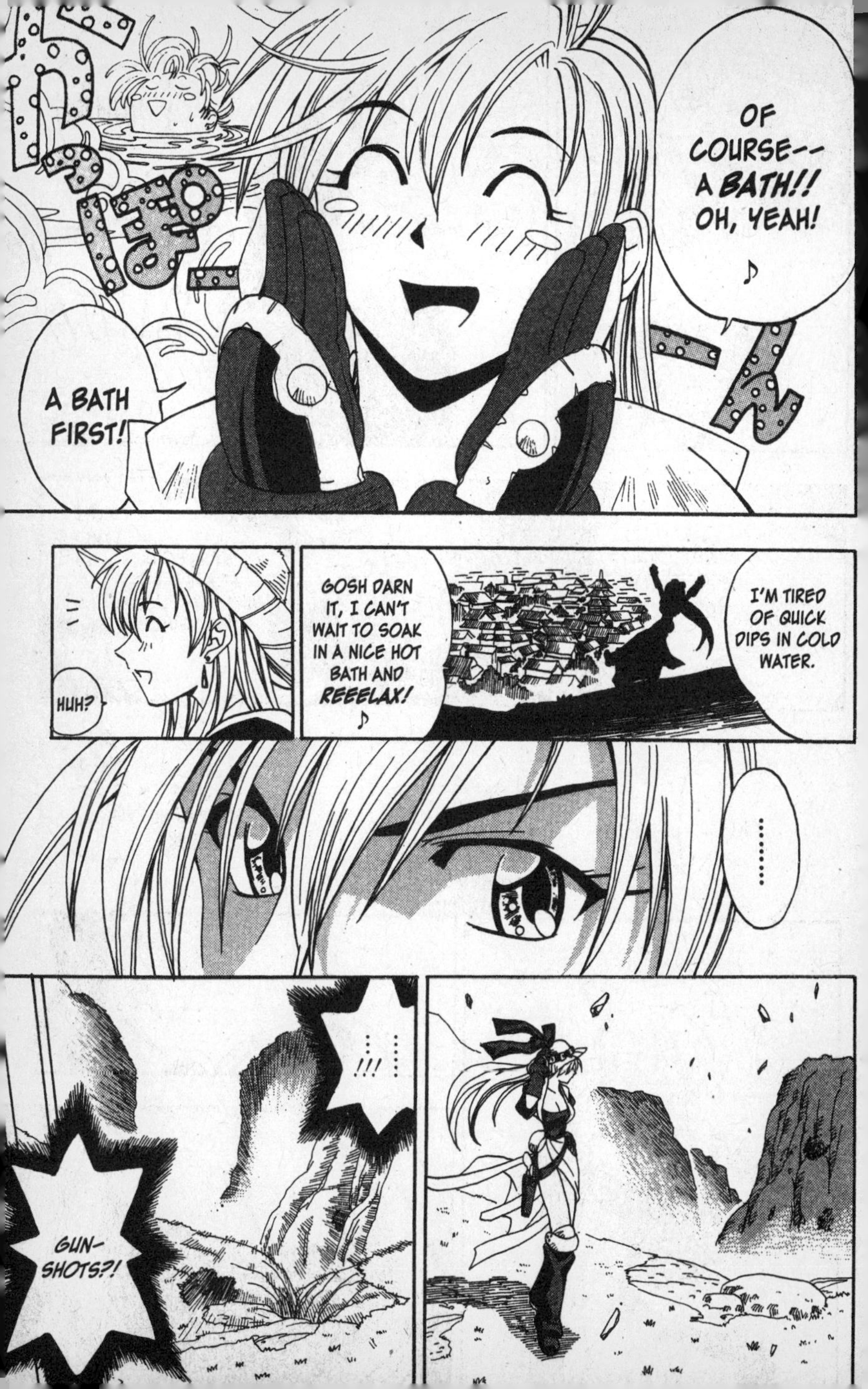
OF COURSE-- A BATH!! OH, YEAH! ♪
A BATH FIRST!
I'M TIRED OF QUICK DIPS IN COLD WATER.
GOSH DARN IT, I CAN'T WAIT TO SOAK IN A NICE HOT BATH AND REEELAX! ♪
HUH?
......
......
!!!
GUN-SHOTS?!

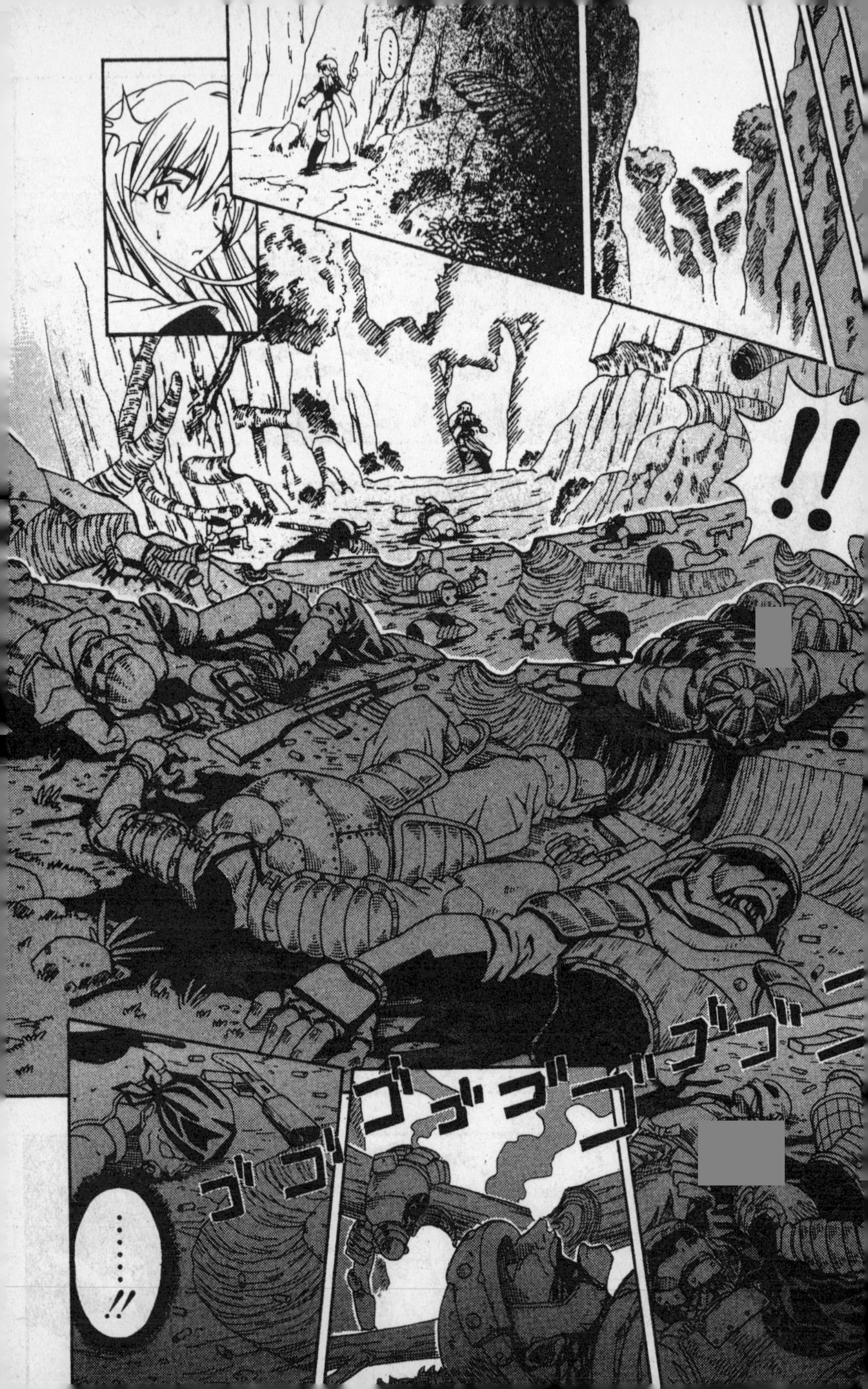
……
!!
ゴゴゴゴゴゴゴゴー
……!!

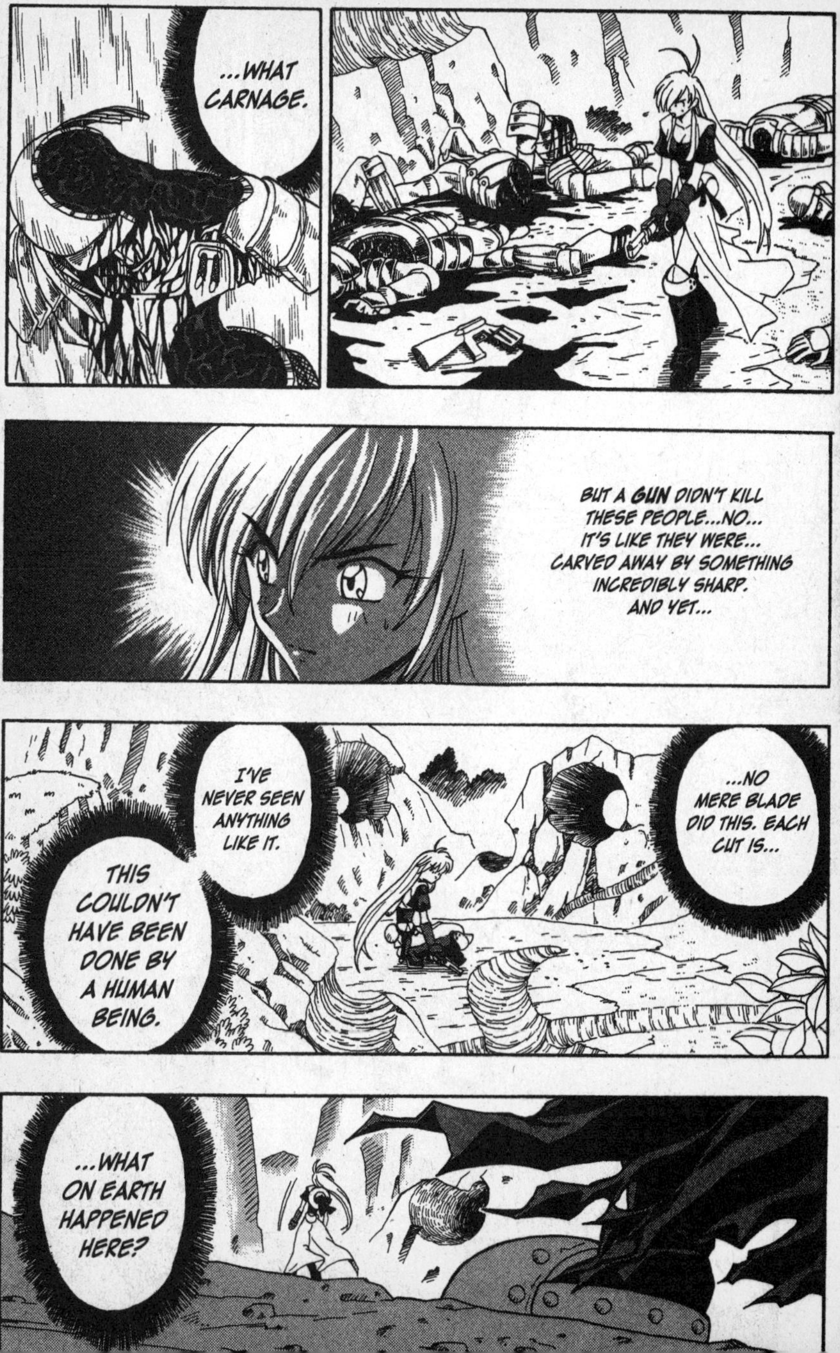
...WHAT CARNAGE.
BUT A GUN DIDN'T KILL THESE PEOPLE...NO... IT'S LIKE THEY WERE... CARVED AWAY BY SOMETHING INCREDIBLY SHARP. AND YET...
...NO MERE BLADE DID THIS. EACH CUT IS...
I'VE NEVER SEEN ANYTHING LIKE IT.
THIS COULDN'T HAVE BEEN DONE BY A HUMAN BEING.
...WHAT ON EARTH HAPPENED HERE?

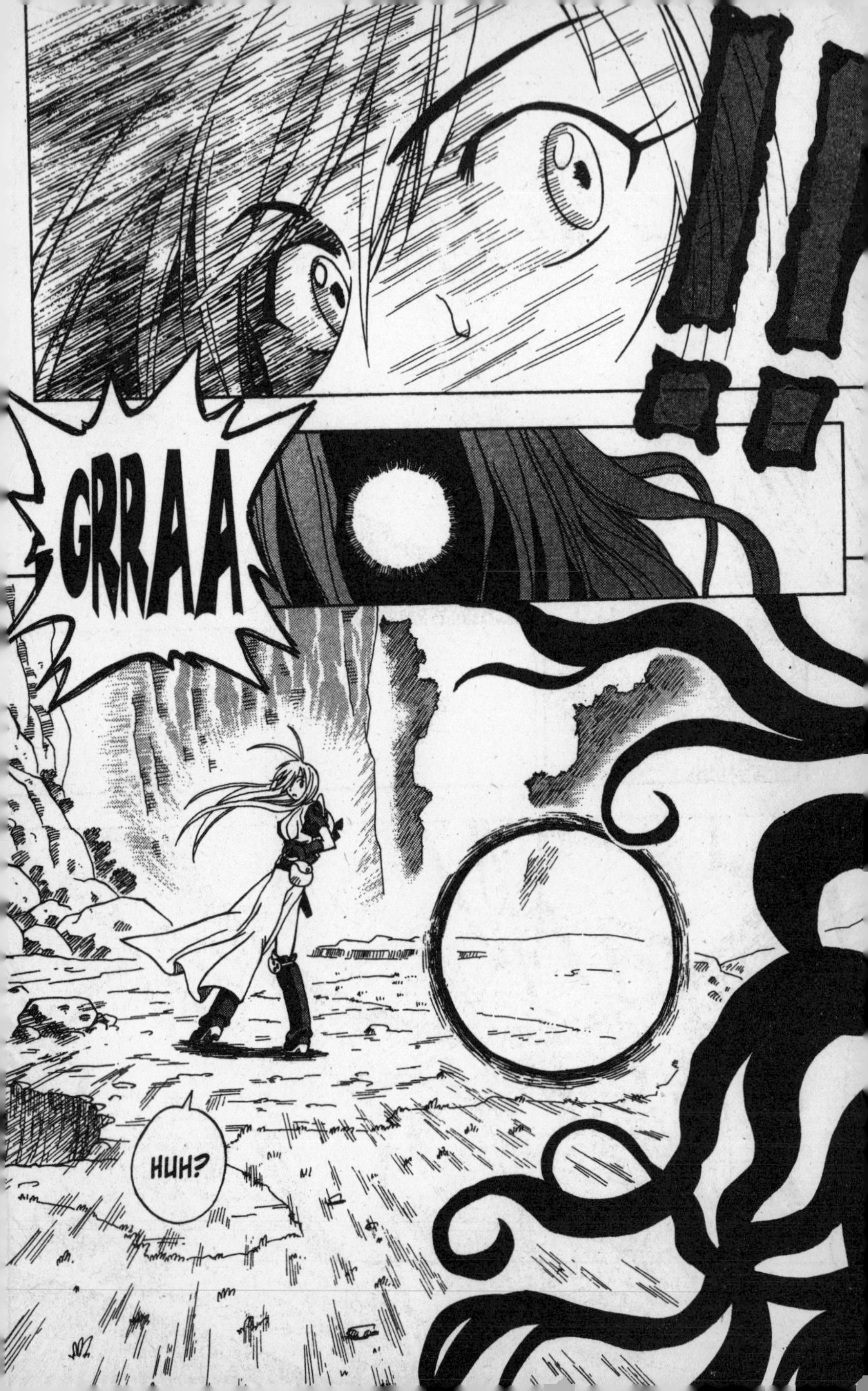
!!
GRRAA
HUH?

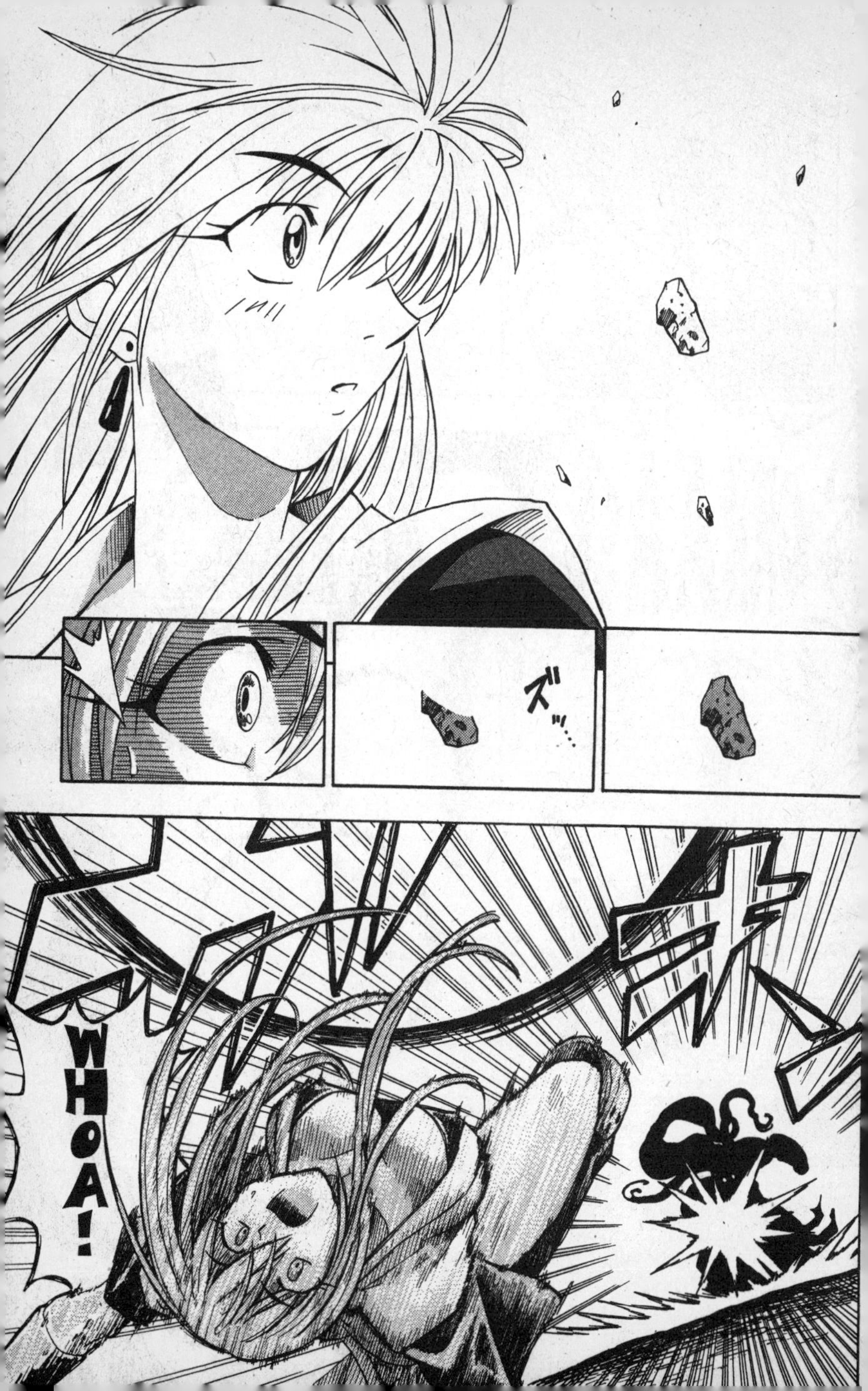
ズッ…
WHOA!

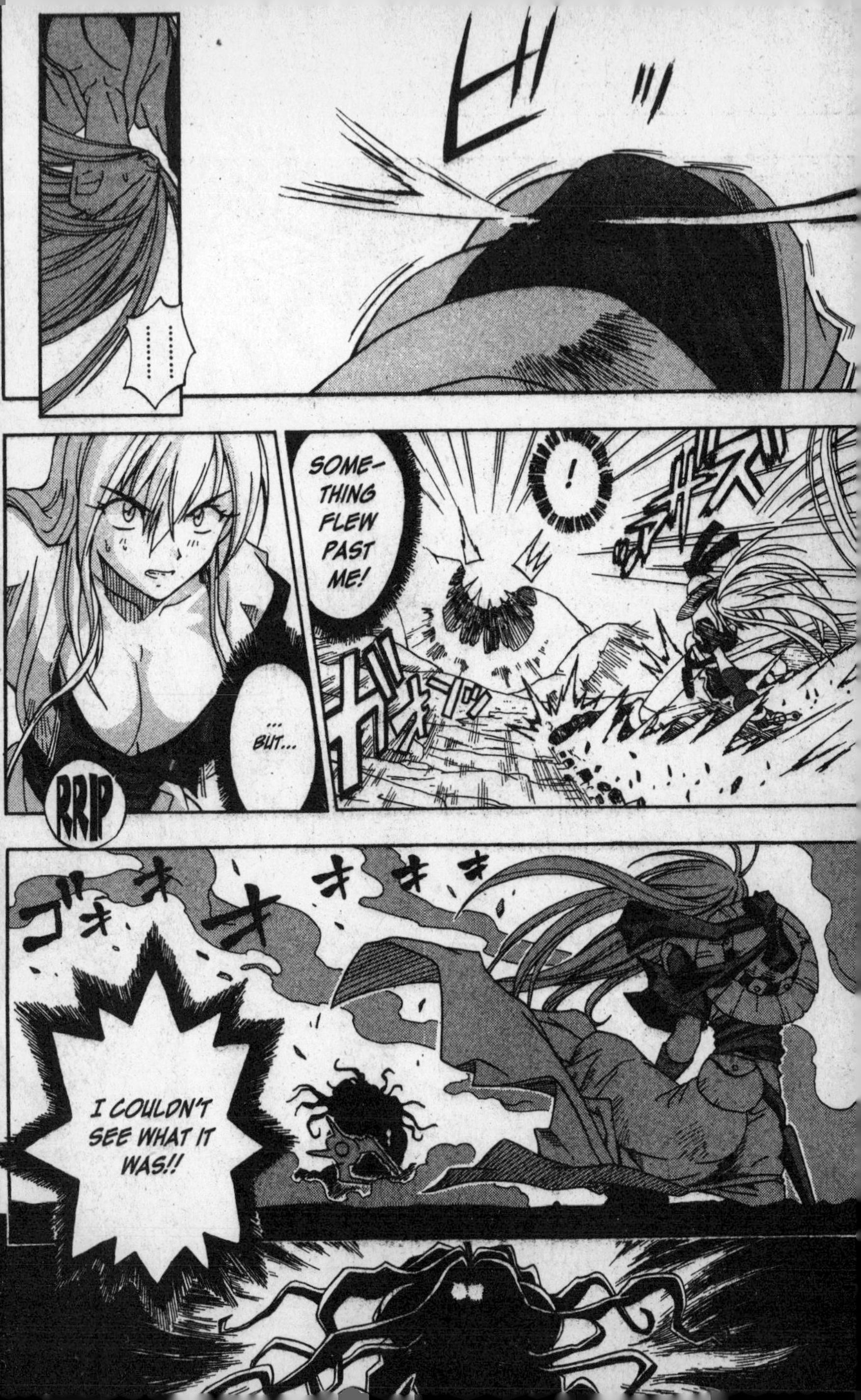
......
!
SOME-THING FLEW PAST ME!
... BUT...
RRIP
I COULDN'T SEE WHAT IT WAS!!

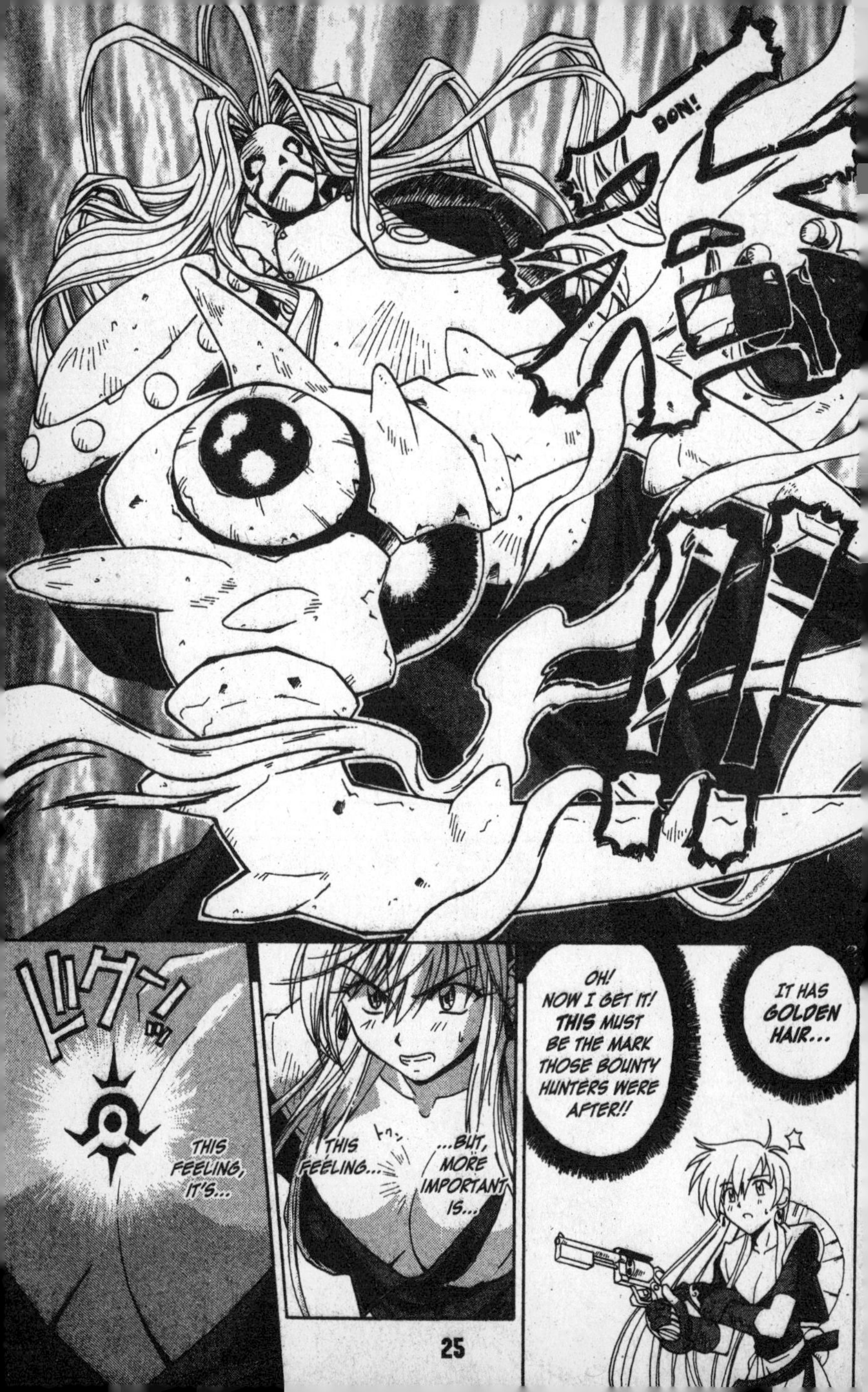
DON!
IT HAS GOLDEN HAIR...
OH! NOW I GET IT! THIS MUST BE THE MARK THOSE BOUNTY HUNTERS WERE AFTER!!
...BUT, MORE IMPORTANT IS...
THIS FEELING...
THIS FEELING, IT'S...

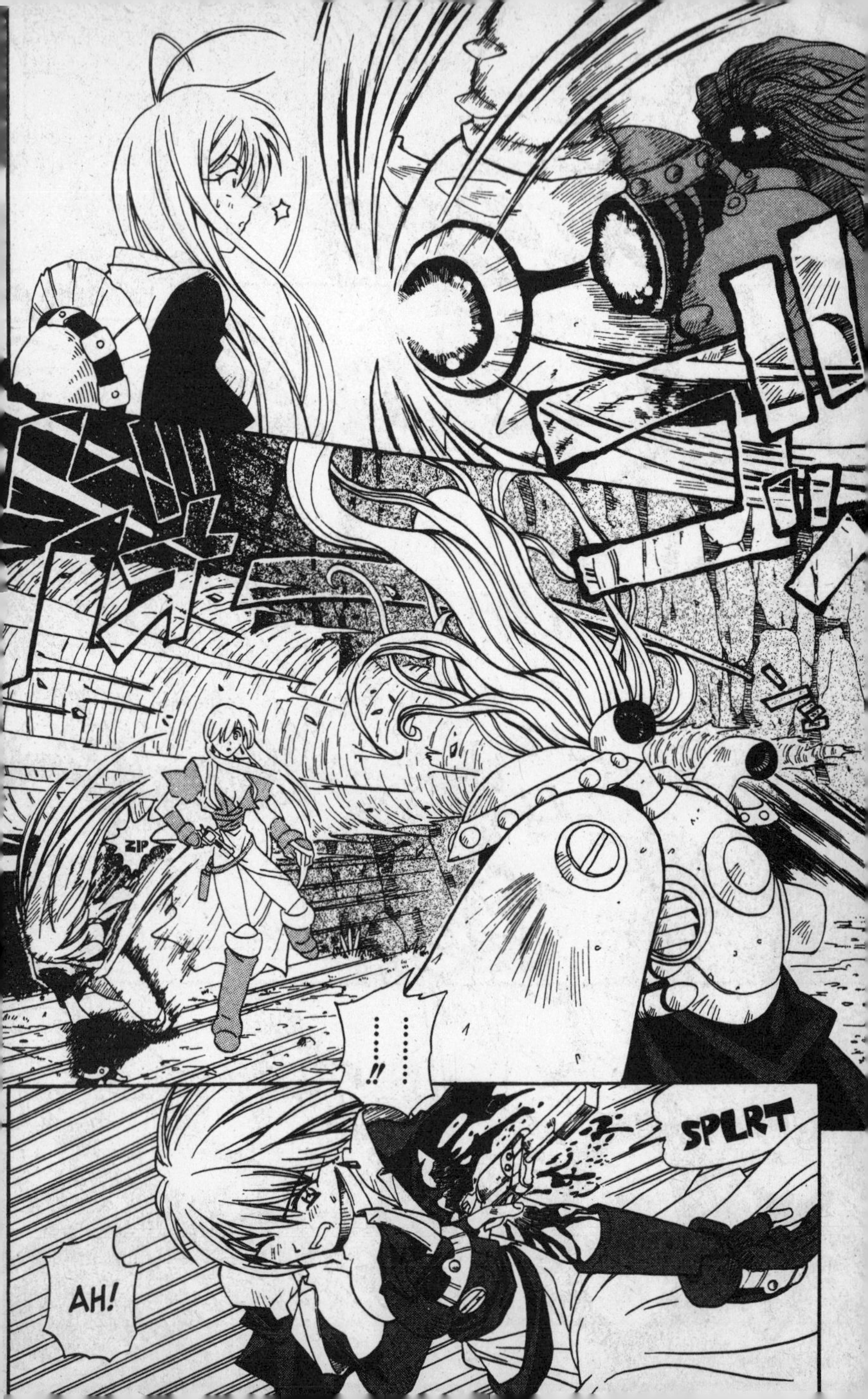
ZIP
......!!
SPLRT
AH!

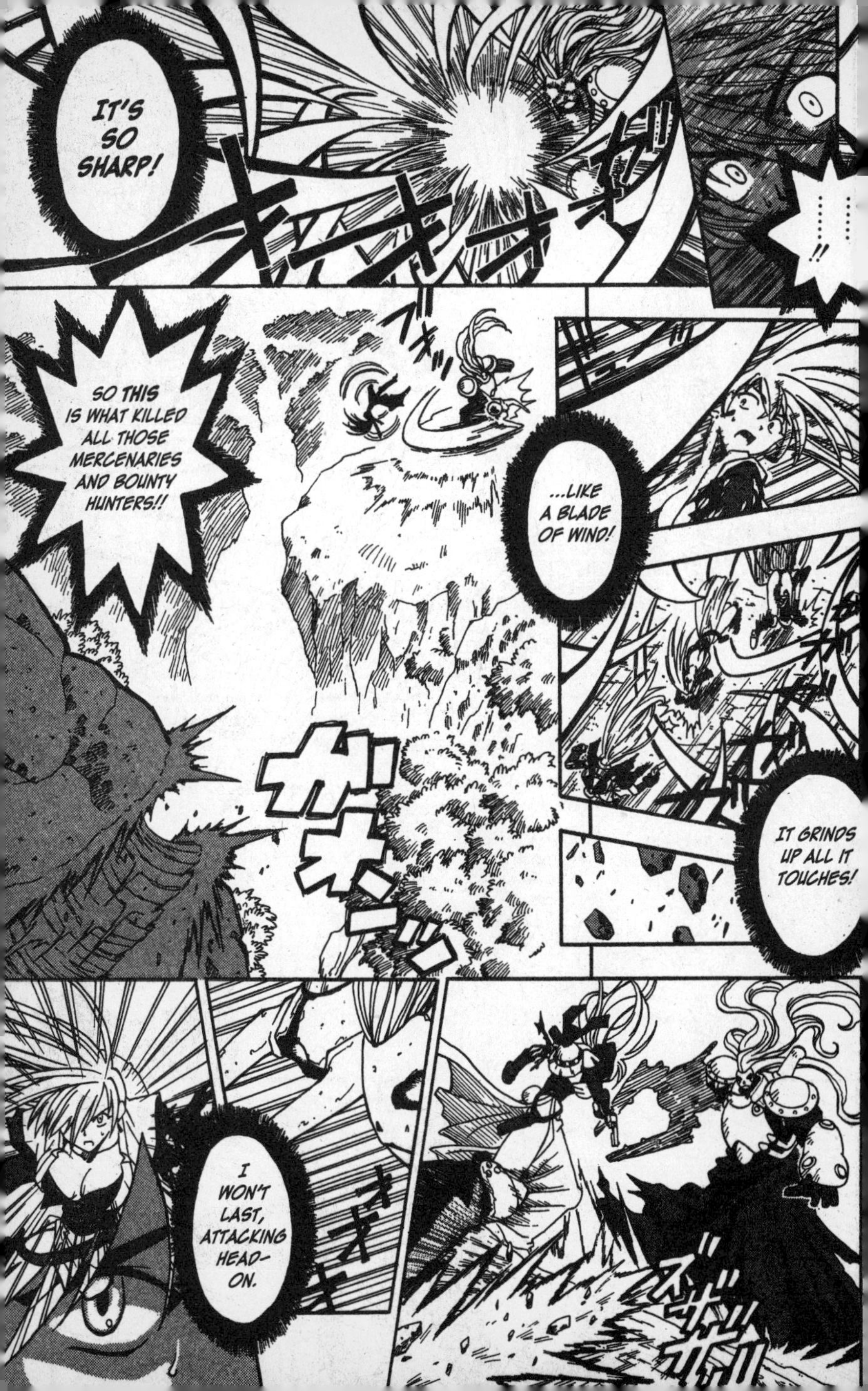
......!!
IT'S SO SHARP!
...LIKE A BLADE OF WIND!
IT GRINDS UP ALL IT TOUCHES!
SO THIS IS WHAT KILLED ALL THOSE MERCENARIES AND BOUNTY HUNTERS!!
I WON'T LAST, ATTACKING HEAD-ON.

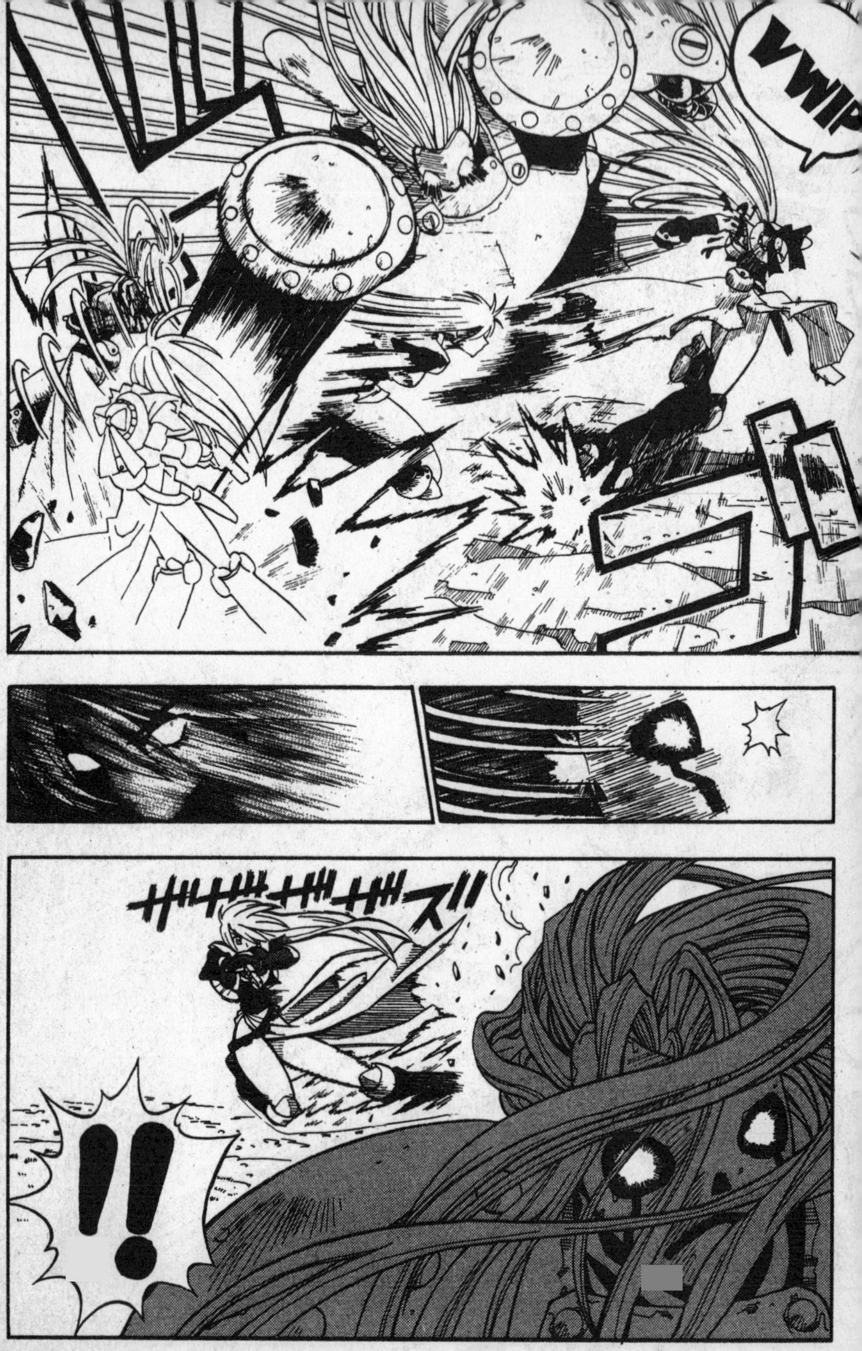
VWIP
!!

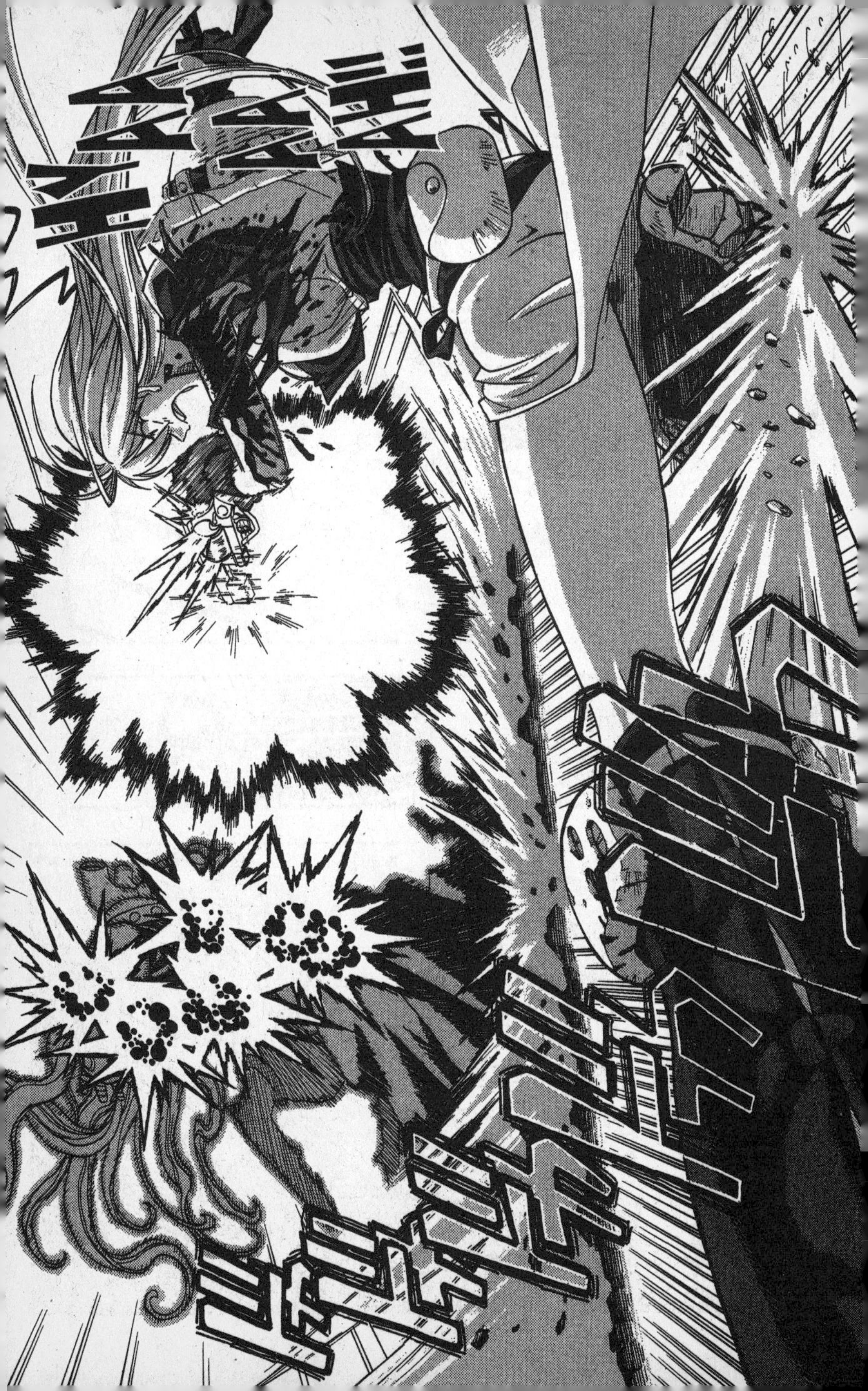

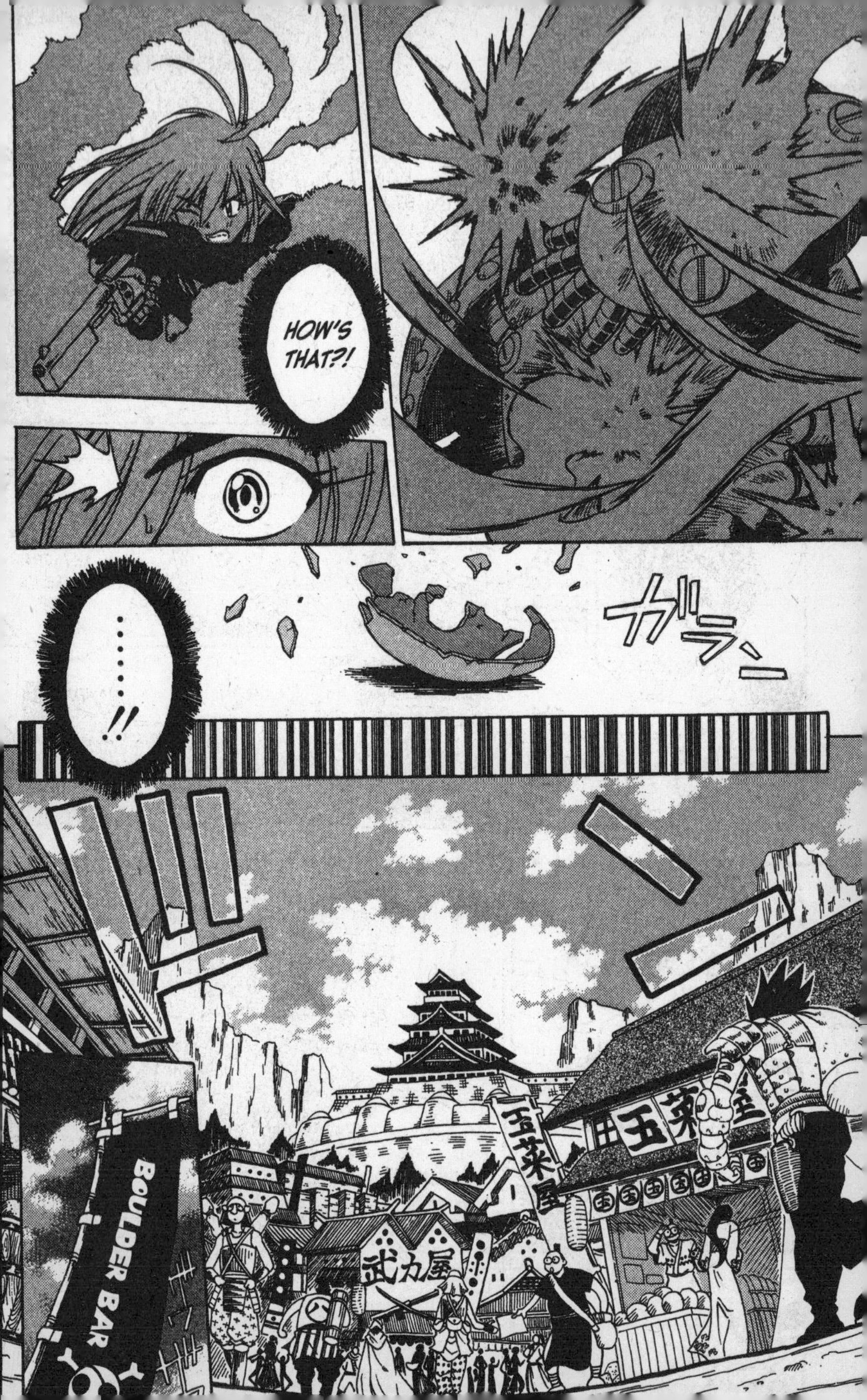
HOW'S THAT?!
......!!
ガラン
!!
五菜屋
武力屋
BOULDER BAR

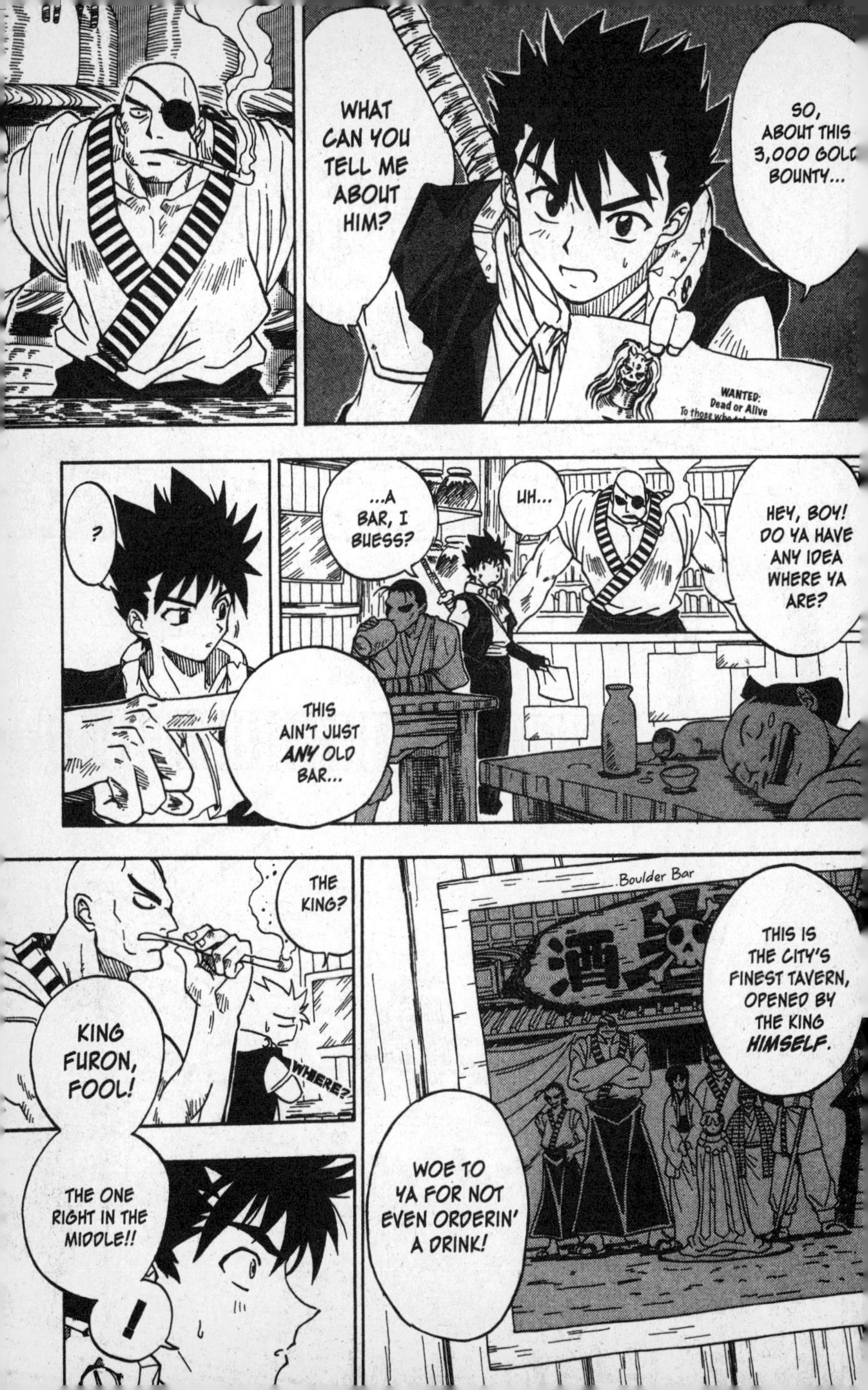
SO, ABOUT THIS 3,000 GOLD BOUNTY...
WHAT CAN YOU TELL ME ABOUT HIM?
WANTED: Dead or Alive
HEY, BOY! DO YA HAVE ANY IDEA WHERE YA ARE?
UH...
...A BAR, I GUESS?
?
THIS AIN'T JUST ANY OLD BAR...
Boulder Bar
THIS IS THE CITY'S FINEST TAVERN, OPENED BY THE KING HIMSELF.
WOE TO YA FOR NOT EVEN ORDERIN' A DRINK!
THE KING?
KING FURON, FOOL!
WHERE?
THE ONE RIGHT IN THE MIDDLE!!
!

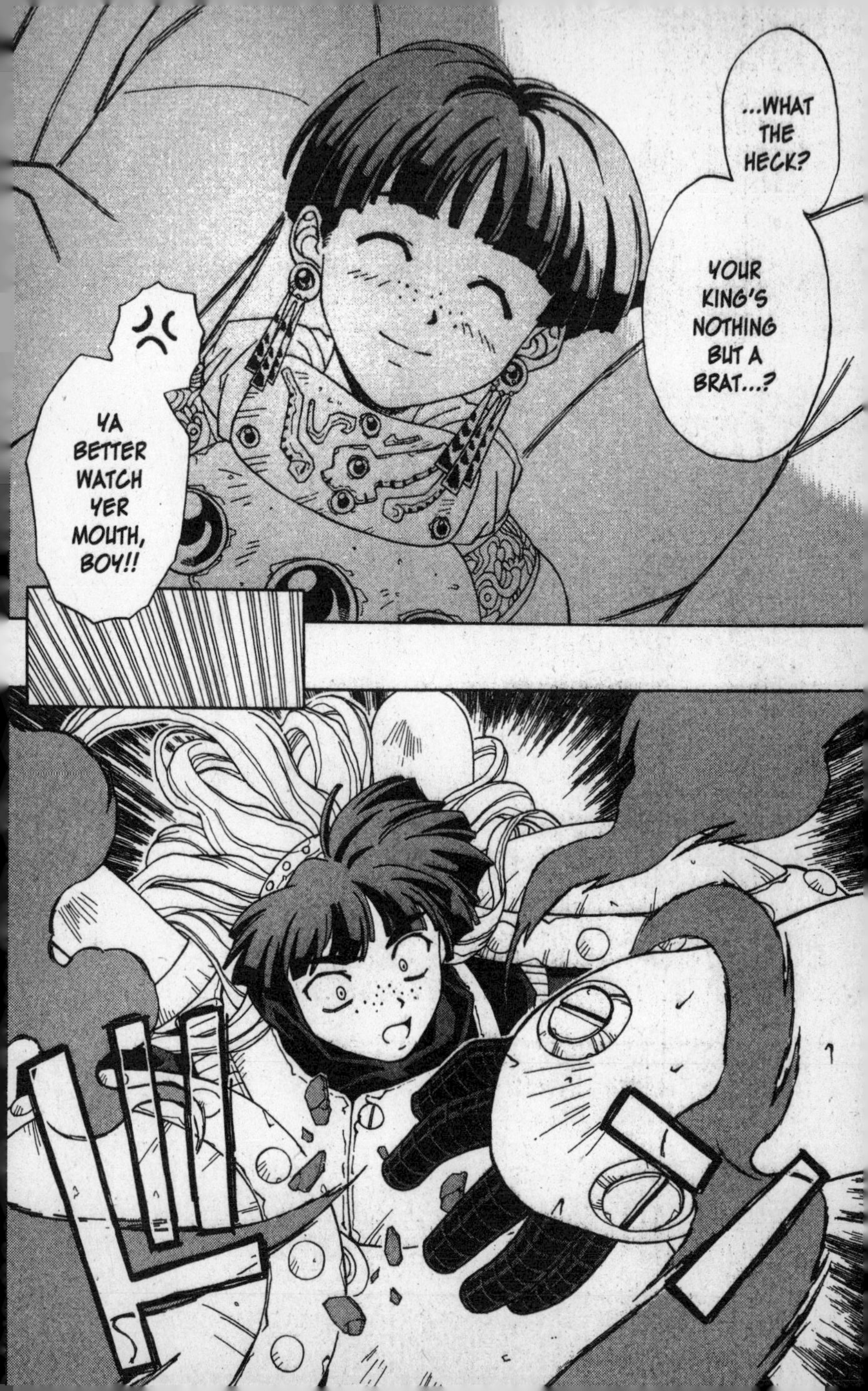
...WHAT THE HECK?
YOUR KING'S NOTHING BUT A BRAT...?
YA BETTER WATCH YER MOUTH, BOY!!

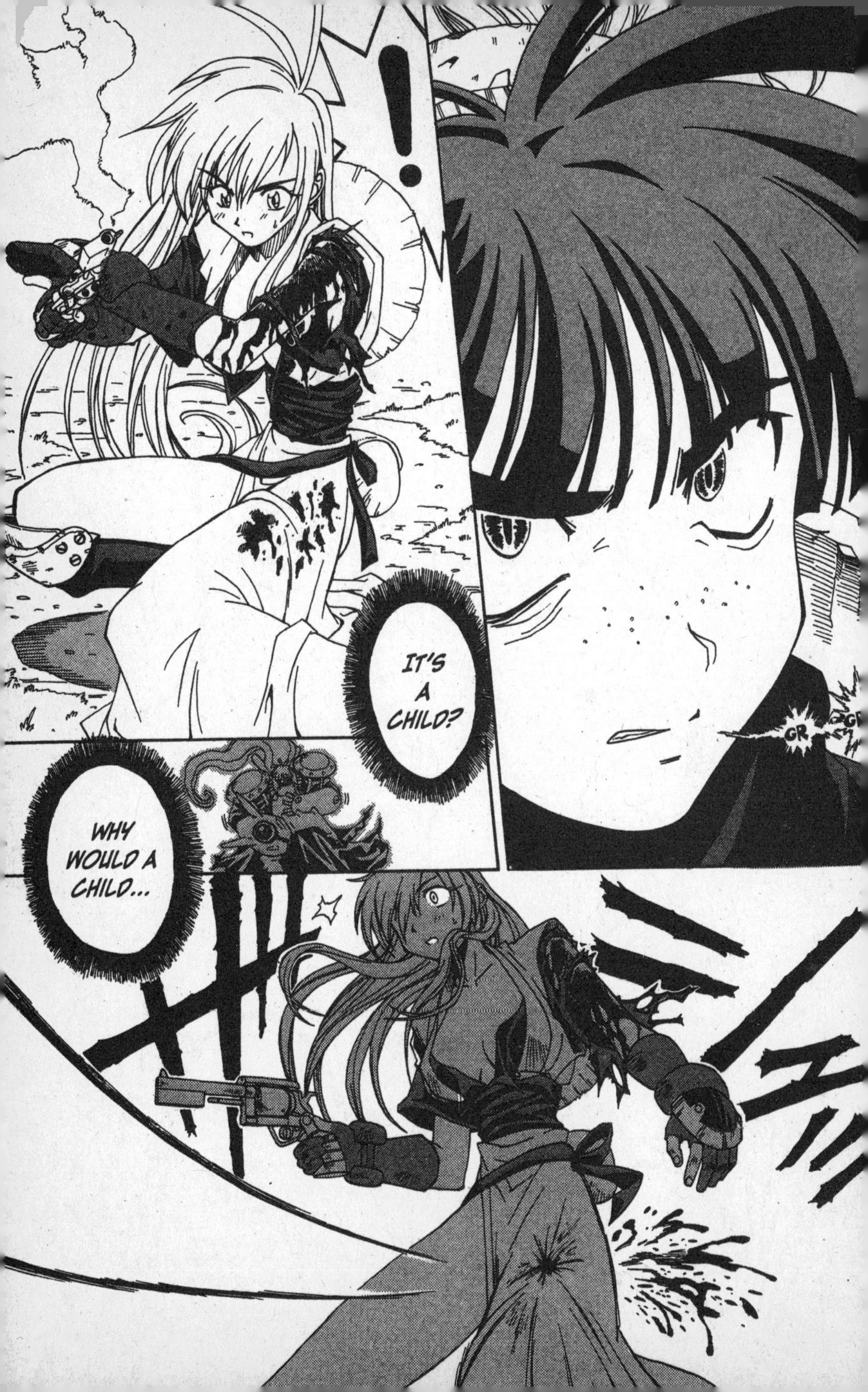
!
IT'S A CHILD?
GR
WHY WOULD A CHILD...

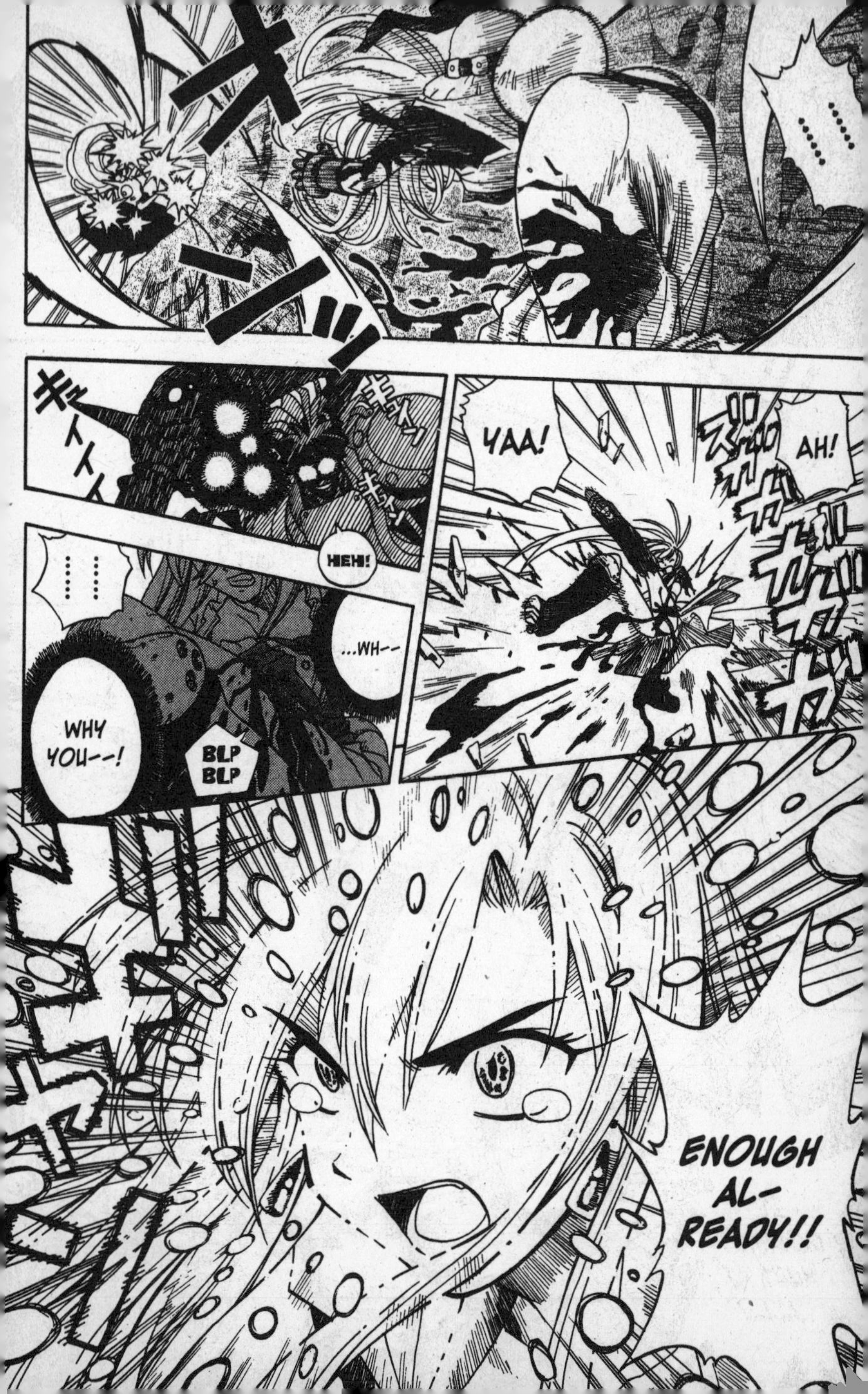
......
AH!
YAA!
HEH!
...WH--
......
WHY YOU--!
BLP BLP
ENOUGH AL-READY!!

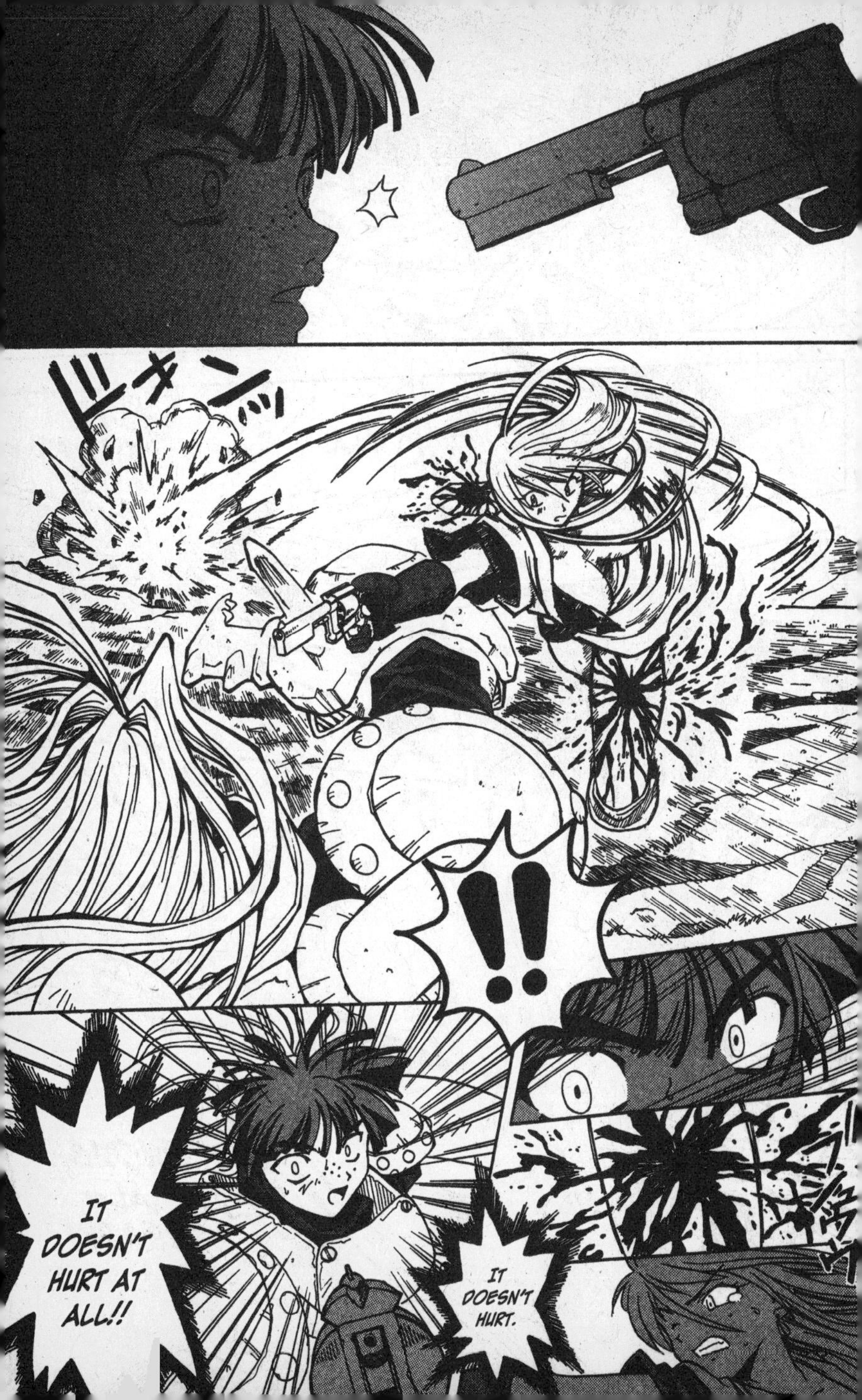
!!
IT DOESN'T HURT.
IT DOESN'T HURT AT ALL!!

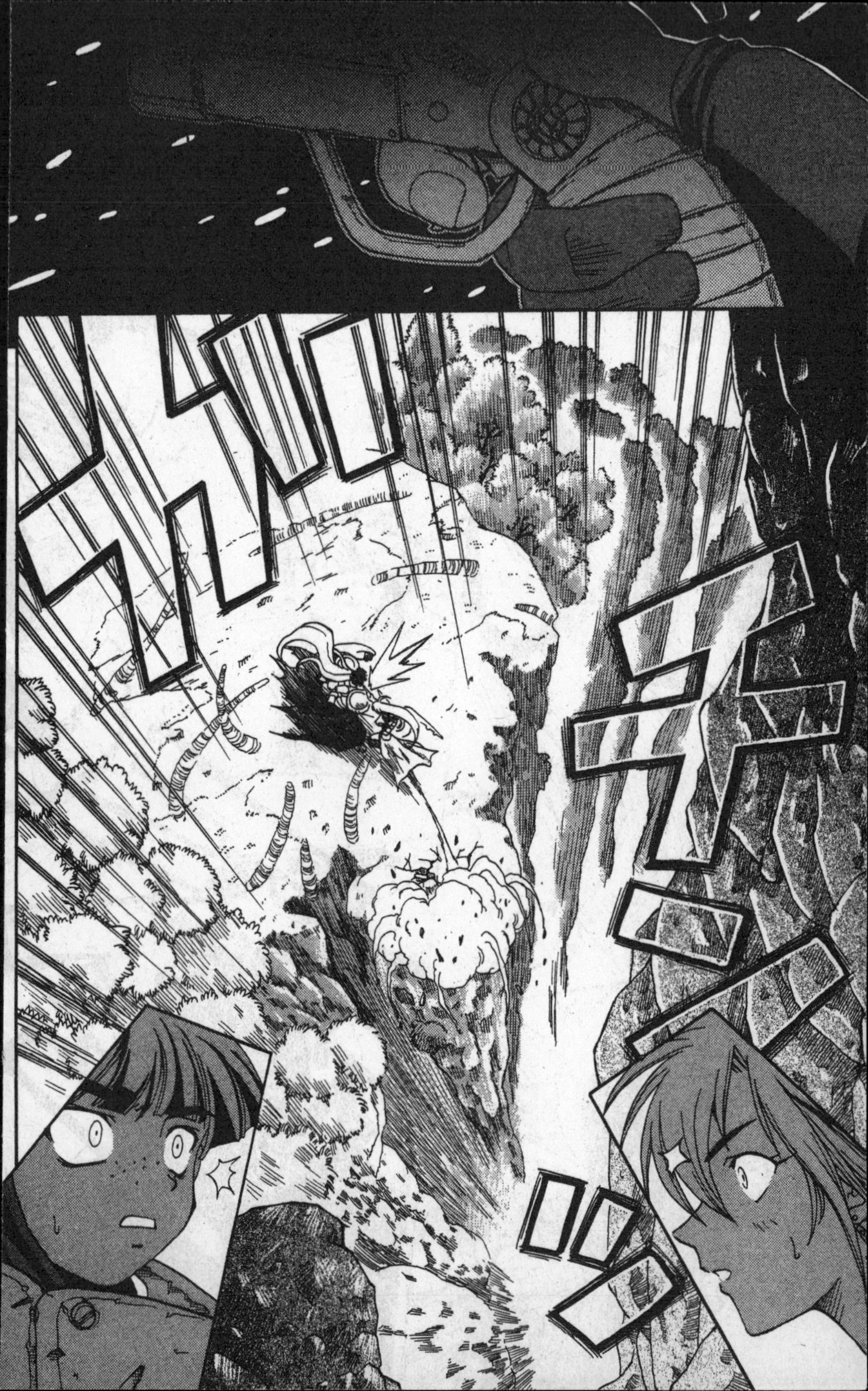

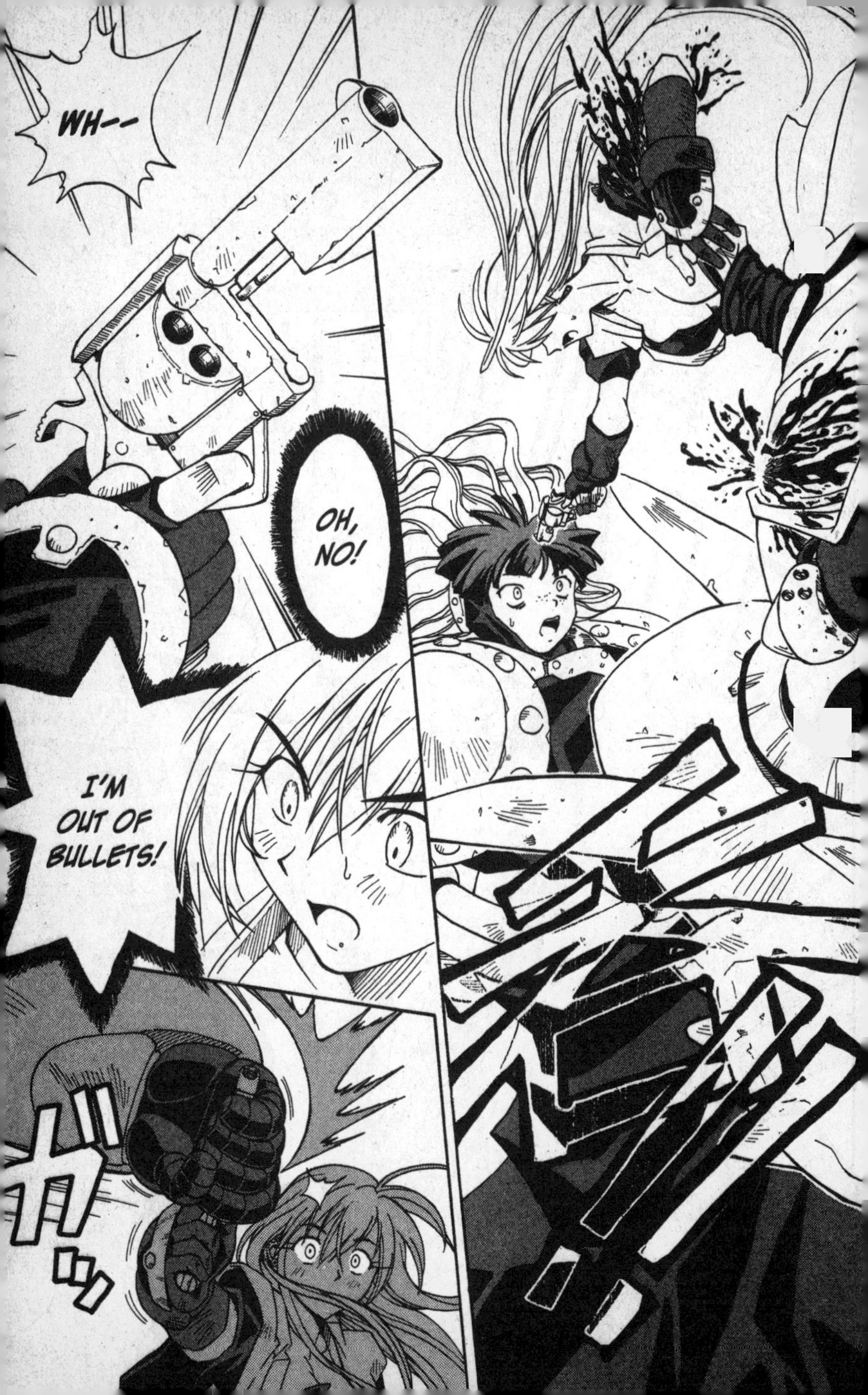
WH--
OH, NO!
I'M OUT OF BULLETS!

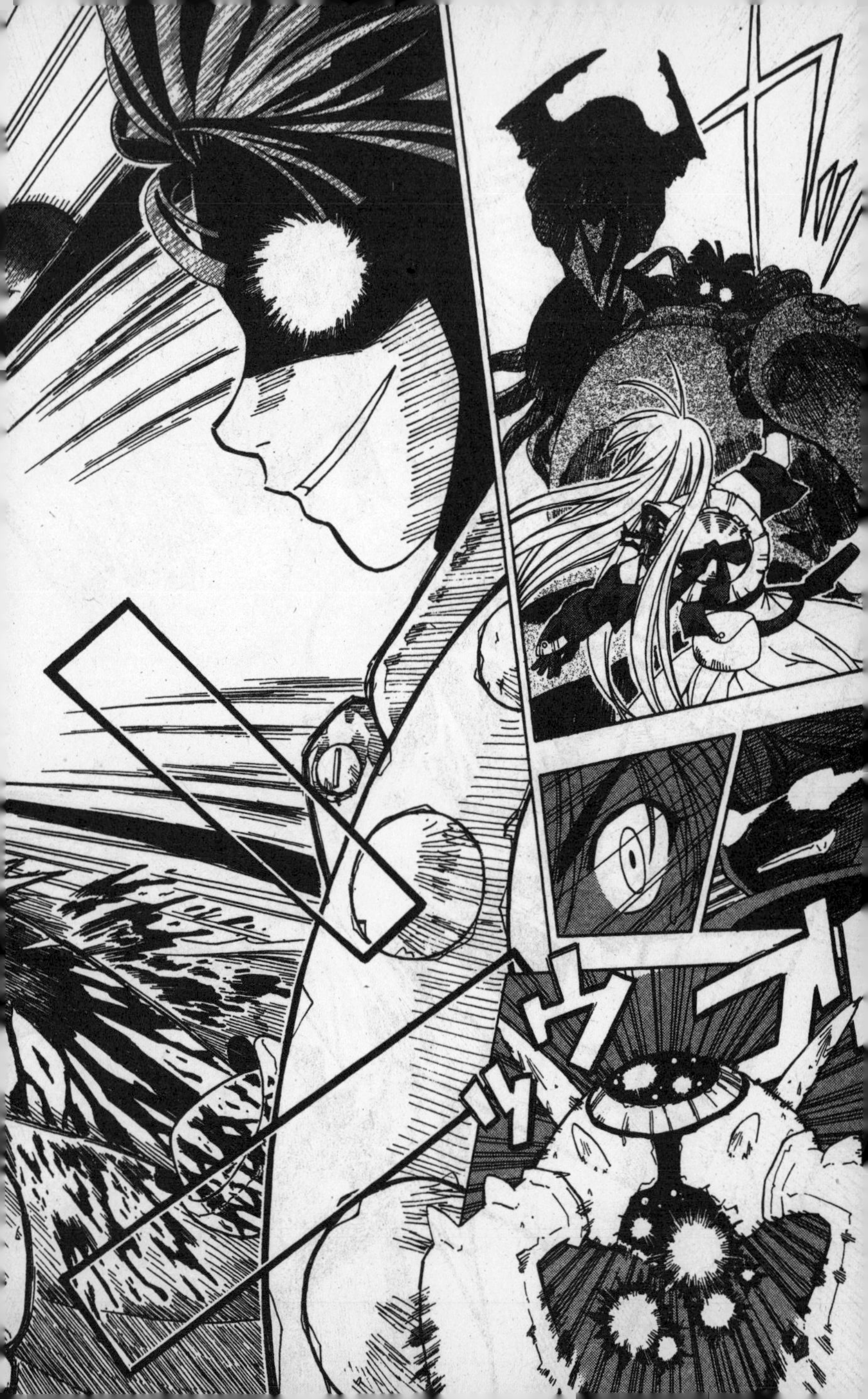

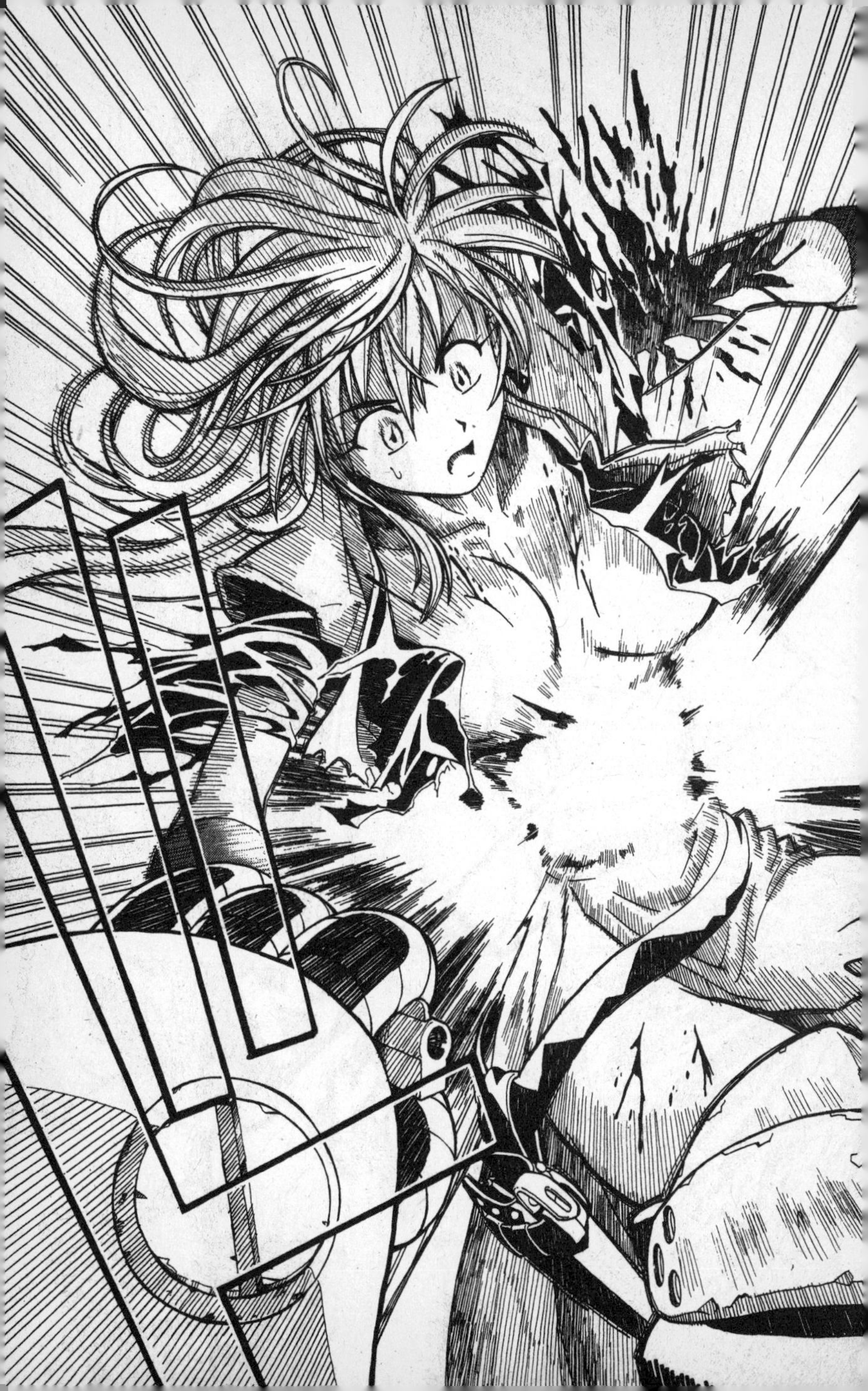
!!

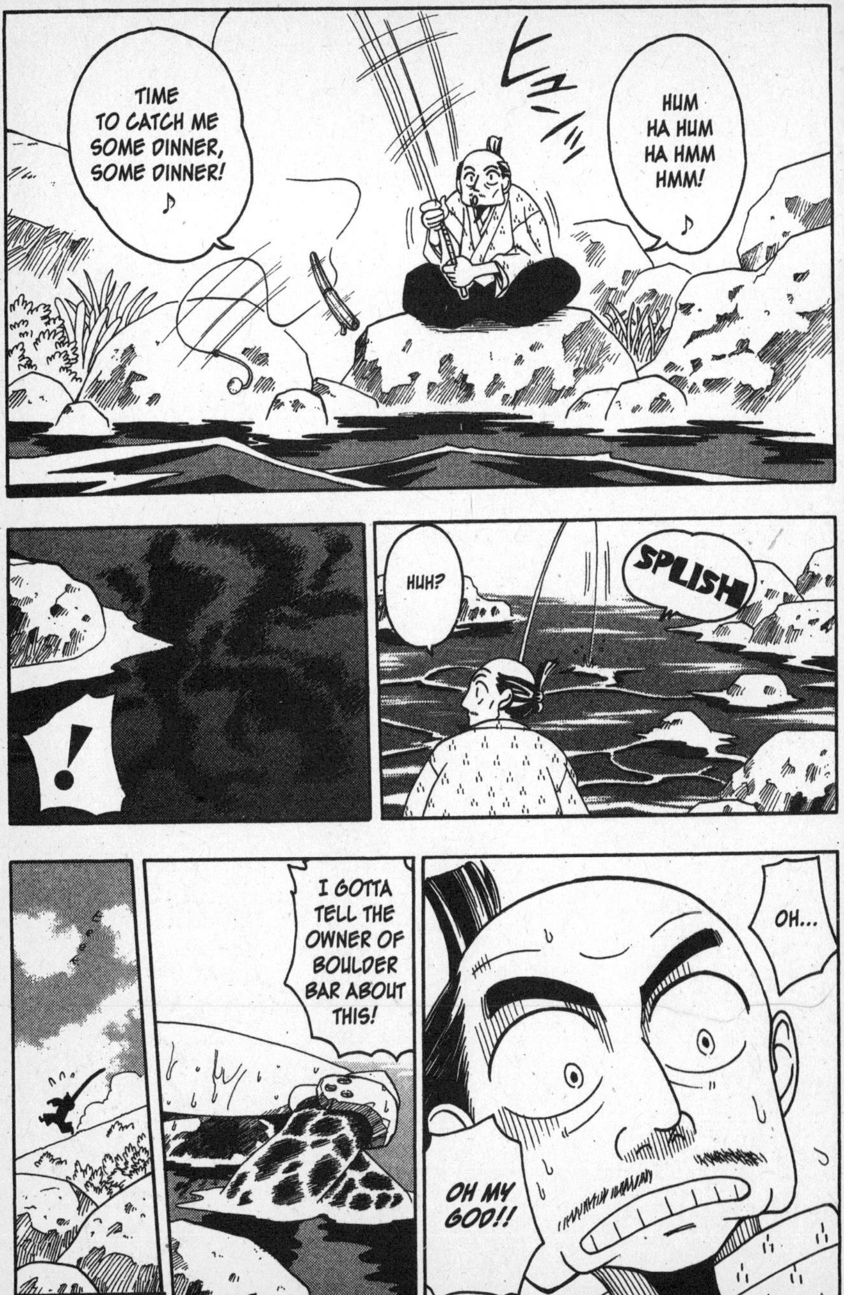
HUM HA HUM HA HMM HMM! ♪
TIME TO CATCH ME SOME DINNER, SOME DINNER! ♪
SPLISH!
HUH?
!
OH...
OH MY GOD!!
I GOTTA TELL THE OWNER OF BOULDER BAR ABOUT THIS!

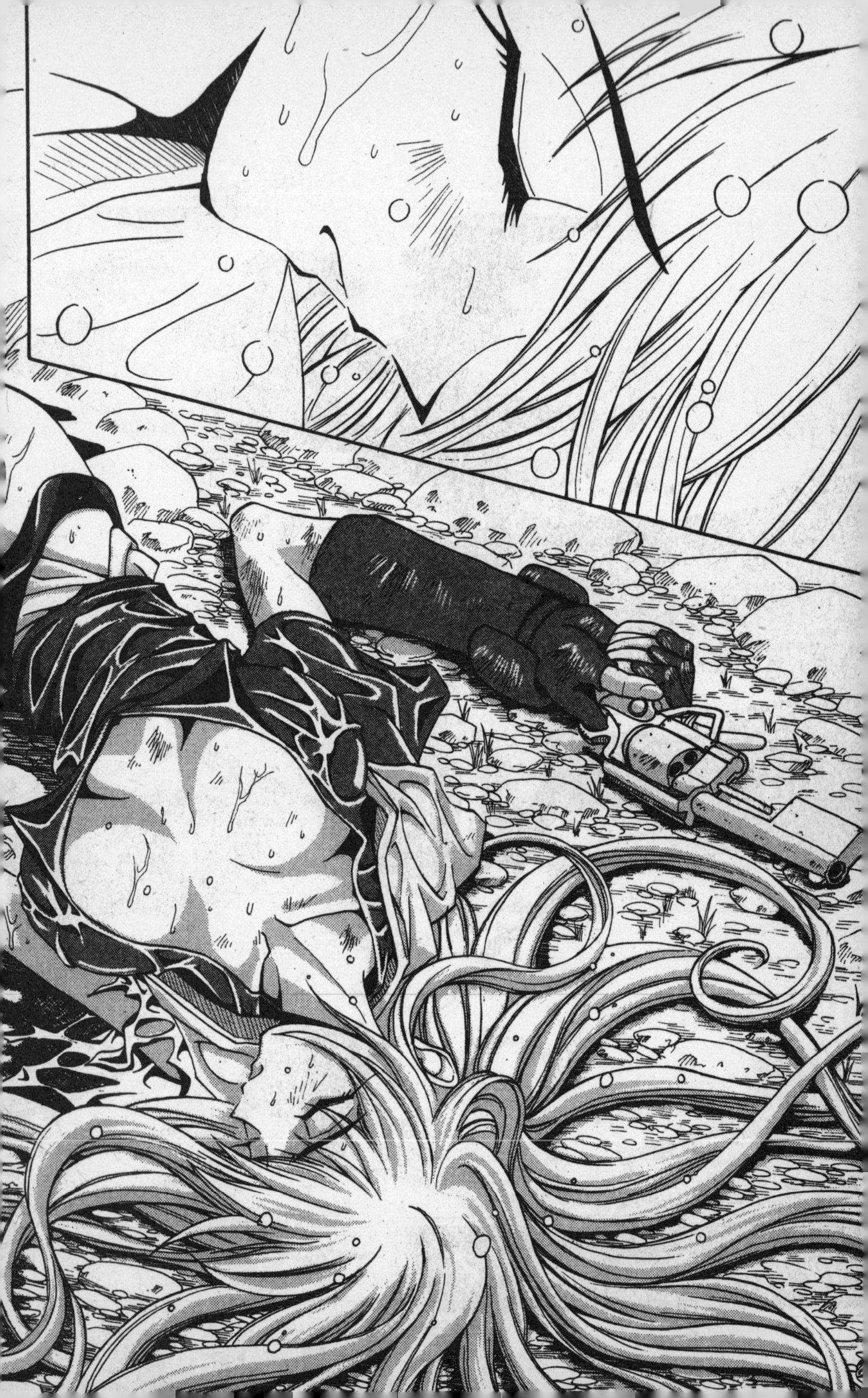

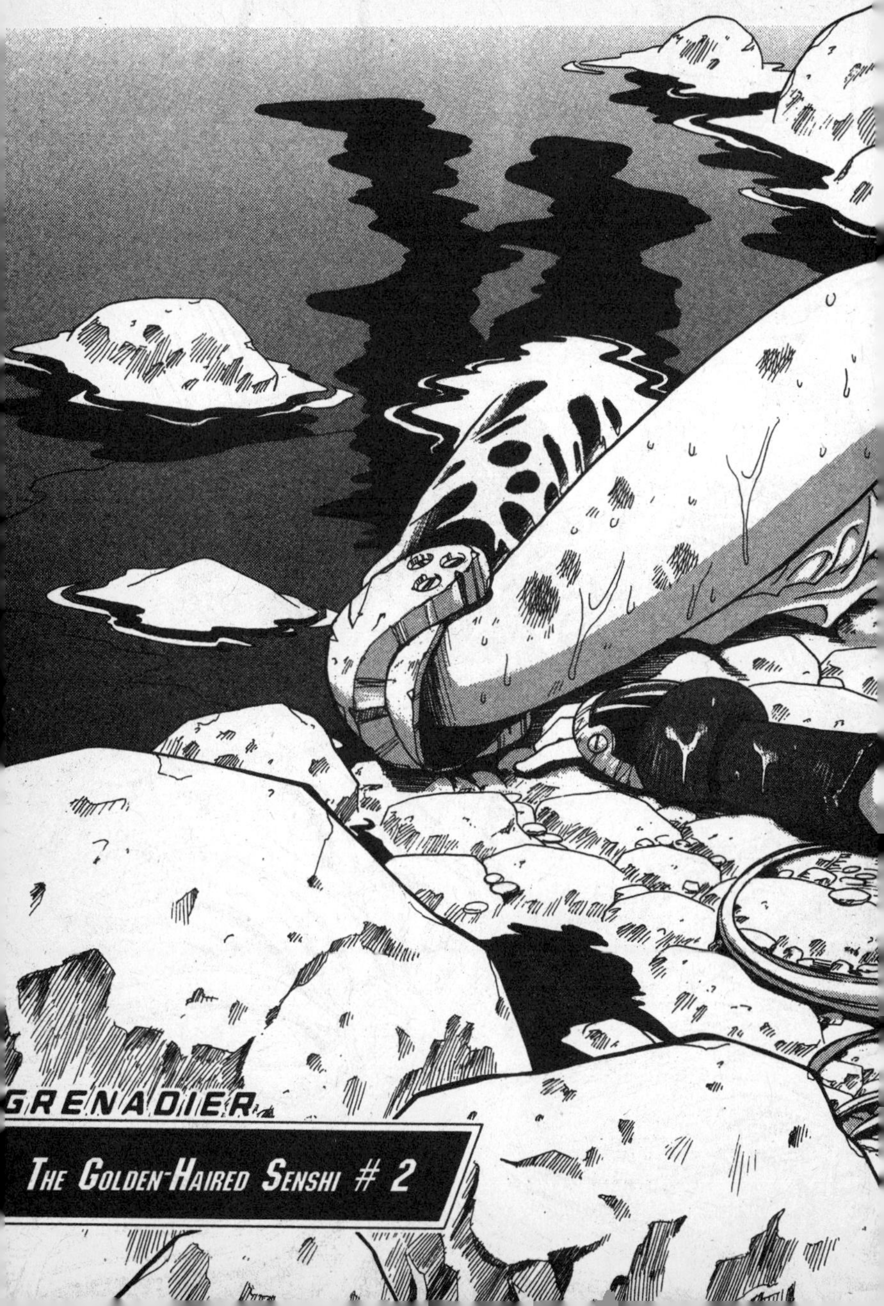
GRENADIER
THE GOLDEN-HAIRED SENSHI # 2

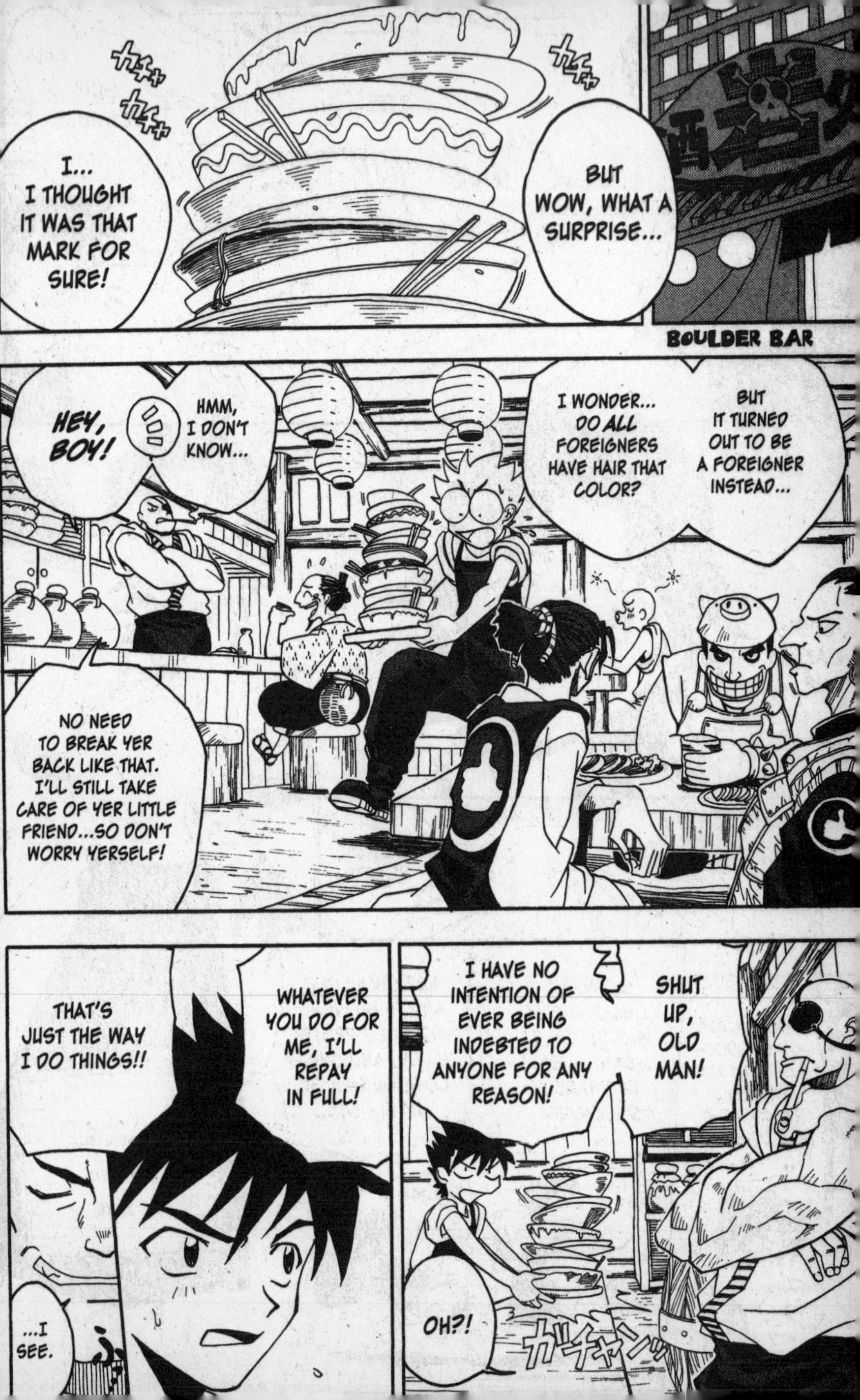
BOULDER BAR
BUT WOW, WHAT A SURPRISE...
I... I THOUGHT IT WAS THAT MARK FOR SURE!
BUT IT TURNED OUT TO BE A FOREIGNER INSTEAD...
I WONDER... DO ALL FOREIGNERS HAVE HAIR THAT COLOR?
HMM, I DON'T KNOW...
HEY, BOY!
NO NEED TO BREAK YER BACK LIKE THAT. I'LL STILL TAKE CARE OF YER LITTLE FRIEND...SO DON'T WORRY YERSELF!
SHUT UP, OLD MAN!
I HAVE NO INTENTION OF EVER BEING INDEBTED TO ANYONE FOR ANY REASON!
OH?!
ガチャンッ
WHATEVER YOU DO FOR ME, I'LL REPAY IN FULL!
THAT'S JUST THE WAY I DO THINGS!!
...I SEE.

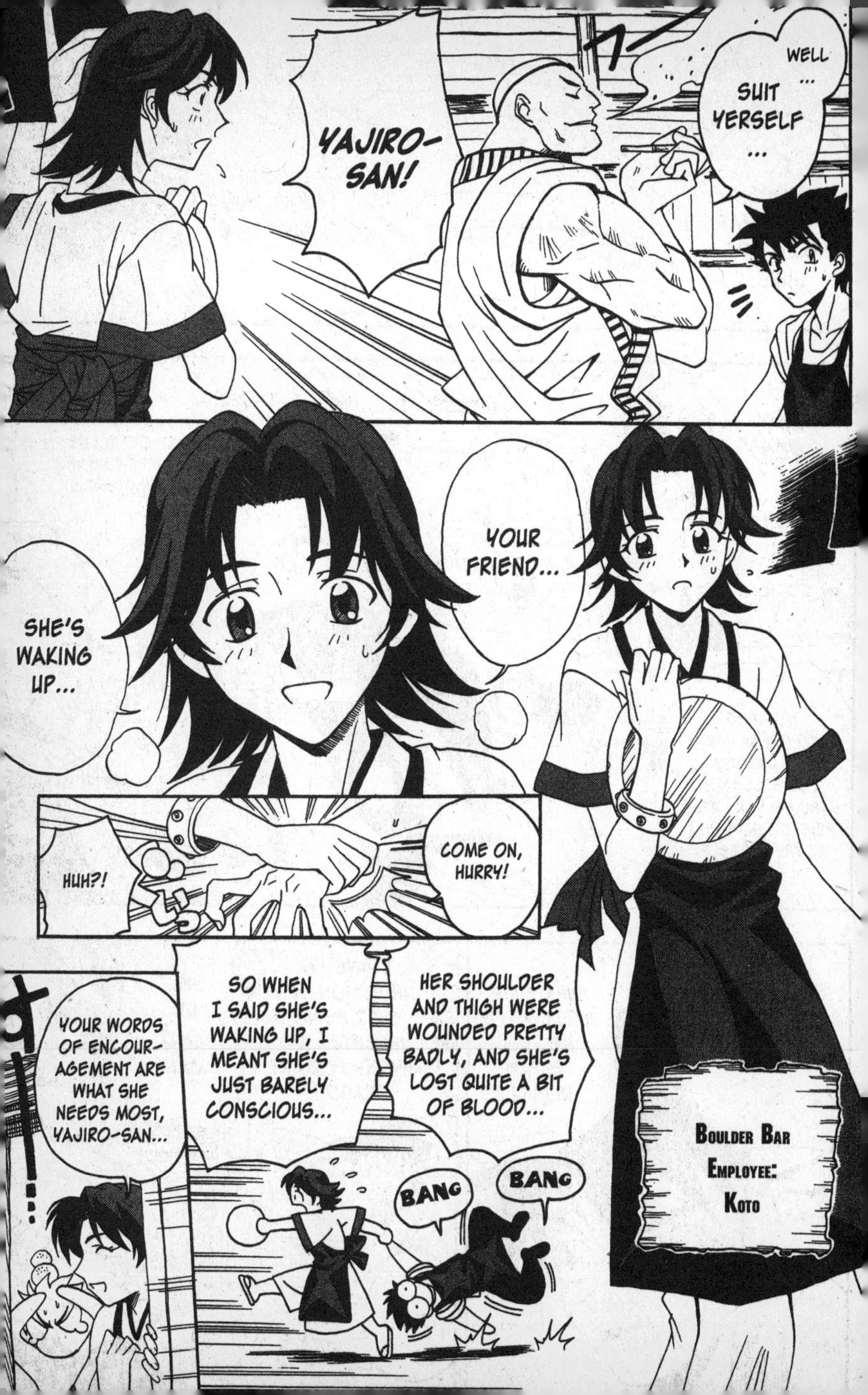

WELL ... SUIT YERSELF ...
YAJIRO-SAN!
YOUR FRIEND...
SHE'S WAKING UP...
BOULDER BAR EMPLOYEE: KOTO
COME ON, HURRY!
HUH?!
HER SHOULDER AND THIGH WERE WOUNDED PRETTY BADLY, AND SHE'S LOST QUITE A BIT OF BLOOD...
SO WHEN I SAID SHE'S WAKING UP, I MEANT SHE'S JUST BARELY CONSCIOUS...
BANG
BANG
YOUR WORDS OF ENCOUR-AGEMENT ARE WHAT SHE NEEDS MOST, YAJIRO-SAN...

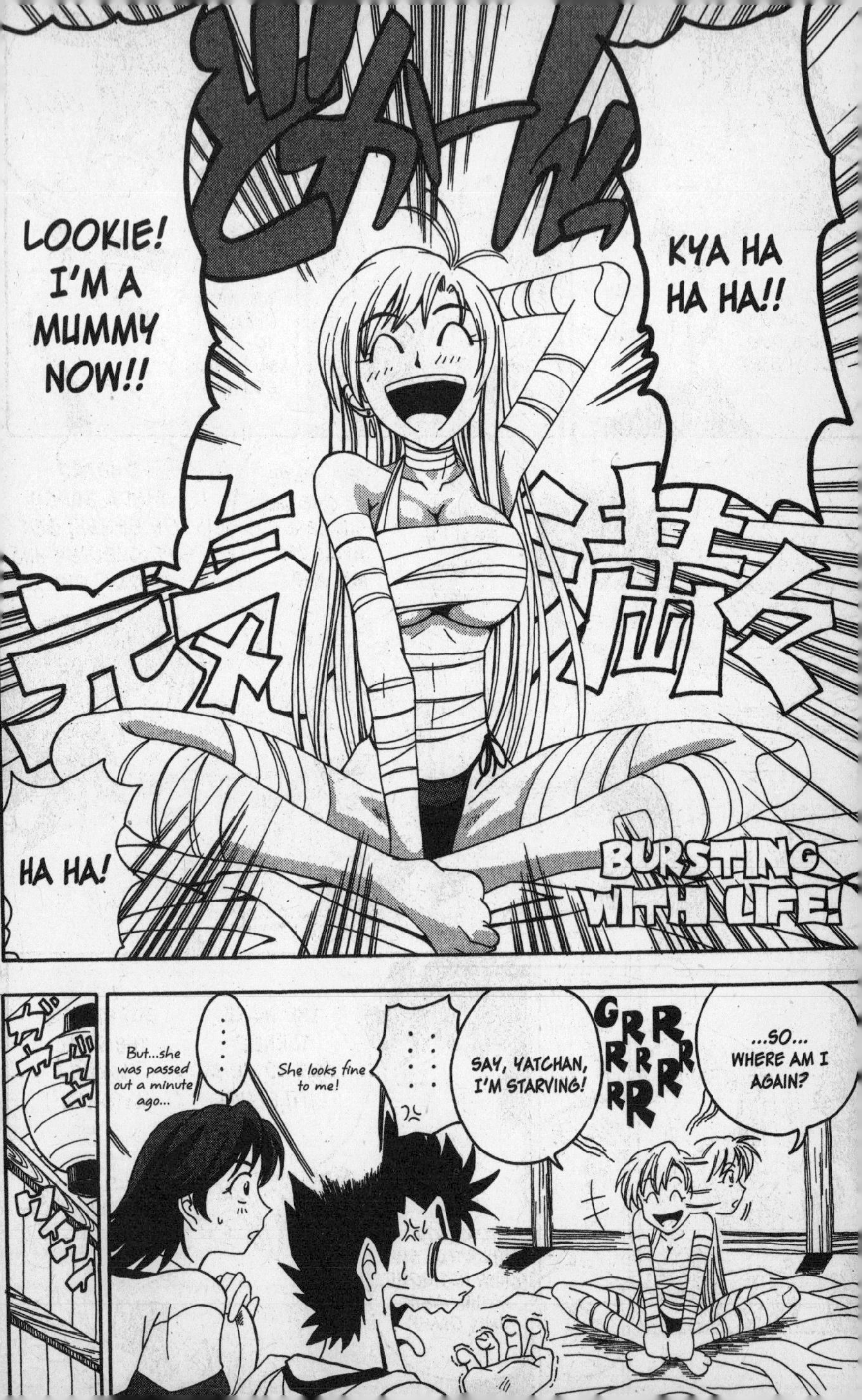
KYA HA
HA HA!!
LOOKIE! I'M A MUMMY NOW!!
BURSTING WITH LIFE!
HA HA!
...SO... WHERE AM I AGAIN?
GRRRRRRRRR
SAY, YATCHAN, I'M STARVING!
......
She looks fine to me!
....
But...she was passed out a minute ago...

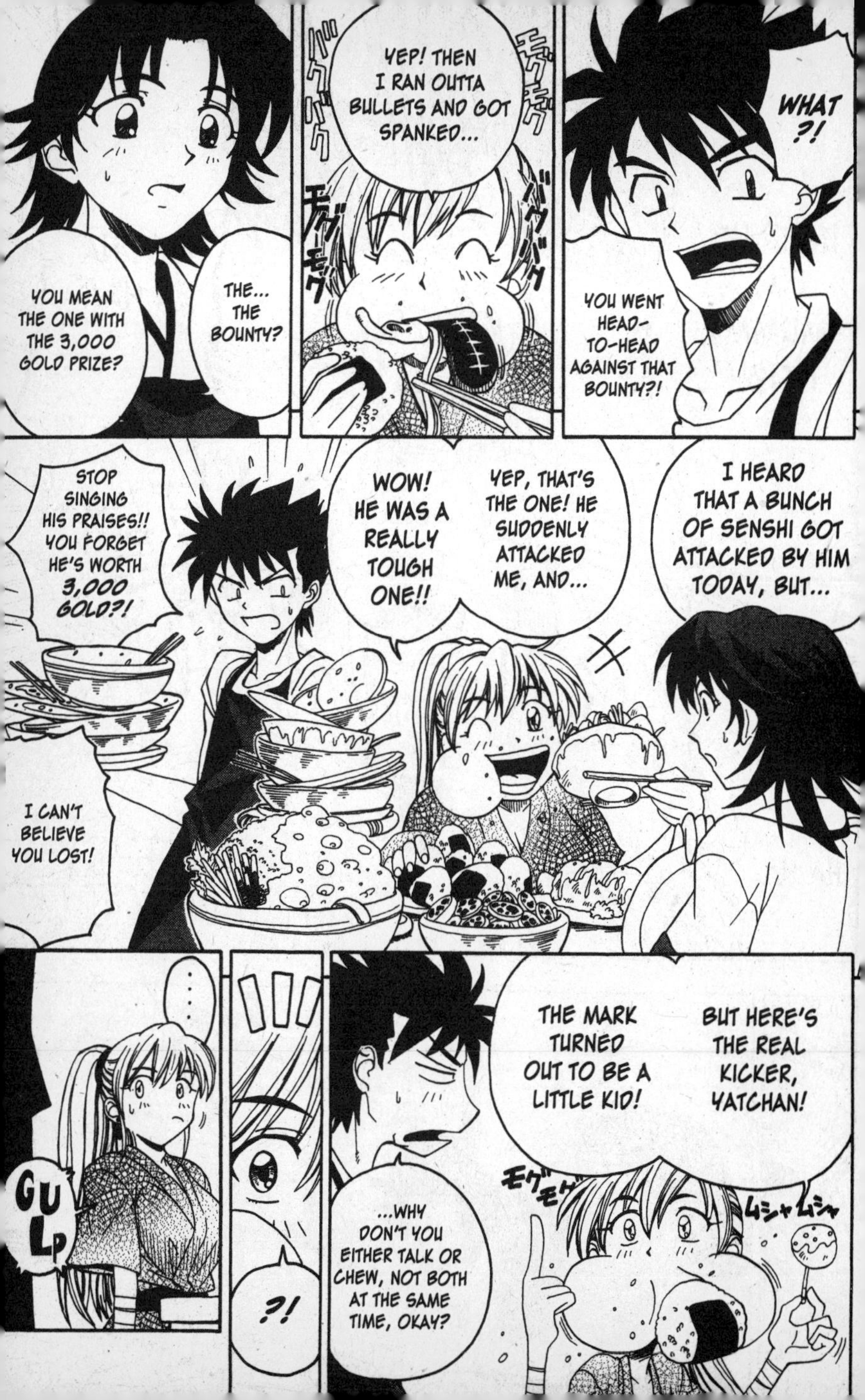
WHAT ?!
YOU WENT HEAD-TO-HEAD AGAINST THAT BOUNTY?!
YEP! THEN I RAN OUTTA BULLETS AND GOT SPANKED...
THE... THE BOUNTY?
YOU MEAN THE ONE WITH THE 3,000 GOLD PRIZE?
I HEARD THAT A BUNCH OF SENSHI GOT ATTACKED BY HIM TODAY, BUT...
YEP, THAT'S THE ONE! HE SUDDENLY ATTACKED ME, AND...
WOW! HE WAS A REALLY TOUGH ONE!!
STOP SINGING HIS PRAISES!! YOU FORGET HE'S WORTH 3,000 GOLD?!
I CAN'T BELIEVE YOU LOST!
BUT HERE'S THE REAL KICKER, YATCHAN!
THE MARK TURNED OUT TO BE A LITTLE KID!
ムシャムシャ
...WHY DON'T YOU EITHER TALK OR CHEW, NOT BOTH AT THE SAME TIME, OKAY?
?!
...
GULP

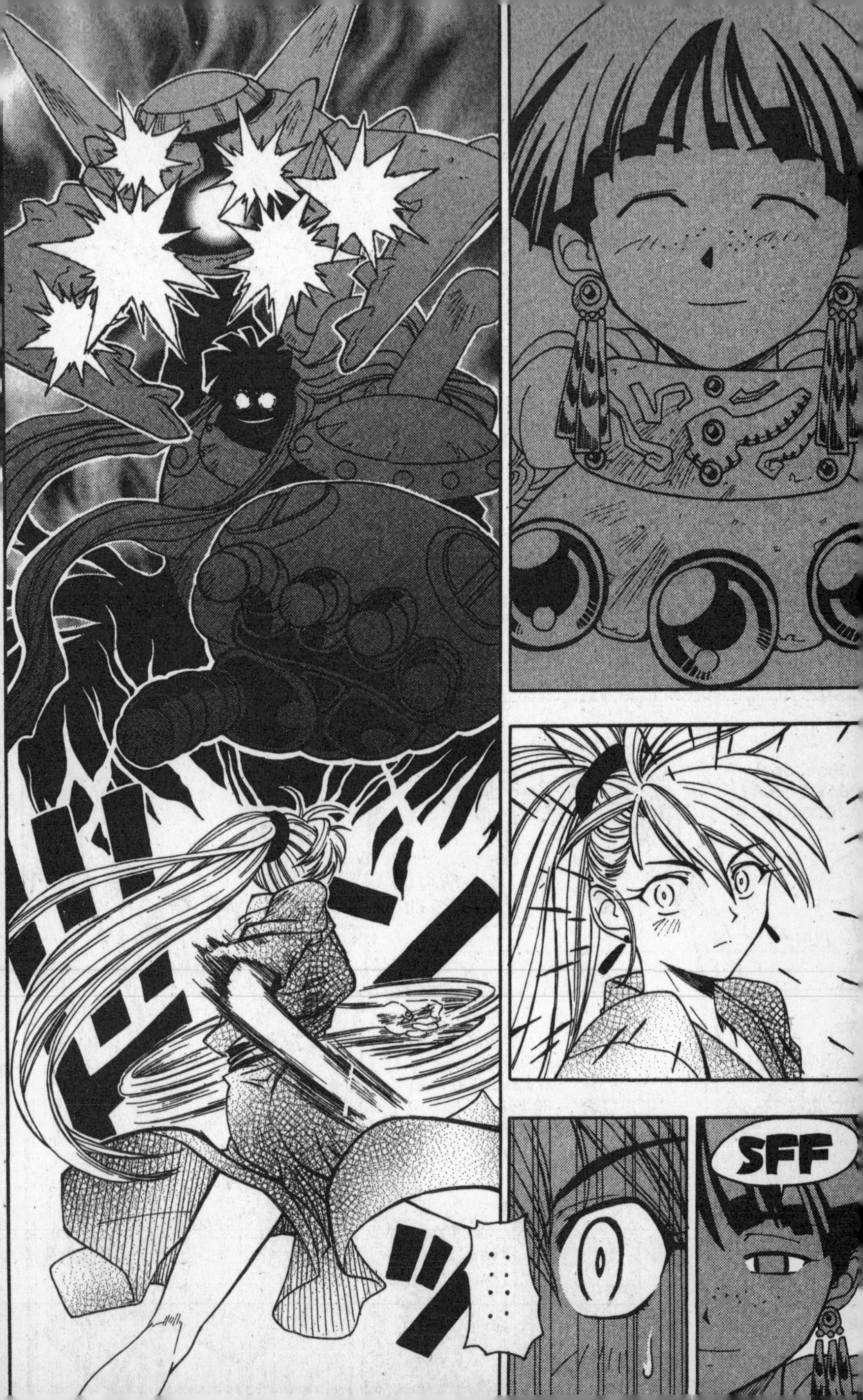
SFF

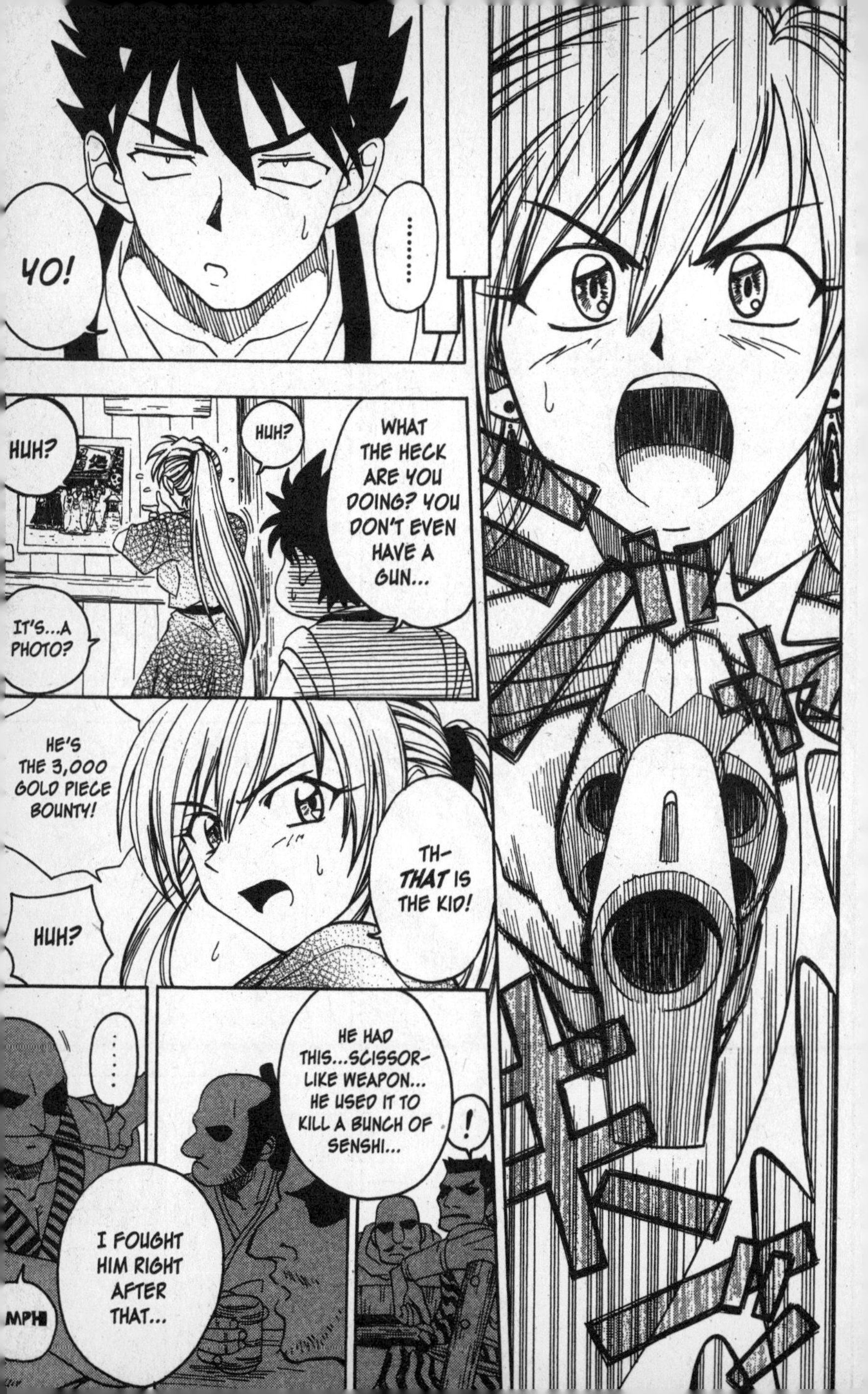
......
YO!
WHAT THE HECK ARE YOU DOING? YOU DON'T EVEN HAVE A GUN...
HUH?
HUH?
IT'S...A PHOTO?
TH- *THAT* IS THE KID!
HE'S THE 3,000 GOLD PIECE BOUNTY!
HUH?
HE HAD THIS...SCISSOR-LIKE WEAPON... HE USED IT TO KILL A BUNCH OF SENSHI...
!
I FOUGHT HIM RIGHT AFTER THAT...
......
MPH

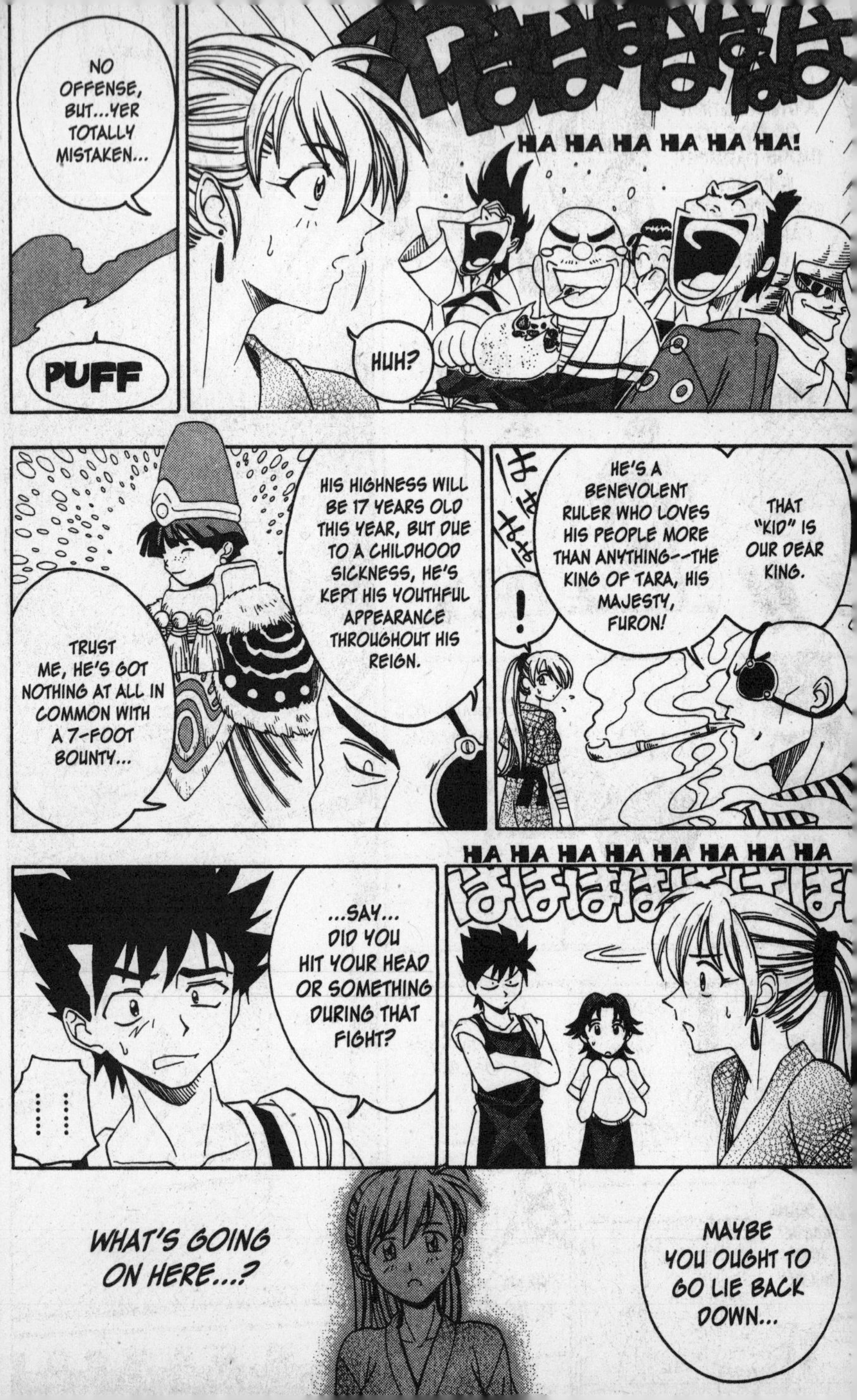
HA HA HA HA HA HA!
HUH?
NO OFFENSE, BUT...YER TOTALLY MISTAKEN...
PUFF
THAT "KID" IS OUR DEAR KING.
HE'S A BENEVOLENT RULER WHO LOVES HIS PEOPLE MORE THAN ANYTHING--THE KING OF TARA, HIS MAJESTY, FURON!
ははは
!
HIS HIGHNESS WILL BE 17 YEARS OLD THIS YEAR, BUT DUE TO A CHILDHOOD SICKNESS, HE'S KEPT HIS YOUTHFUL APPEARANCE THROUGHOUT HIS REIGN.
TRUST ME, HE'S GOT NOTHING AT ALL IN COMMON WITH A 7-FOOT BOUNTY...
HA HA HA HA HA HA HA HA
...SAY... DID YOU HIT YOUR HEAD OR SOMETHING DURING THAT FIGHT?
......
MAYBE YOU OUGHT TO GO LIE BACK DOWN...
WHAT'S GOING ON HERE...?

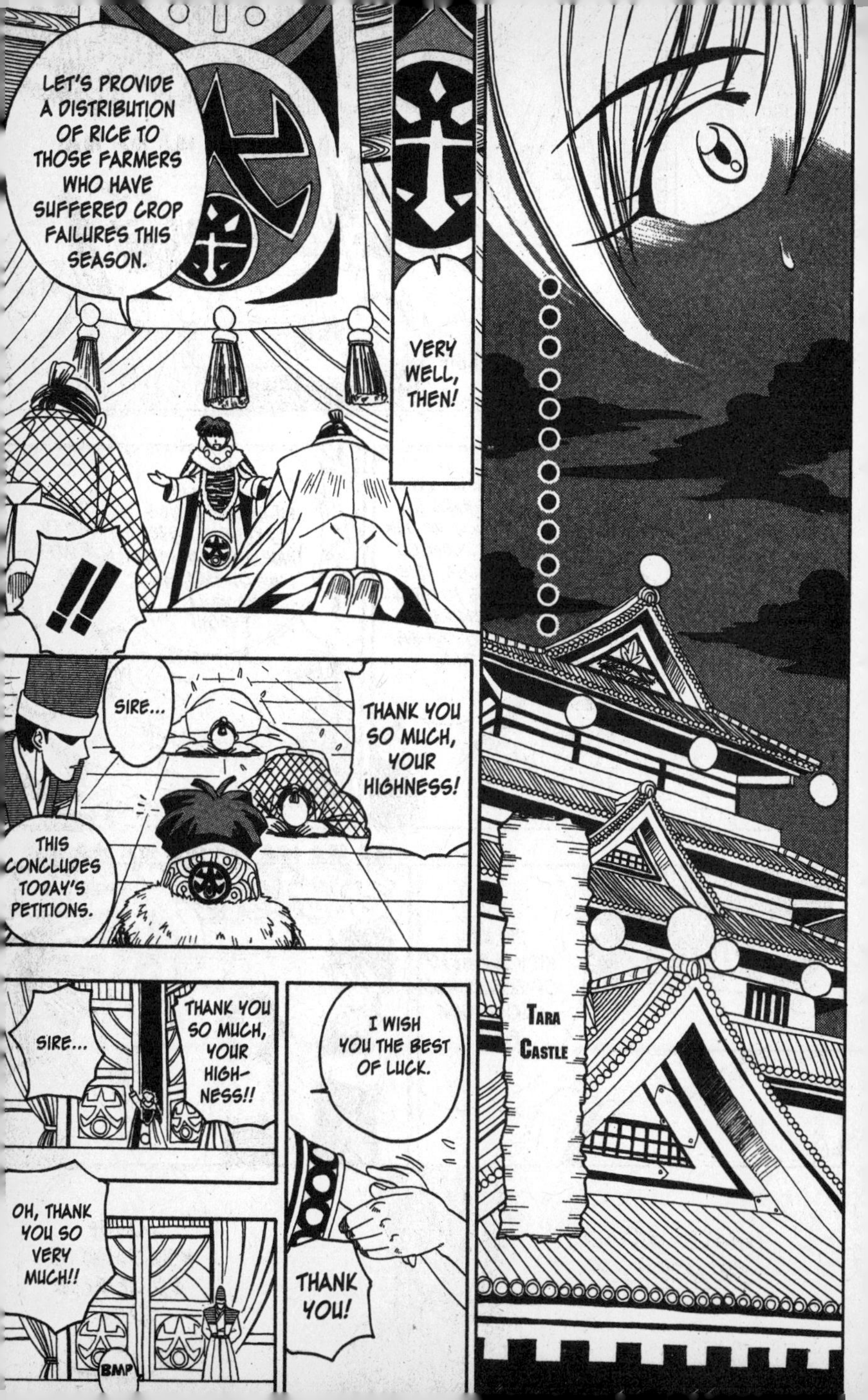
TARA CASTLE
LET'S PROVIDE A DISTRIBUTION OF RICE TO THOSE FARMERS WHO HAVE SUFFERED CROP FAILURES THIS SEASON.
VERY WELL, THEN!
!!
THANK YOU SO MUCH, YOUR HIGHNESS!
SIRE...
THIS CONCLUDES TODAY'S PETITIONS.
I WISH YOU THE BEST OF LUCK.
THANK YOU!
THANK YOU SO MUCH, YOUR HIGH-NESS!!
SIRE...
OH, THANK YOU SO VERY MUCH!!
BMP

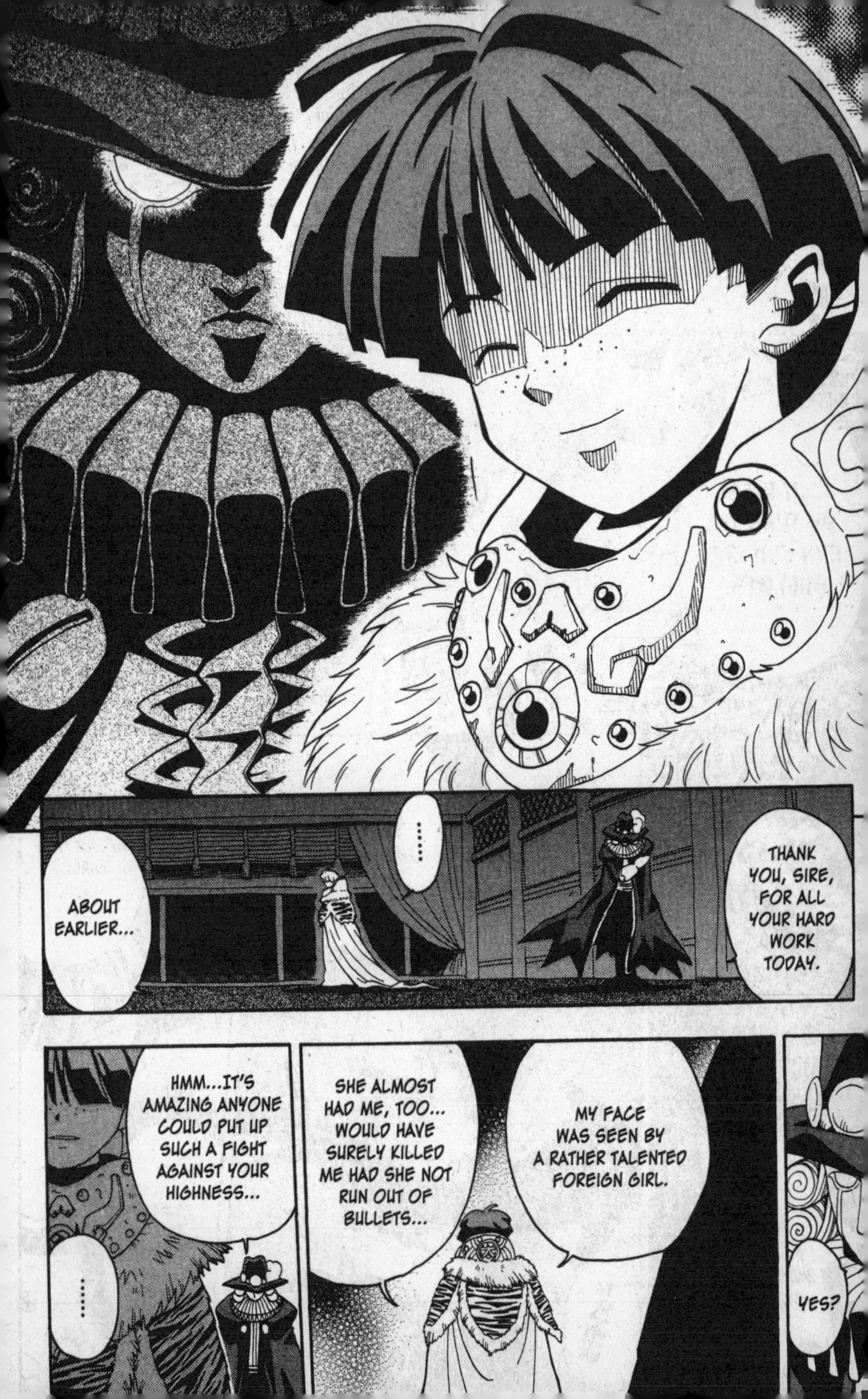
THANK YOU, SIRE, FOR ALL YOUR HARD WORK TODAY.
......
ABOUT EARLIER...
YES?
MY FACE WAS SEEN BY A RATHER TALENTED FOREIGN GIRL.
SHE ALMOST HAD ME, TOO... WOULD HAVE SURELY KILLED ME HAD SHE NOT RUN OUT OF BULLETS...
HMM...IT'S AMAZING ANYONE COULD PUT UP SUCH A FIGHT AGAINST YOUR HIGHNESS...
......

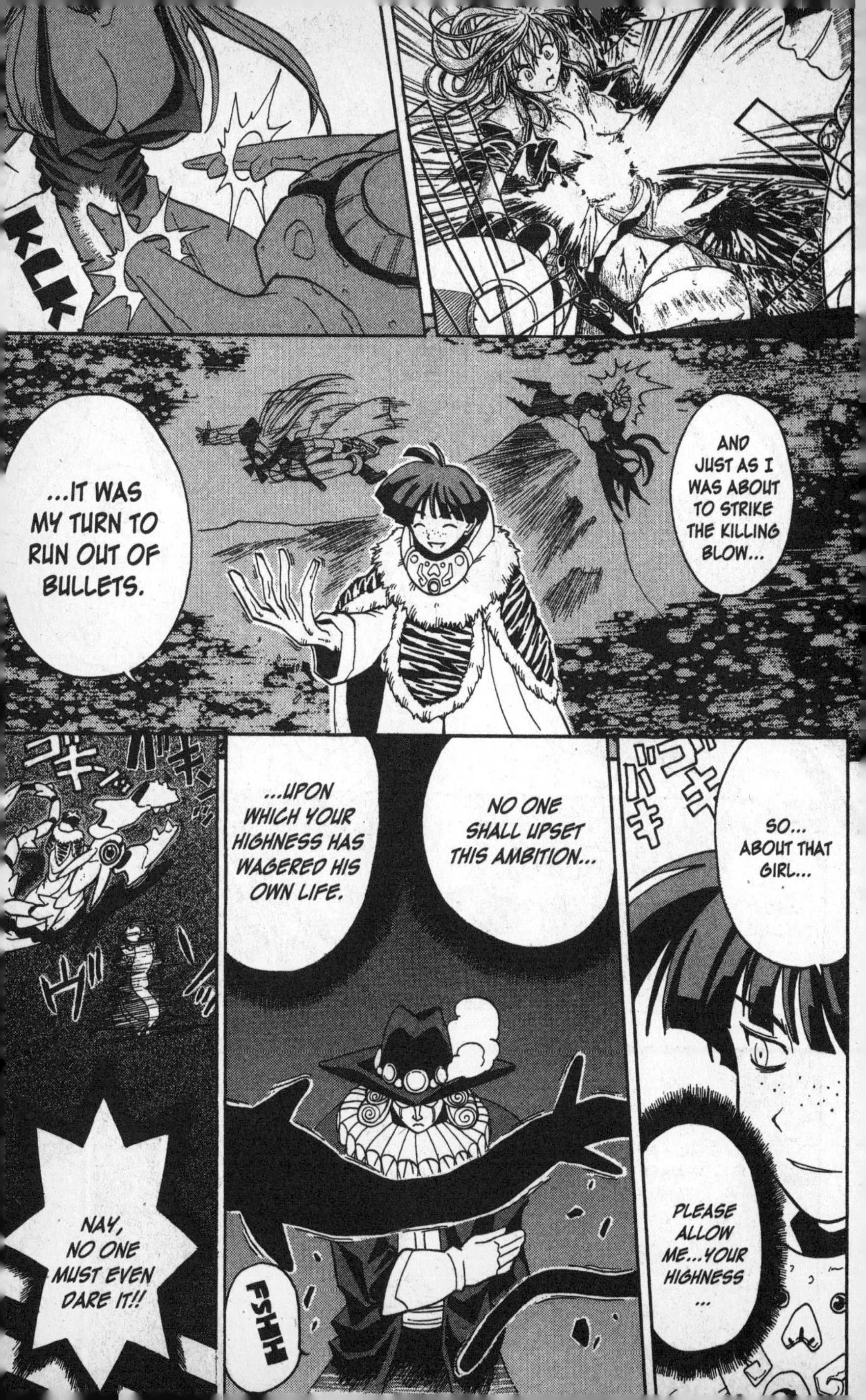
KLK
AND JUST AS I WAS ABOUT TO STRIKE THE KILLING BLOW...
...IT WAS MY TURN TO RUN OUT OF BULLETS.
SO... ABOUT THAT GIRL...
PLEASE ALLOW ME...YOUR HIGHNESS ...
NO ONE SHALL UPSET THIS AMBITION...
...UPON WHICH YOUR HIGHNESS HAS WAGERED HIS OWN LIFE.
FSHHH
NAY, NO ONE MUST EVEN DARE IT!!

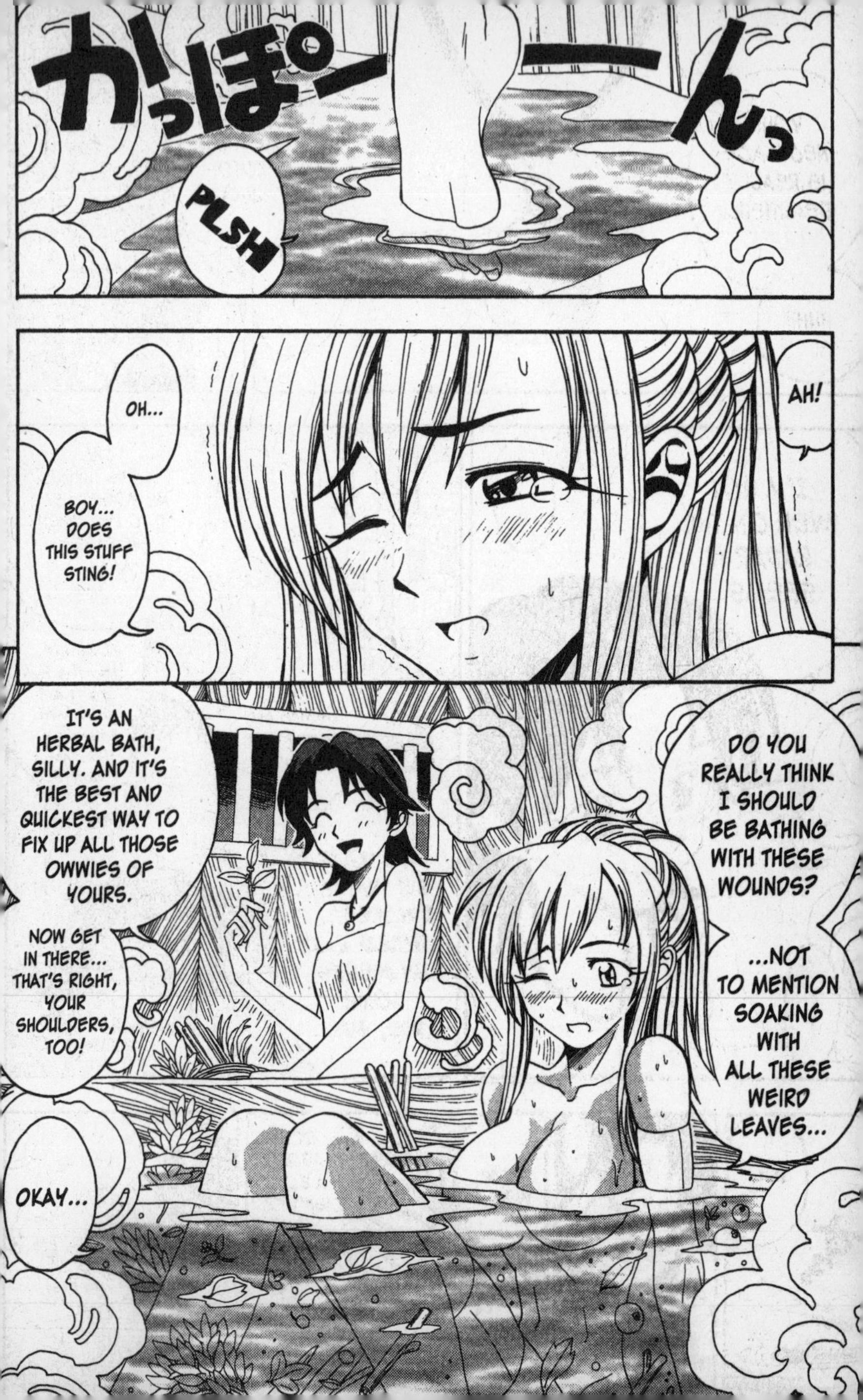
かっぽーーんっ
PLSH
AH!
OH...
BOY... DOES THIS STUFF STING!
DO YOU REALLY THINK I SHOULD BE BATHING WITH THESE WOUNDS?
...NOT TO MENTION SOAKING WITH ALL THESE WEIRD LEAVES...
IT'S AN HERBAL BATH, SILLY. AND IT'S THE BEST AND QUICKEST WAY TO FIX UP ALL THOSE OWWIES OF YOURS.
NOW GET IN THERE... THAT'S RIGHT, YOUR SHOULDERS, TOO!
OKAY...

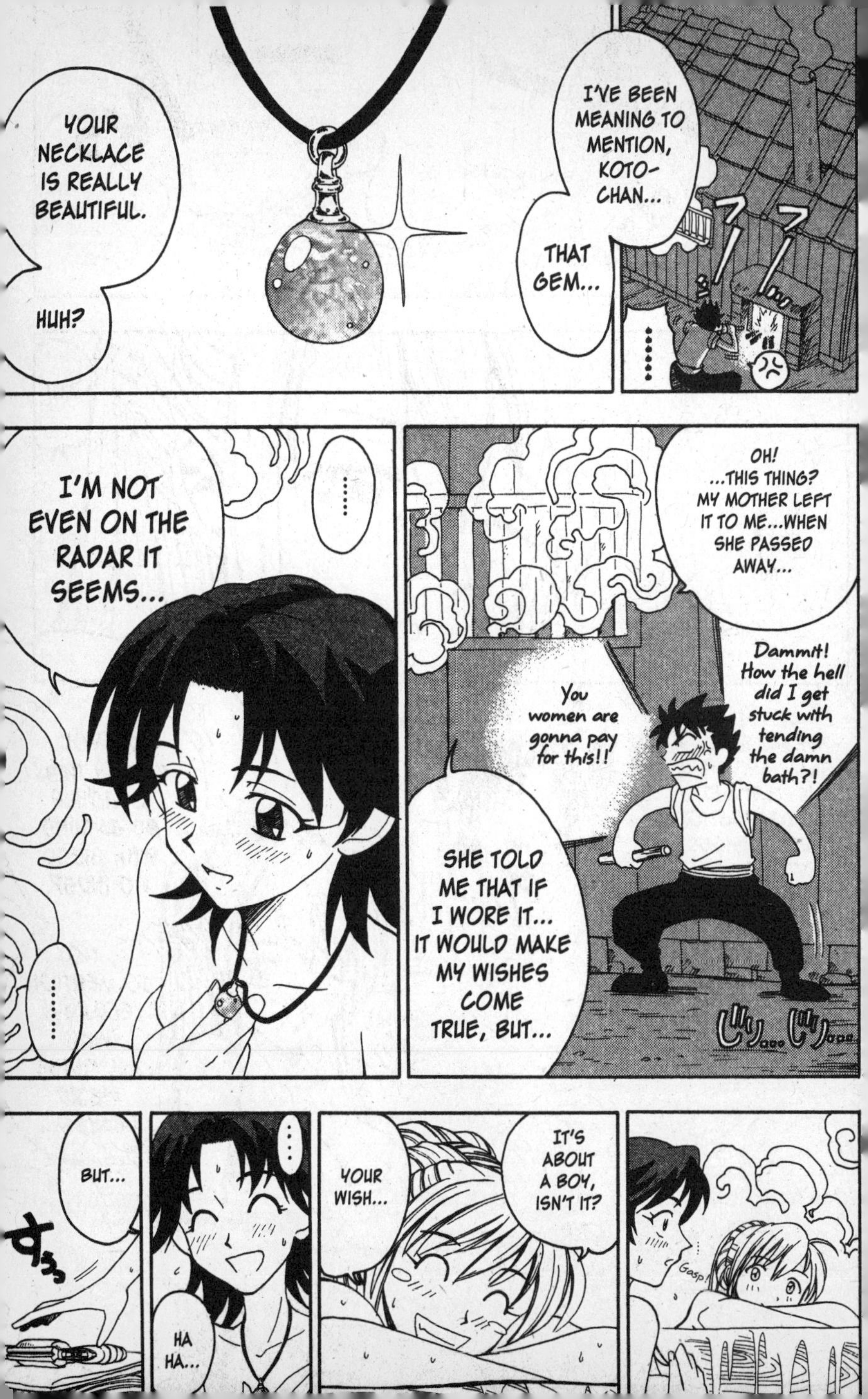
I'VE BEEN MEANING TO MENTION, KOTO-CHAN...
THAT GEM...
......
YOUR NECKLACE IS REALLY BEAUTIFUL.
HUH?
OH! ...THIS THING? MY MOTHER LEFT IT TO ME...WHEN SHE PASSED AWAY...
Dammit! How the hell did I get stuck with tending the damn bath?!
You women are gonna pay for this!!
SHE TOLD ME THAT IF I WORE IT... IT WOULD MAKE MY WISHES COME TRUE, BUT...
じり...じり...
......
I'M NOT EVEN ON THE RADAR IT SEEMS...
......
Gasp!
IT'S ABOUT A BOY, ISN'T IT?
YOUR WISH...
...
HA HA...
BUT...
すっ

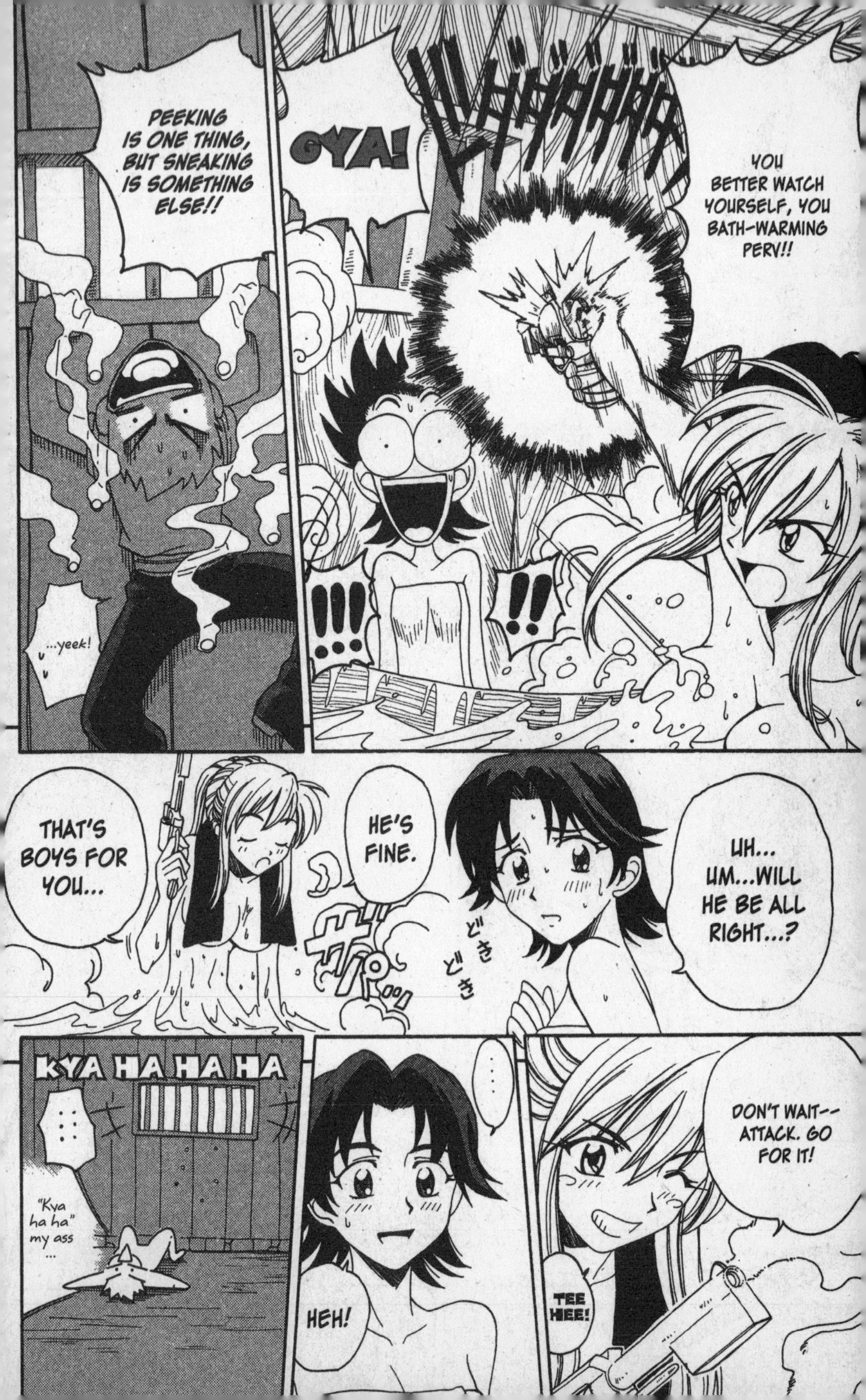
YOU BETTER WATCH YOURSELF, YOU BATH-WARMING PERV!!
GYA!
!!
!!!
PEEKING IS ONE THING, BUT SNEAKING IS SOMETHING ELSE!!
...yeek!
UH... UM...WILL HE BE ALL RIGHT...?
どき どき
HE'S FINE.
THAT'S BOYS FOR YOU...
DON'T WAIT-- ATTACK. GO FOR IT!
TEE HEE!
...
HEH!
KYA HA HA HA
...
"Kya ha ha" my ass ...

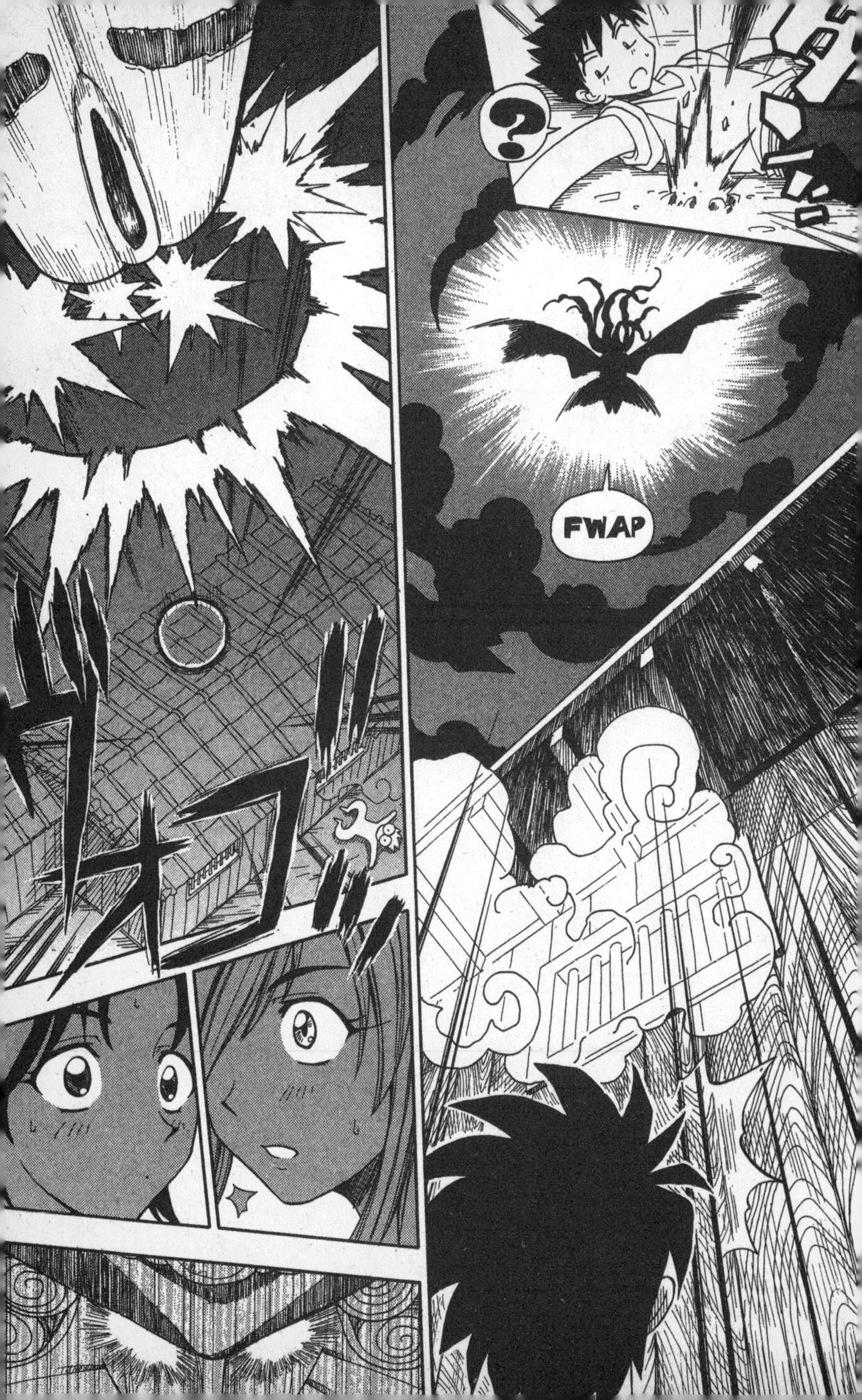
?
FWAP

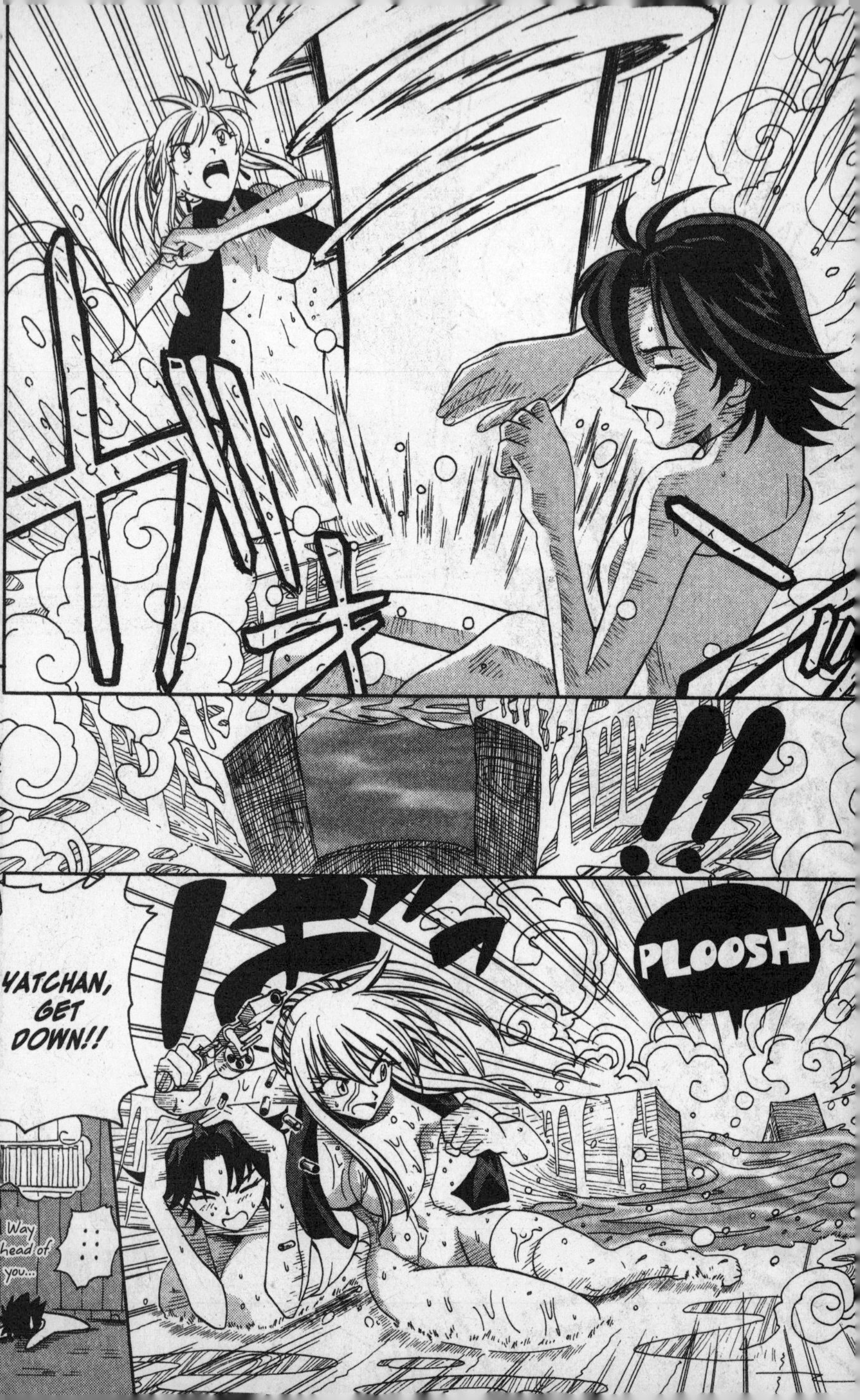
PLOOSH
YATCHAN, GET DOWN!!
Way ahead of you...

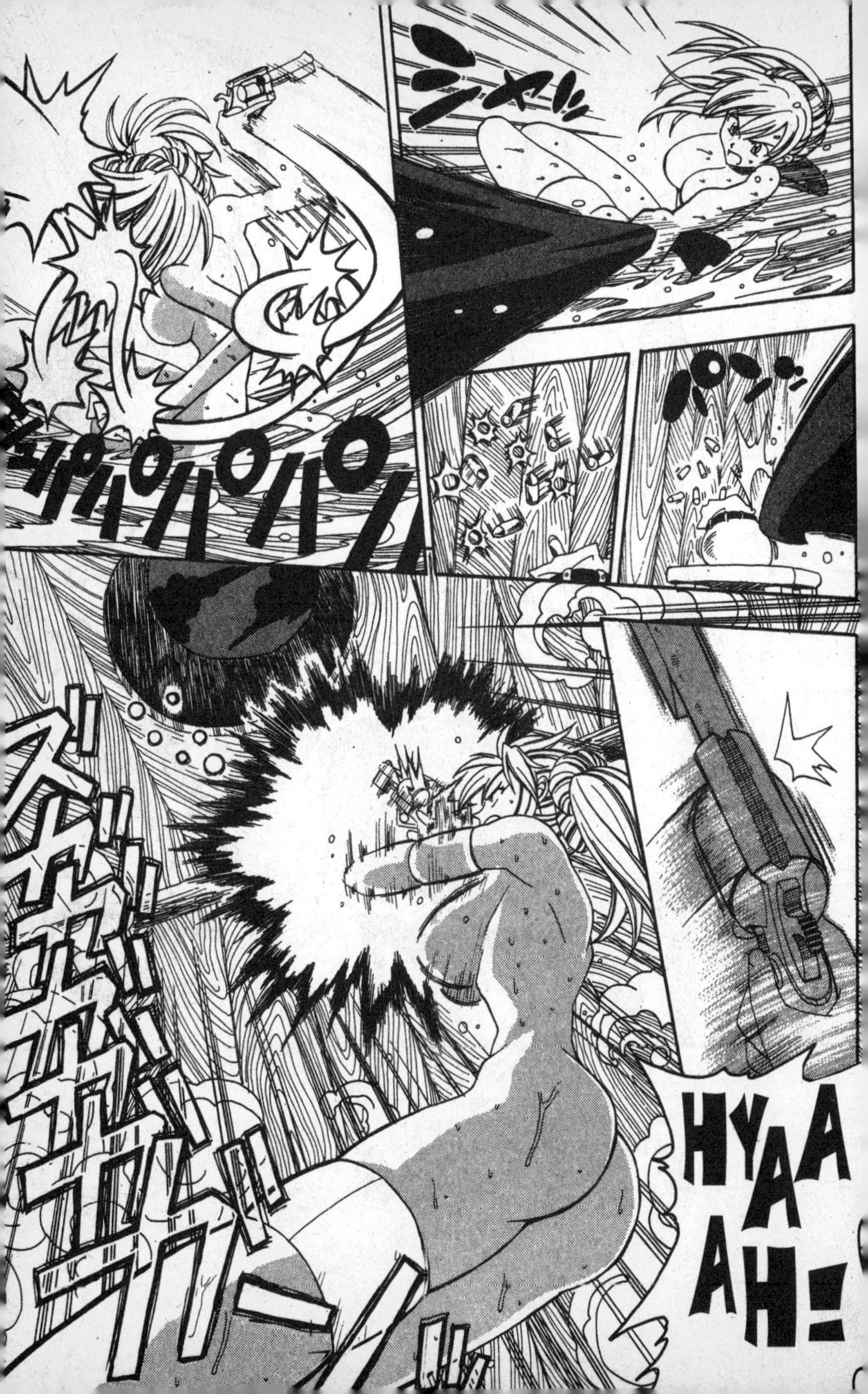
シャッ
パンッ
HYAAAAH!!

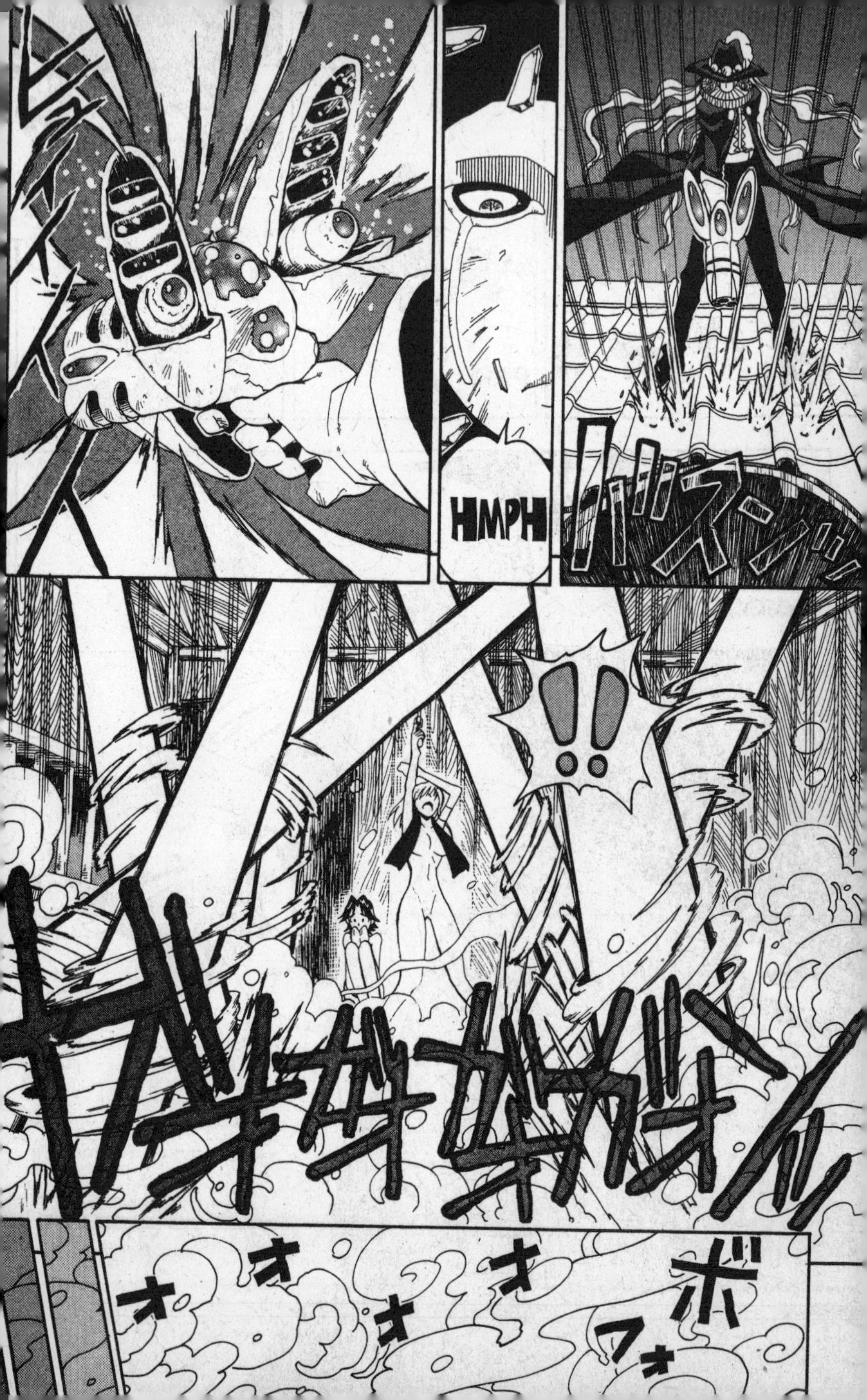
HMPH
!!

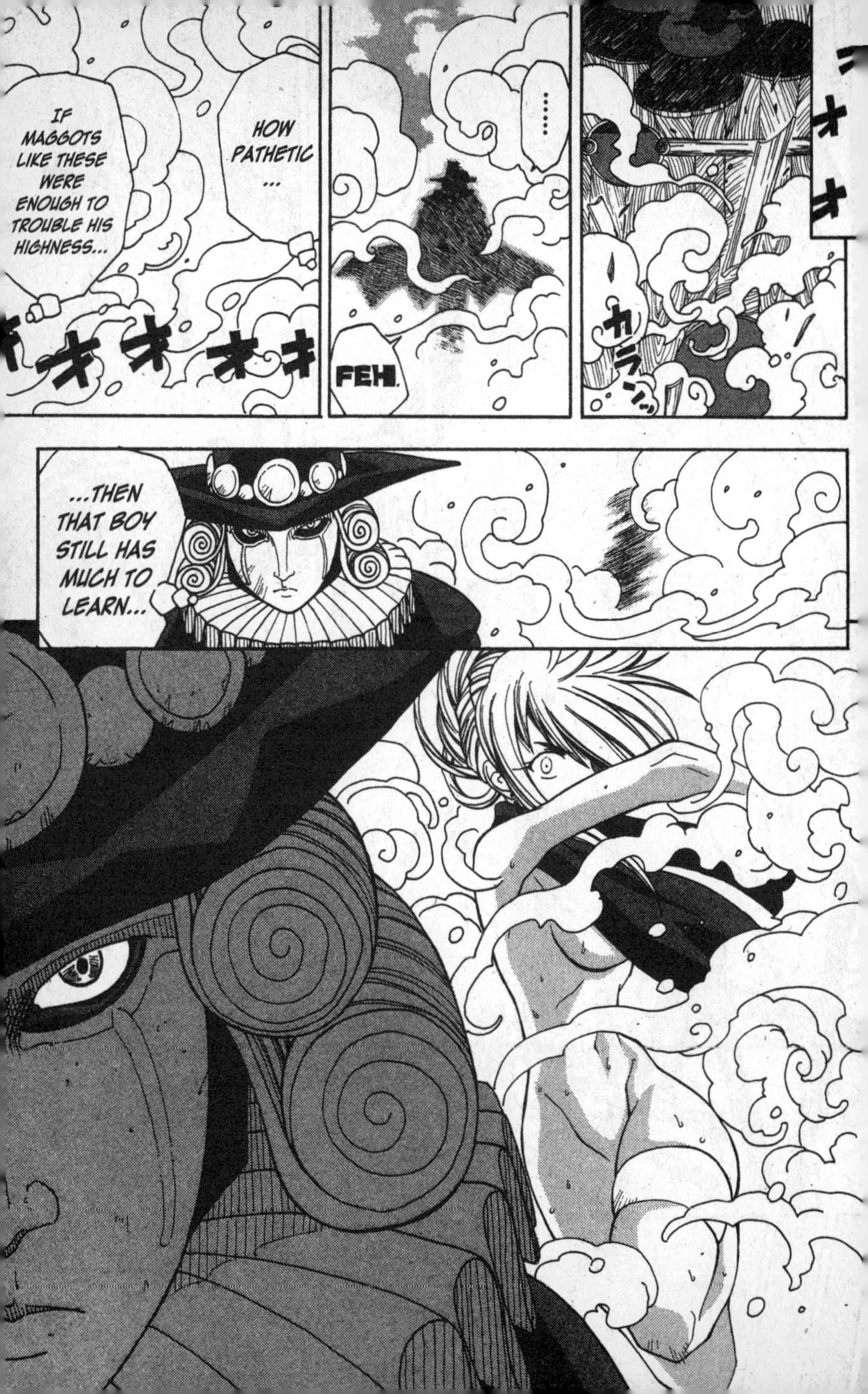
オオオ
カラン…
......
FEH.
HOW PATHETIC ...
IF MAGGOTS LIKE THESE WERE ENOUGH TO TROUBLE HIS HIGHNESS...
オオオオ
...THEN THAT BOY STILL HAS MUCH TO LEARN...

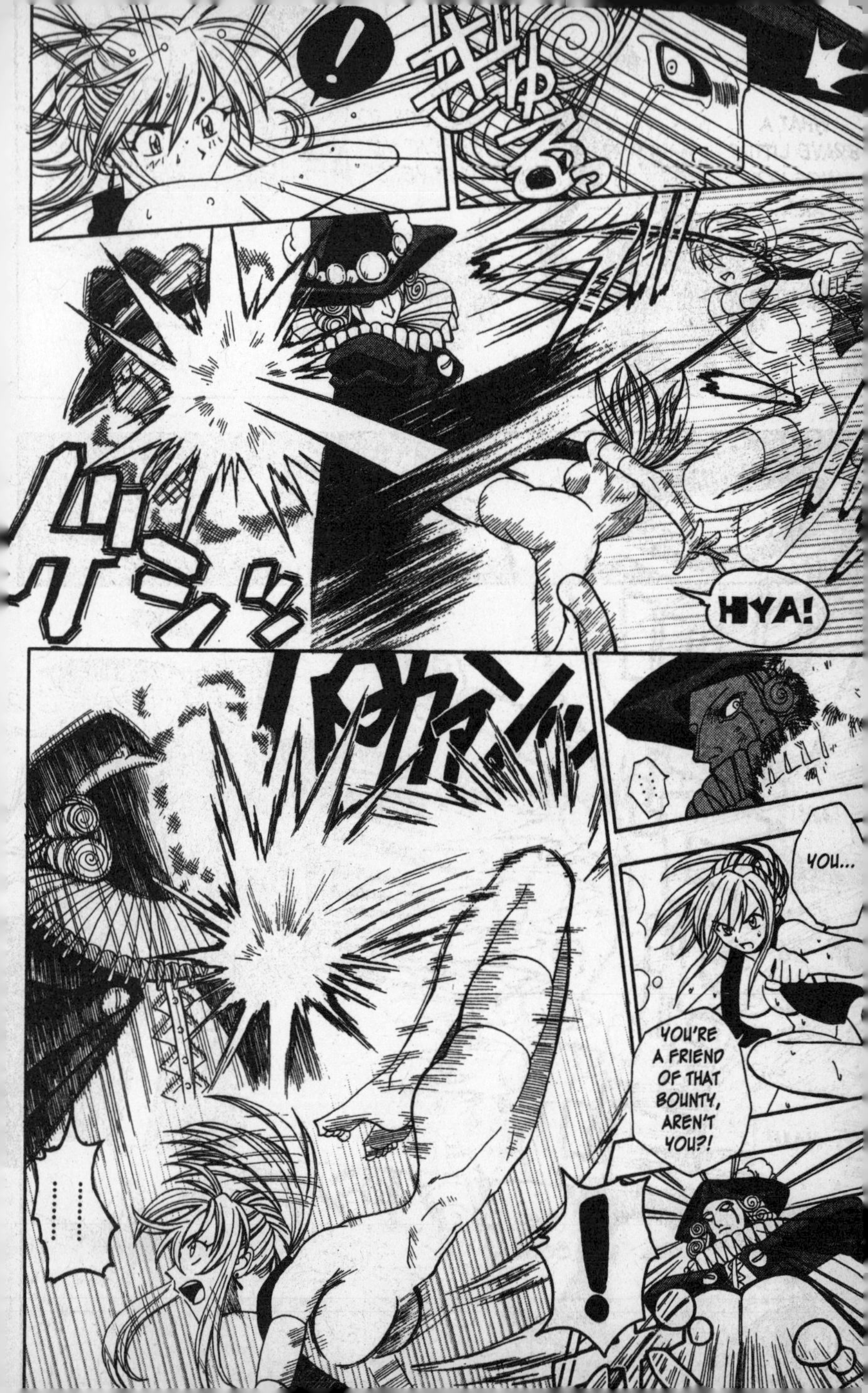
!
HYA!
. . .
YOU...
YOU'RE A FRIEND OF THAT BOUNTY, AREN'T YOU?!
!
......

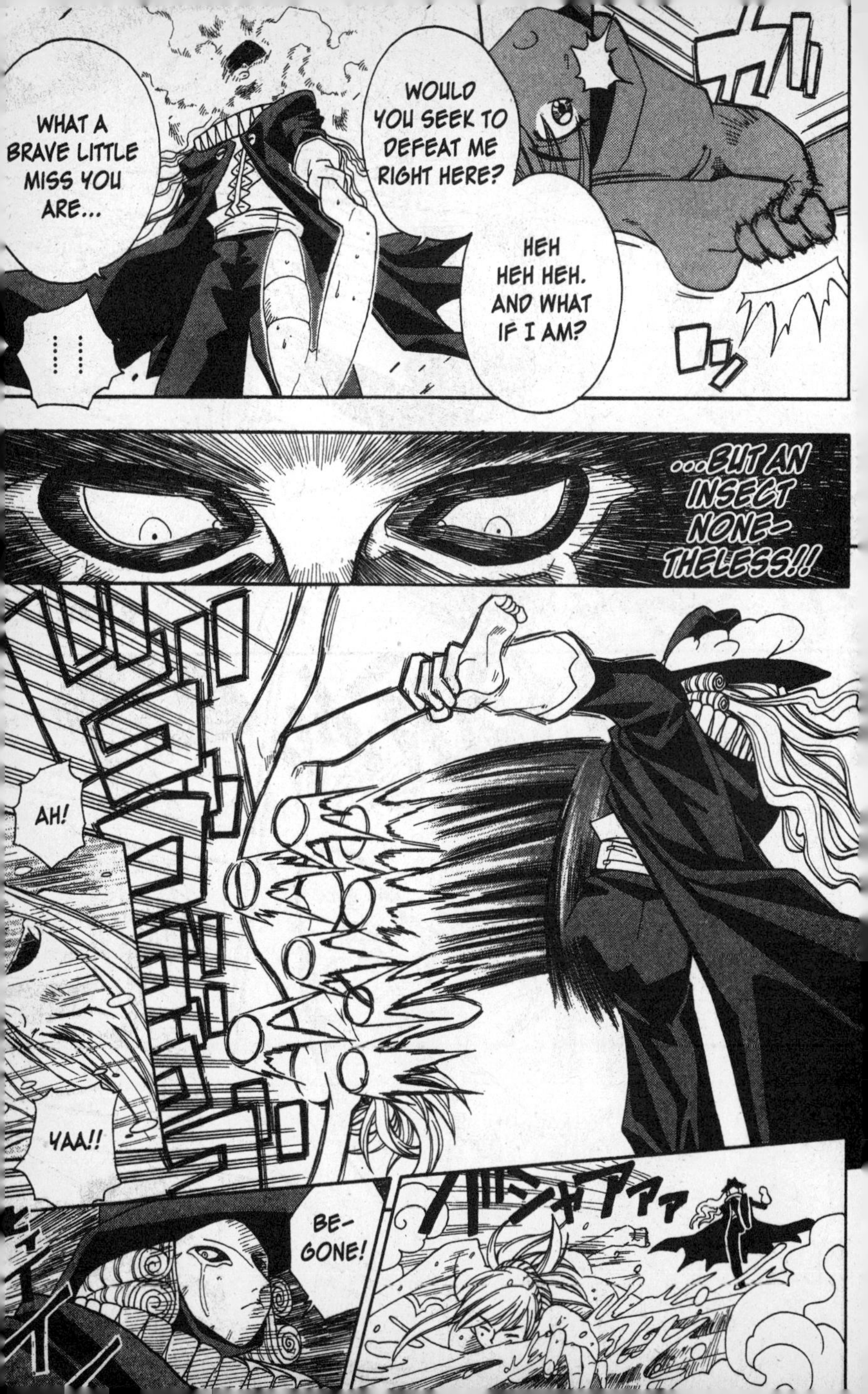

WOULD YOU SEEK TO DEFEAT ME RIGHT HERE?
HEH HEH HEH. AND WHAT IF I AM?
WHAT A BRAVE LITTLE MISS YOU ARE...
......
...BUT AN INSECT NONE-THELESS!!
AH!
YAA!!
BE-GONE!

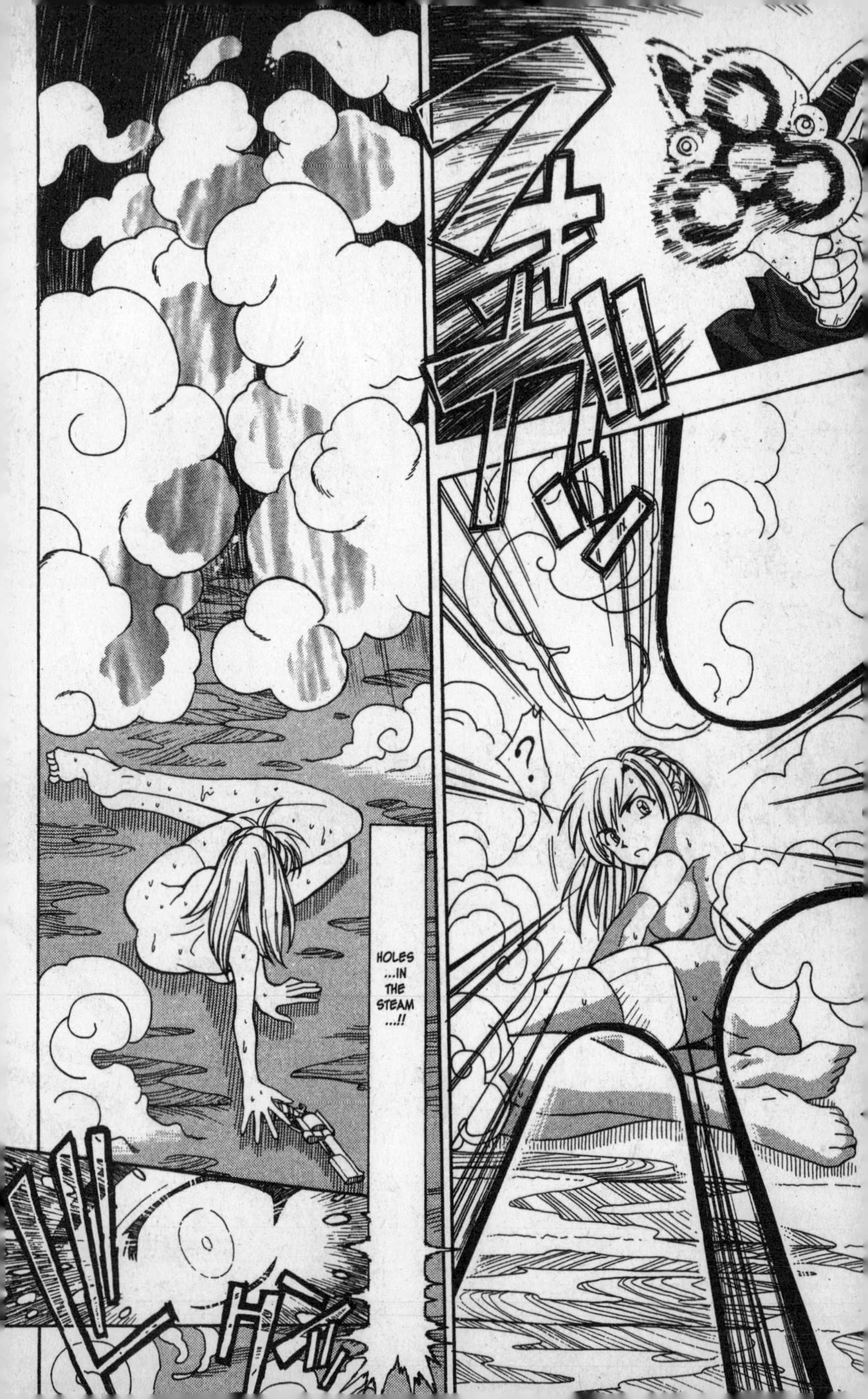
?
HOLES ...IN THE STEAM ...!!

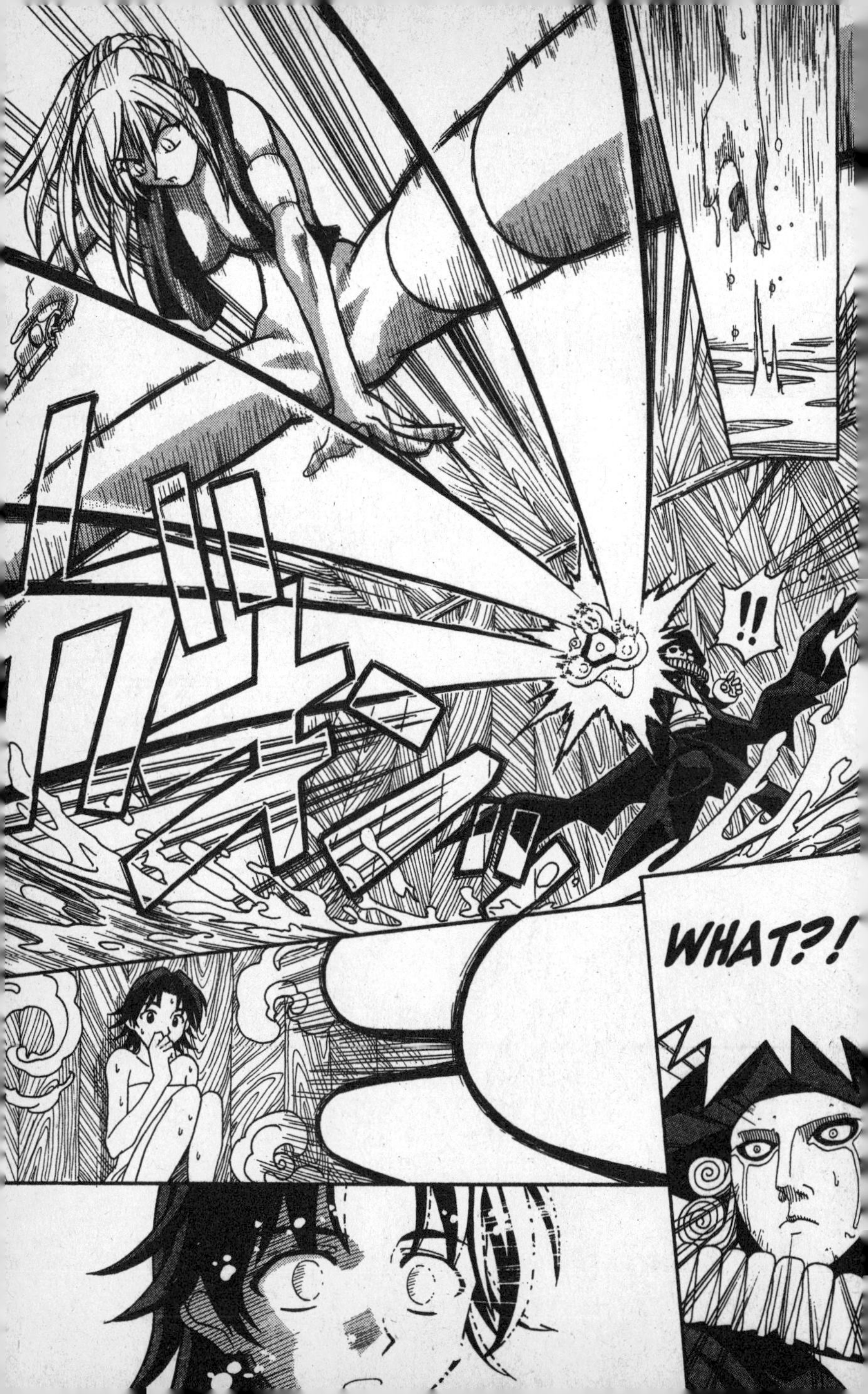
!!
WHAT?!

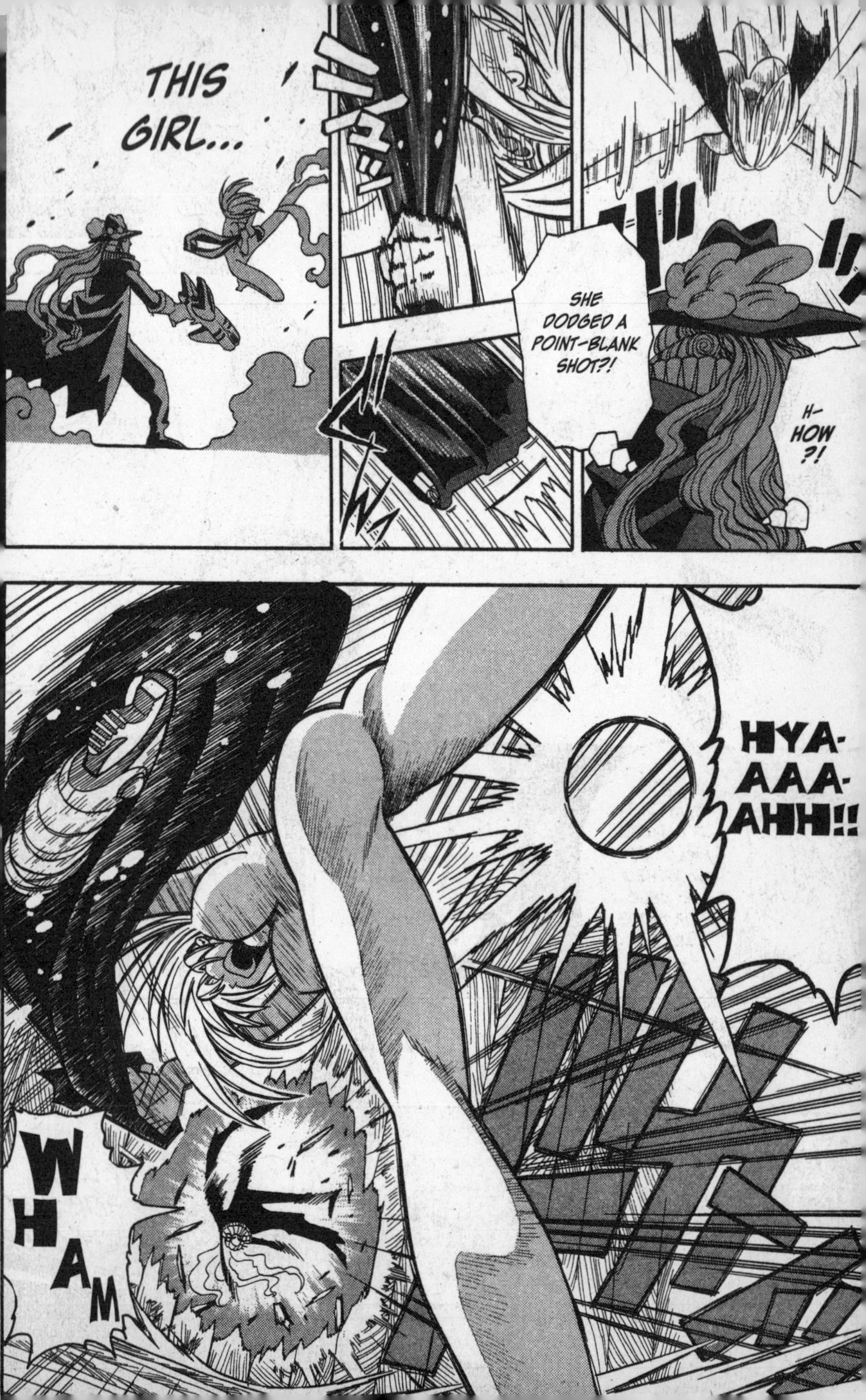
SHE DODGED A POINT-BLANK SHOT?!
H-HOW?!
THIS GIRL...
HYA-AAA-AHH!!
WHAM

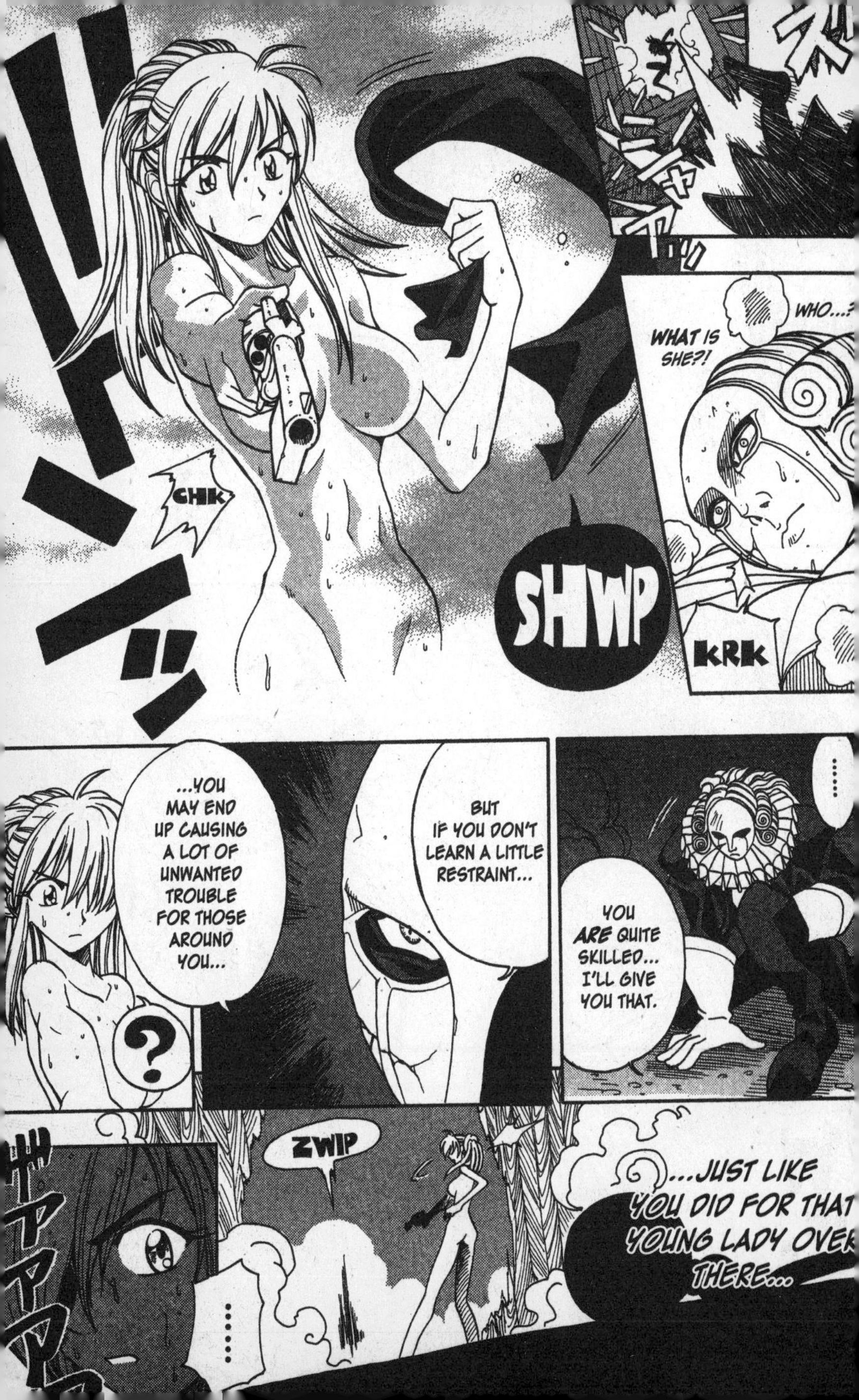
WHO...?
WHAT IS SHE?!
KRK
SHWP
CHK
......
YOU ARE QUITE SKILLED... I'LL GIVE YOU THAT.
BUT IF YOU DON'T LEARN A LITTLE RESTRAINT...
...YOU MAY END UP CAUSING A LOT OF UNWANTED TROUBLE FOR THOSE AROUND YOU...
?
...JUST LIKE YOU DID FOR THAT YOUNG LADY OVER THERE...
ZWIP
......

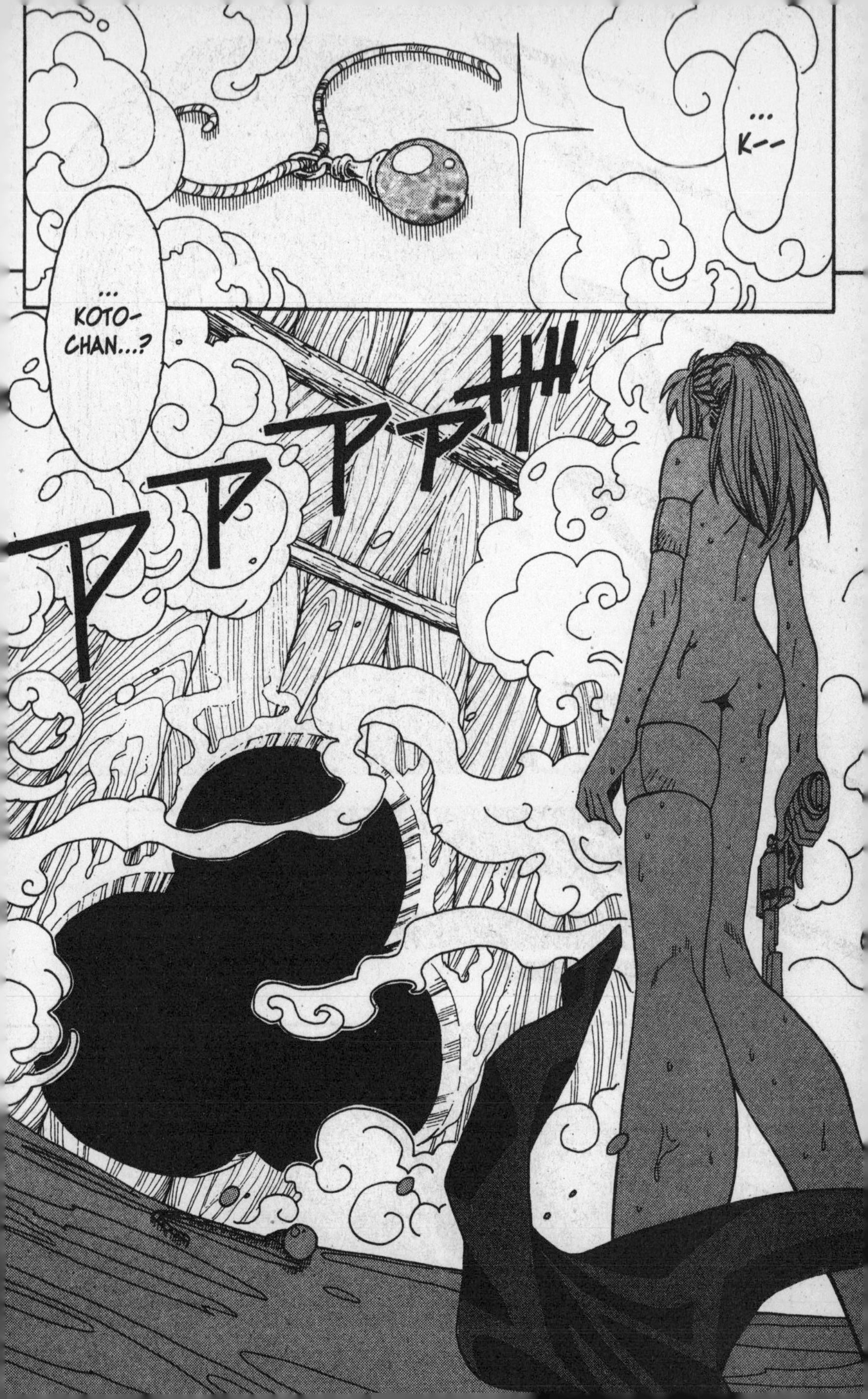

... K--
... KOTO-CHAN...?

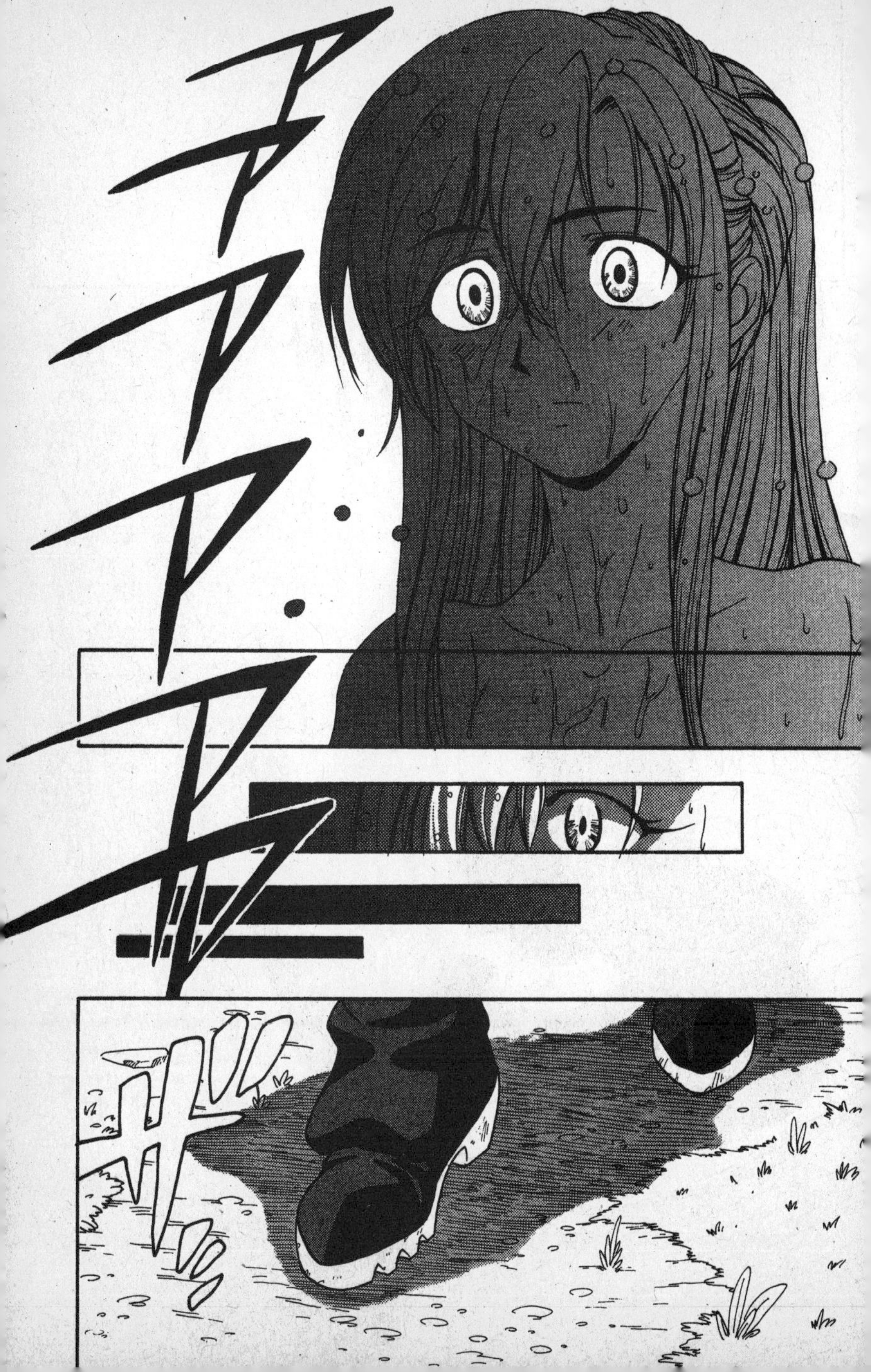

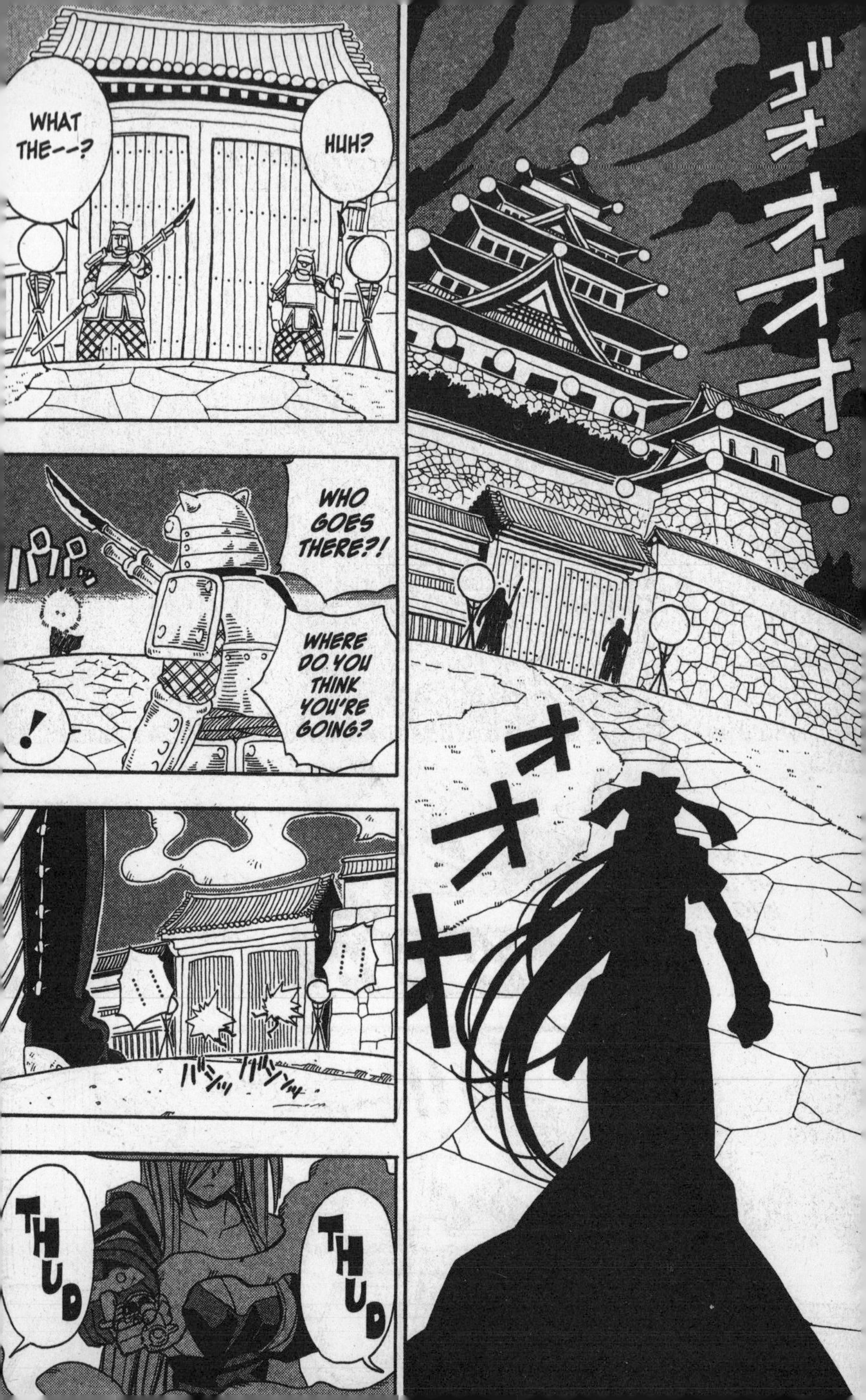
ゴォオオオ
オオオ
HUH?
WHAT THE--?
WHO GOES THERE?!
WHERE DO YOU THINK YOU'RE GOING?
!
THUD
THUD

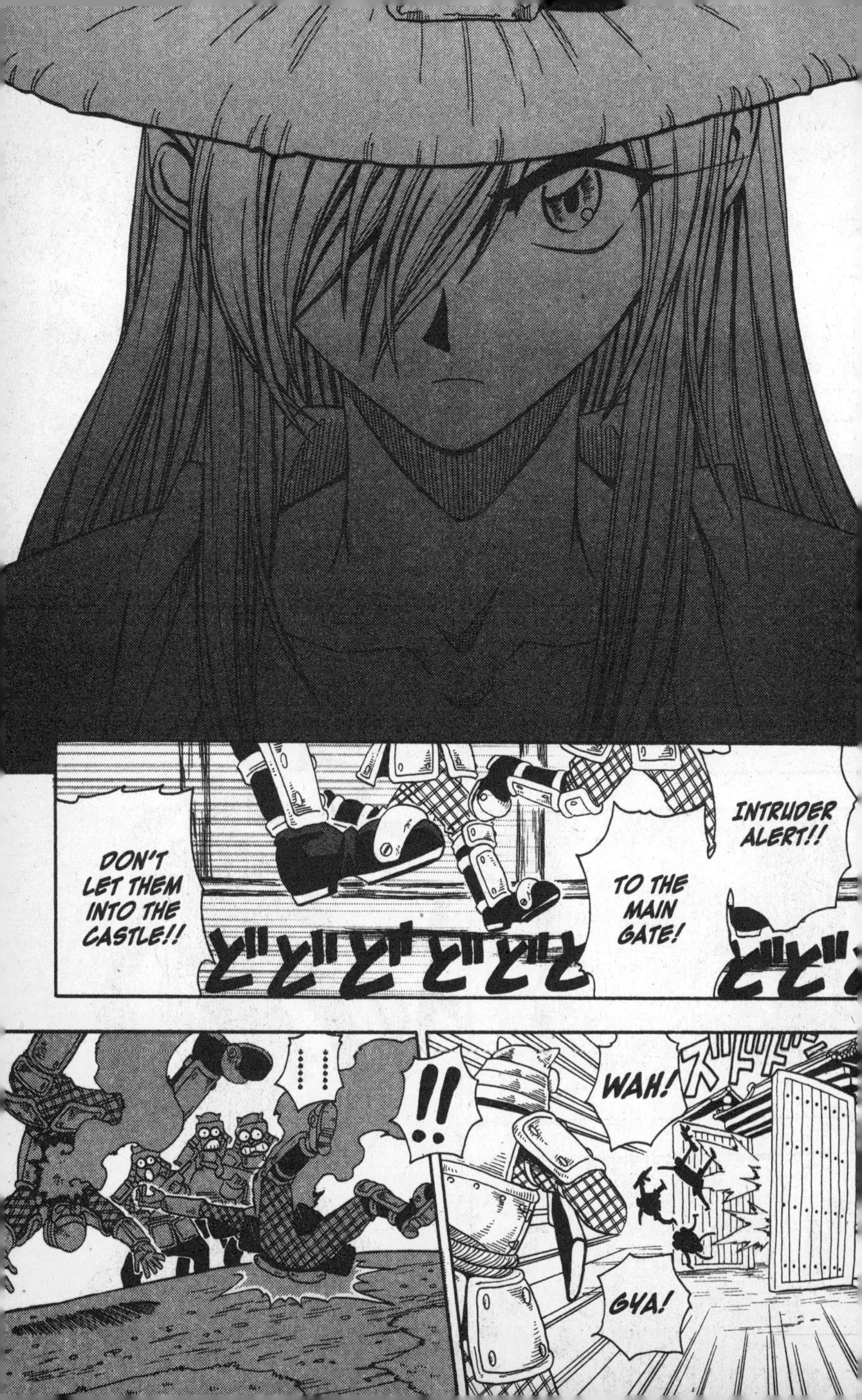
INTRUDER ALERT!!
どど
TO THE MAIN GATE!
DON'T LET THEM INTO THE CASTLE!!
どどどどど
WAH!
GYA!
!!
......

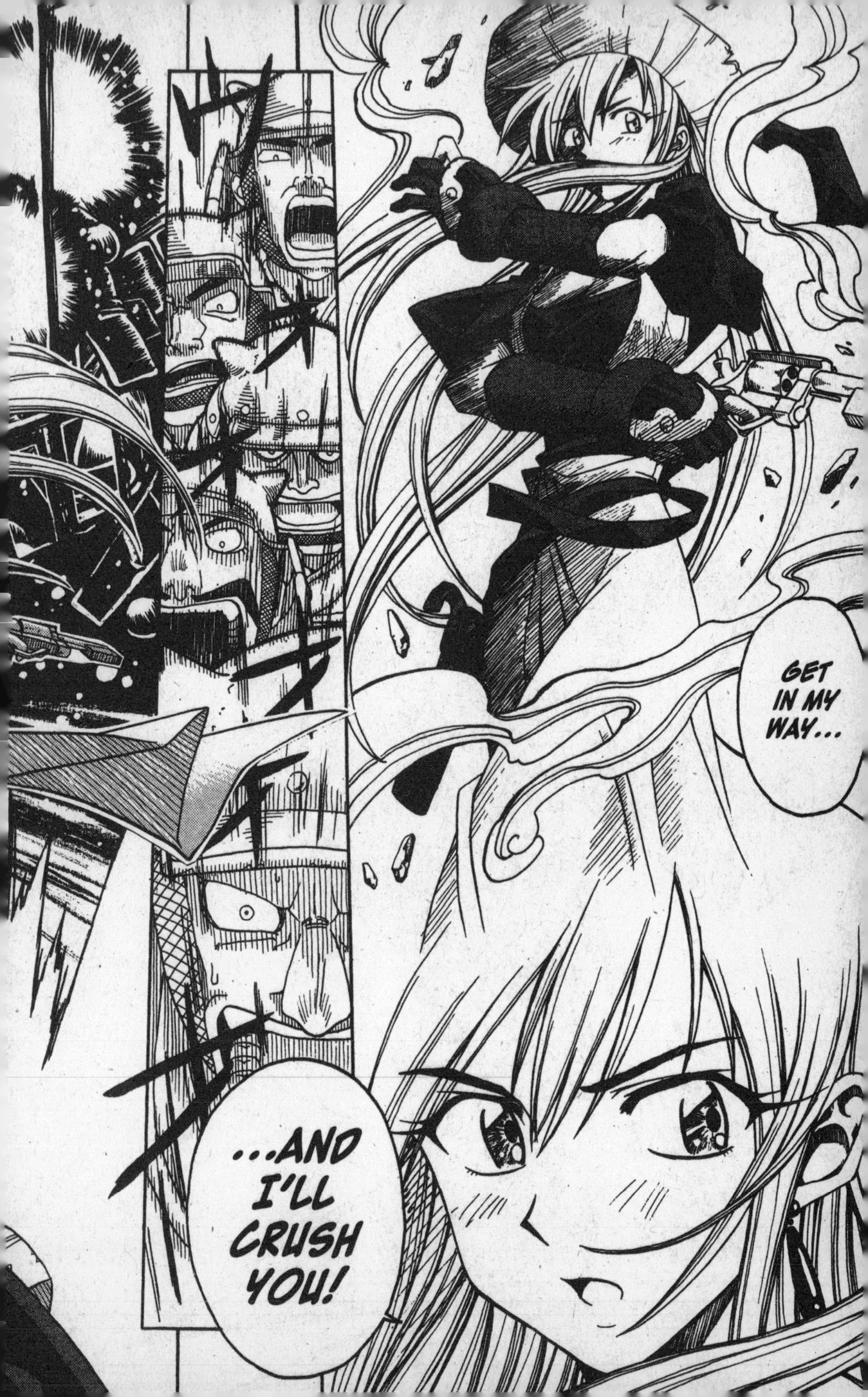
GET IN MY WAY...
...AND I'LL CRUSH YOU!

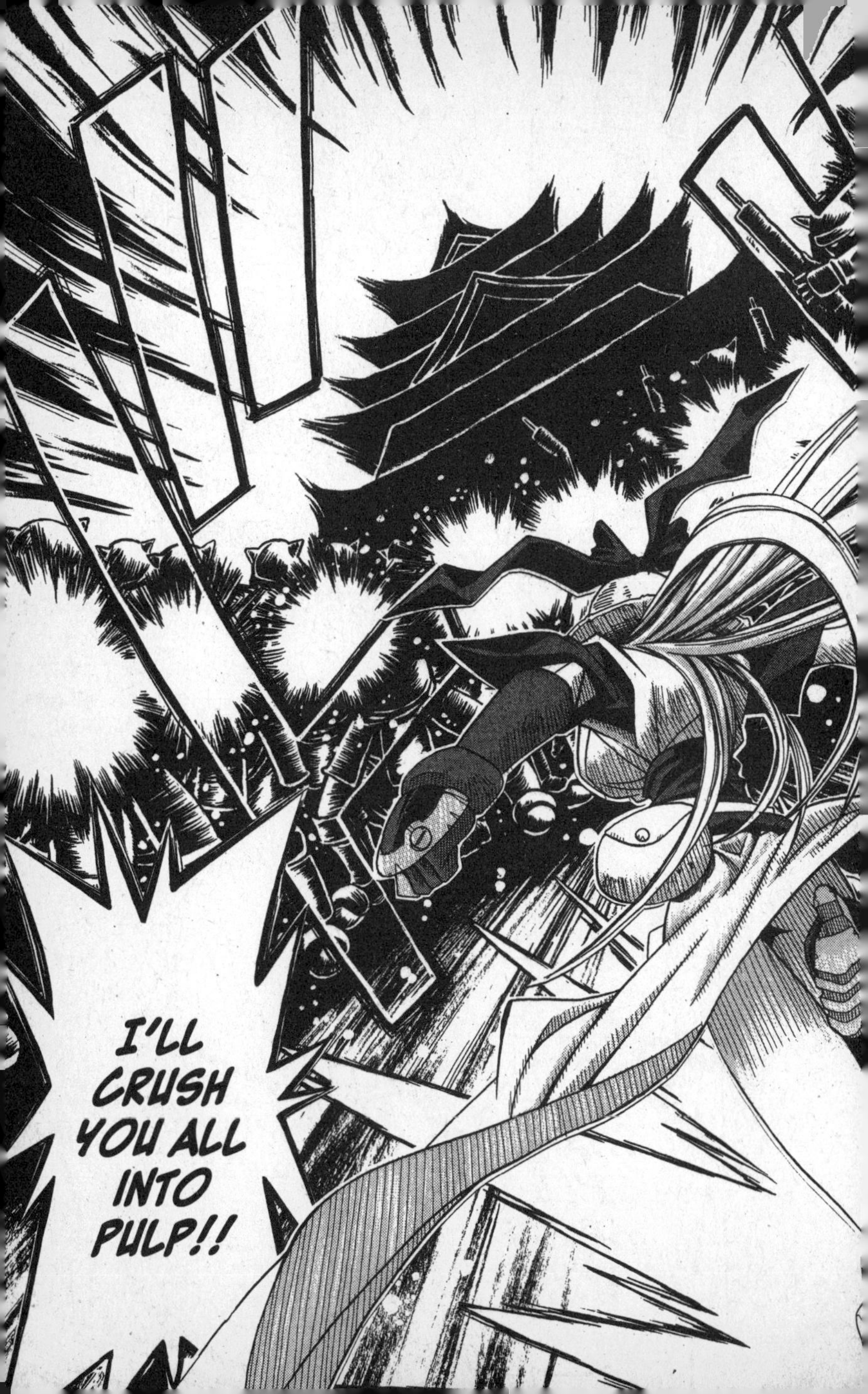
I'LL CRUSH YOU ALL INTO PULP!!

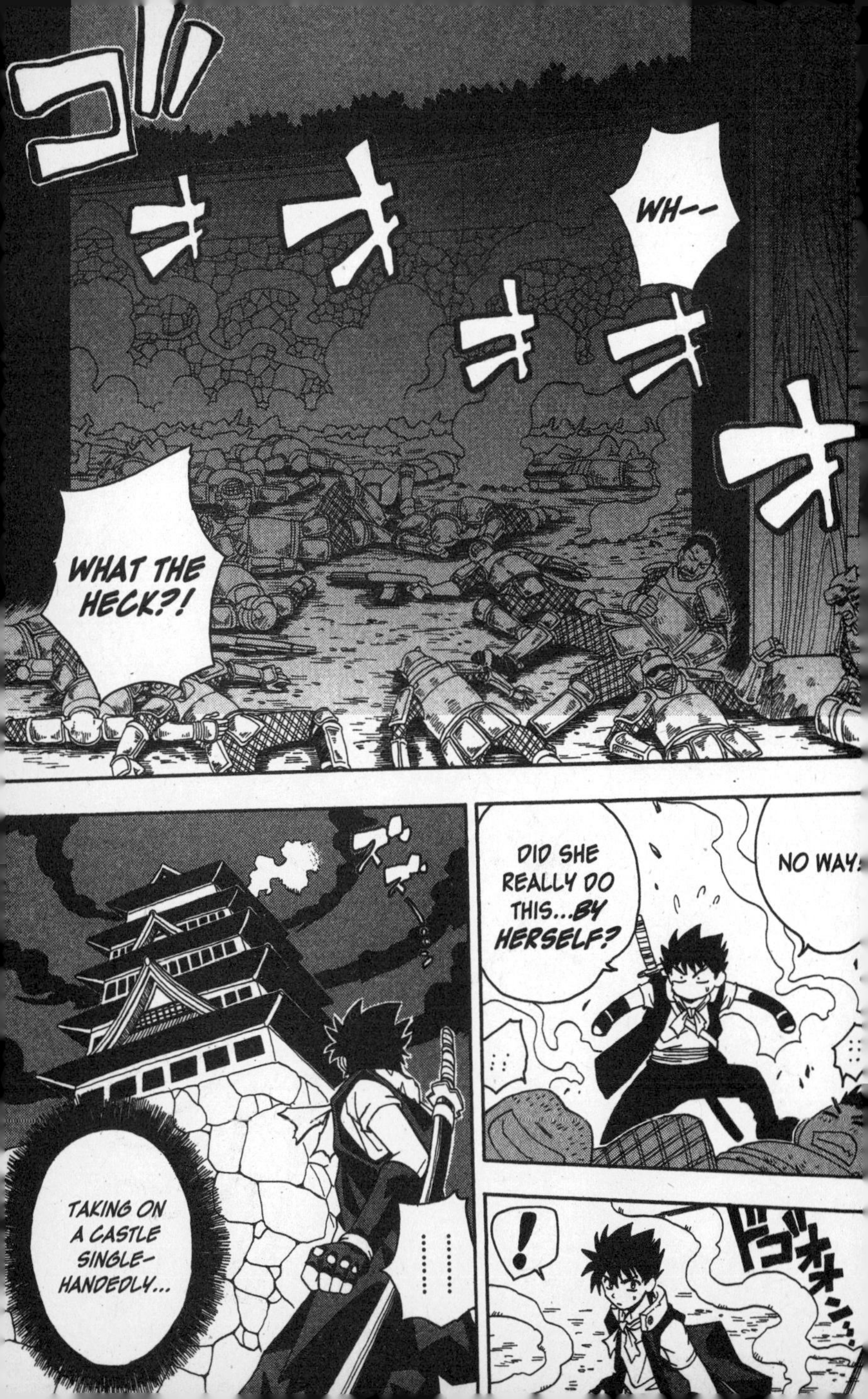
WH--
WHAT THE HECK?!
NO WAY
DID SHE REALLY DO THIS...BY HERSELF?
!
TAKING ON A CASTLE SINGLE-HANDEDLY...
......

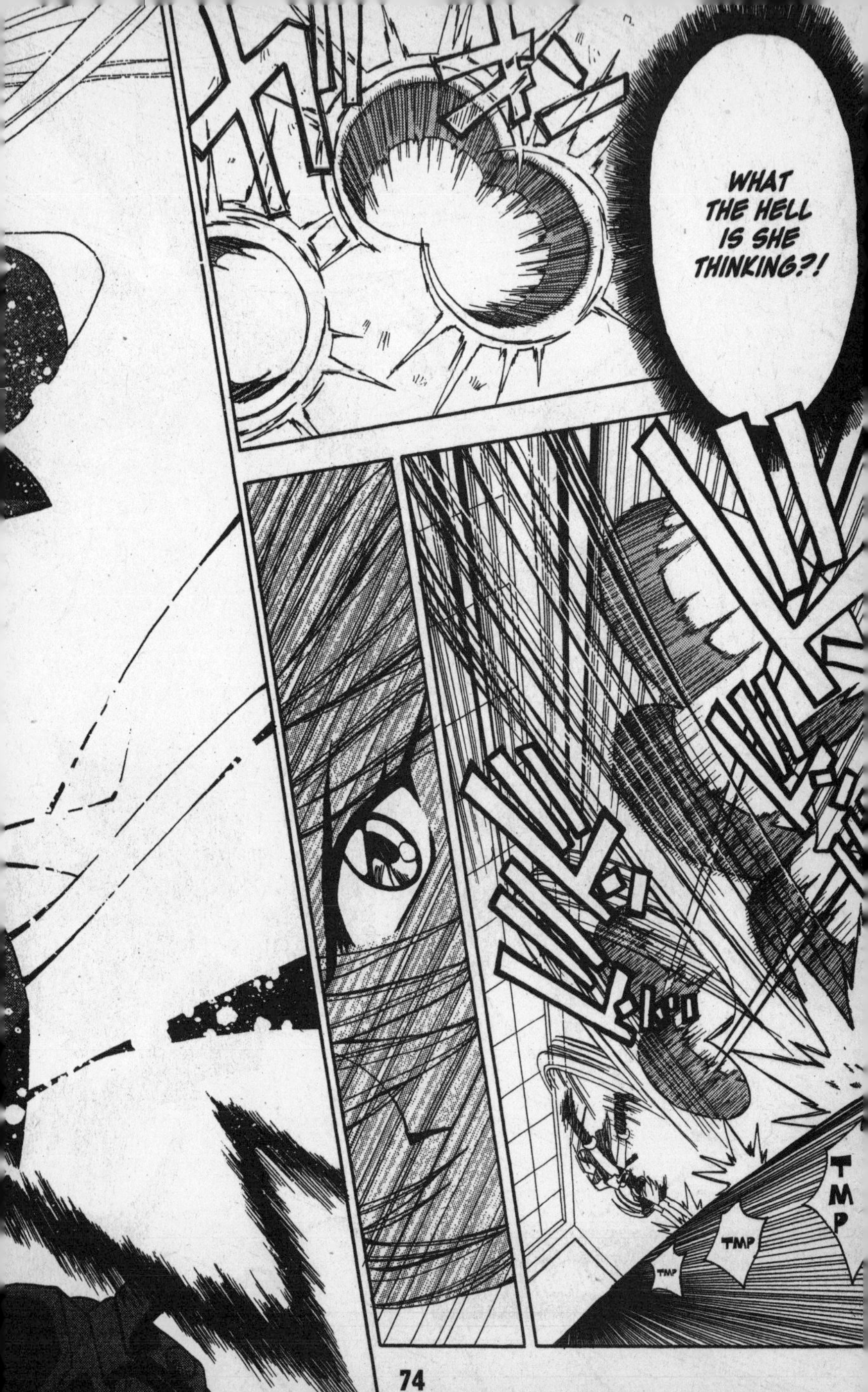
WHAT THE HELL IS SHE THINKING?!
TMP
TMP
TMP

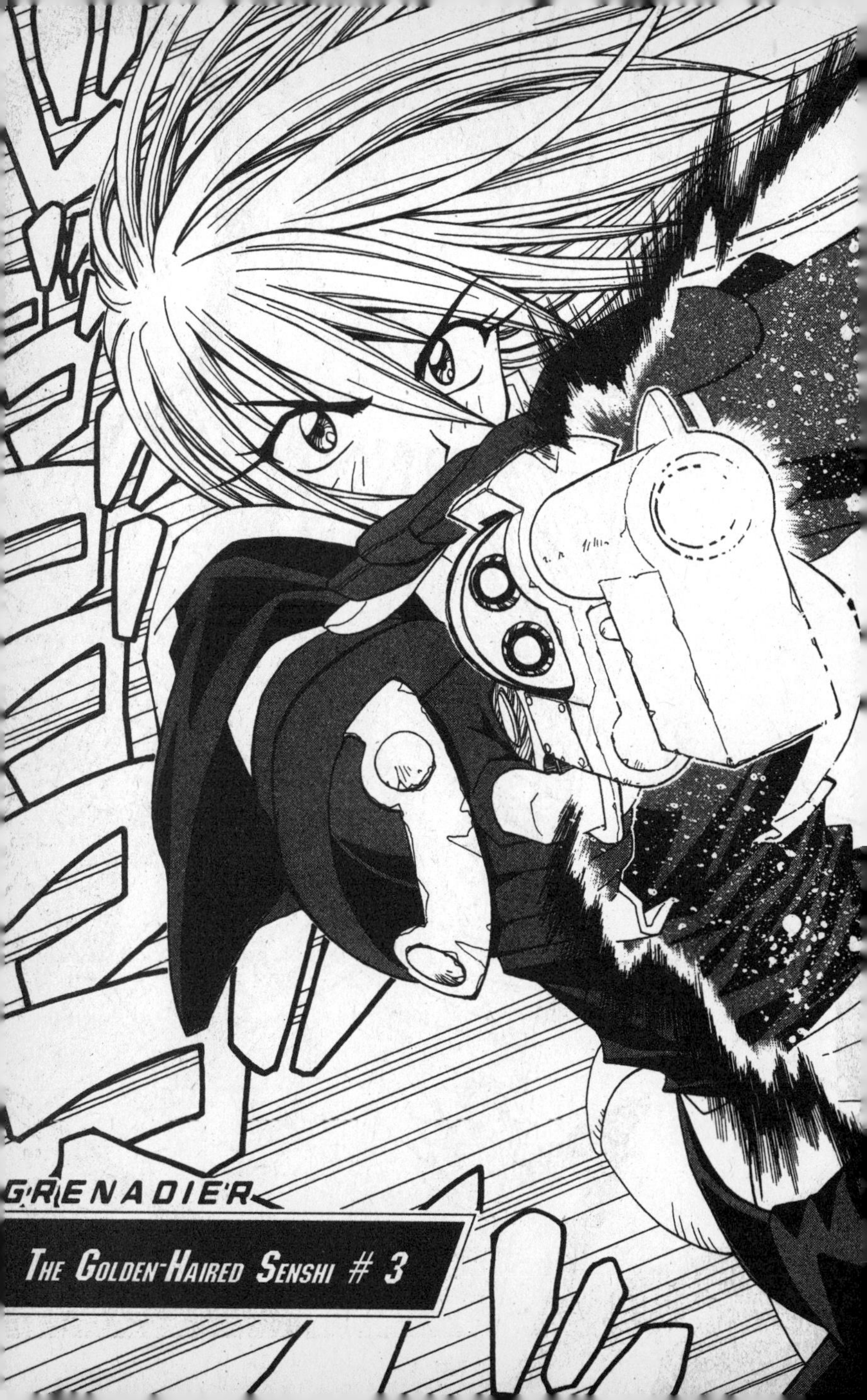
GRENADIER
THE GOLDEN-HAIRED SENSHI # 3

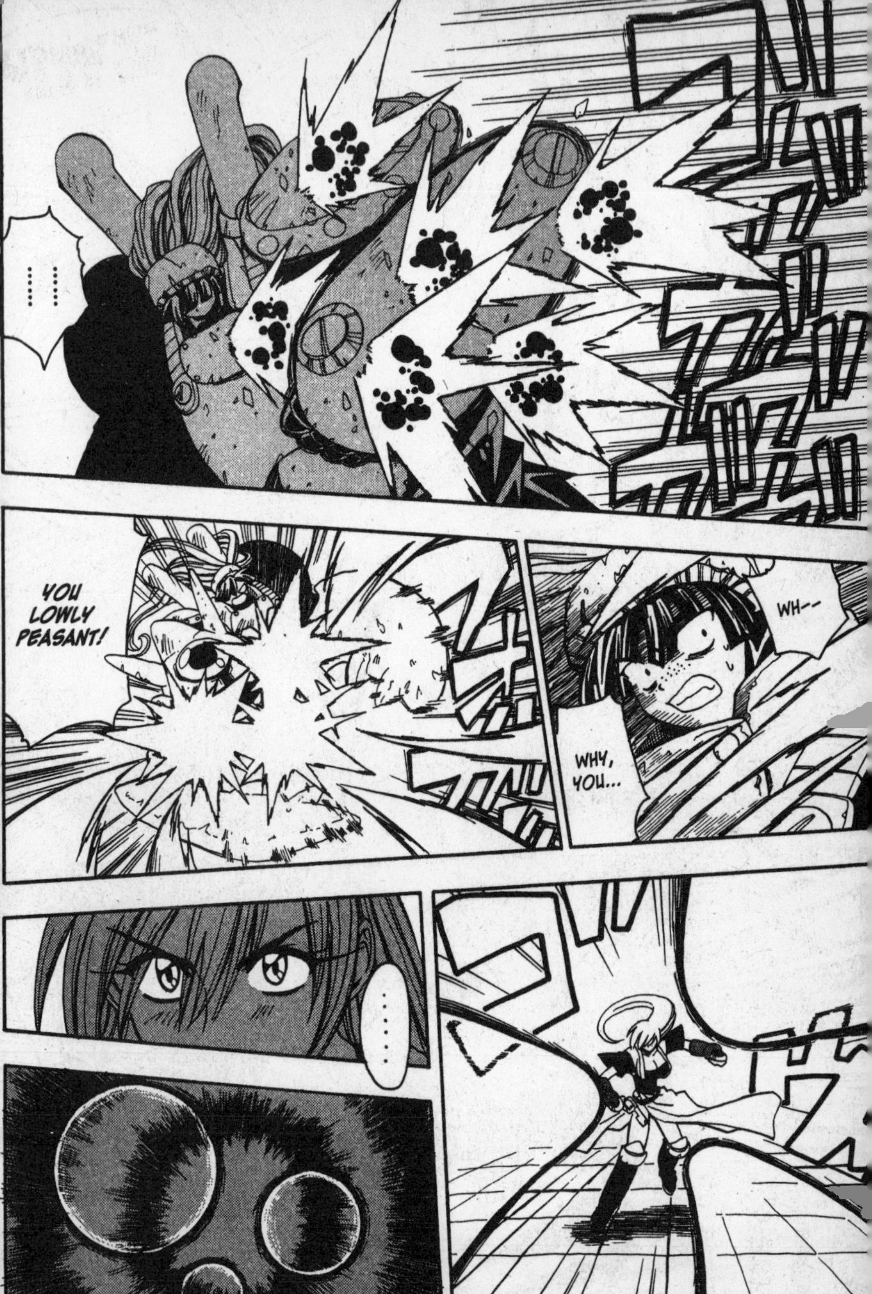
......
WH--
WHY, YOU...
YOU LOWLY PEASANT!
......

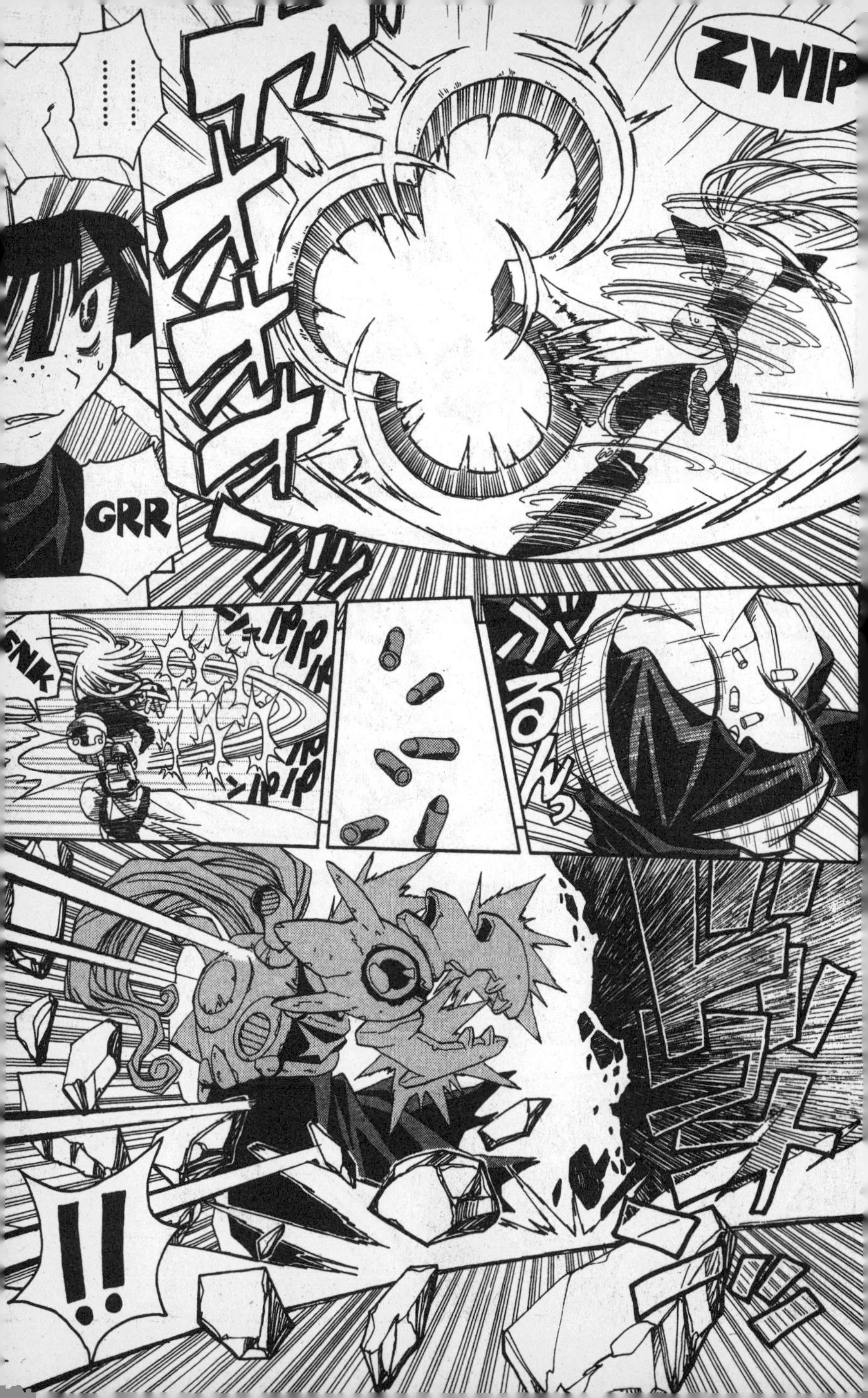
ZWIP
GRR
SNK
!!

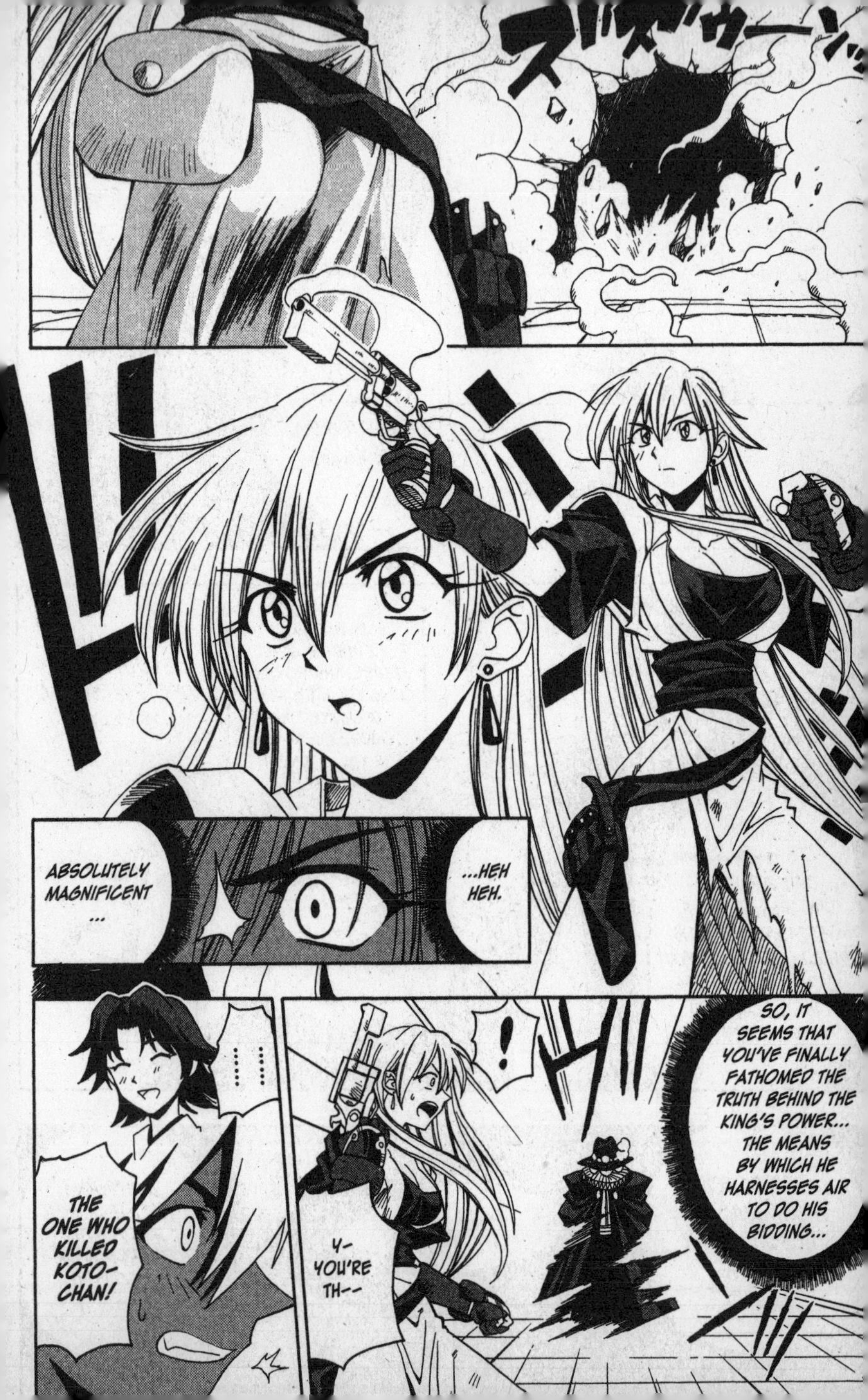
...HEH HEH.
ABSOLUTELY MAGNIFICENT ...
SO, IT SEEMS THAT YOU'VE FINALLY FATHOMED THE TRUTH BEHIND THE KING'S POWER... THE MEANS BY WHICH HE HARNESSES AIR TO DO HIS BIDDING...
!
Y- YOU'RE TH--
......
THE ONE WHO KILLED KOTO-CHAN!

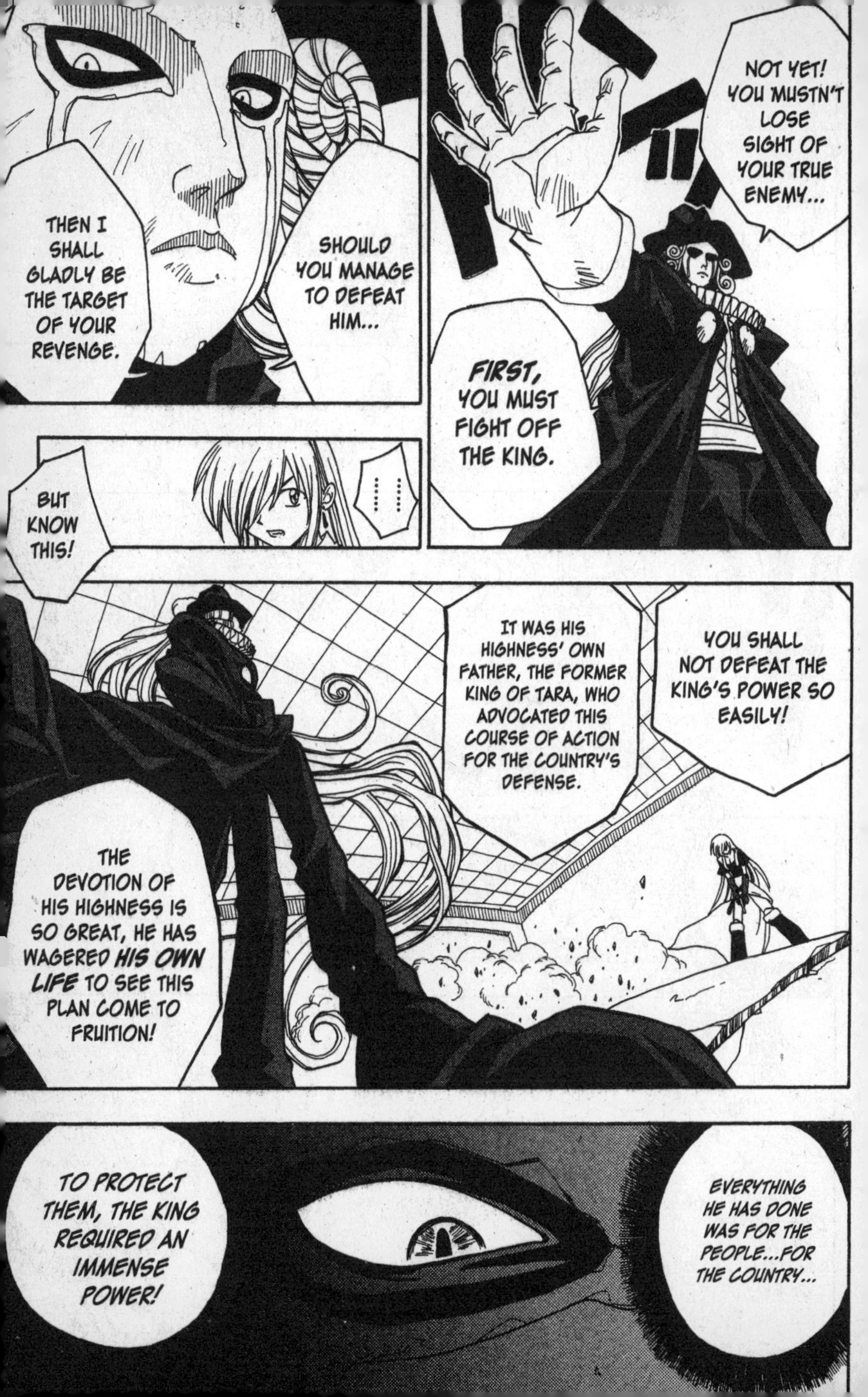
NOT YET! YOU MUSTN'T LOSE SIGHT OF YOUR TRUE ENEMY...
FIRST, YOU MUST FIGHT OFF THE KING.
SHOULD YOU MANAGE TO DEFEAT HIM...
THEN I SHALL GLADLY BE THE TARGET OF YOUR REVENGE.
......
BUT KNOW THIS!
YOU SHALL NOT DEFEAT THE KING'S POWER SO EASILY!
IT WAS HIS HIGHNESS' OWN FATHER, THE FORMER KING OF TARA, WHO ADVOCATED THIS COURSE OF ACTION FOR THE COUNTRY'S DEFENSE.
THE DEVOTION OF HIS HIGHNESS IS SO GREAT, HE HAS WAGERED HIS OWN LIFE TO SEE THIS PLAN COME TO FRUITION!
EVERYTHING HE HAS DONE WAS FOR THE PEOPLE...FOR THE COUNTRY...
TO PROTECT THEM, THE KING REQUIRED AN IMMENSE POWER!

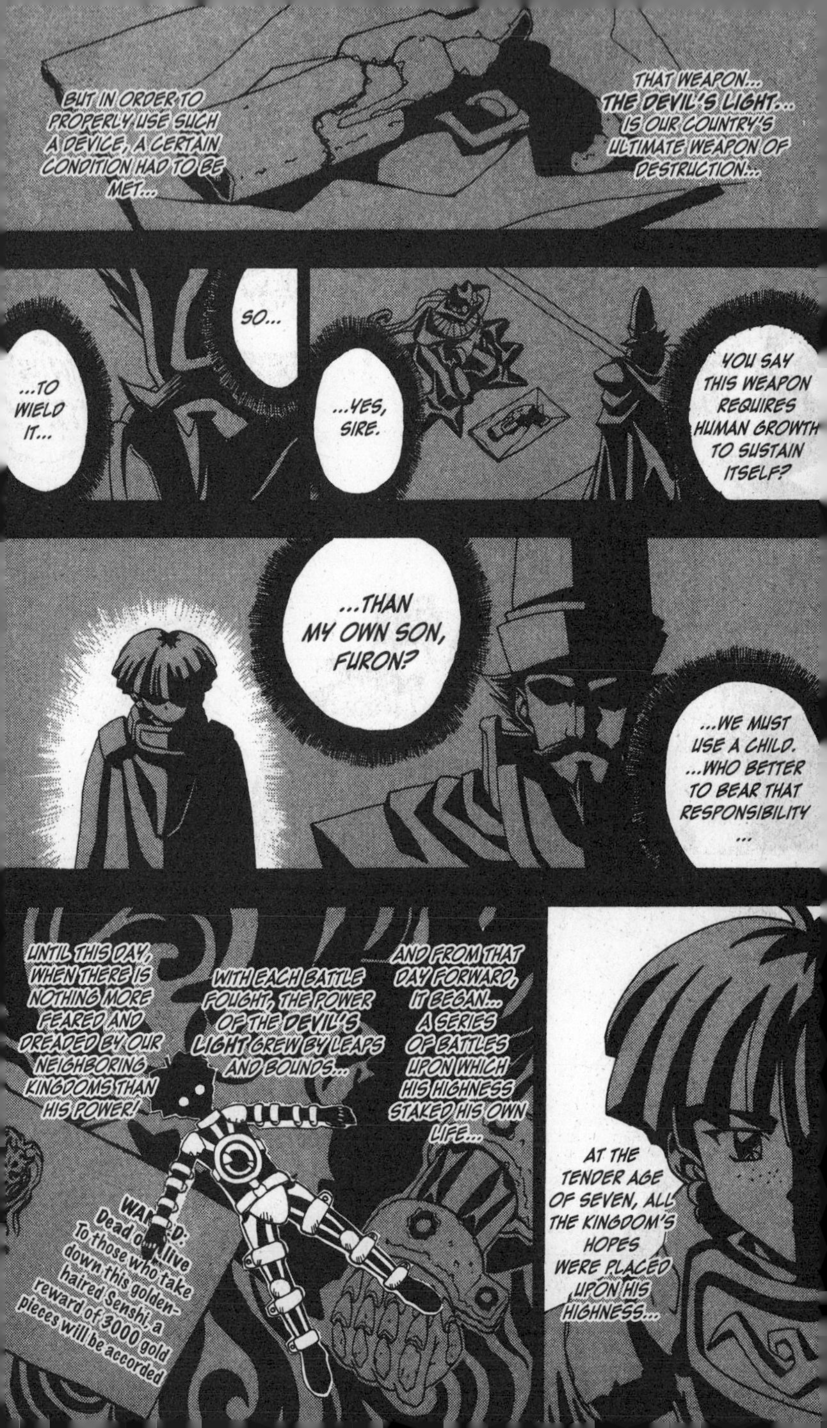
THAT WEAPON... THE DEVIL'S LIGHT... IS OUR COUNTRY'S ULTIMATE WEAPON OF DESTRUCTION...
BUT IN ORDER TO PROPERLY USE SUCH A DEVICE, A CERTAIN CONDITION HAD TO BE MET...
YOU SAY THIS WEAPON REQUIRES HUMAN GROWTH TO SUSTAIN ITSELF?
...YES, SIRE.
SO...
...TO WIELD IT...
...WE MUST USE A CHILD. ...WHO BETTER TO BEAR THAT RESPONSIBILITY ...
...THAN MY OWN SON, FURON?
AT THE TENDER AGE OF SEVEN, ALL THE KINGDOM'S HOPES WERE PLACED UPON HIS HIGHNESS...
AND FROM THAT DAY FORWARD, IT BEGAN... A SERIES OF BATTLES UPON WHICH HIS HIGHNESS STAKED HIS OWN LIFE...
WITH EACH BATTLE FOUGHT, THE POWER OF THE DEVIL'S LIGHT GREW BY LEAPS AND BOUNDS...
UNTIL THIS DAY, WHEN THERE IS NOTHING MORE FEARED AND DREADED BY OUR NEIGHBORING KINGDOMS THAN HIS POWER!
To those who take down this golden-haired Senshi, a reward of 3000 gold pieces will be accorded

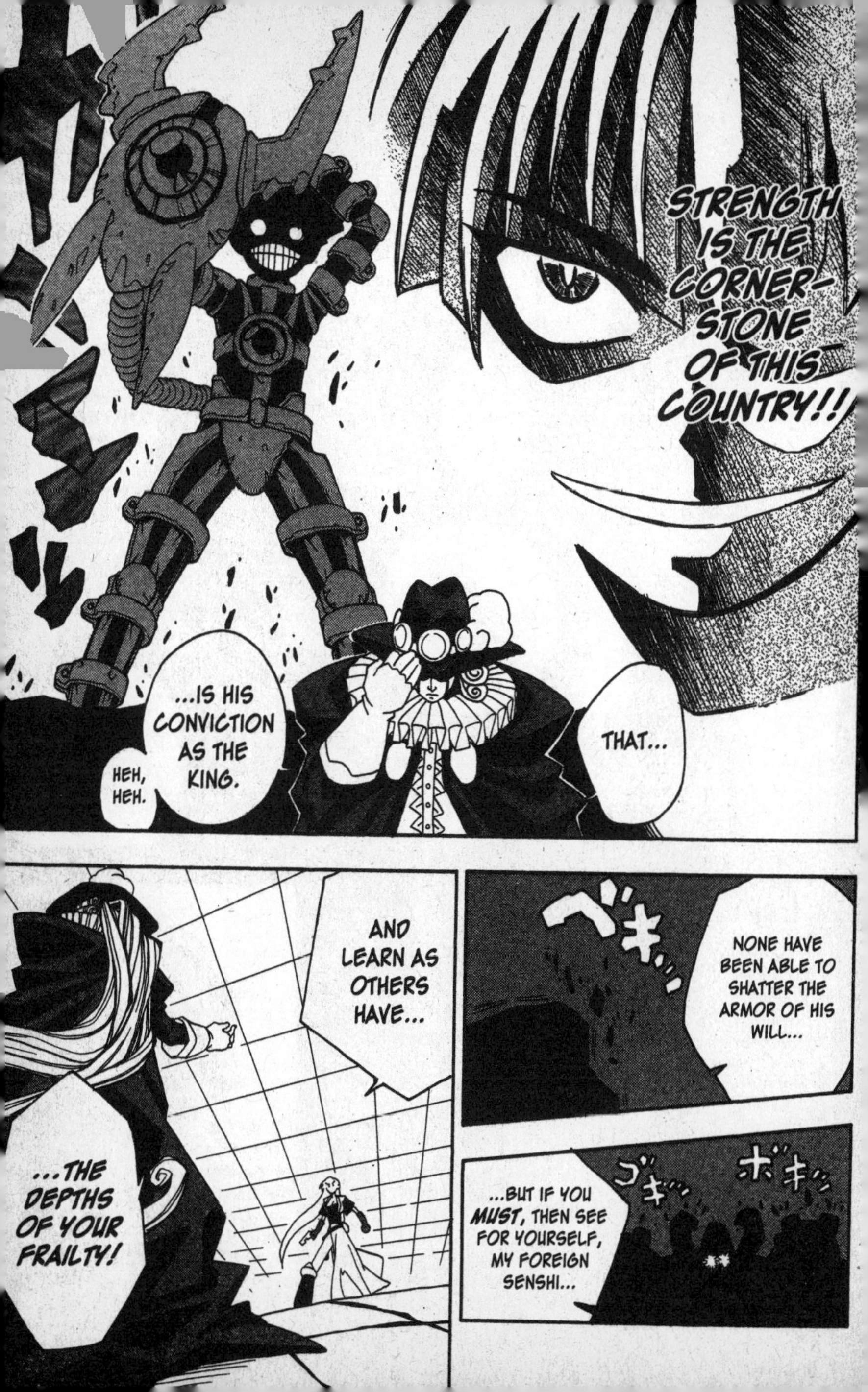
STRENGTH IS THE CORNER-STONE OF THIS COUNTRY!!
THAT...
...IS HIS CONVICTION AS THE KING.
HEH, HEH.
ベキ
NONE HAVE BEEN ABLE TO SHATTER THE ARMOR OF HIS WILL...
ゴキ
ボキ
...BUT IF YOU *MUST*, THEN SEE FOR YOURSELF, MY FOREIGN SENSHI...
AND LEARN AS OTHERS HAVE...
...THE DEPTHS OF YOUR FRAILTY!

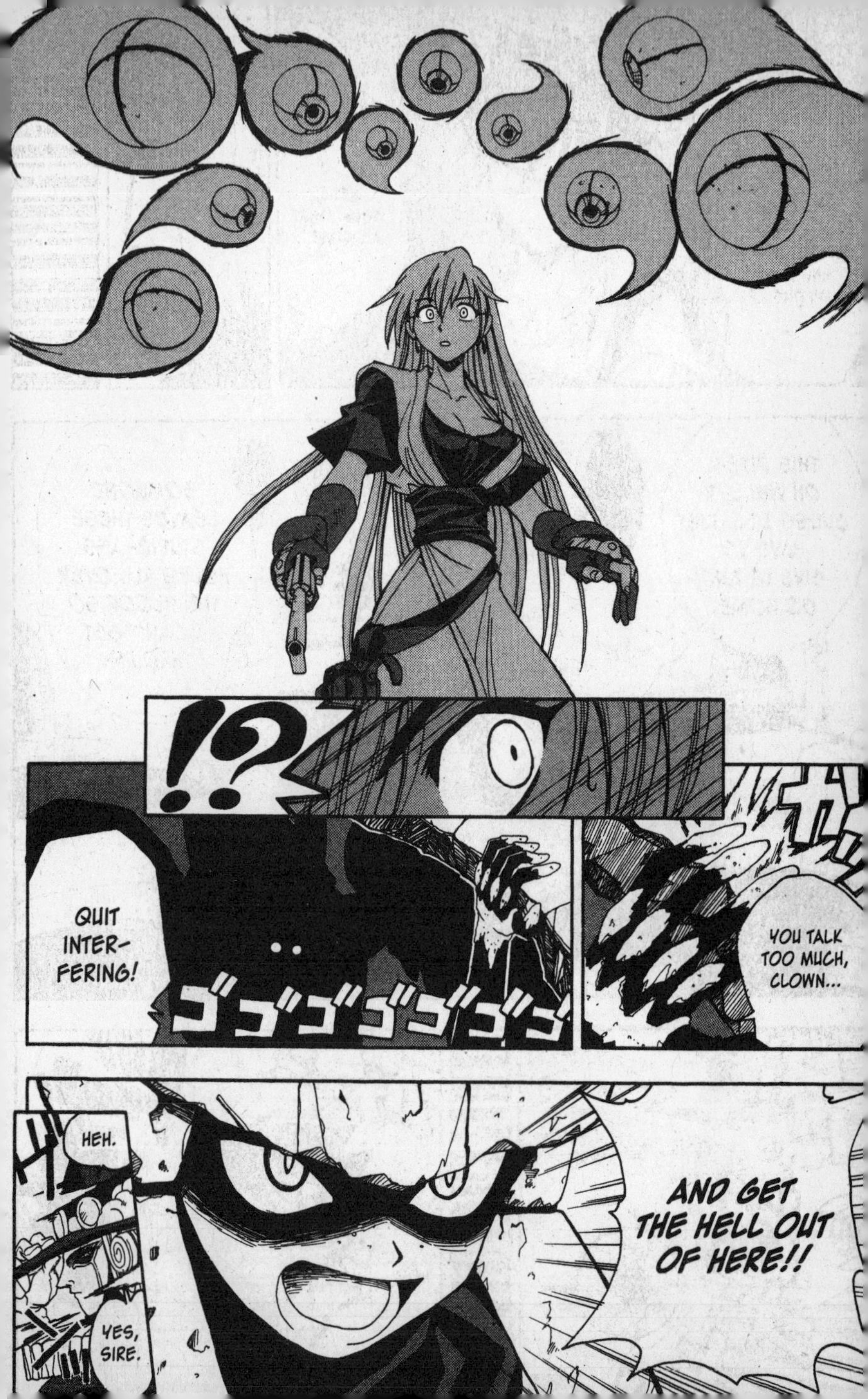
!?
YOU TALK TOO MUCH, CLOWN...
QUIT INTER-FERING!
ゴゴゴゴゴゴ
AND GET THE HELL OUT OF HERE!!
HEH.
YES, SIRE.

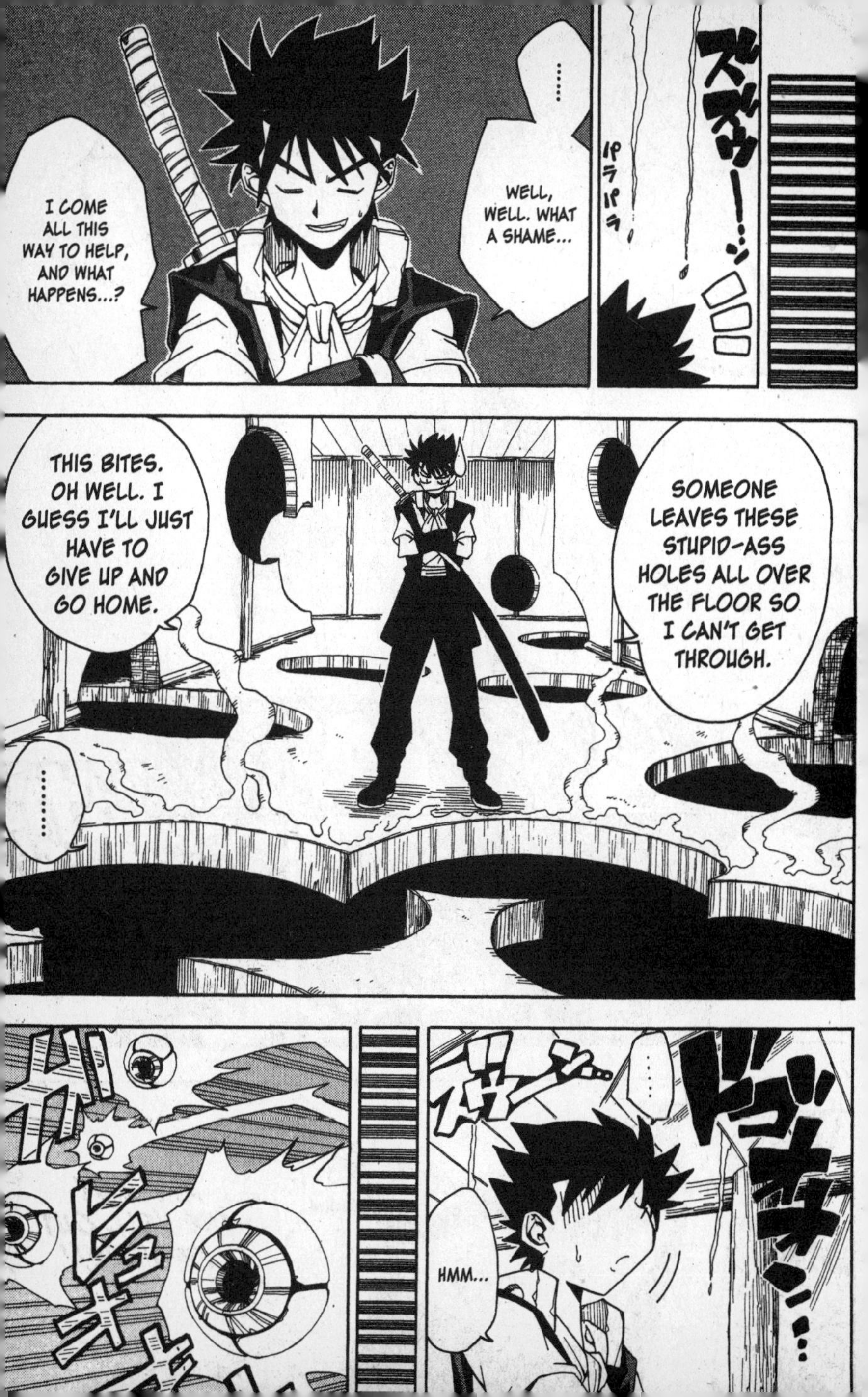
パラパラ
......
WELL, WELL. WHAT A SHAME...
I COME ALL THIS WAY TO HELP, AND WHAT HAPPENS...?
SOMEONE LEAVES THESE STUPID-ASS HOLES ALL OVER THE FLOOR SO I CAN'T GET THROUGH.
THIS BITES. OH WELL. I GUESS I'LL JUST HAVE TO GIVE UP AND GO HOME.
......
......
HMM...

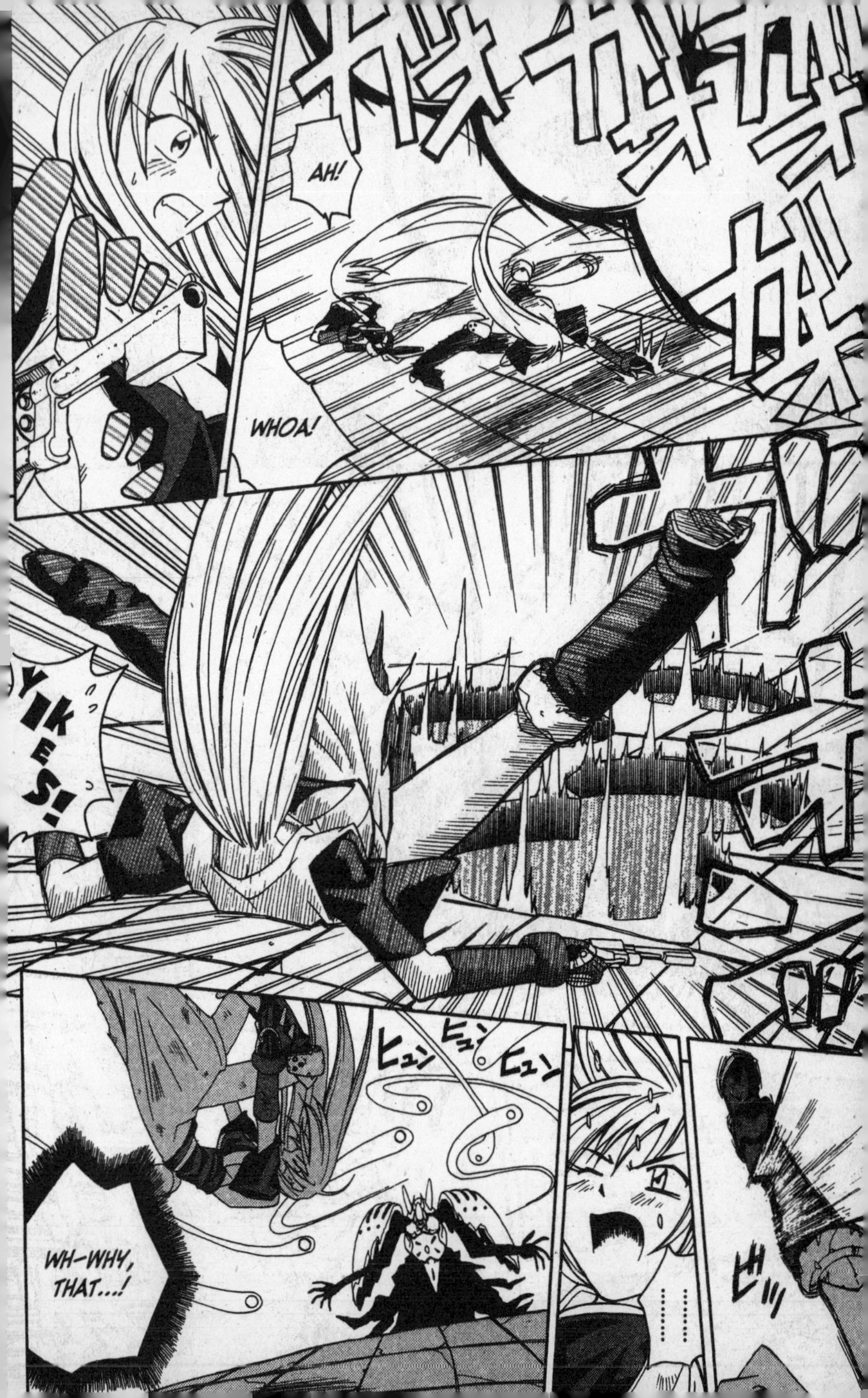
AH!
WHOA!
YIKES!
ビッ
……
ヒュン
ヒュン
ヒュン
ヒュン
WH-WHY, THAT...!

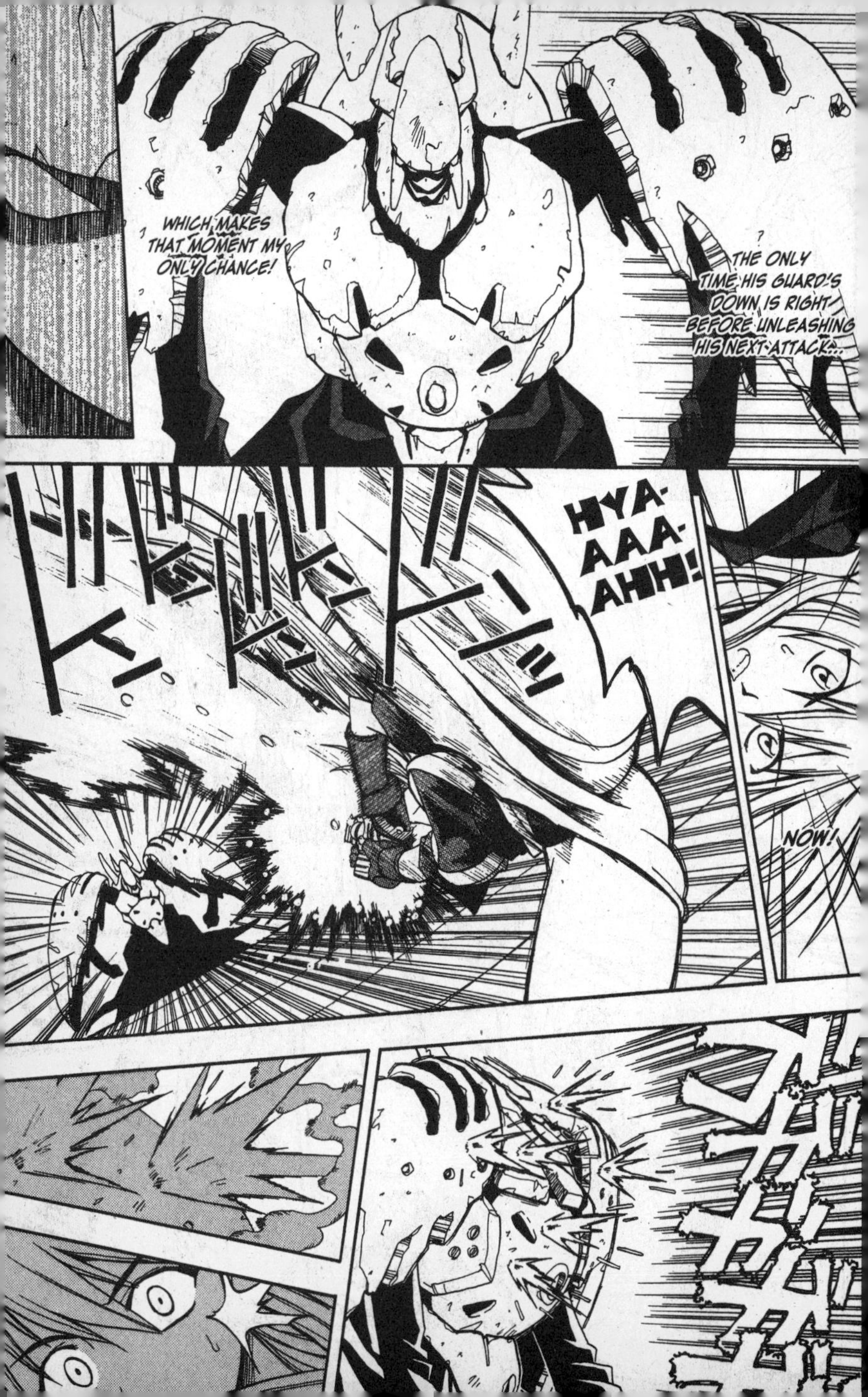
THE ONLY TIME HIS GUARD'S DOWN IS RIGHT BEFORE UNLEASHING HIS NEXT ATTACK...
WHICH MAKES THAT MOMENT MY ONLY CHANCE!
NOW!
HYA-AAA-AHH!

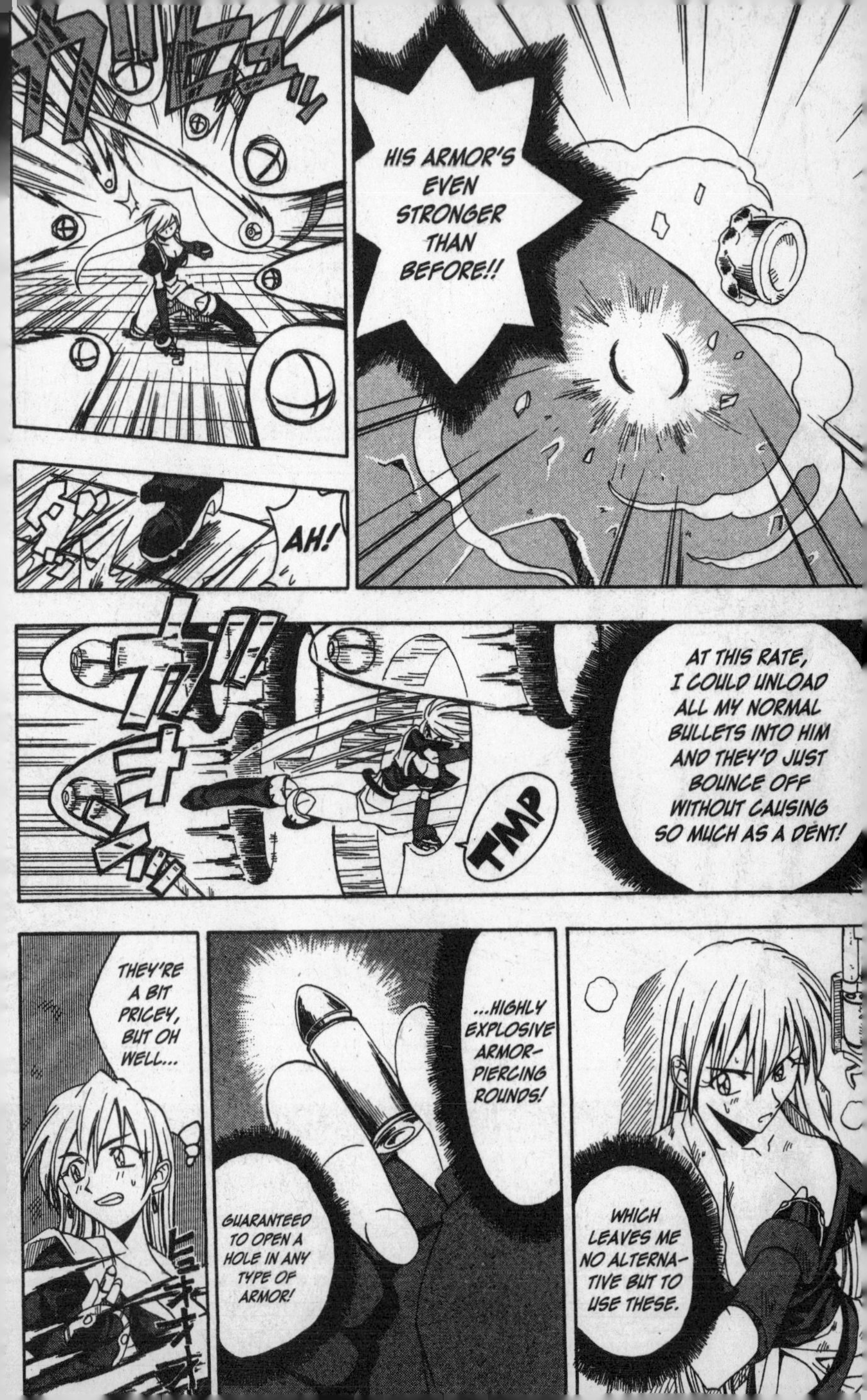
HIS ARMOR'S EVEN STRONGER THAN BEFORE!!
AH!
AT THIS RATE, I COULD UNLOAD ALL MY NORMAL BULLETS INTO HIM AND THEY'D JUST BOUNCE OFF WITHOUT CAUSING SO MUCH AS A DENT!
TMP
WHICH LEAVES ME NO ALTERNA-TIVE BUT TO USE THESE.
...HIGHLY EXPLOSIVE ARMOR-PIERCING ROUNDS!
GUARANTEED TO OPEN A HOLE IN ANY TYPE OF ARMOR!
THEY'RE A BIT PRICEY, BUT OH WELL...

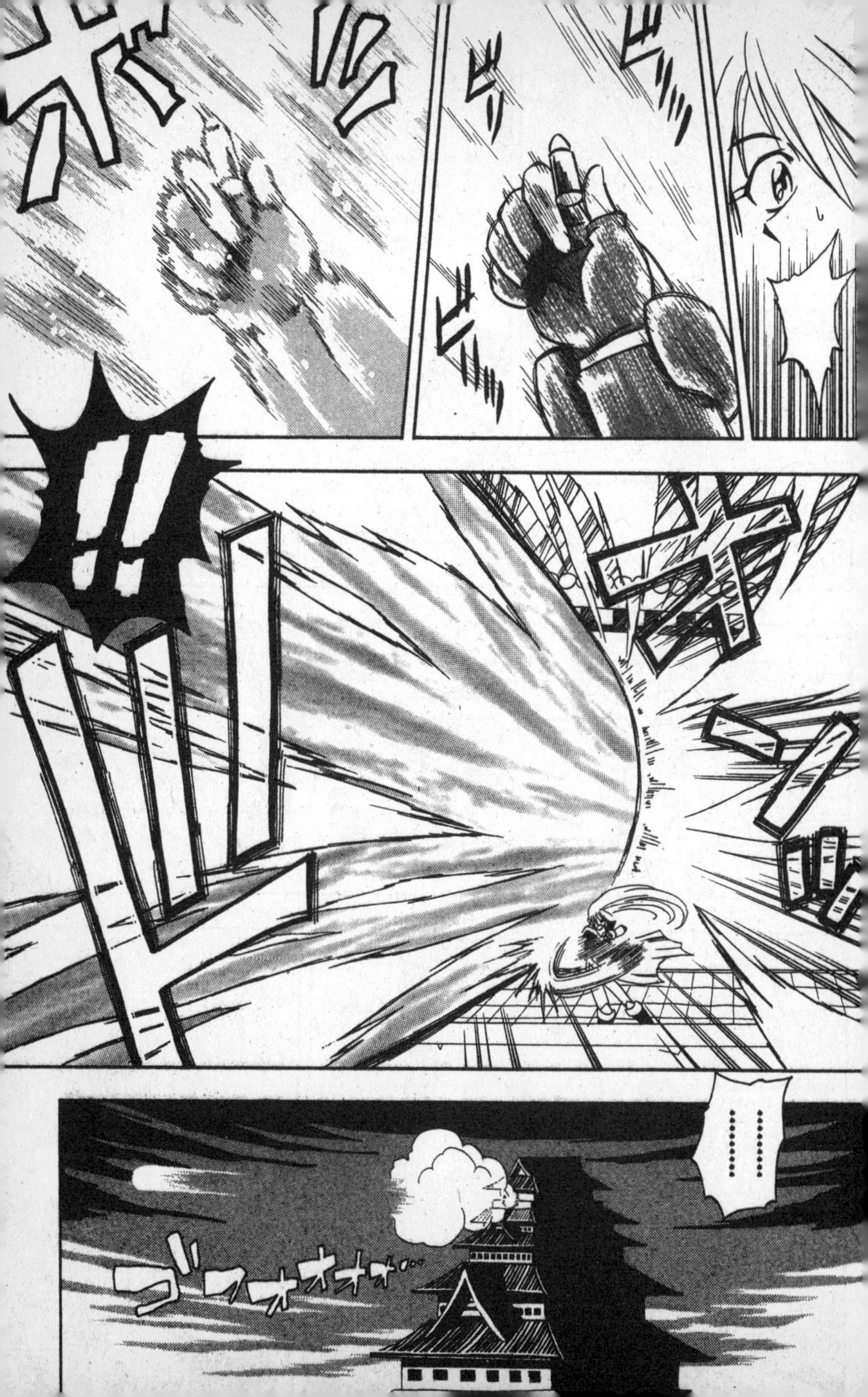
ギリ…
ギリ…
!!
……
ゴォオオオ…

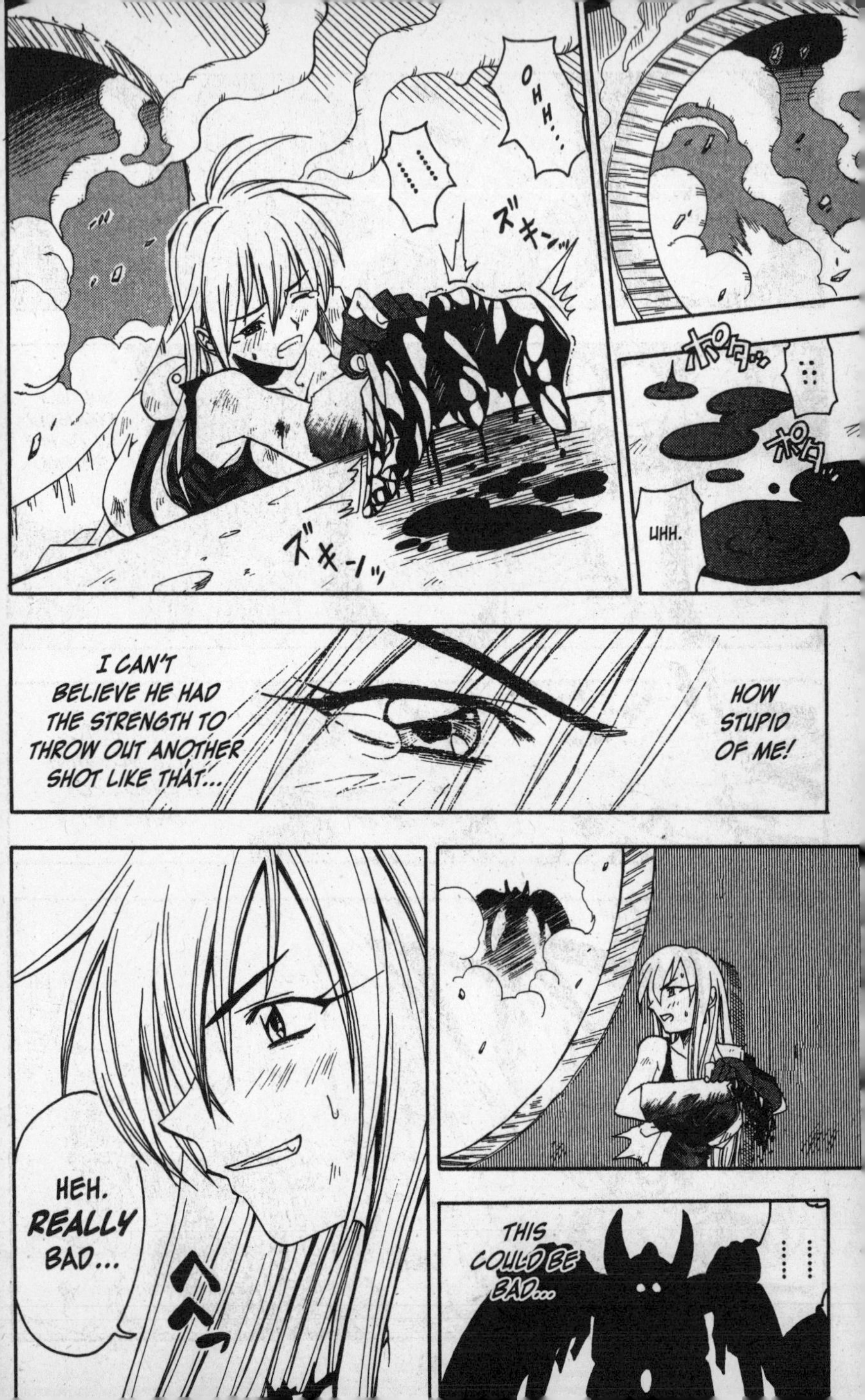

ポタッ…
…
ポタ…
UHH.
……
OHH…
ズキーンッ
ズキーンッ
HOW STUPID OF ME!
I CAN'T BELIEVE HE HAD THE STRENGTH TO THROW OUT ANOTHER SHOT LIKE THAT…
……
THIS COULD BE BAD…
HEH. REALLY BAD…
へへっ

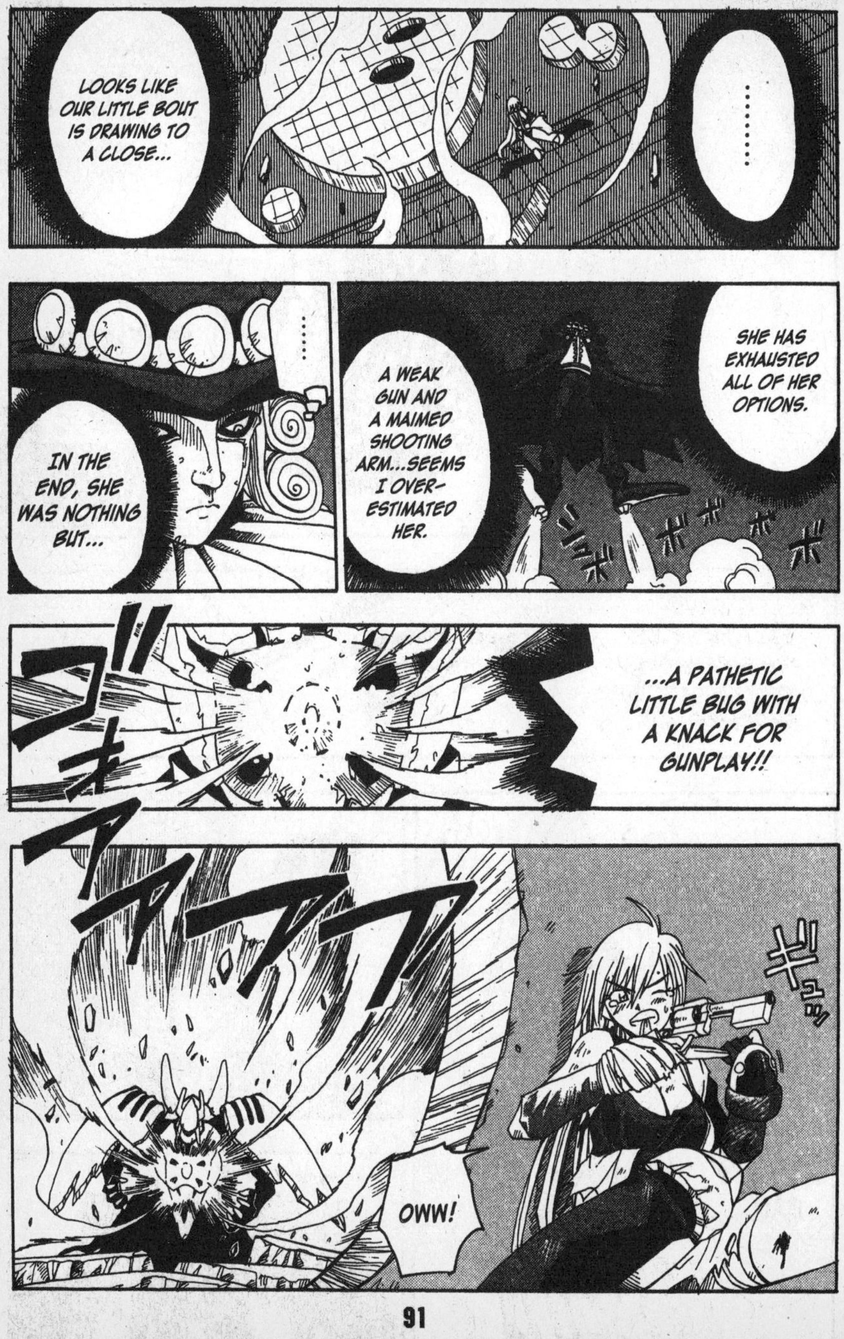
......
LOOKS LIKE OUR LITTLE BOUT IS DRAWING TO A CLOSE...
SHE HAS EXHAUSTED ALL OF HER OPTIONS.
A WEAK GUN AND A MAIMED SHOOTING ARM...SEEMS I OVER-ESTIMATED HER.
......
IN THE END, SHE WAS NOTHING BUT...
...A PATHETIC LITTLE BUG WITH A KNACK FOR GUNPLAY!!
OWW!

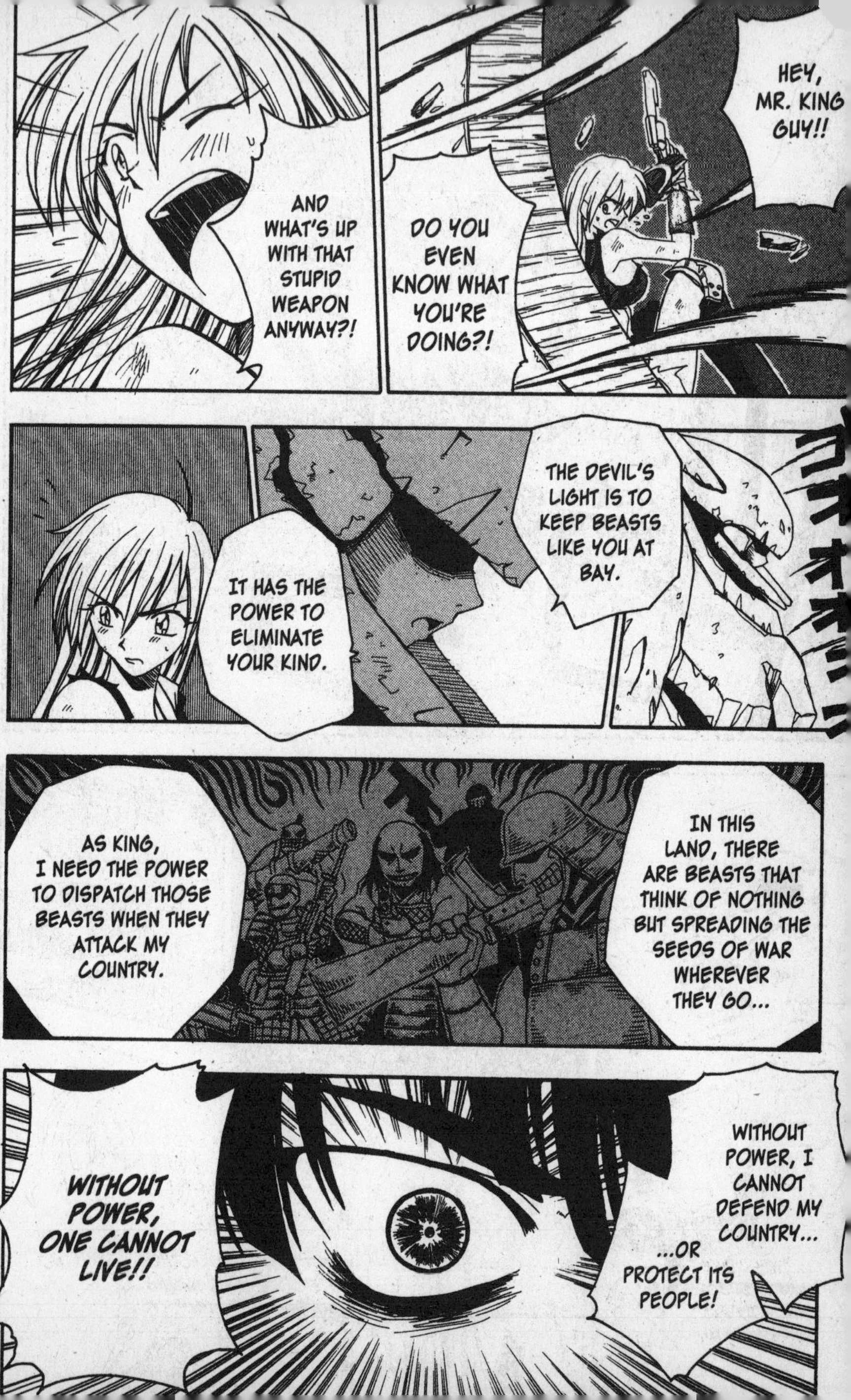
HEY, MR. KING GUY!!
DO YOU EVEN KNOW WHAT YOU'RE DOING?!
AND WHAT'S UP WITH THAT STUPID WEAPON ANYWAY?!
THE DEVIL'S LIGHT IS TO KEEP BEASTS LIKE YOU AT BAY.
IT HAS THE POWER TO ELIMINATE YOUR KIND.
IN THIS LAND, THERE ARE BEASTS THAT THINK OF NOTHING BUT SPREADING THE SEEDS OF WAR WHEREVER THEY GO...
AS KING, I NEED THE POWER TO DISPATCH THOSE BEASTS WHEN THEY ATTACK MY COUNTRY.
WITHOUT POWER, I CANNOT DEFEND MY COUNTRY...
...OR PROTECT ITS PEOPLE!
WITHOUT POWER, ONE CANNOT LIVE!!

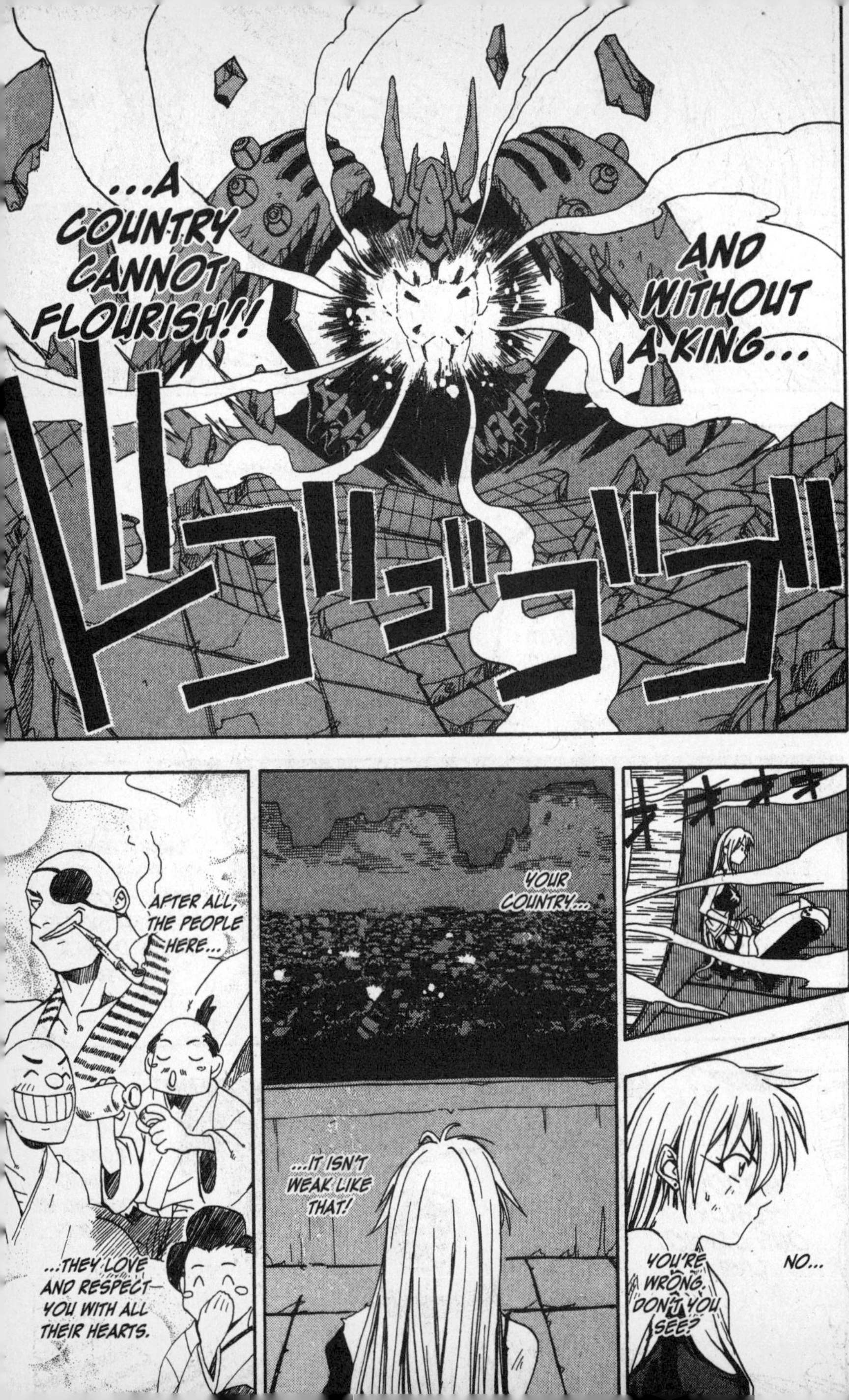
AND WITHOUT A KING...
...A COUNTRY CANNOT FLOURISH!!
ドゴゴゴゴ
NO...
YOU'RE WRONG, DON'T YOU SEE?
YOUR COUNTRY...
...IT ISN'T WEAK LIKE THAT!
AFTER ALL, THE PEOPLE HERE...
...THEY LOVE AND RESPECT YOU WITH ALL THEIR HEARTS.

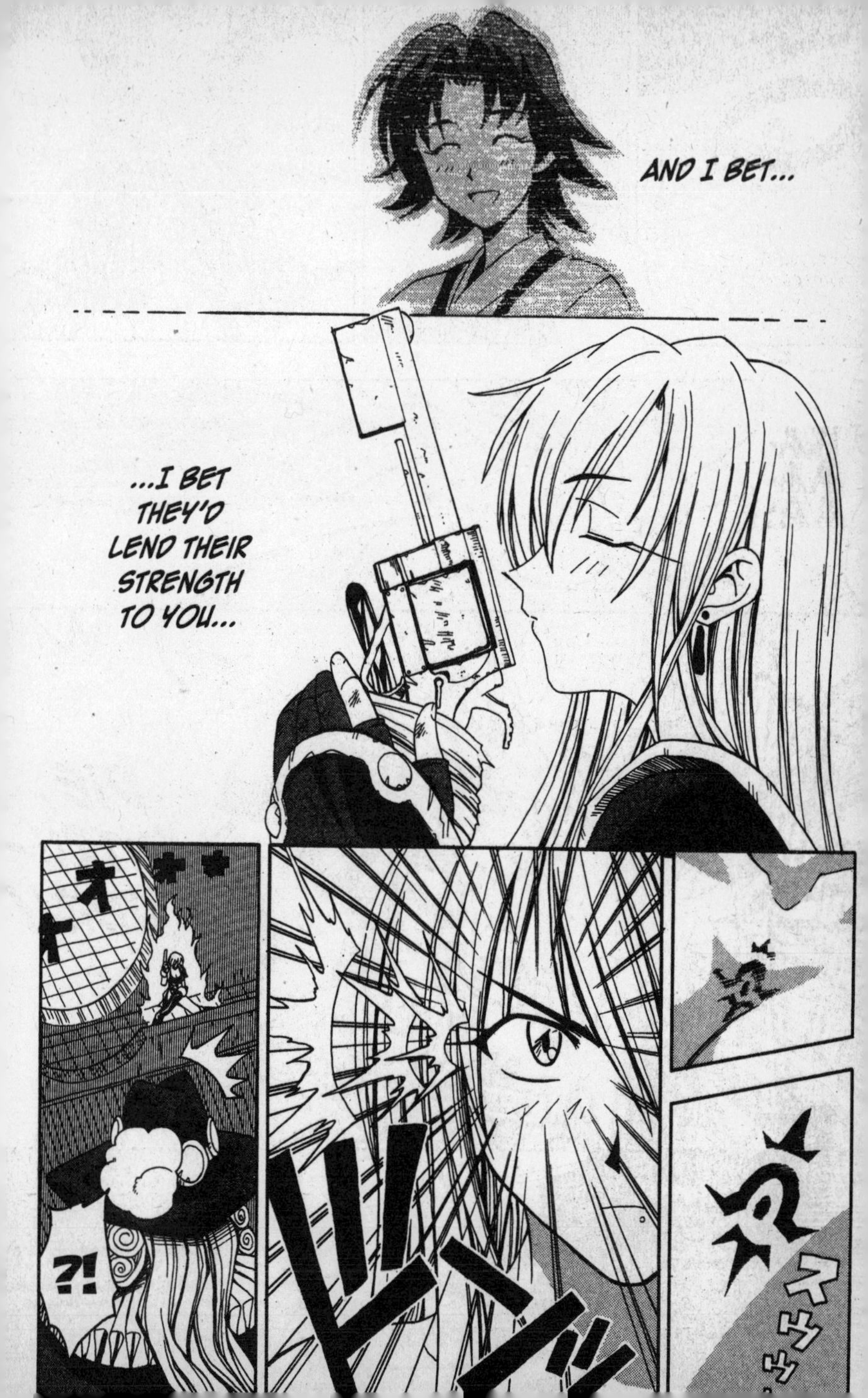
AND I BET...
...I BET THEY'D LEND THEIR STRENGTH TO YOU...
?!

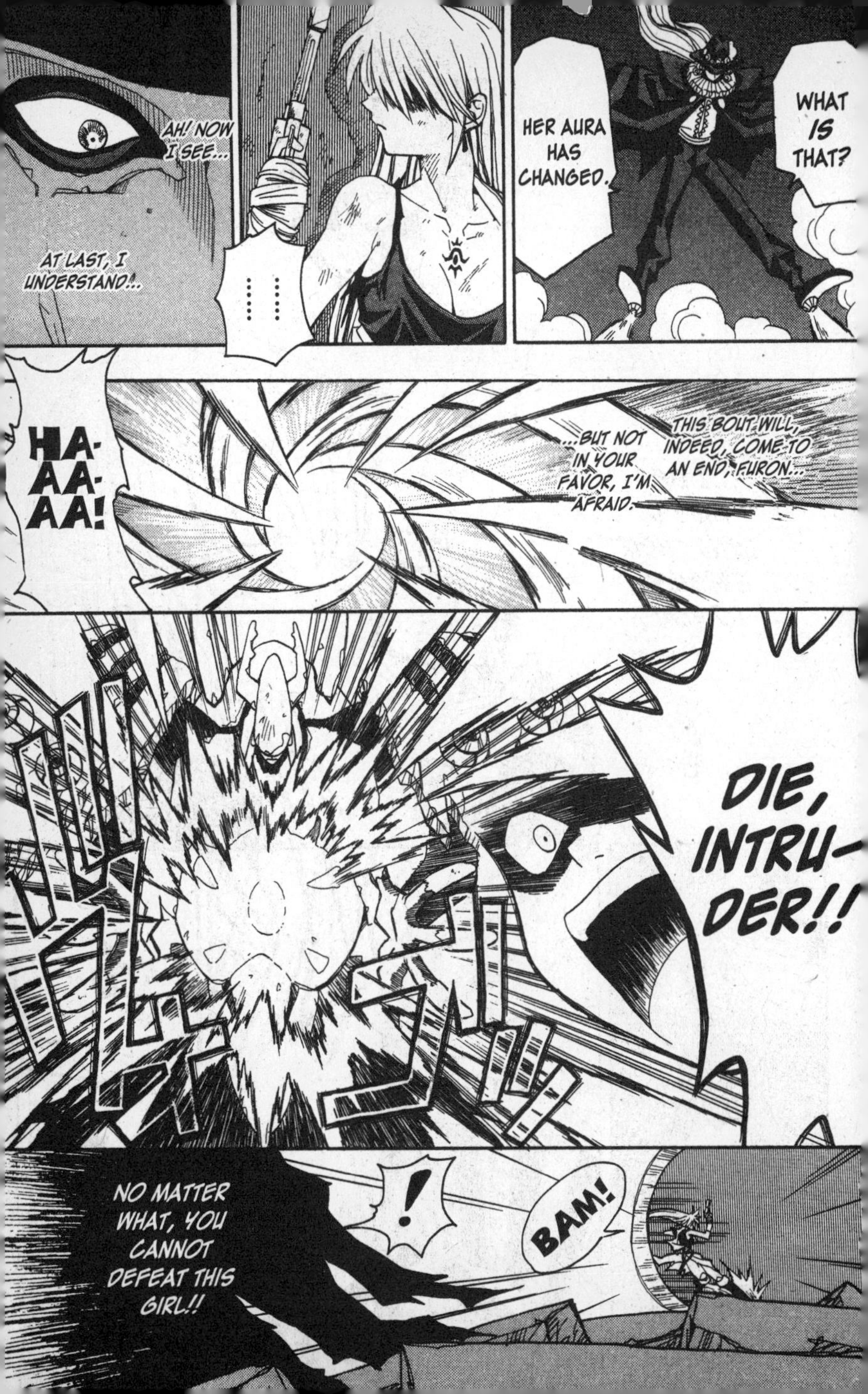
WHAT IS THAT?
HER AURA HAS CHANGED.
......
AH! NOW I SEE...
AT LAST, I UNDERSTAND...
THIS BOUT WILL, INDEED, COME TO AN END, FURON...
...BUT NOT IN YOUR FAVOR, I'M AFRAID.
HA-AA-AA!
DIE, INTRUDER!!
BAM!
!
NO MATTER WHAT, YOU CANNOT DEFEAT THIS GIRL!!

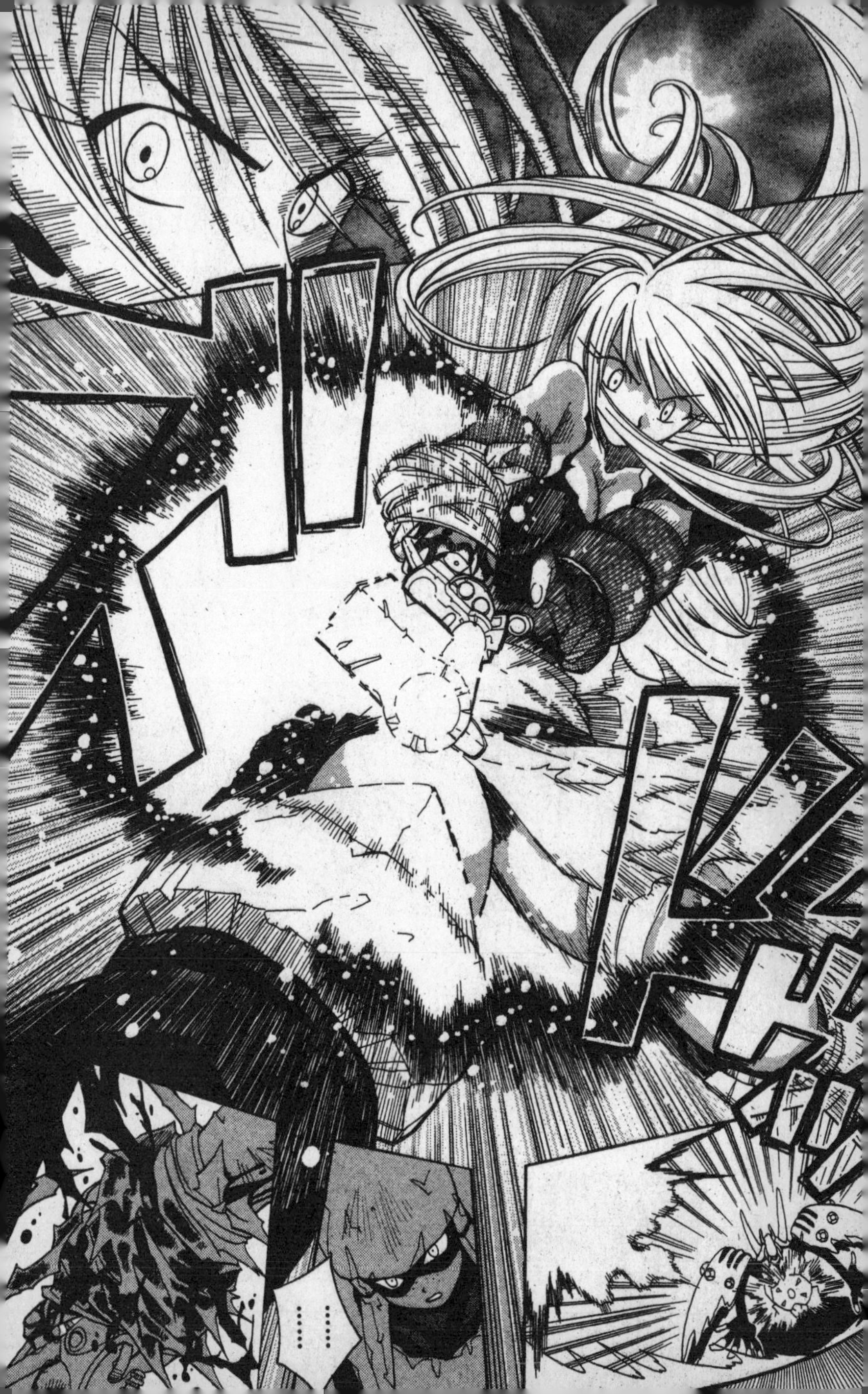
......

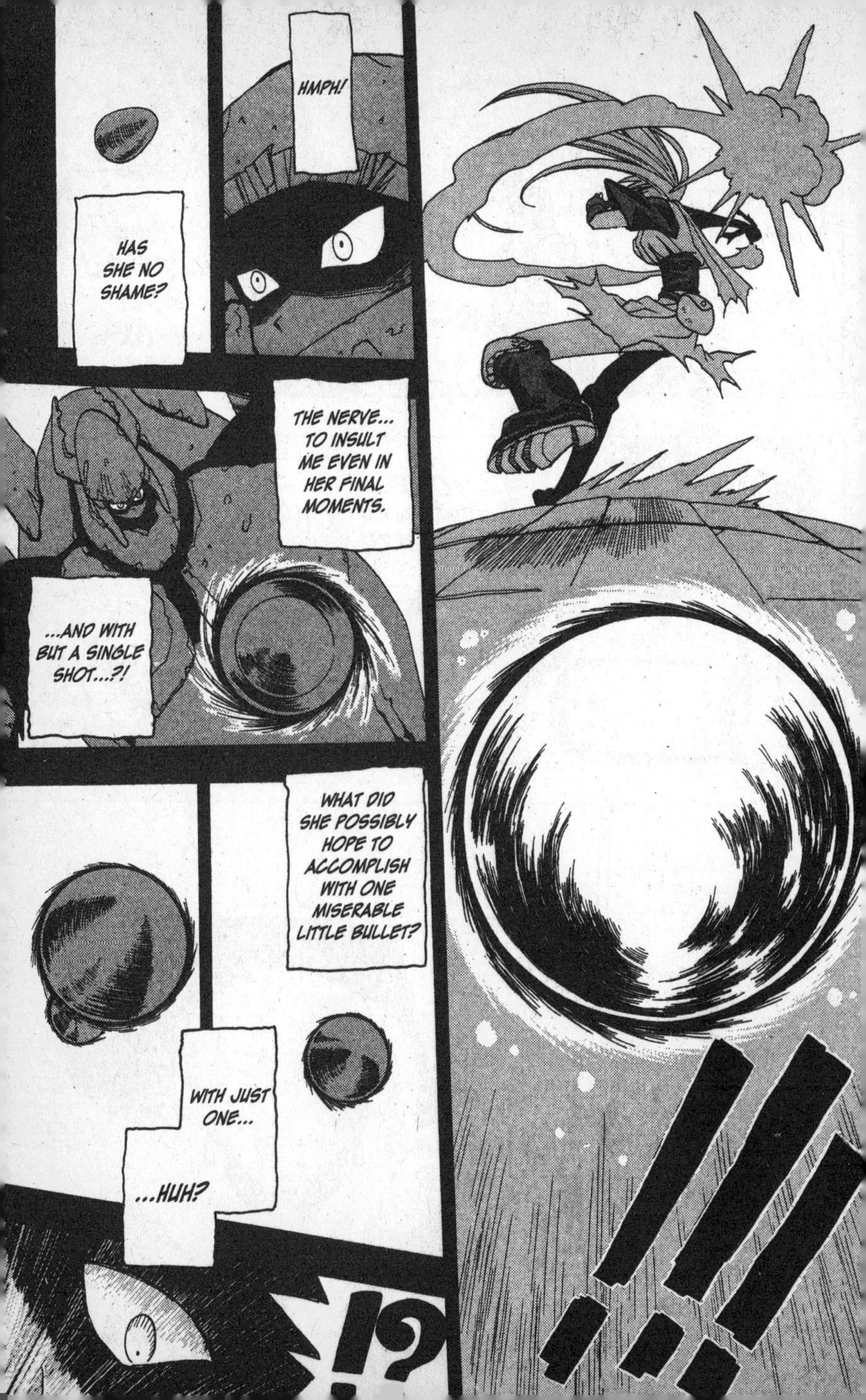
!!!
HMPH!
HAS SHE NO SHAME?
THE NERVE... TO INSULT ME EVEN IN HER FINAL MOMENTS.
...AND WITH BUT A SINGLE SHOT...?!
WHAT DID SHE POSSIBLY HOPE TO ACCOMPLISH WITH ONE MISERABLE LITTLE BULLET?
WITH JUST ONE...
...HUH?
!?

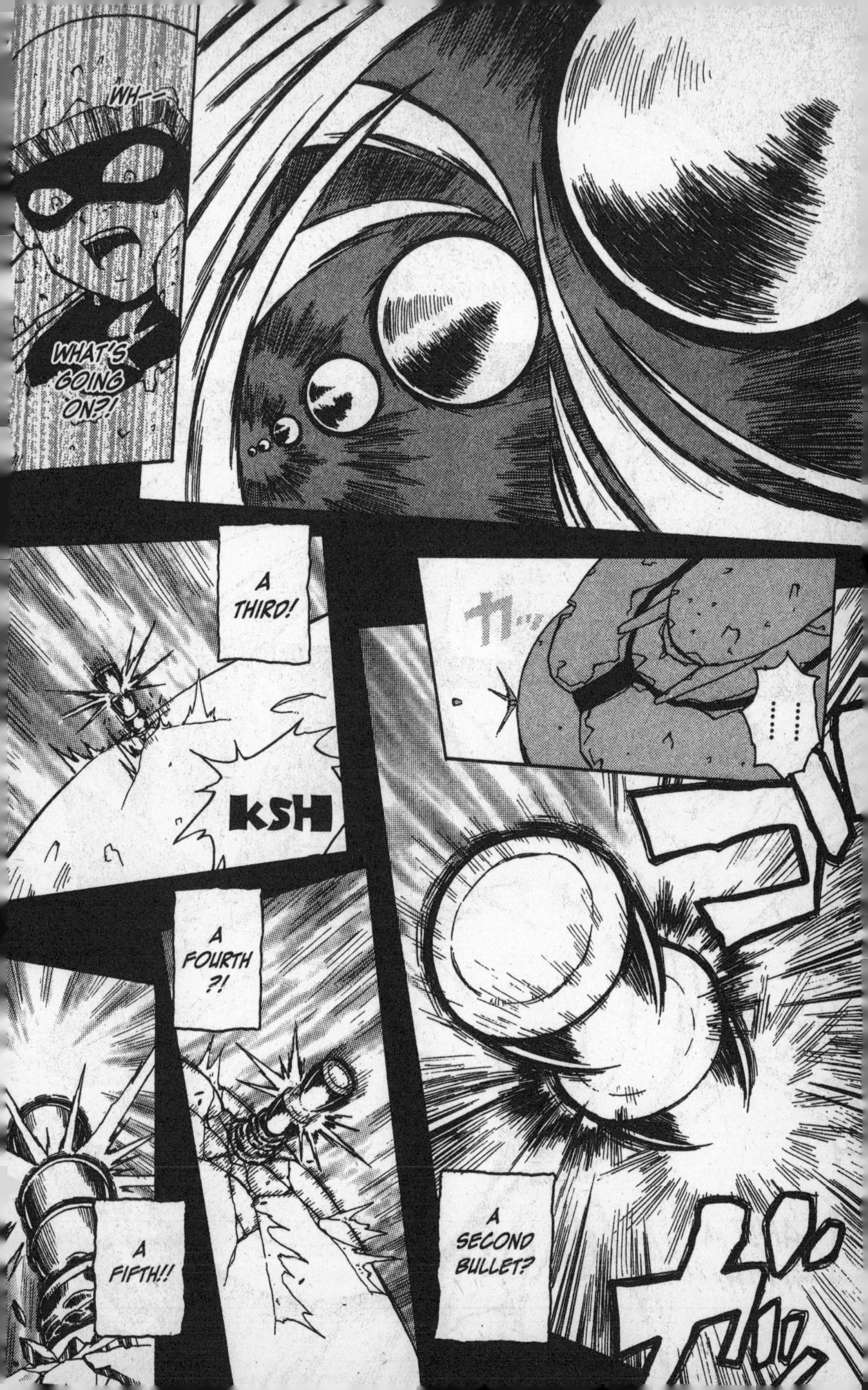
WH—
WHAT'S GOING ON?!
カッ
......
A SECOND BULLET?
A THIRD!
KSH
A FOURTH?!
A FIFTH!!

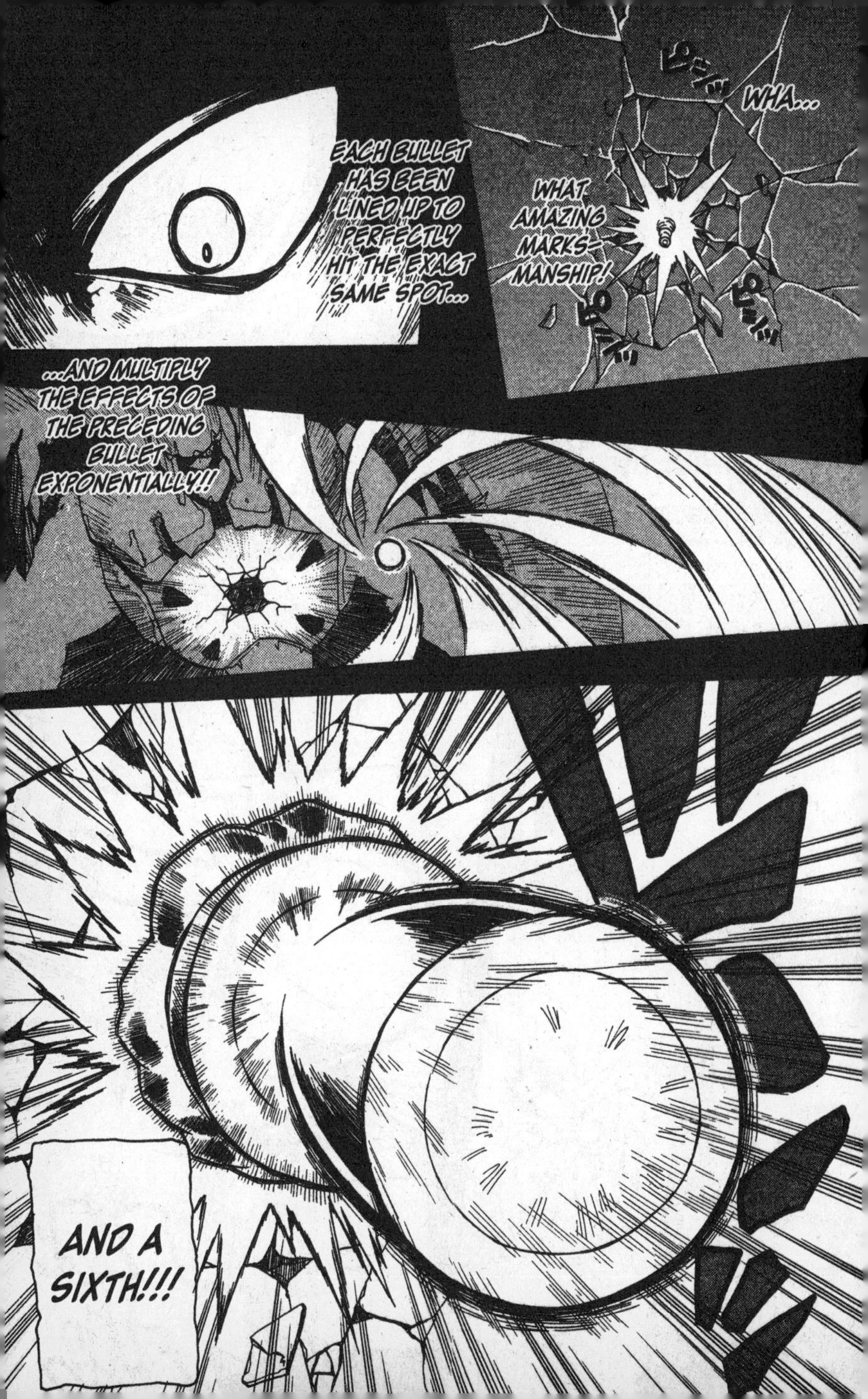
WHA...
WHAT AMAZING MARKS-MANSHIP!
EACH BULLET HAS BEEN LINED UP TO PERFECTLY HIT THE EXACT SAME SPOT...
...AND MULTIPLY THE EFFECTS OF THE PRECEDING BULLET EXPONENTIALLY!!
AND A SIXTH!!!

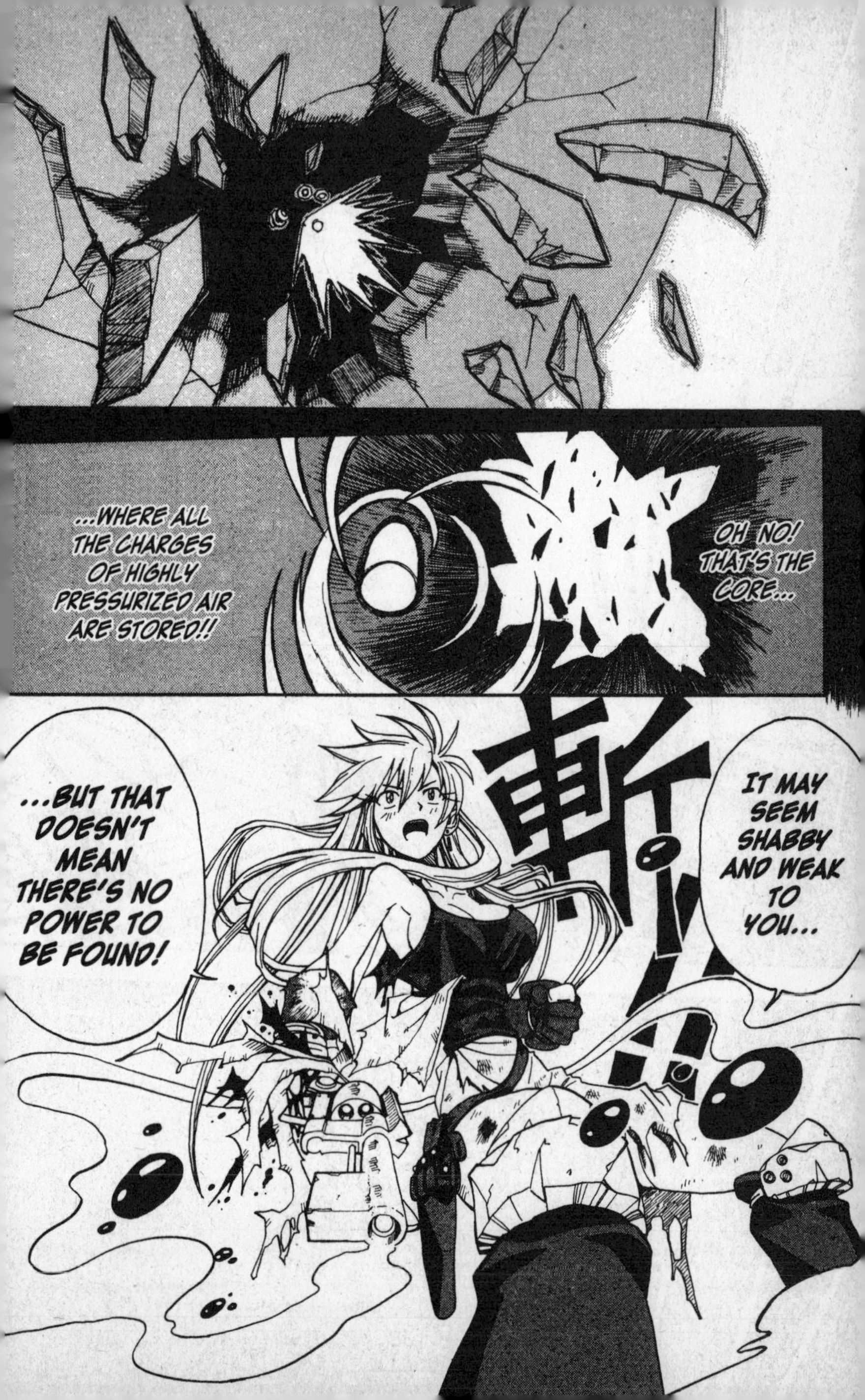
OH NO! THAT'S THE CORE...
...WHERE ALL THE CHARGES OF HIGHLY PRESSURIZED AIR ARE STORED!!
斬ッ!!
IT MAY SEEM SHABBY AND WEAK TO YOU...
...BUT THAT DOESN'T MEAN THERE'S NO POWER TO BE FOUND!

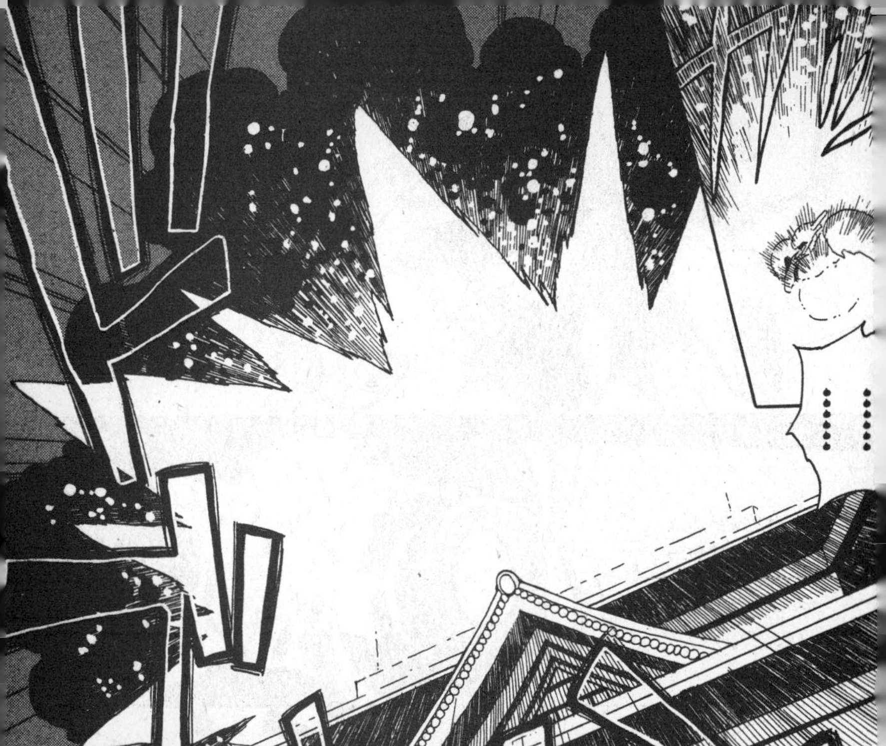
……
……

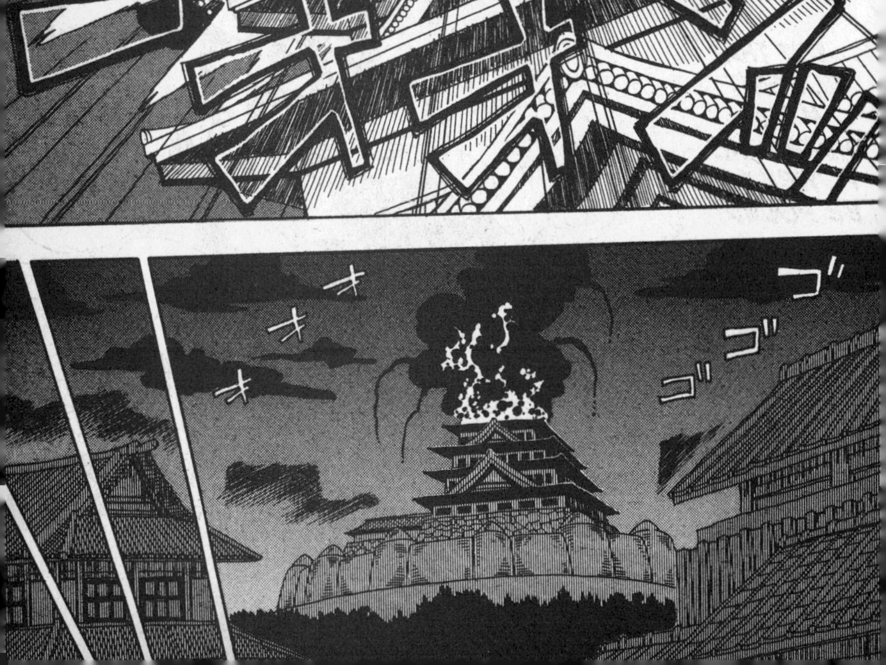
ゴゴゴ
オオオ

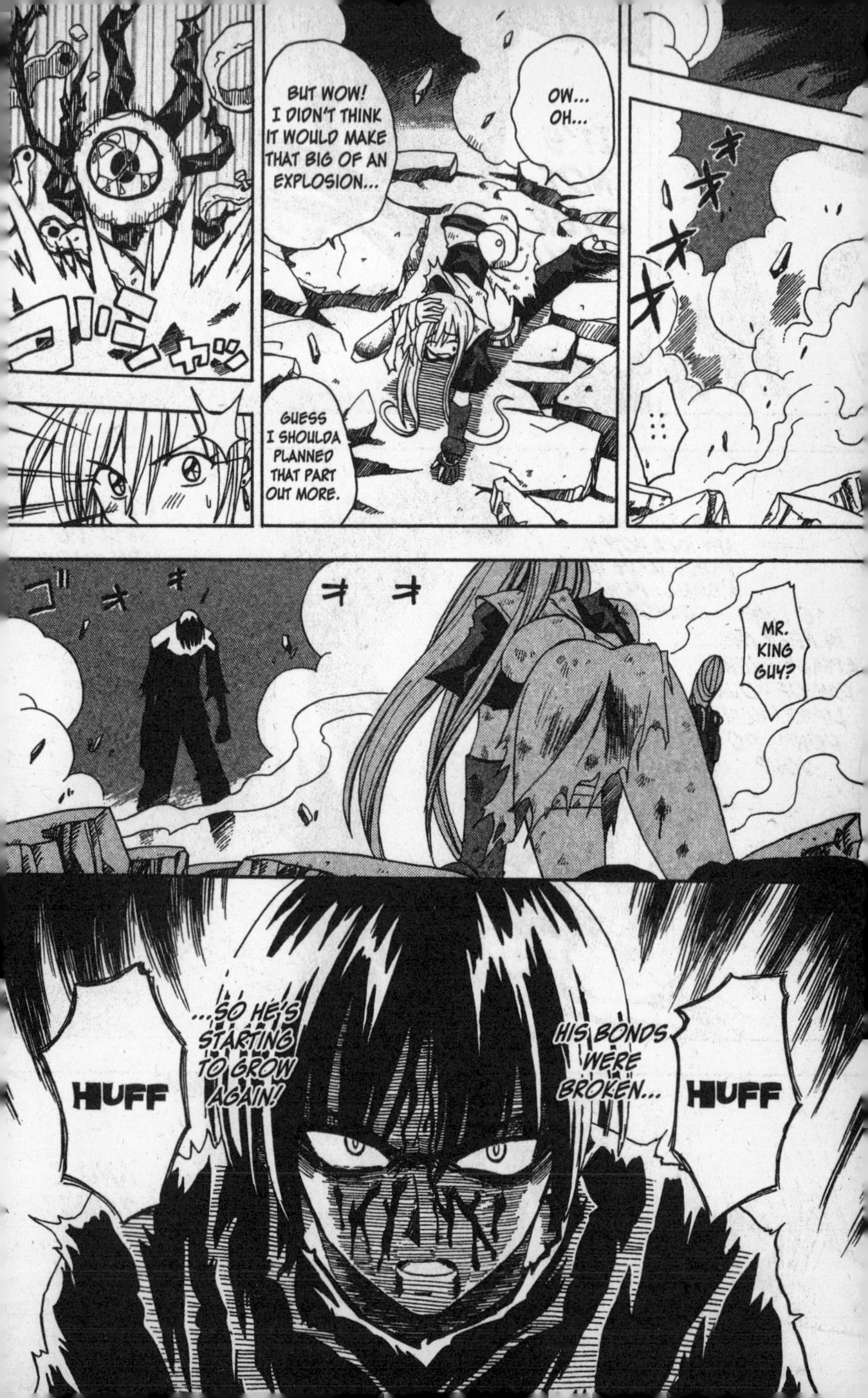

OW... OH...
BUT WOW! I DIDN'T THINK IT WOULD MAKE THAT BIG OF AN EXPLOSION...
GUESS I SHOULDA PLANNED THAT PART OUT MORE.
MR. KING GUY?
HUFF
HIS BONDS WERE BROKEN...
...SO HE'S STARTING TO GROW AGAIN!
HUFF

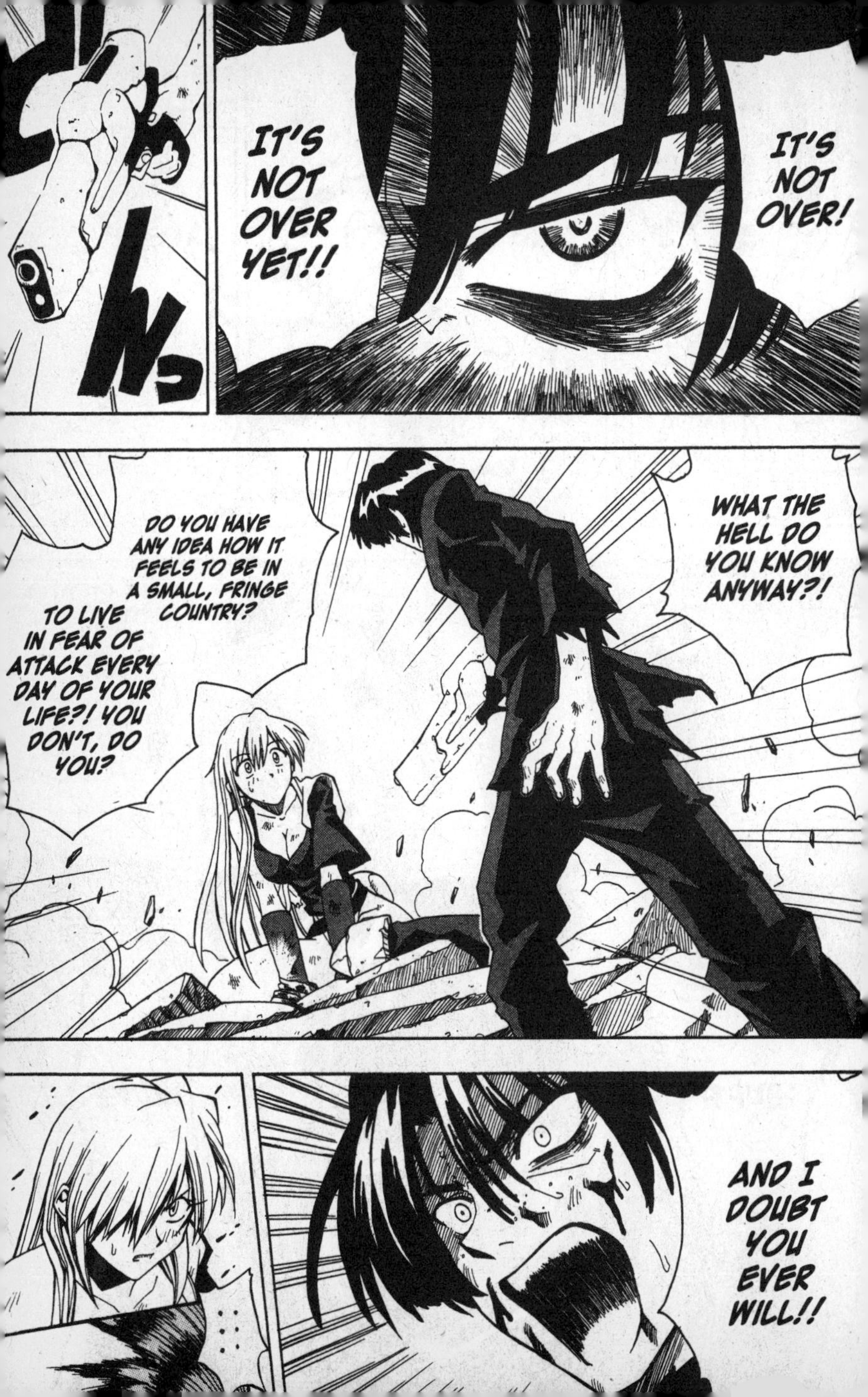

IT'S NOT OVER!
IT'S NOT OVER YET!!
WHAT THE HELL DO YOU KNOW ANYWAY?!
DO YOU HAVE ANY IDEA HOW IT FEELS TO BE IN A SMALL, FRINGE COUNTRY?
TO LIVE IN FEAR OF ATTACK EVERY DAY OF YOUR LIFE?! YOU DON'T, DO YOU?
AND I DOUBT YOU EVER WILL!!

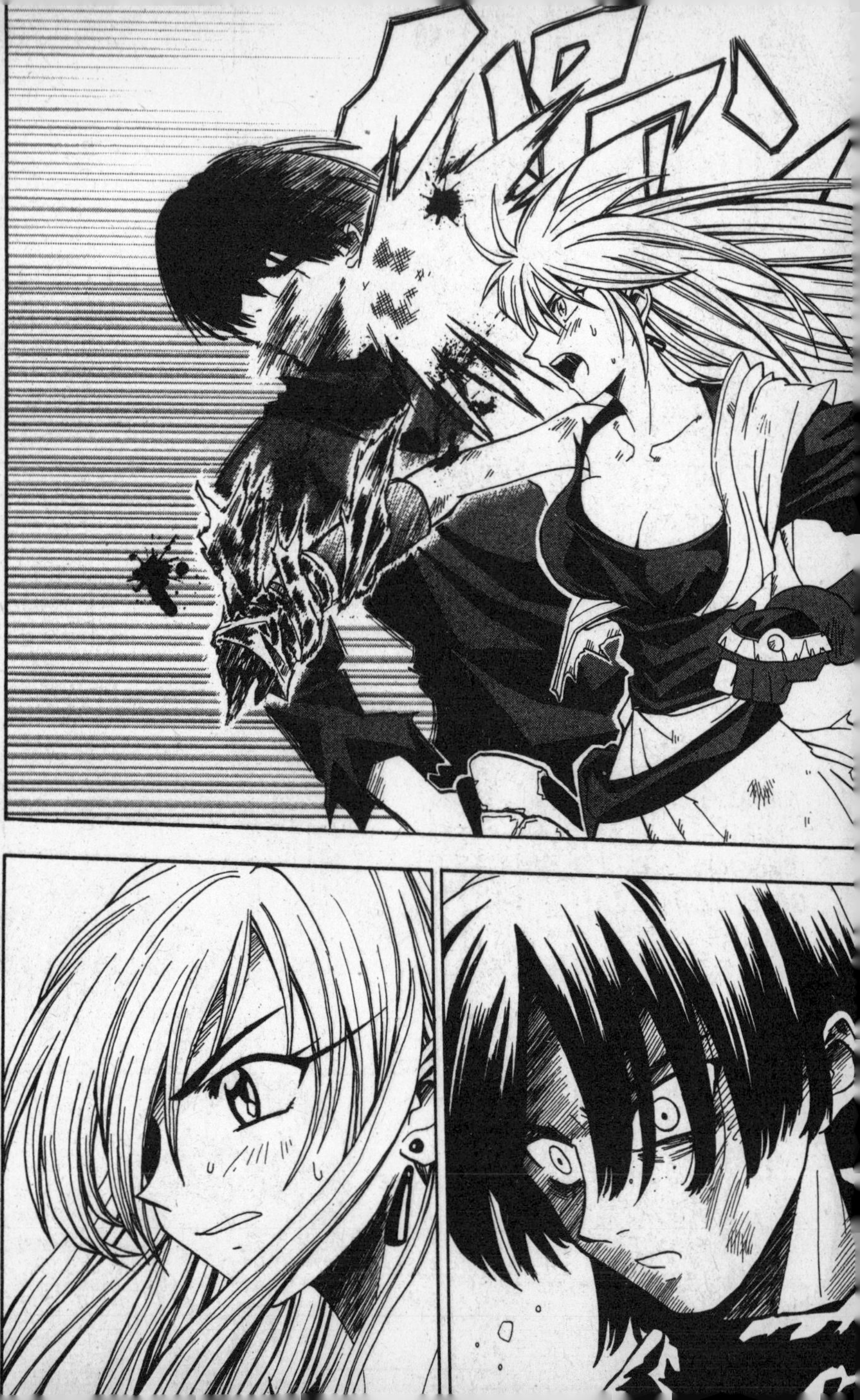

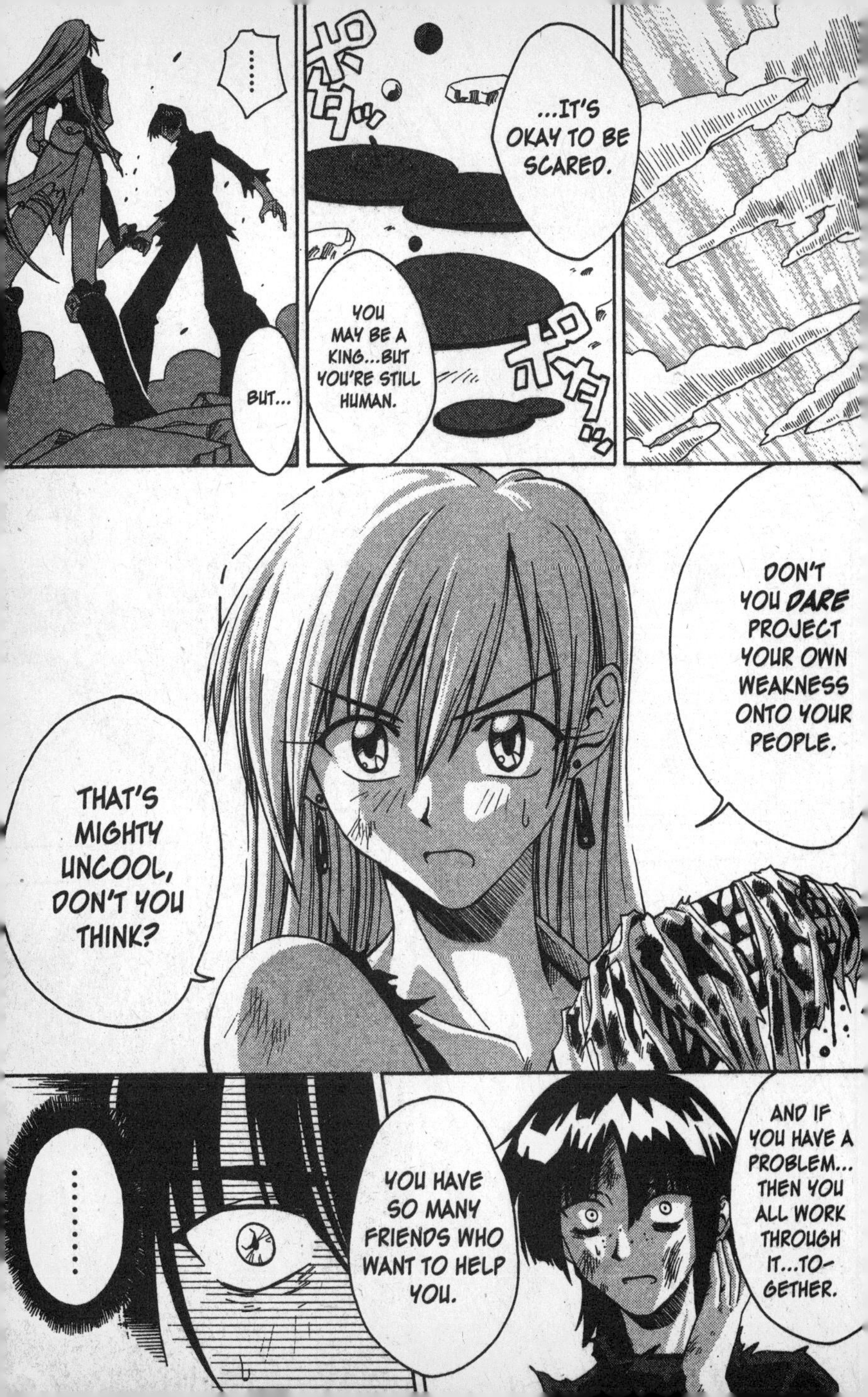

ポタッ
...IT'S OKAY TO BE SCARED.
YOU MAY BE A KING...BUT YOU'RE STILL HUMAN.
ポタッ
......
BUT...
DON'T YOU DARE PROJECT YOUR OWN WEAKNESS ONTO YOUR PEOPLE.
THAT'S MIGHTY UNCOOL, DON'T YOU THINK?
AND IF YOU HAVE A PROBLEM... THEN YOU ALL WORK THROUGH IT...TO-GETHER.
YOU HAVE SO MANY FRIENDS WHO WANT TO HELP YOU.
......

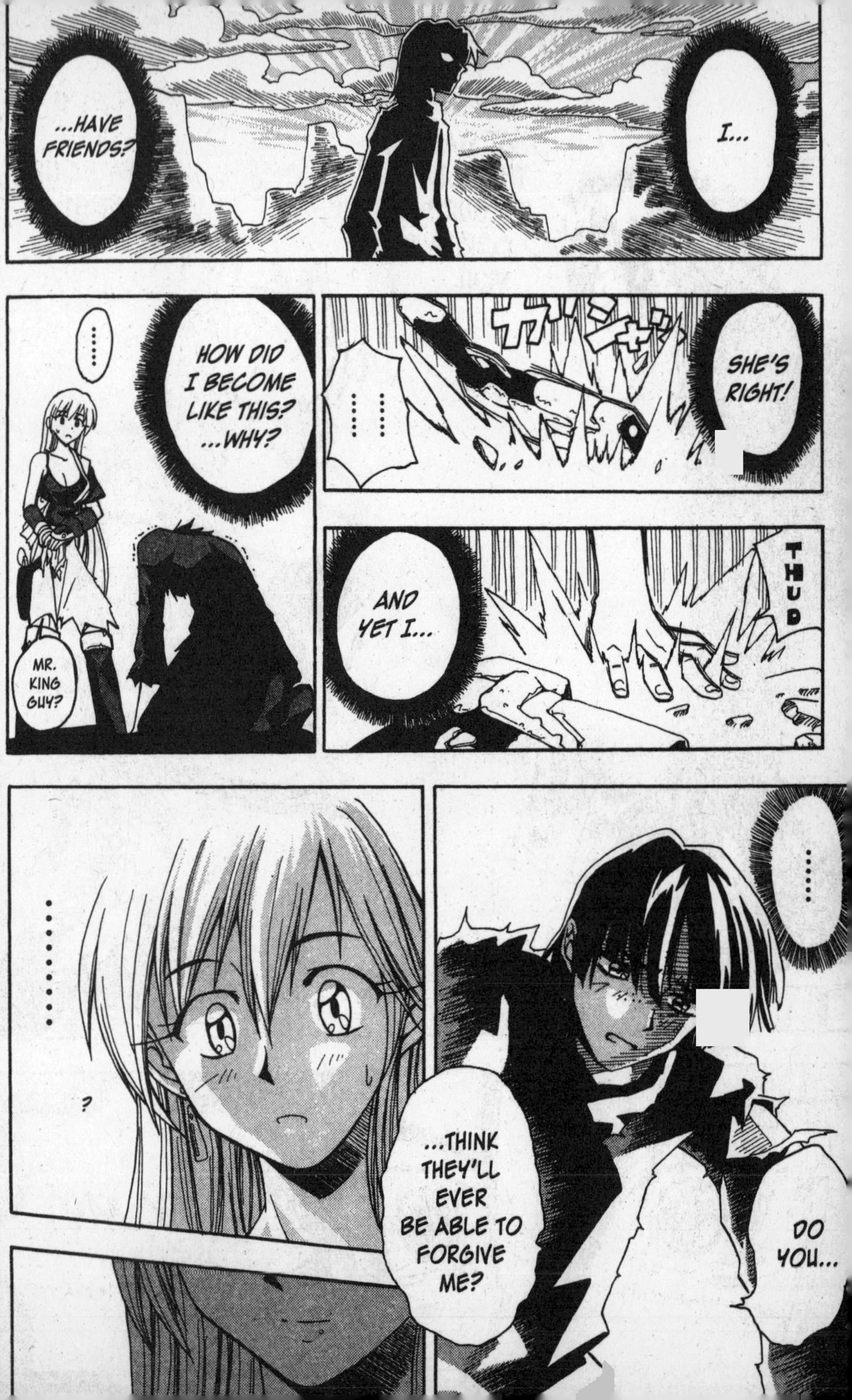
I...
...HAVE FRIENDS?
SHE'S RIGHT!
......
THUD
AND YET I...
HOW DID I BECOME LIKE THIS? ...WHY?
......
MR. KING GUY?
......
DO YOU...
...THINK THEY'LL EVER BE ABLE TO FORGIVE ME?
......
?

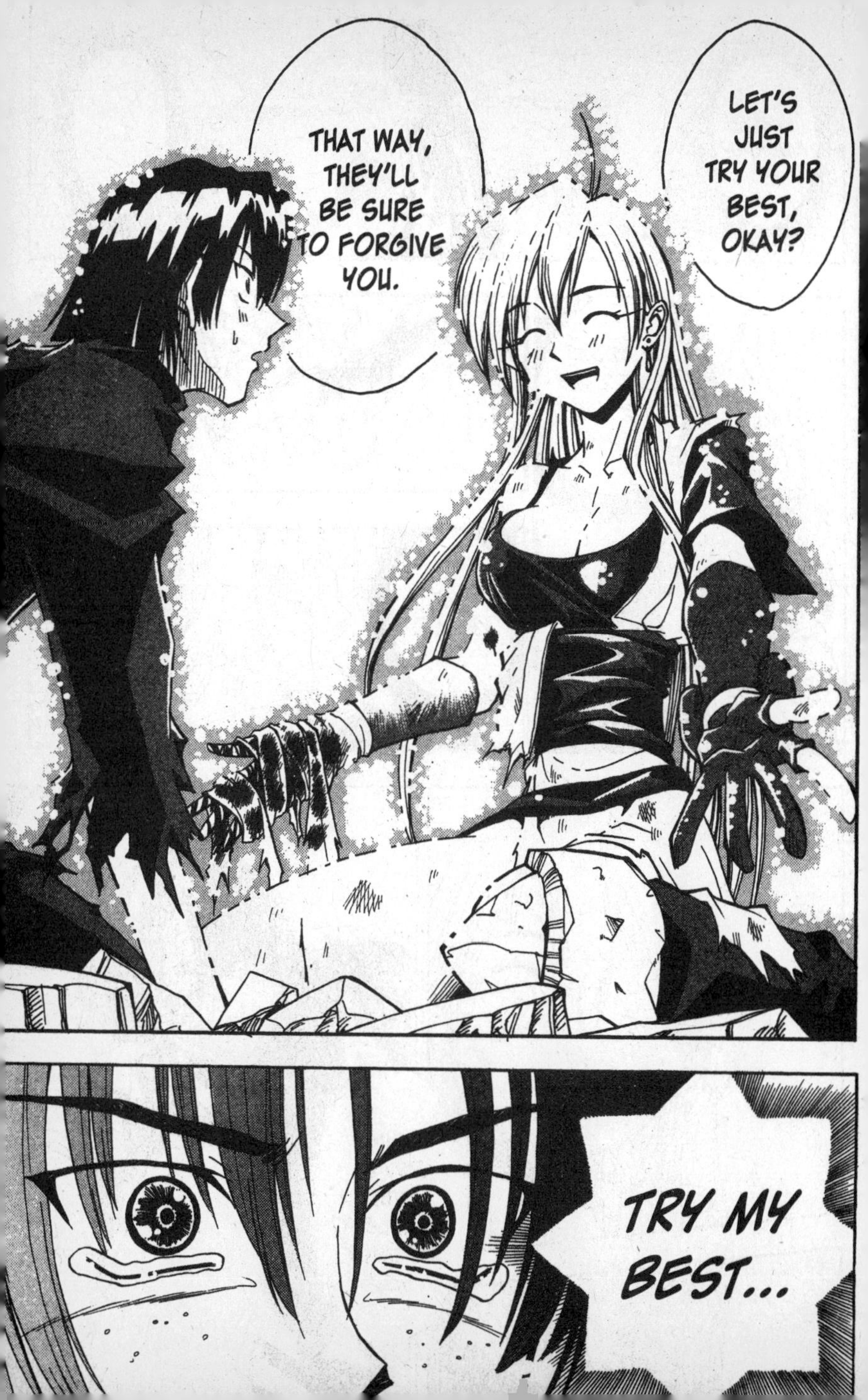
LET'S JUST TRY YOUR BEST, OKAY?
THAT WAY, THEY'LL BE SURE TO FORGIVE YOU.
TRY MY BEST...

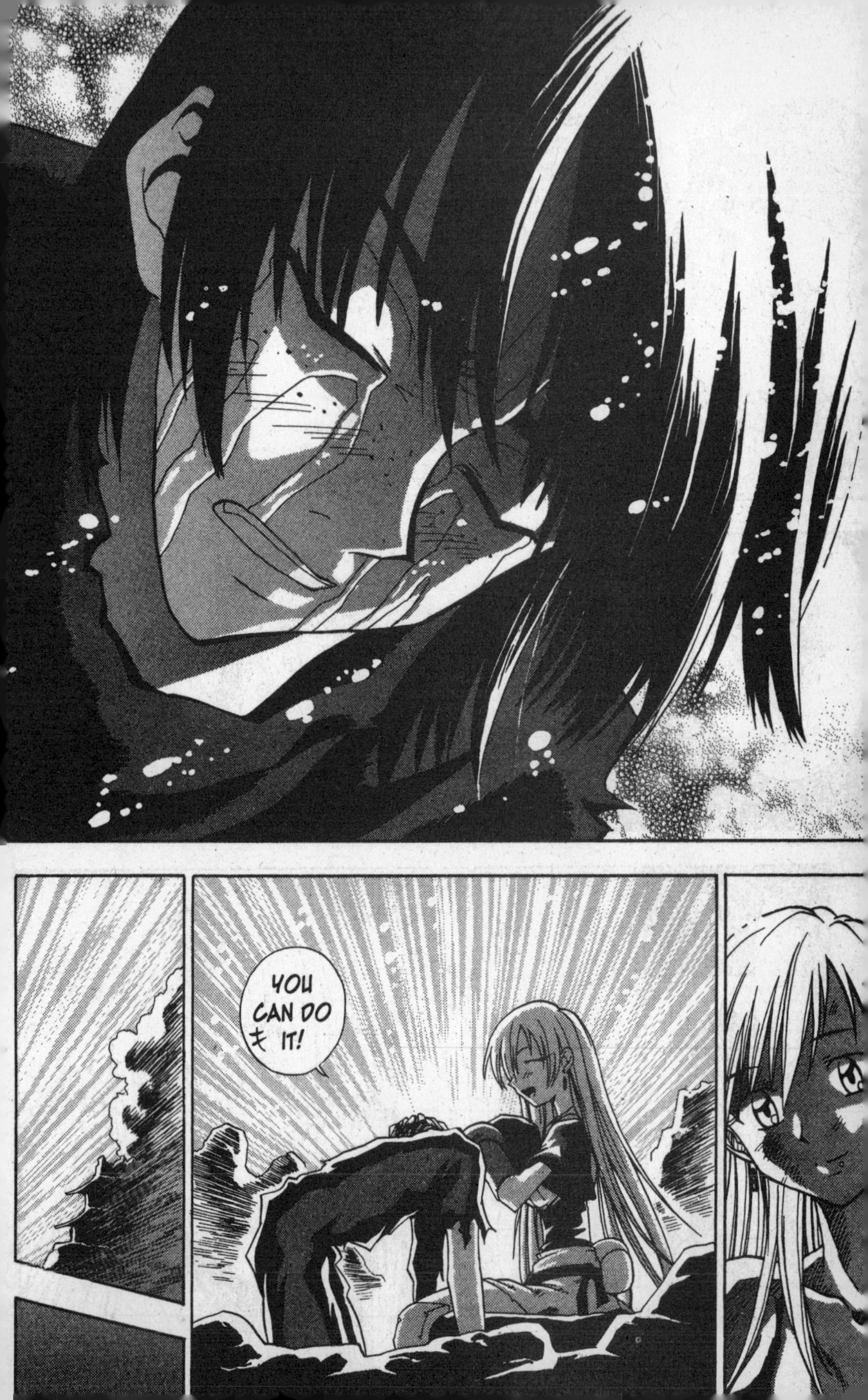
YOU CAN DO IT!

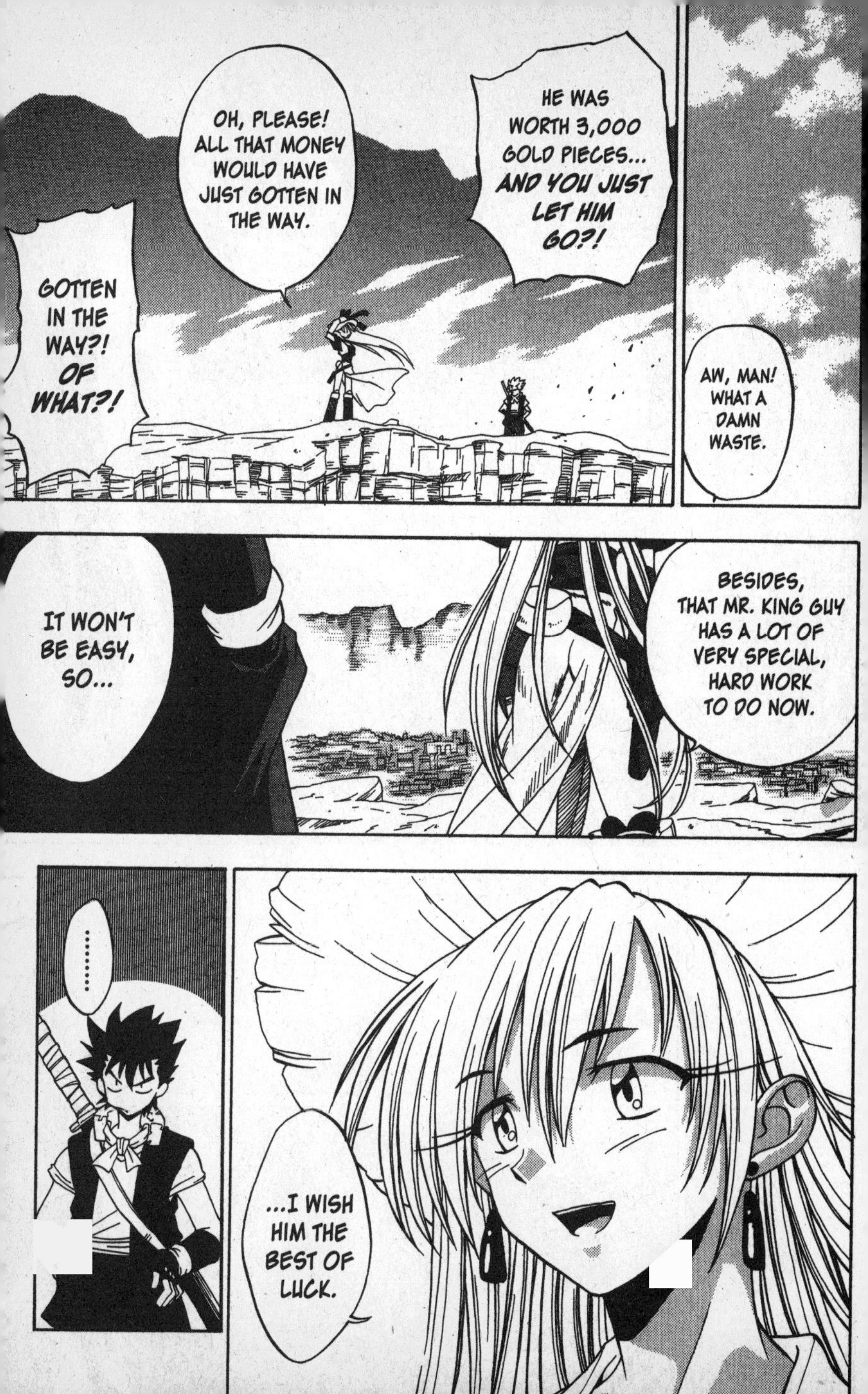
AW, MAN! WHAT A DAMN WASTE.
HE WAS WORTH 3,000 GOLD PIECES... AND YOU JUST LET HIM GO?!
OH, PLEASE! ALL THAT MONEY WOULD HAVE JUST GOTTEN IN THE WAY.
GOTTEN IN THE WAY?! OF WHAT?!
BESIDES, THAT MR. KING GUY HAS A LOT OF VERY SPECIAL, HARD WORK TO DO NOW.
IT WON'T BE EASY, SO...
...I WISH HIM THE BEST OF LUCK.
......

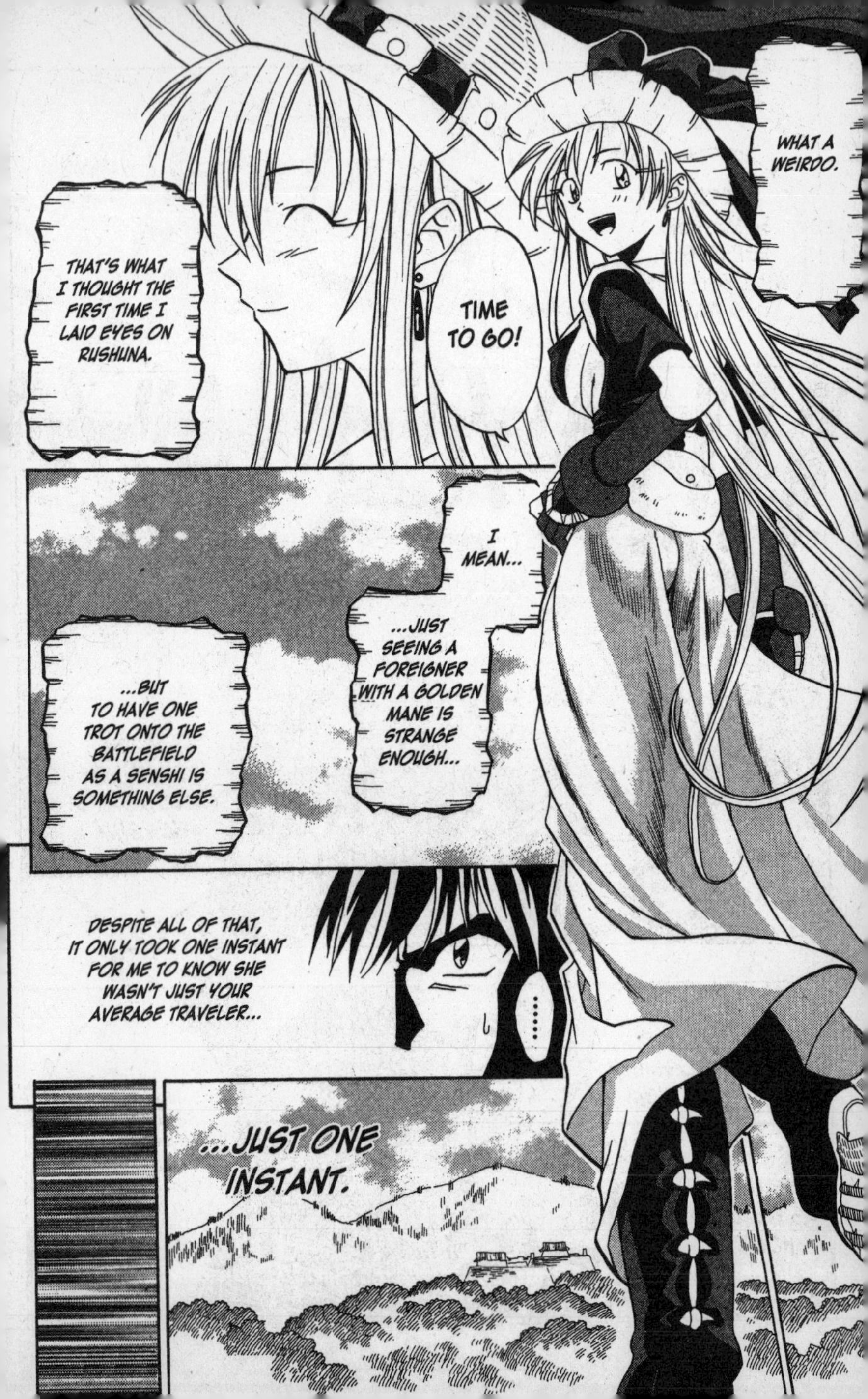
WHAT A WEIRDO.
TIME TO GO!
THAT'S WHAT I THOUGHT THE FIRST TIME I LAID EYES ON RUSHUNA.
I MEAN...
...JUST SEEING A FOREIGNER WITH A GOLDEN MANE IS STRANGE ENOUGH...
...BUT TO HAVE ONE TROT ONTO THE BATTLEFIELD AS A SENSHI IS SOMETHING ELSE.
......
DESPITE ALL OF THAT, IT ONLY TOOK ONE INSTANT FOR ME TO KNOW SHE WASN'T JUST YOUR AVERAGE TRAVELER...
...JUST ONE INSTANT.

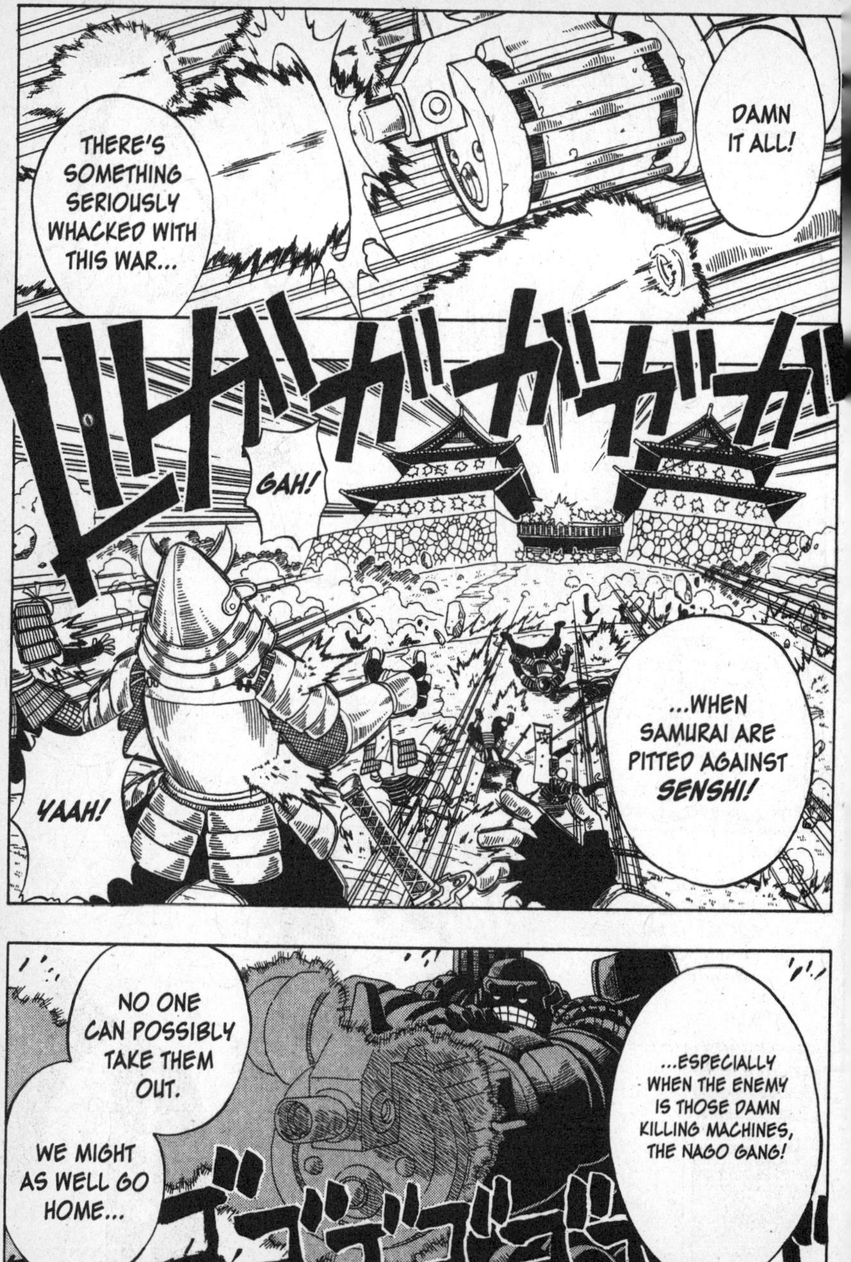

DAMN IT ALL!
THERE'S SOMETHING SERIOUSLY WHACKED WITH THIS WAR...
...WHEN SAMURAI ARE PITTED AGAINST SENSHI!
GAH!
YAAH!
...ESPECIALLY WHEN THE ENEMY IS THOSE DAMN KILLING MACHINES, THE NAGO GANG!
NO ONE CAN POSSIBLY TAKE THEM OUT.
WE MIGHT AS WELL GO HOME...

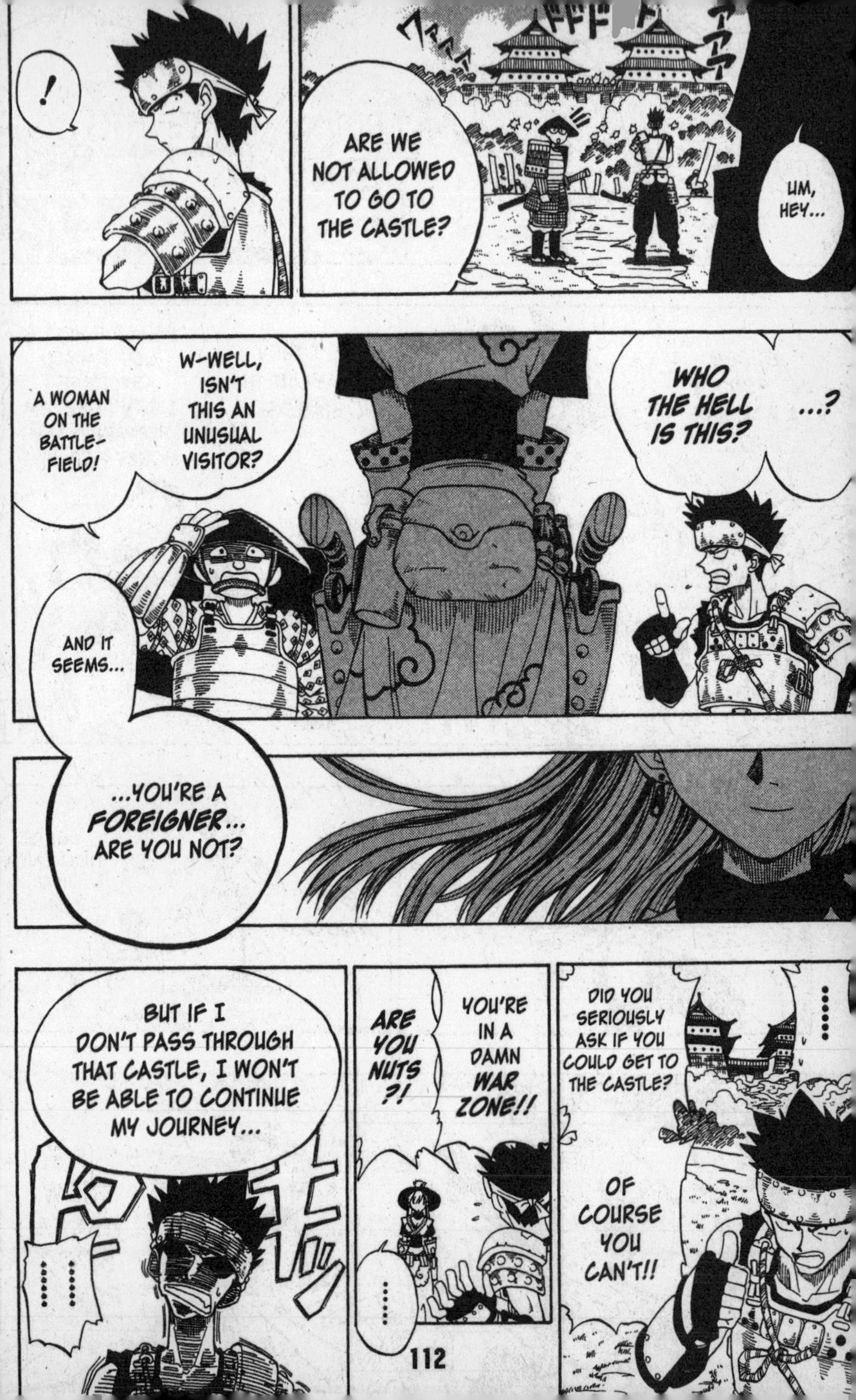
UM, HEY...
ARE WE NOT ALLOWED TO GO TO THE CASTLE?
!
...?
WHO THE HELL IS THIS?
W-WELL, ISN'T THIS AN UNUSUAL VISITOR?
A WOMAN ON THE BATTLE-FIELD!
AND IT SEEMS...
...YOU'RE A FOREIGNER... ARE YOU NOT?
......
DID YOU SERIOUSLY ASK IF YOU COULD GET TO THE CASTLE?
OF COURSE YOU CAN'T!!
YOU'RE IN A DAMN WAR ZONE!!
ARE YOU NUTS?!
......
BUT IF I DON'T PASS THROUGH THAT CASTLE, I WON'T BE ABLE TO CONTINUE MY JOURNEY...
......

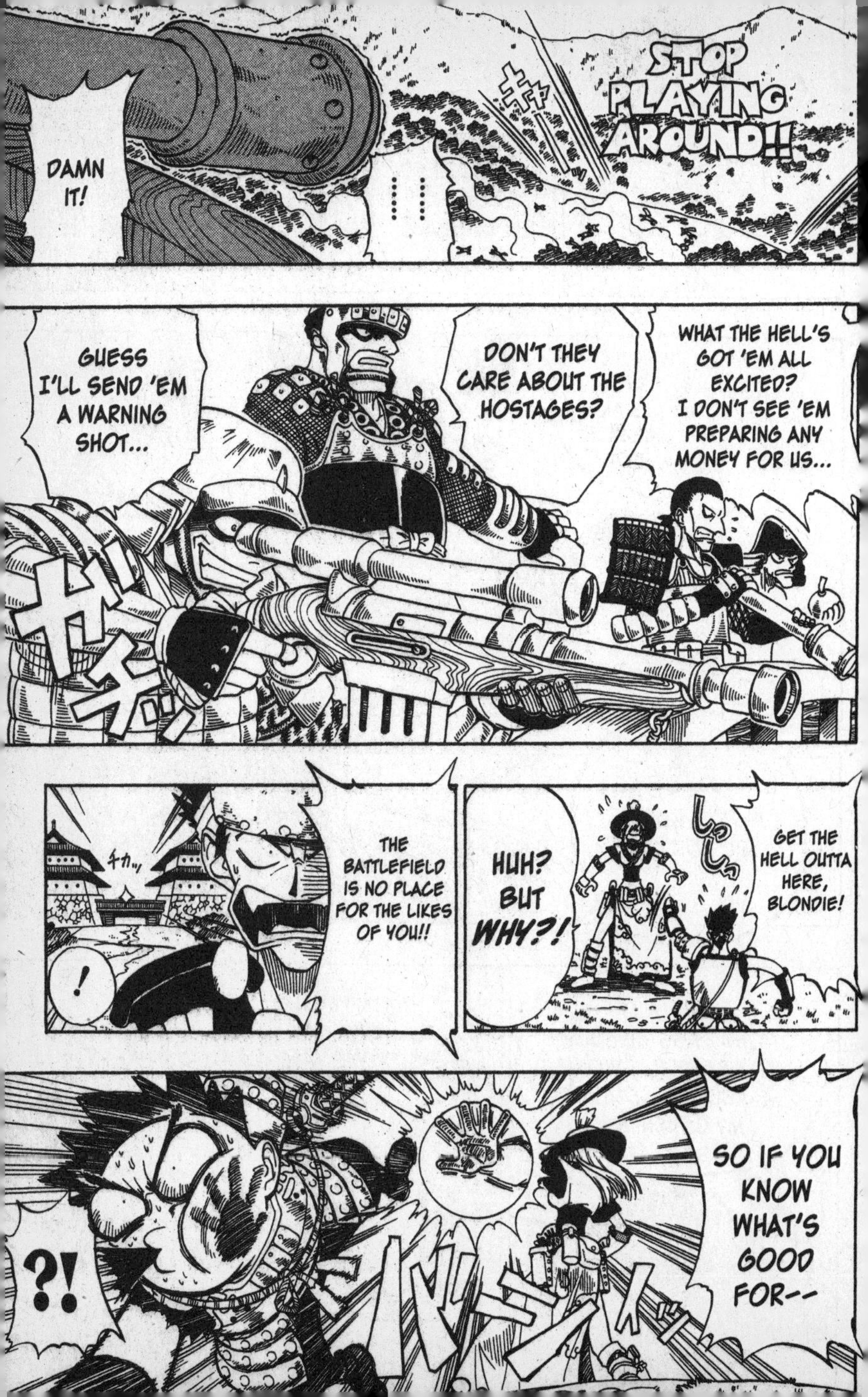
STOP PLAYING AROUND!!
......
DAMN IT!
WHAT THE HELL'S GOT 'EM ALL EXCITED? I DON'T SEE 'EM PREPARING ANY MONEY FOR US...
DON'T THEY CARE ABOUT THE HOSTAGES?
GUESS I'LL SEND 'EM A WARNING SHOT...
GET THE HELL OUTTA HERE, BLONDIE!
HUH? BUT WHY?!
THE BATTLEFIELD IS NO PLACE FOR THE LIKES OF YOU!!
!
SO IF YOU KNOW WHAT'S GOOD FOR--
?!

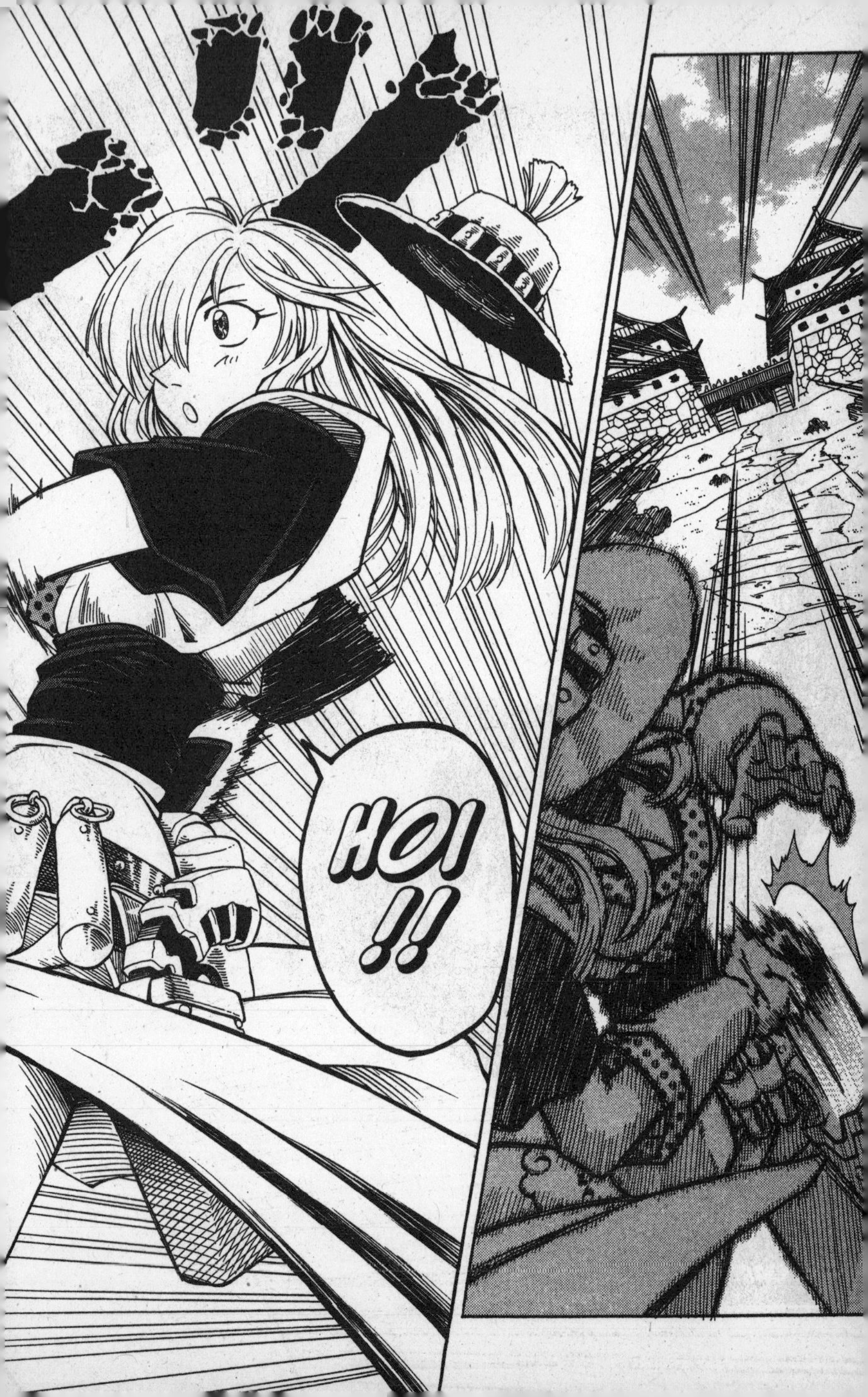
HOI !!

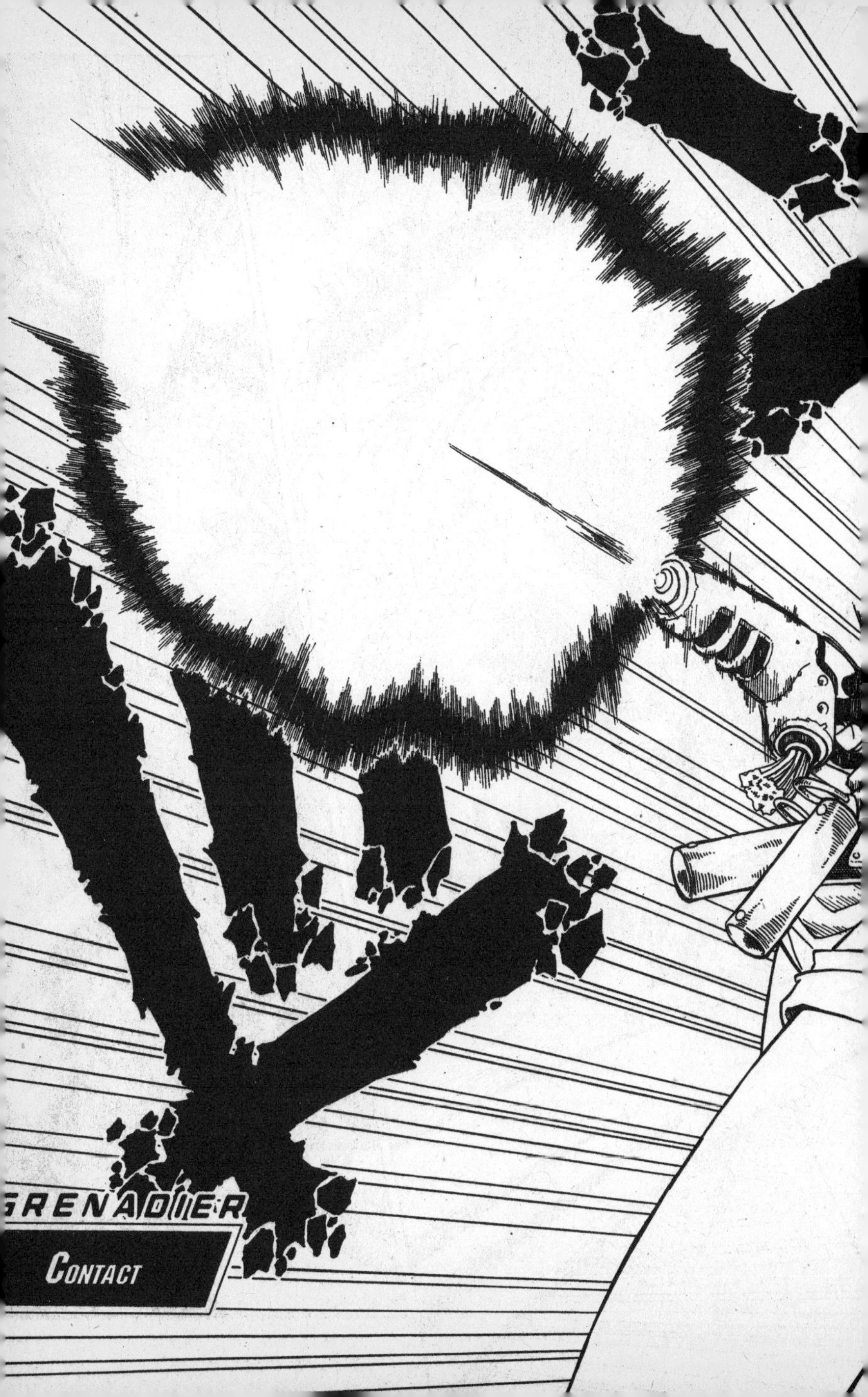
GRENADIER
CONTACT

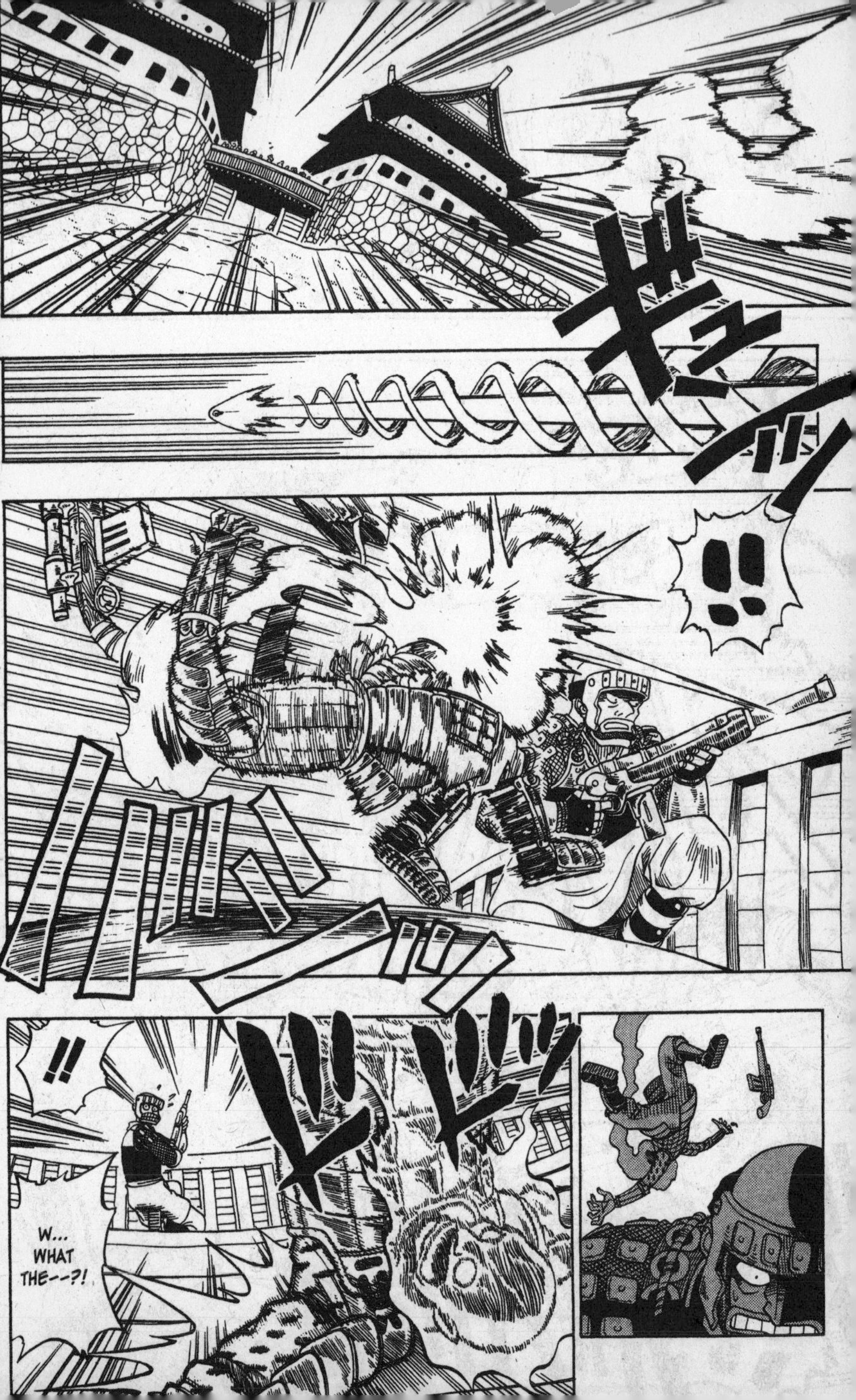
!!
!!
W... WHAT THE--?!

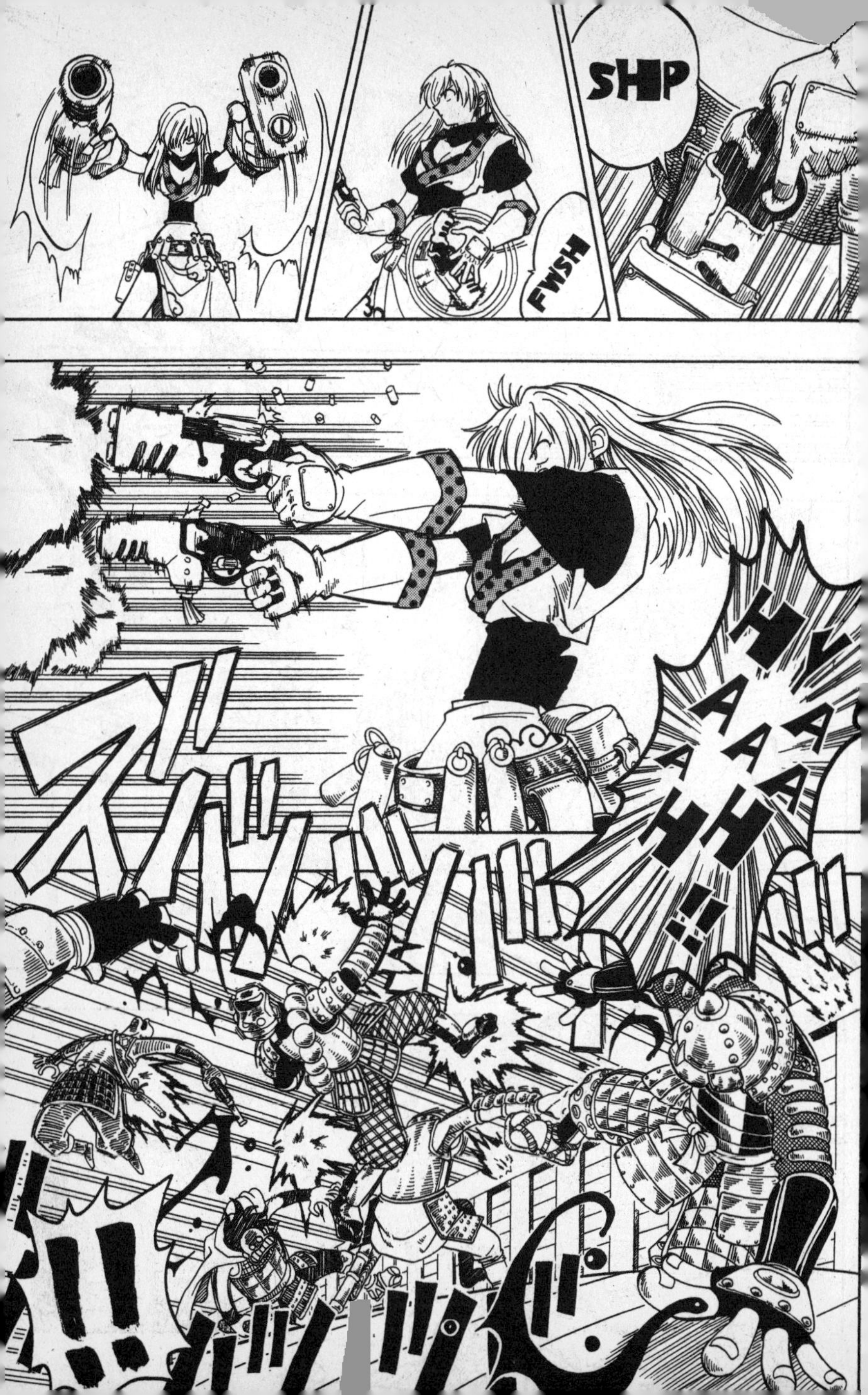
SHP
FWSH
HYAAAAAHH!!

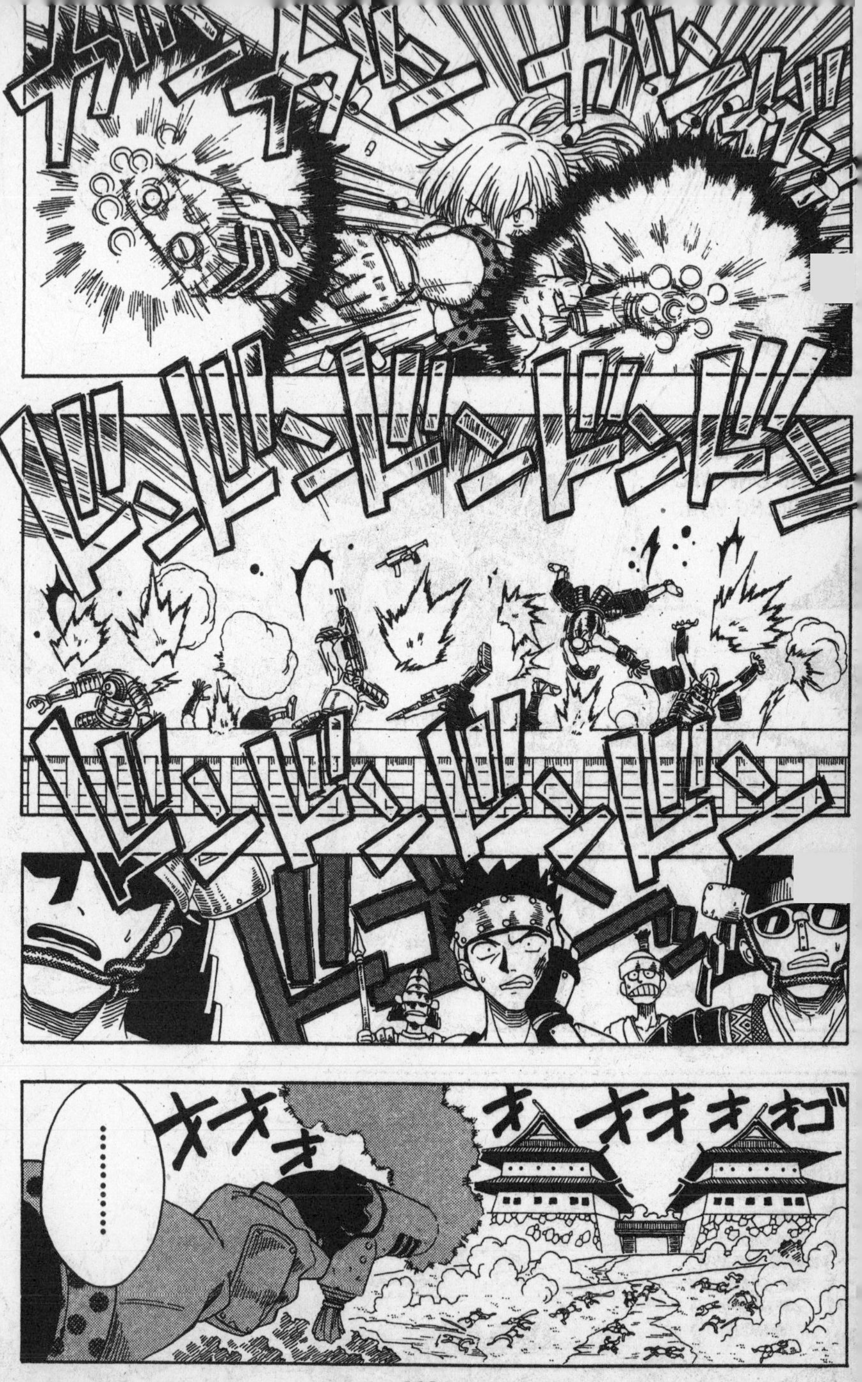
ガガガッ
ガガン
ダダン
ダダン
ドンドンドンドン
ドドドドドン
ドン
……
ゴオオオオオオ

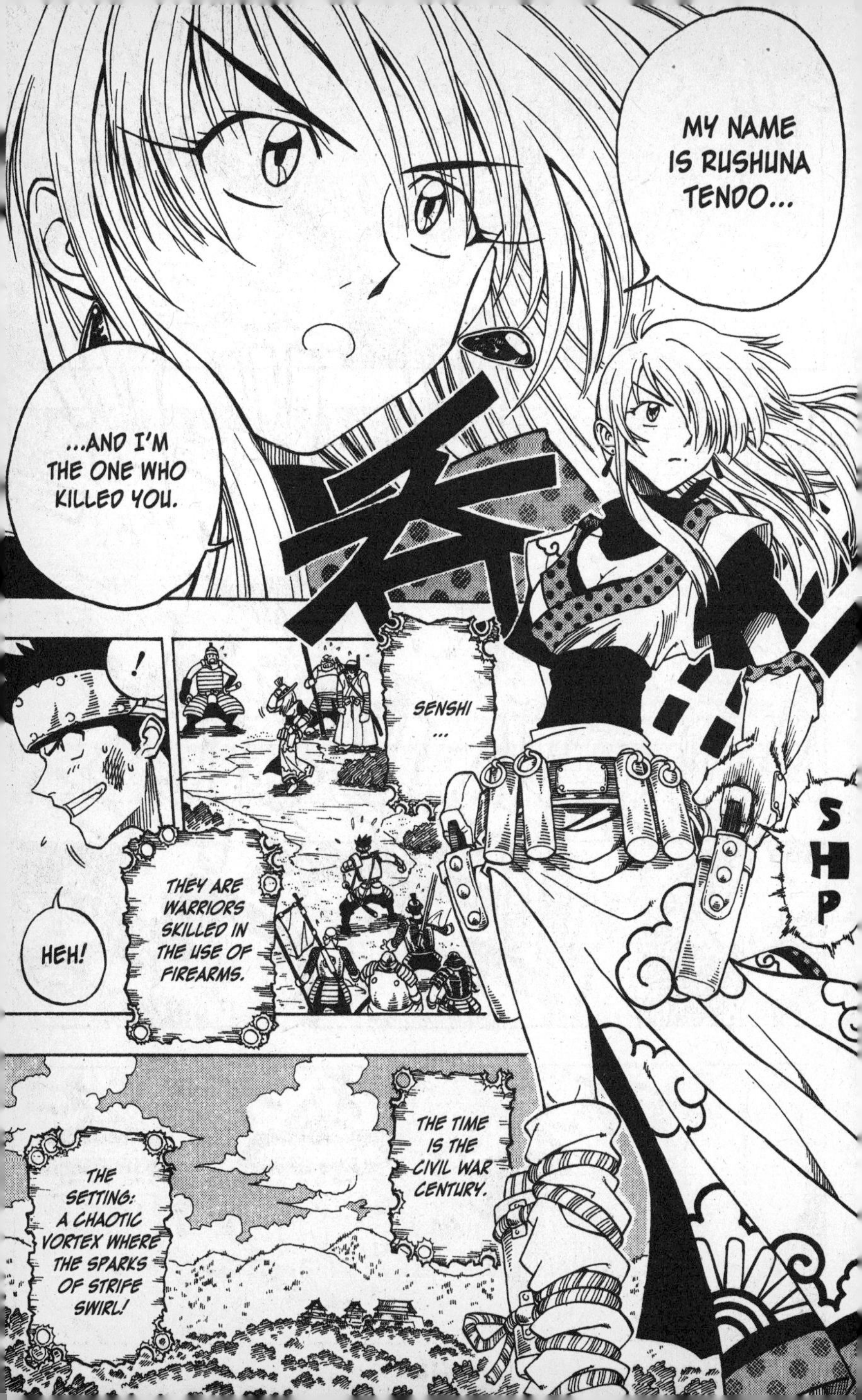
MY NAME IS RUSHUNA TENDO...
...AND I'M THE ONE WHO KILLED YOU.
SHP
SENSHI ...
THEY ARE WARRIORS SKILLED IN THE USE OF FIREARMS.
!
HEH!
THE TIME IS THE CIVIL WAR CENTURY.
THE SETTING: A CHAOTIC VORTEX WHERE THE SPARKS OF STRIFE SWIRL!

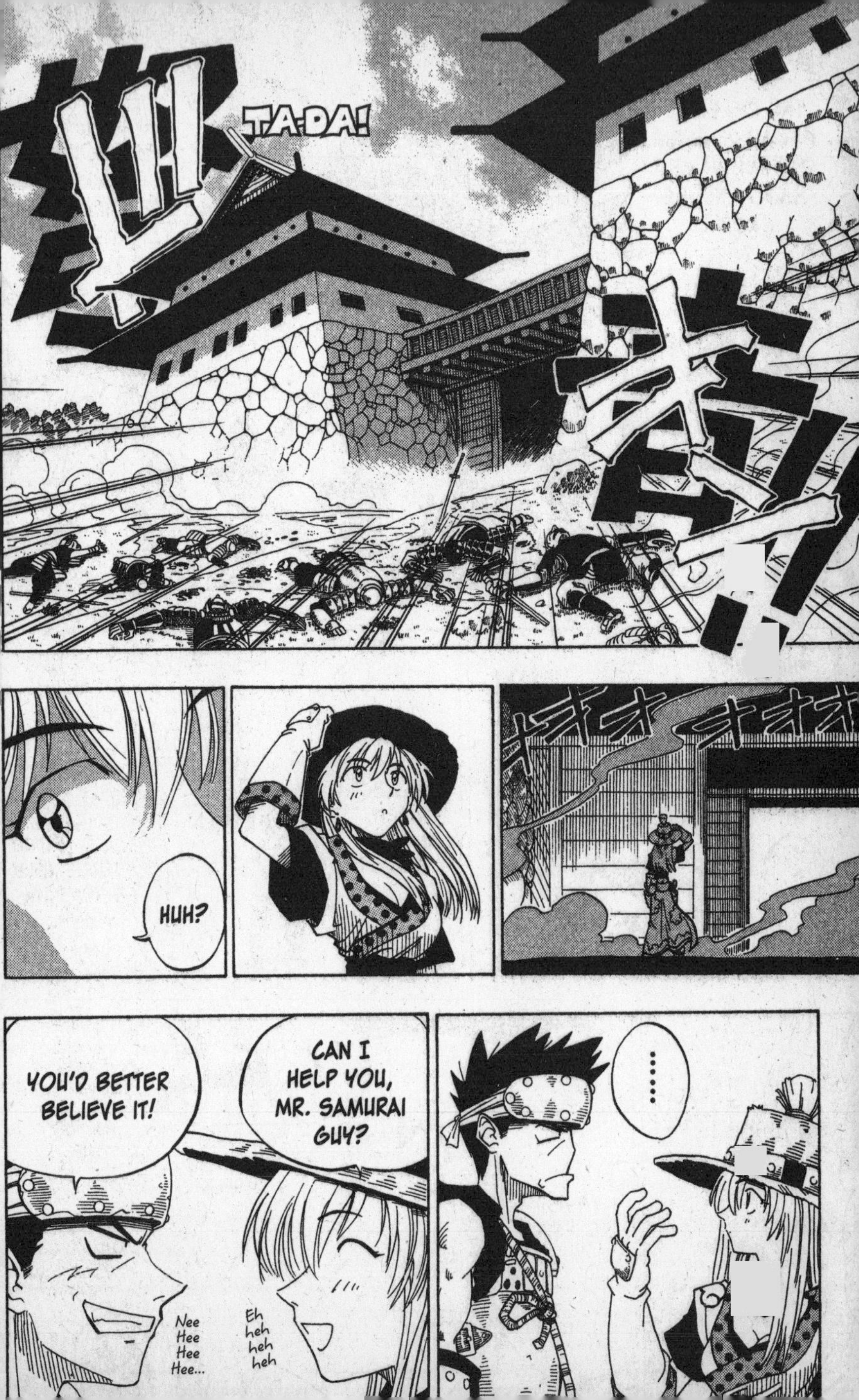
TA-DA!
HUH?
......
CAN I HELP YOU, MR. SAMURAI GUY?
YOU'D BETTER BELIEVE IT!
Eh heh heh heh
Nee Hee Hee Hee...

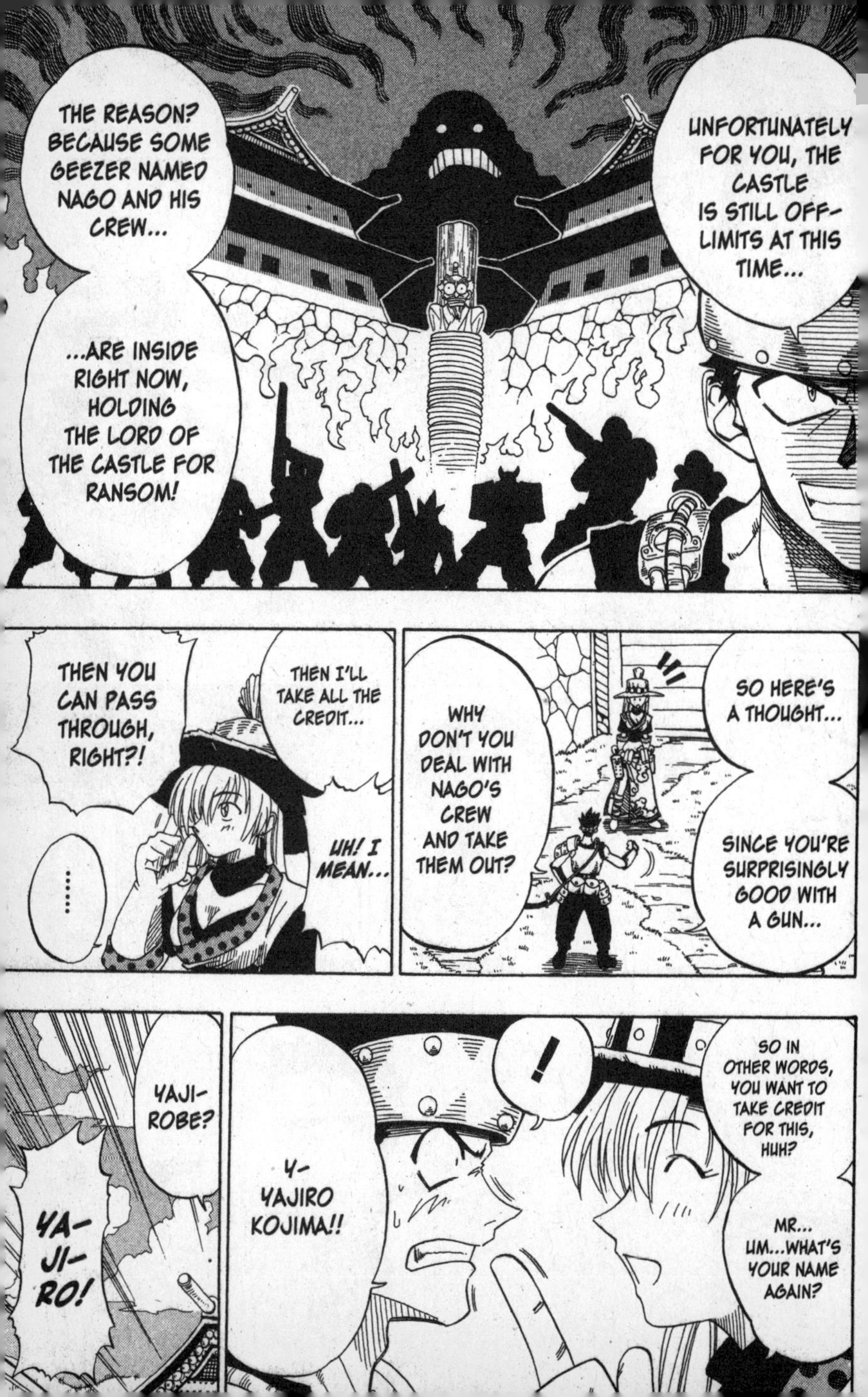
UNFORTUNATELY FOR YOU, THE CASTLE IS STILL OFF-LIMITS AT THIS TIME...
THE REASON? BECAUSE SOME GEEZER NAMED NAGO AND HIS CREW...
...ARE INSIDE RIGHT NOW, HOLDING THE LORD OF THE CASTLE FOR RANSOM!
SO HERE'S A THOUGHT...
SINCE YOU'RE SURPRISINGLY GOOD WITH A GUN...
WHY DON'T YOU DEAL WITH NAGO'S CREW AND TAKE THEM OUT?
THEN I'LL TAKE ALL THE CREDIT...
UH! I MEAN...
THEN YOU CAN PASS THROUGH, RIGHT?!
......
SO IN OTHER WORDS, YOU WANT TO TAKE CREDIT FOR THIS, HUH?
!
MR... UM...WHAT'S YOUR NAME AGAIN?
Y- YAJIRO KOJIMA!!
YAJI-ROBE?
YA-JI-RO!

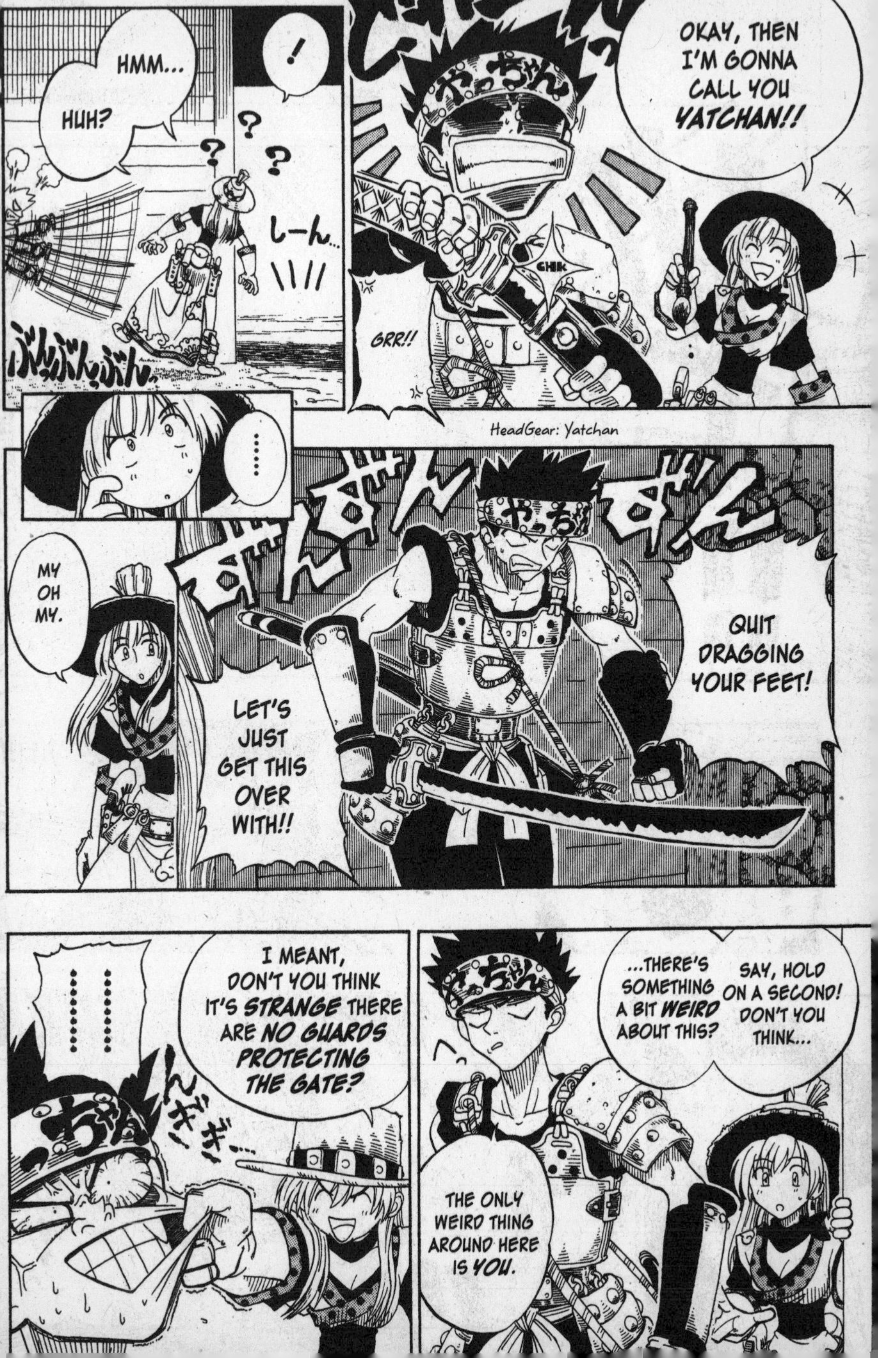
どかーん
OKAY, THEN I'M GONNA CALL YOU YATCHAN!!
CHK
GRR!!
HeadGear: Yatchan
!
HMM...
HUH?
? ? ?
しーん...
ぶんぶんぶん
......
ずんずんずん
QUIT DRAGGING YOUR FEET!
LET'S JUST GET THIS OVER WITH!!
MY OH MY.
SAY, HOLD ON A SECOND! DON'T YOU THINK...
...THERE'S SOMETHING A BIT WEIRD ABOUT THIS?
THE ONLY WEIRD THING AROUND HERE IS YOU.
I MEANT, DON'T YOU THINK IT'S STRANGE THERE ARE NO GUARDS PROTECTING THE GATE?
んぎぎ...
......

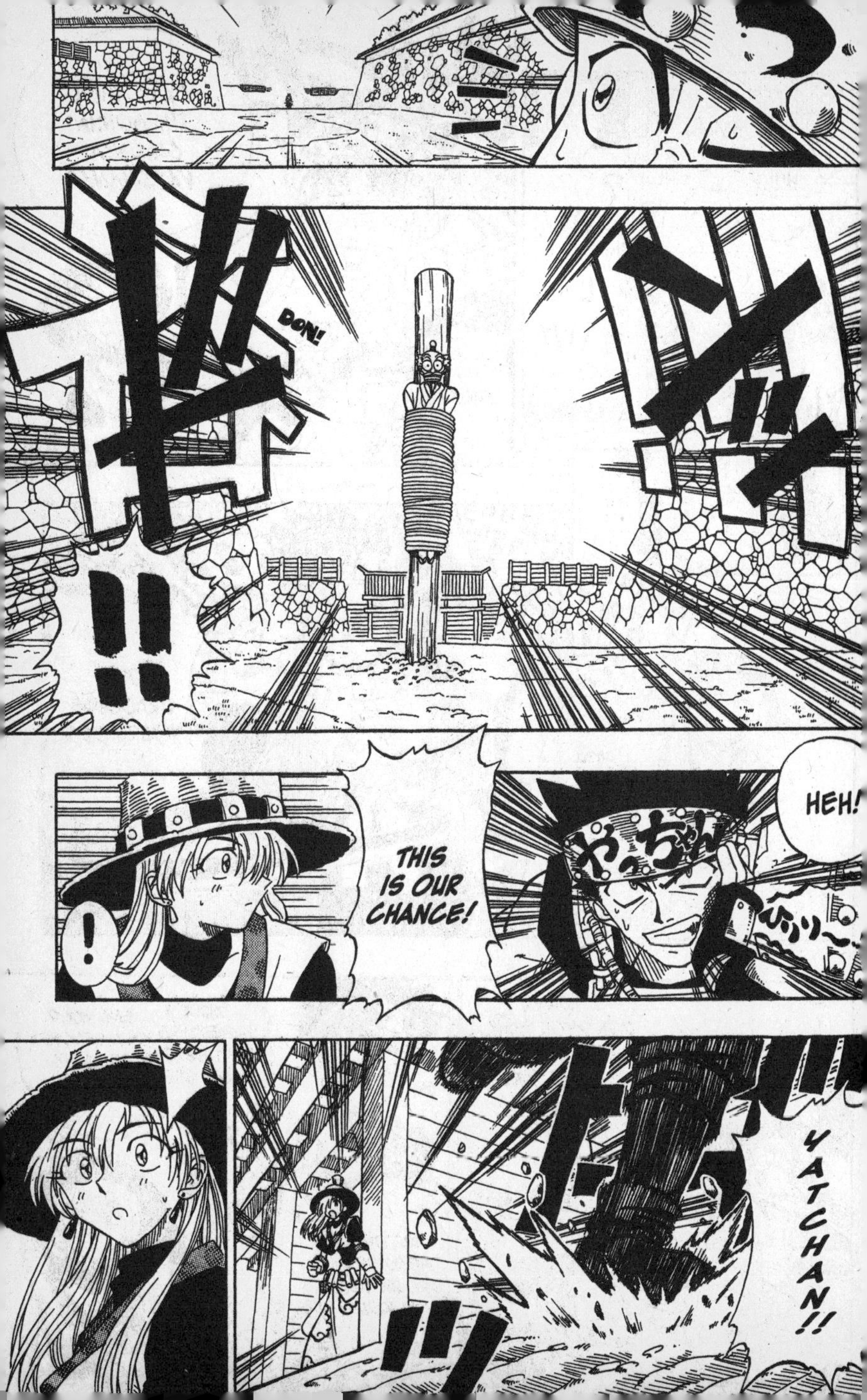
DON!
HEH!
やっちゃん
THIS IS OUR CHANCE!
!
YATCHAN!!

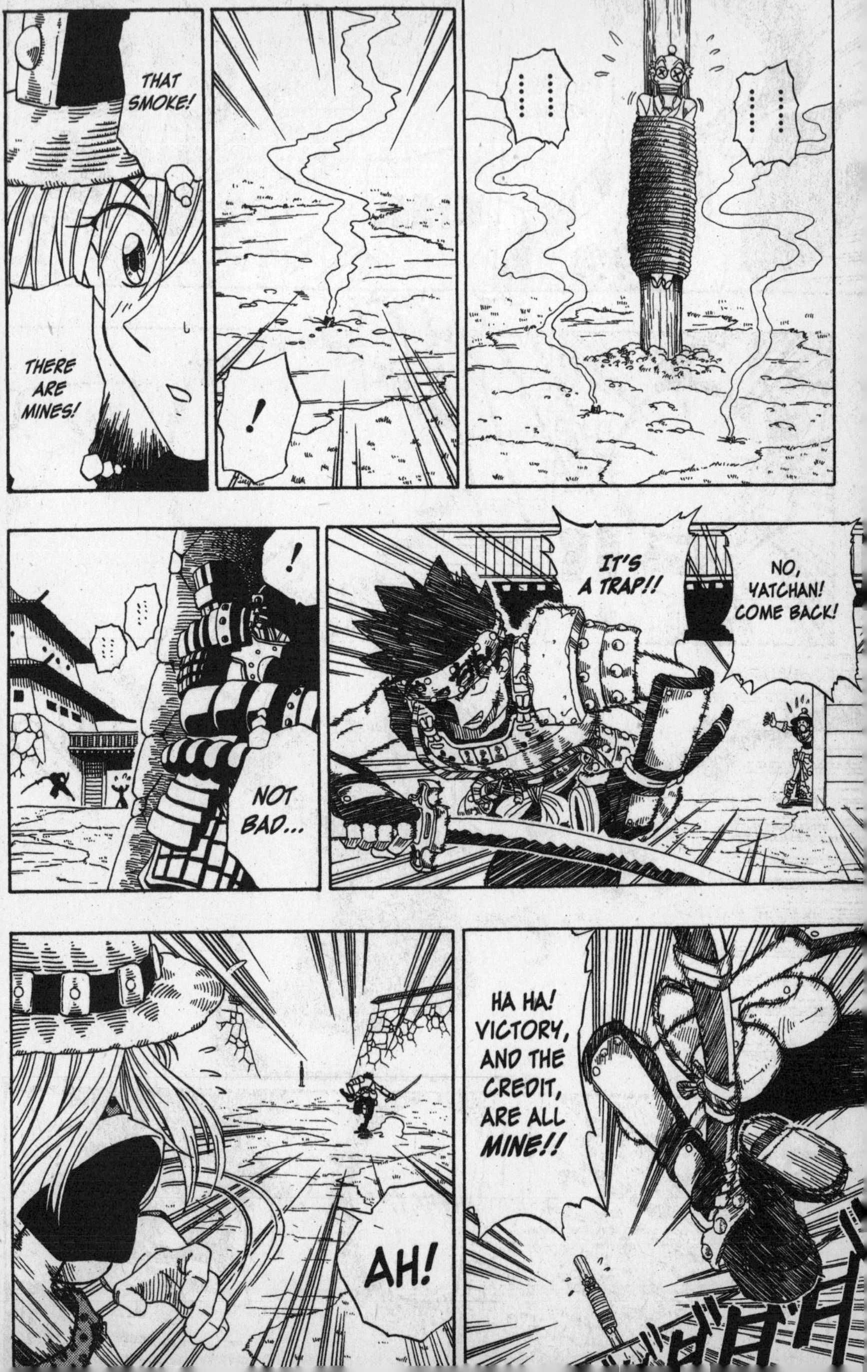
……
……
!
THAT SMOKE!
THERE ARE MINES!
NO, YATCHAN! COME BACK!
IT'S A TRAP!!
!
……
NOT BAD...
HA HA! VICTORY, AND THE CREDIT, ARE ALL MINE!!
AH!

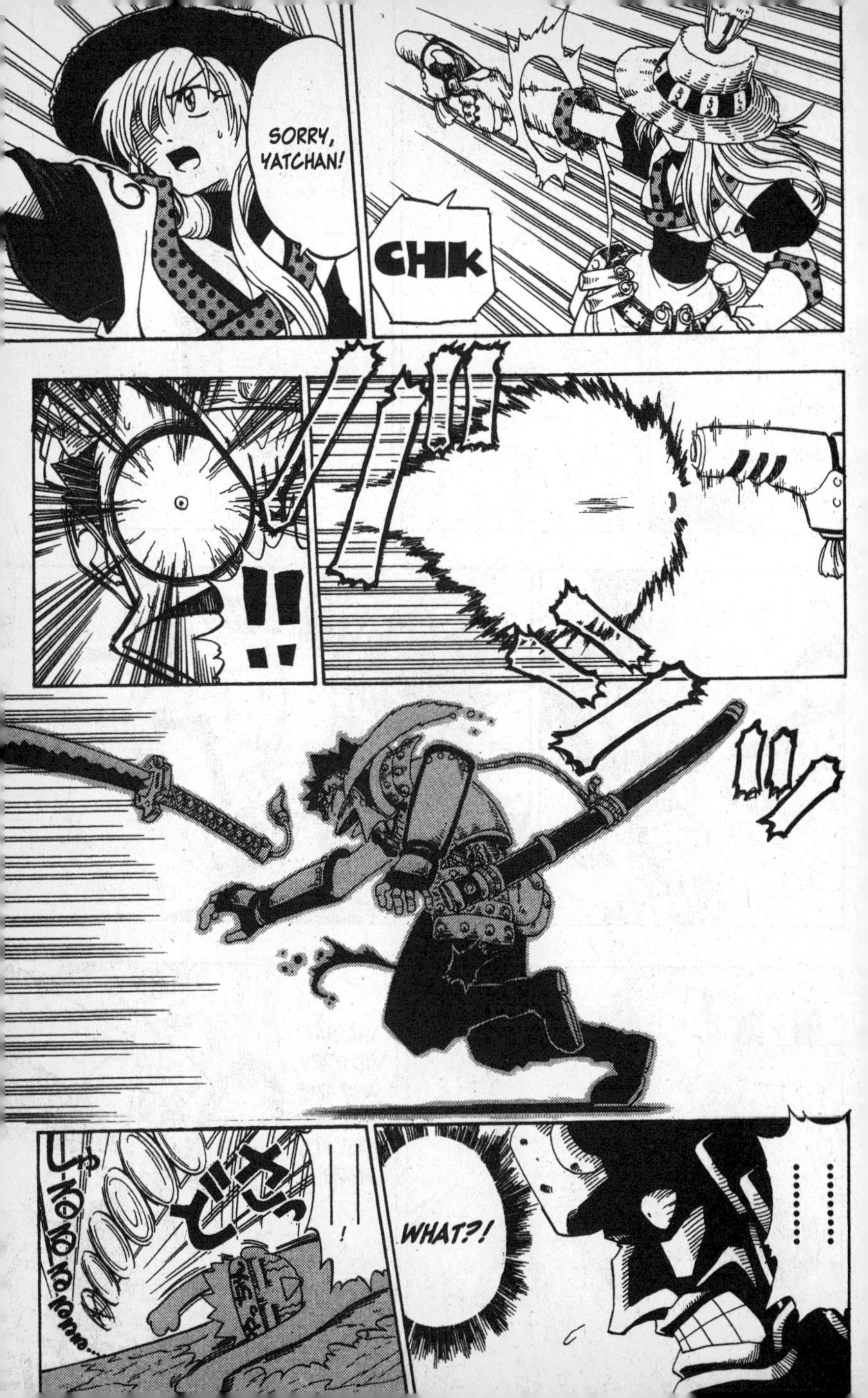
CHK
SORRY, YATCHAN!
!!
......
WHAT?!
!
どさっ

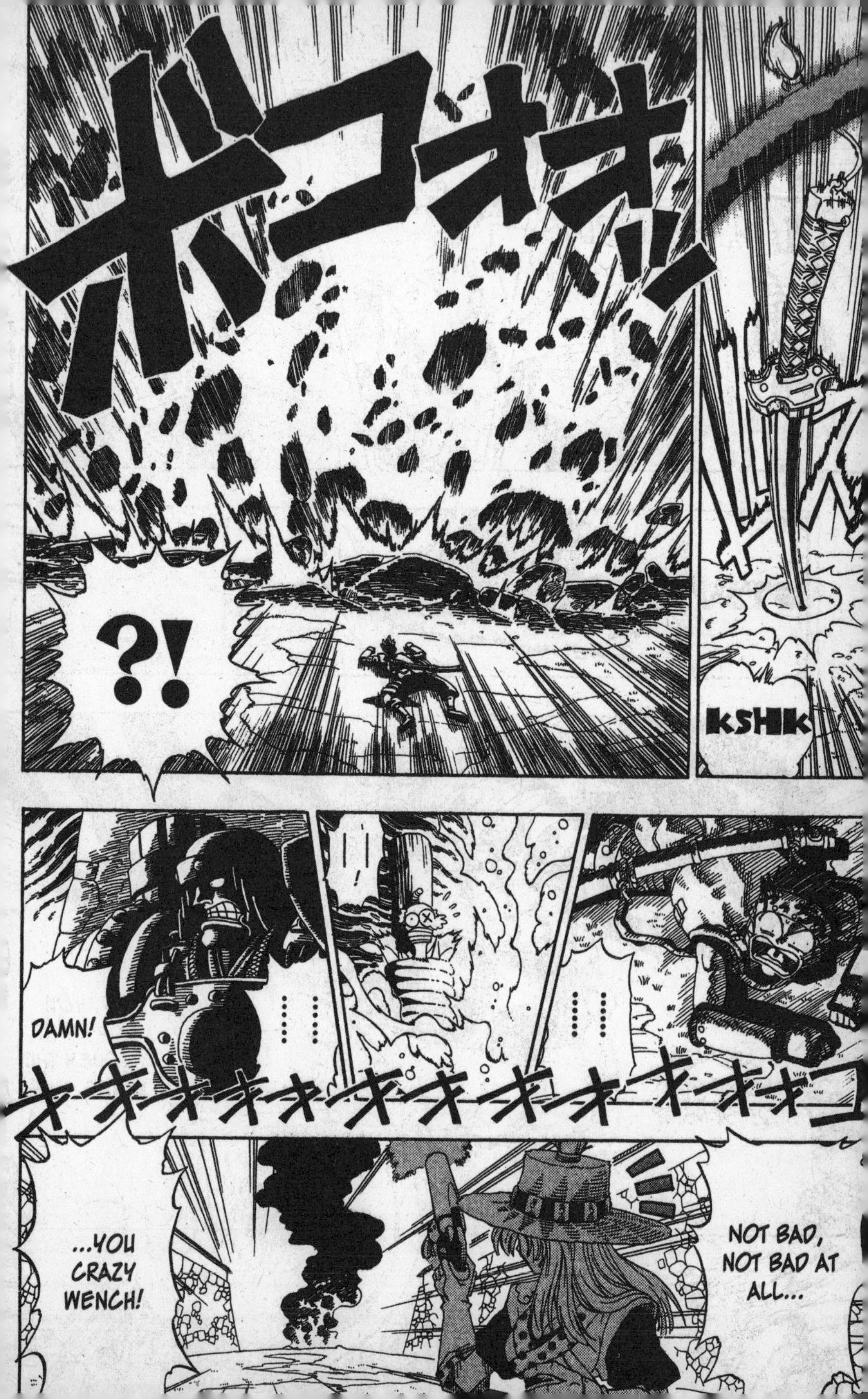
KSHIK
?!
DAMN!
NOT BAD, NOT BAD AT ALL...
...YOU CRAZY WENCH!

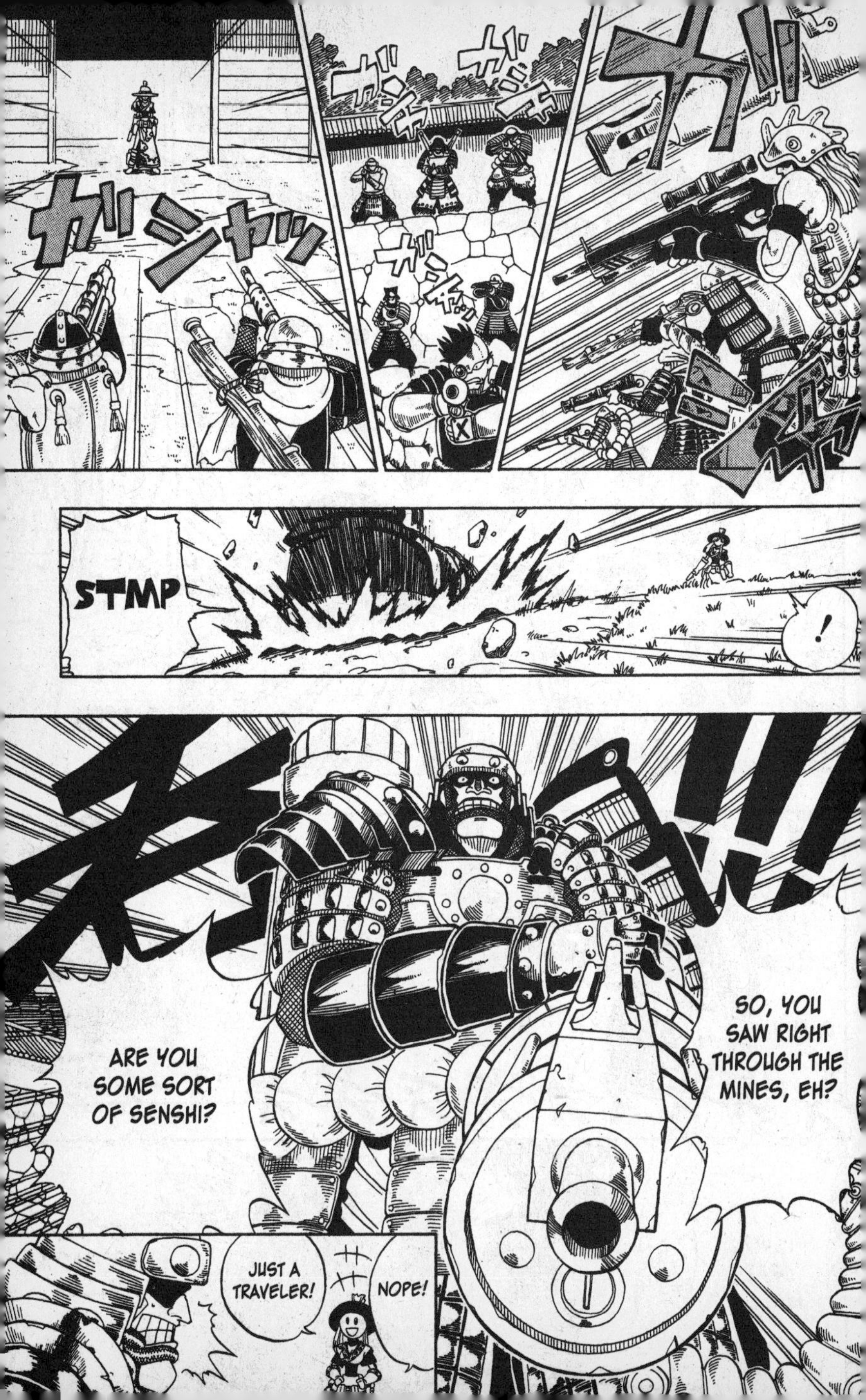
!
STMP
SO, YOU SAW RIGHT THROUGH THE MINES, EH?
ARE YOU SOME SORT OF SENSHI?
NOPE!
JUST A TRAVELER!

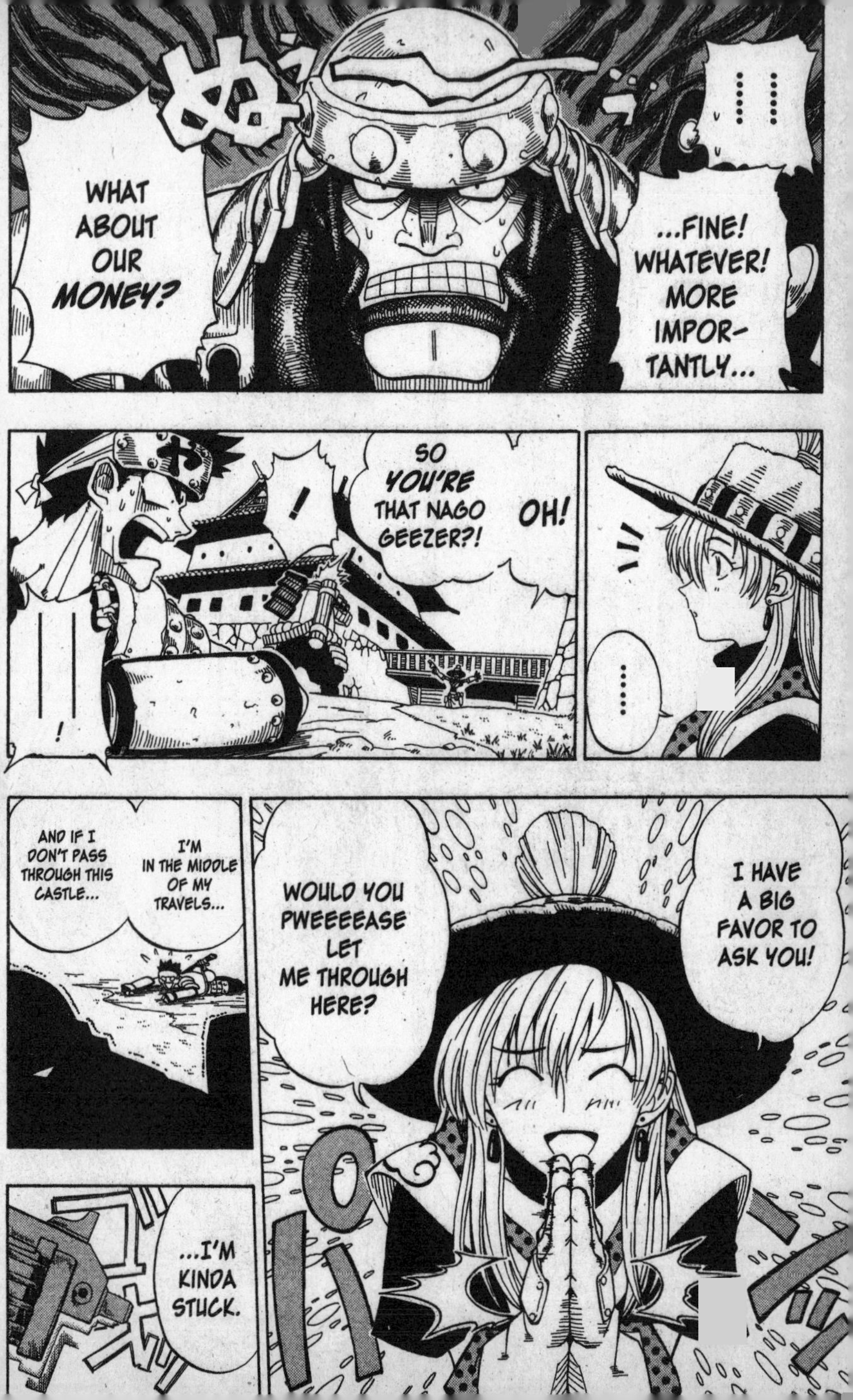
......
...FINE! WHATEVER! MORE IMPORTANTLY...
ぬ
WHAT ABOUT OUR *MONEY?*
......
OH!
SO *YOU'RE* THAT NAGO GEEZER?!
!
!
I HAVE A BIG FAVOR TO ASK YOU!
WOULD YOU PWEEEEASE LET ME THROUGH HERE?
I'M IN THE MIDDLE OF MY TRAVELS...
AND IF I DON'T PASS THROUGH THIS CASTLE...
...I'M KINDA STUCK.

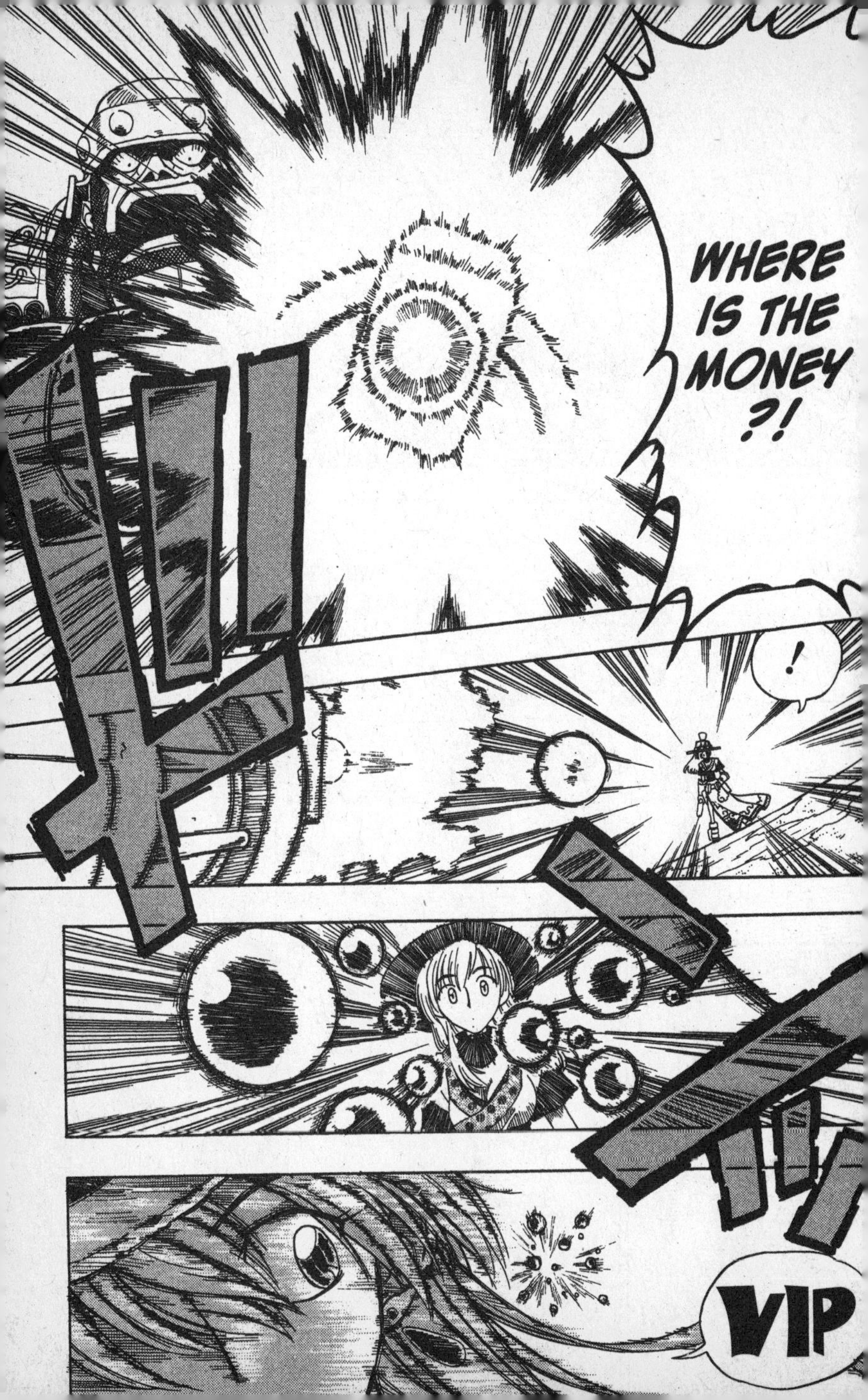
WHERE IS THE MONEY ?!
!
VIP

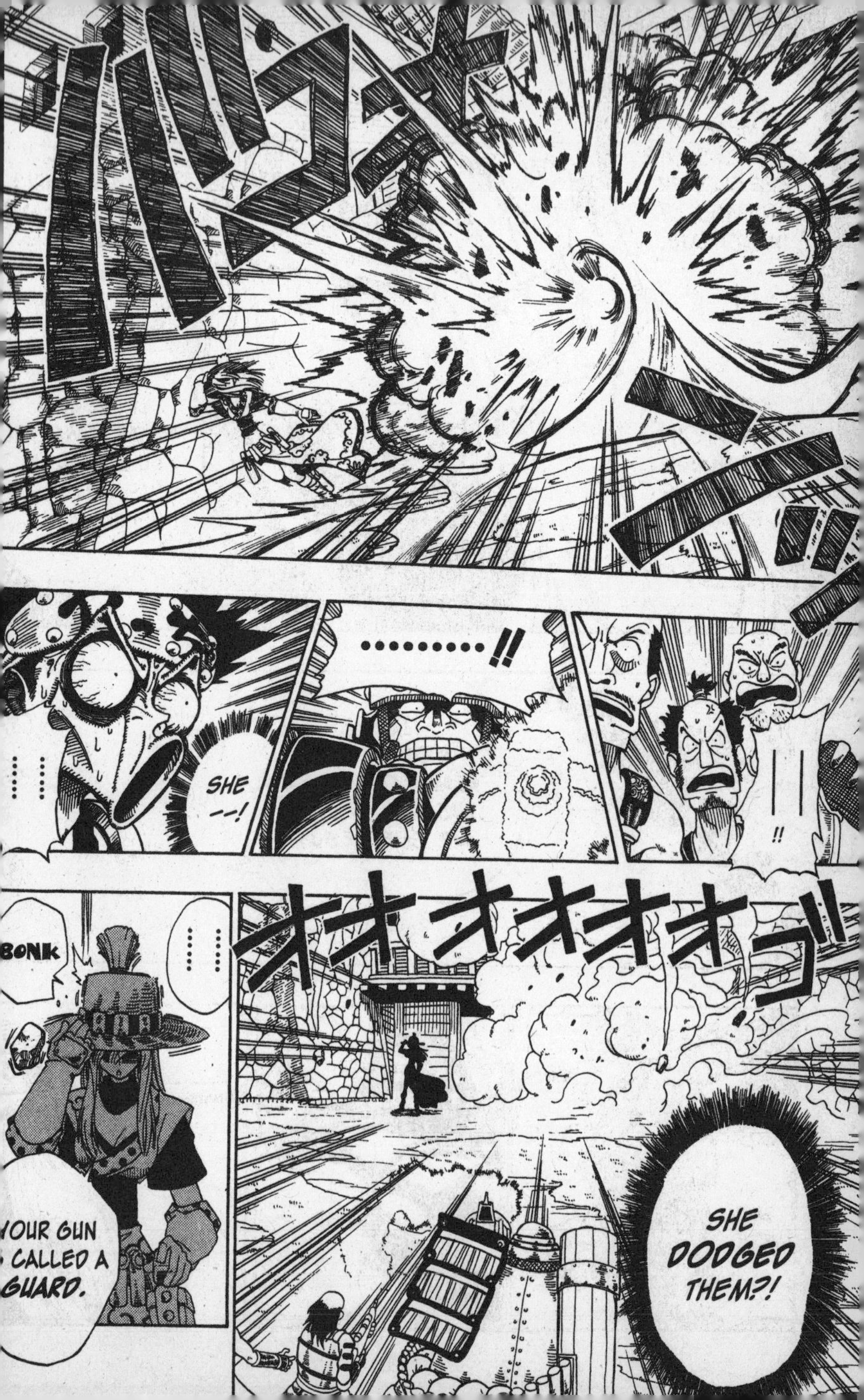
!!
..........!!
SHE --!
......
SHE DODGED THEM?!
......
BONK
YOUR GUN CALLED A GUARD.

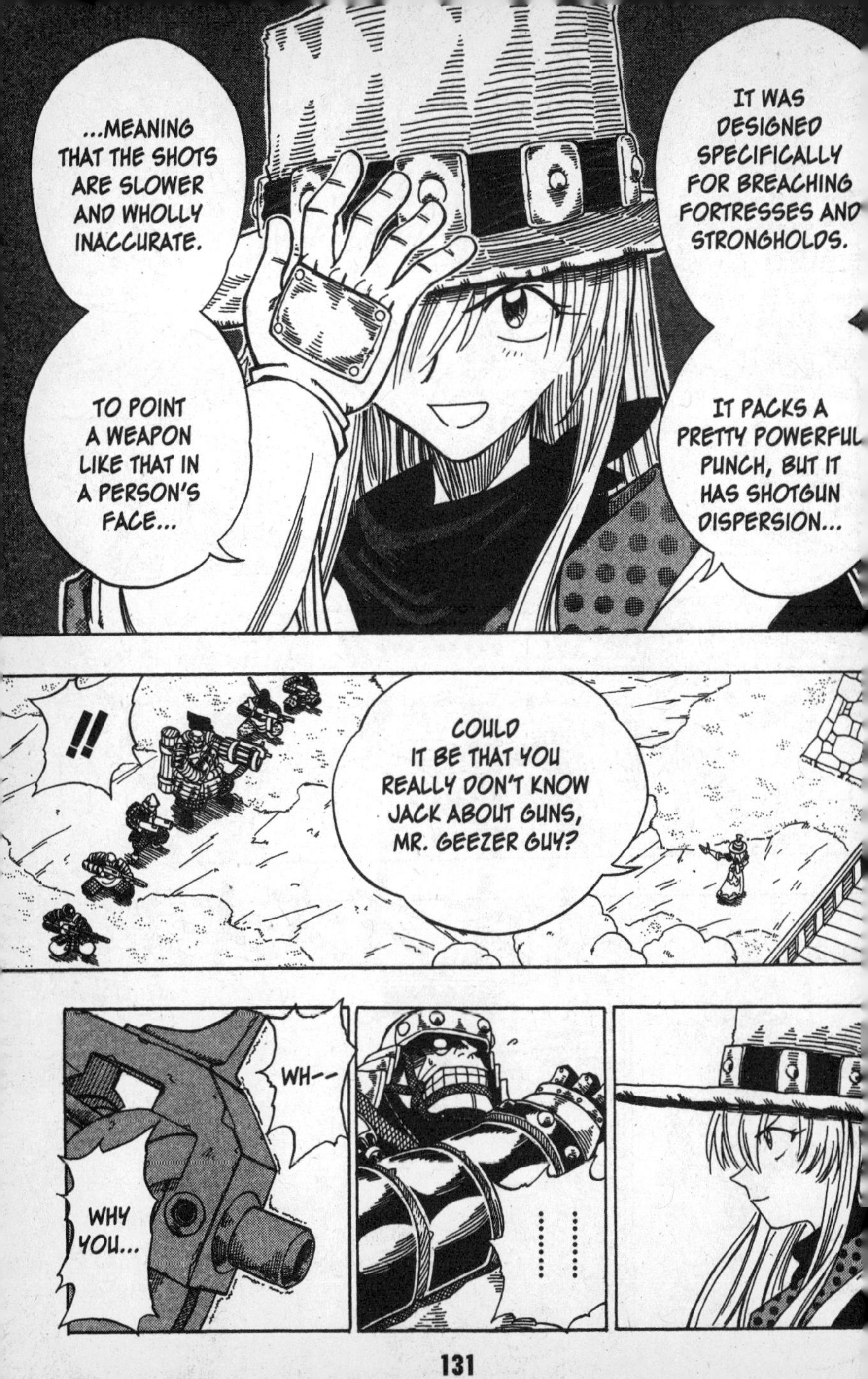
IT WAS DESIGNED SPECIFICALLY FOR BREACHING FORTRESSES AND STRONGHOLDS.
IT PACKS A PRETTY POWERFUL PUNCH, BUT IT HAS SHOTGUN DISPERSION...
...MEANING THAT THE SHOTS ARE SLOWER AND WHOLLY INACCURATE.
TO POINT A WEAPON LIKE THAT IN A PERSON'S FACE...
COULD IT BE THAT YOU REALLY DON'T KNOW JACK ABOUT GUNS, MR. GEEZER GUY?
!!
......
WH--
WHY YOU...

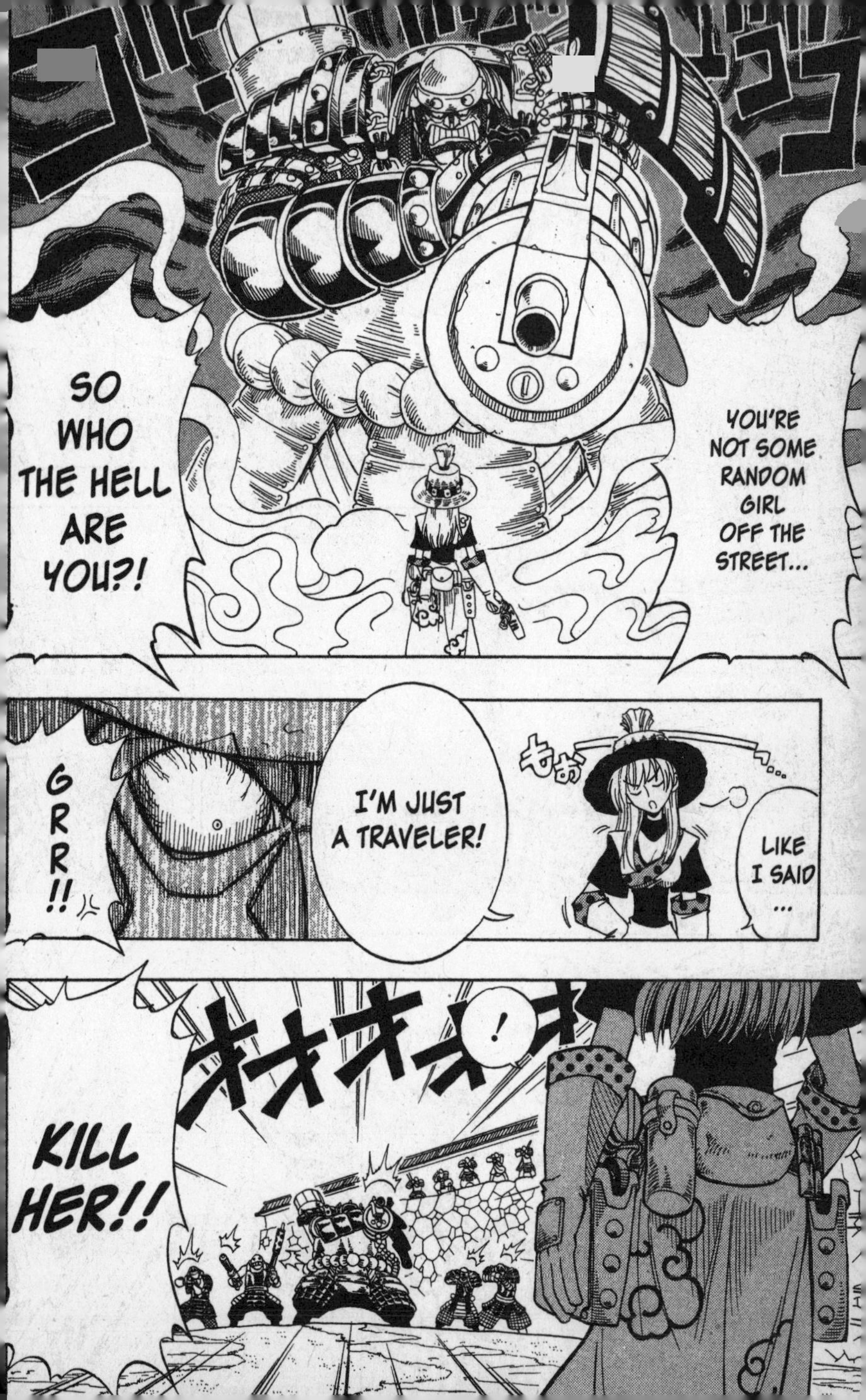
YOU'RE NOT SOME RANDOM GIRL OFF THE STREET...
SO WHO THE HELL ARE YOU?!
もぉ
LIKE I SAID ...
I'M JUST A TRAVELER!
GRRR!!
!
KILL HER!!

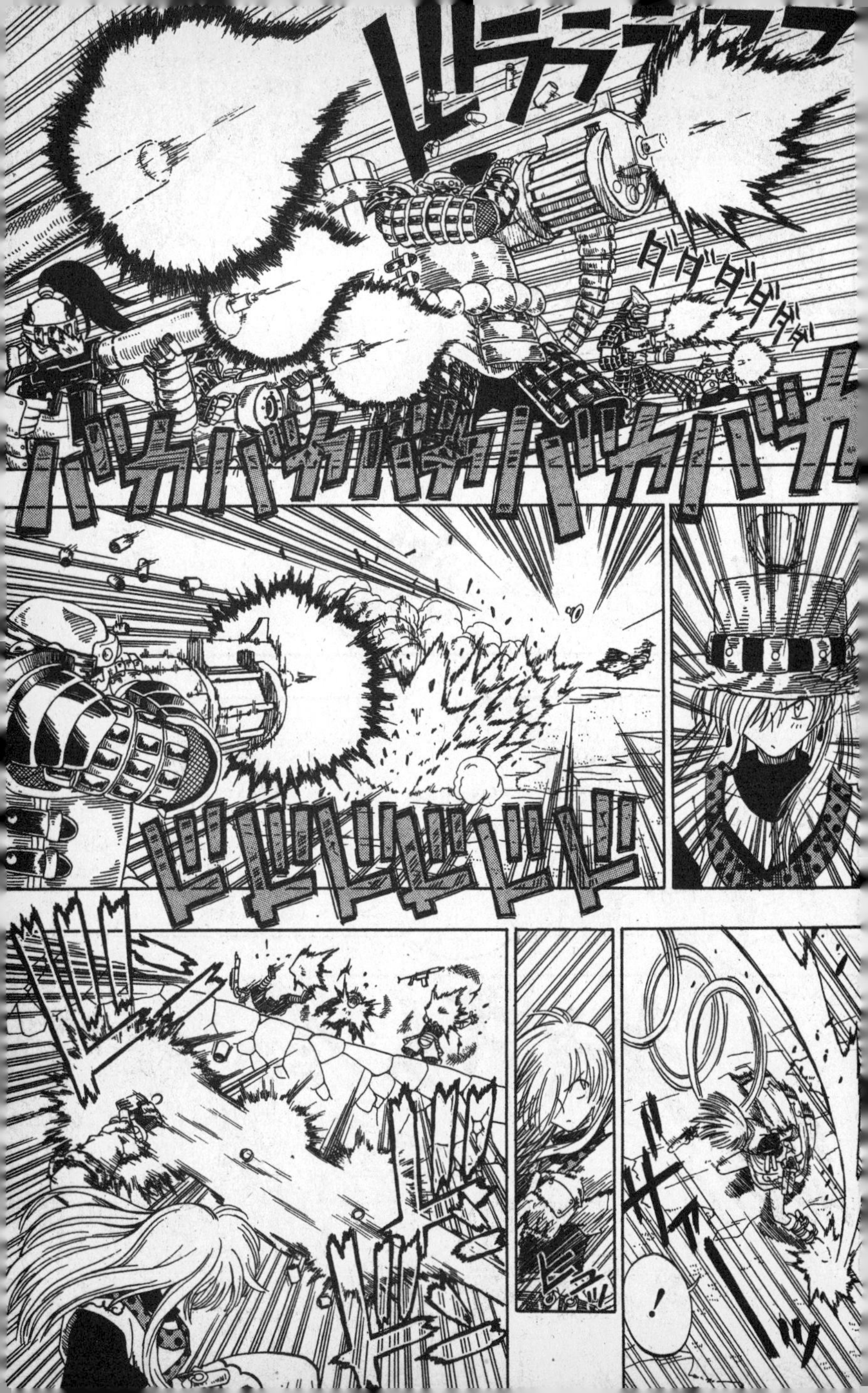
ダダダダダダ
ドドドドドドド
!

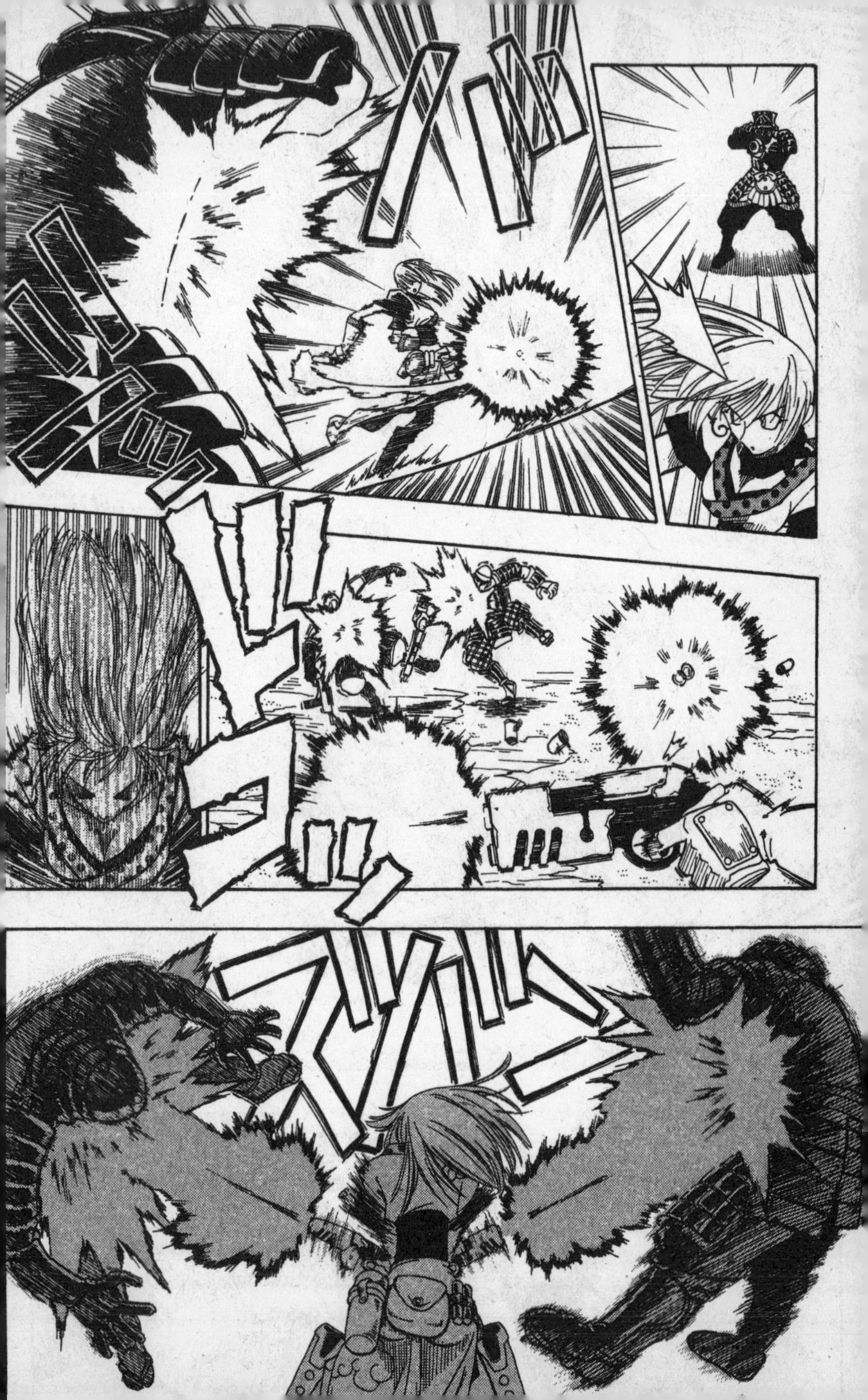

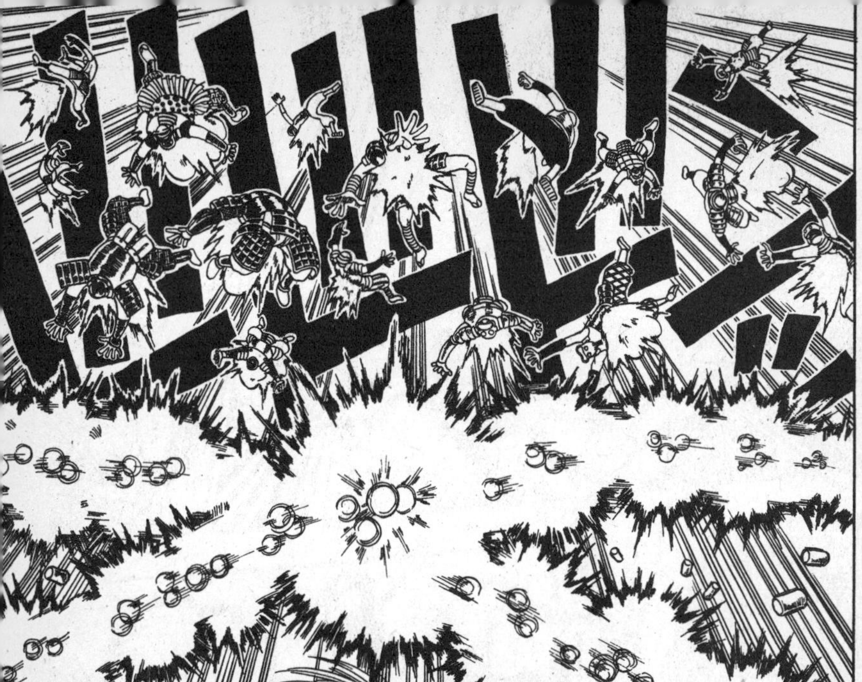
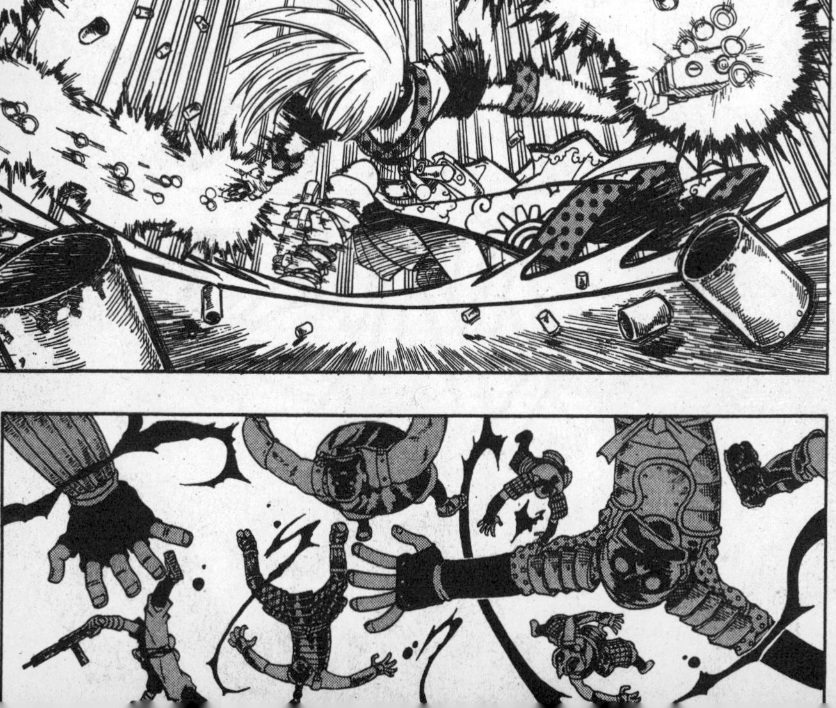

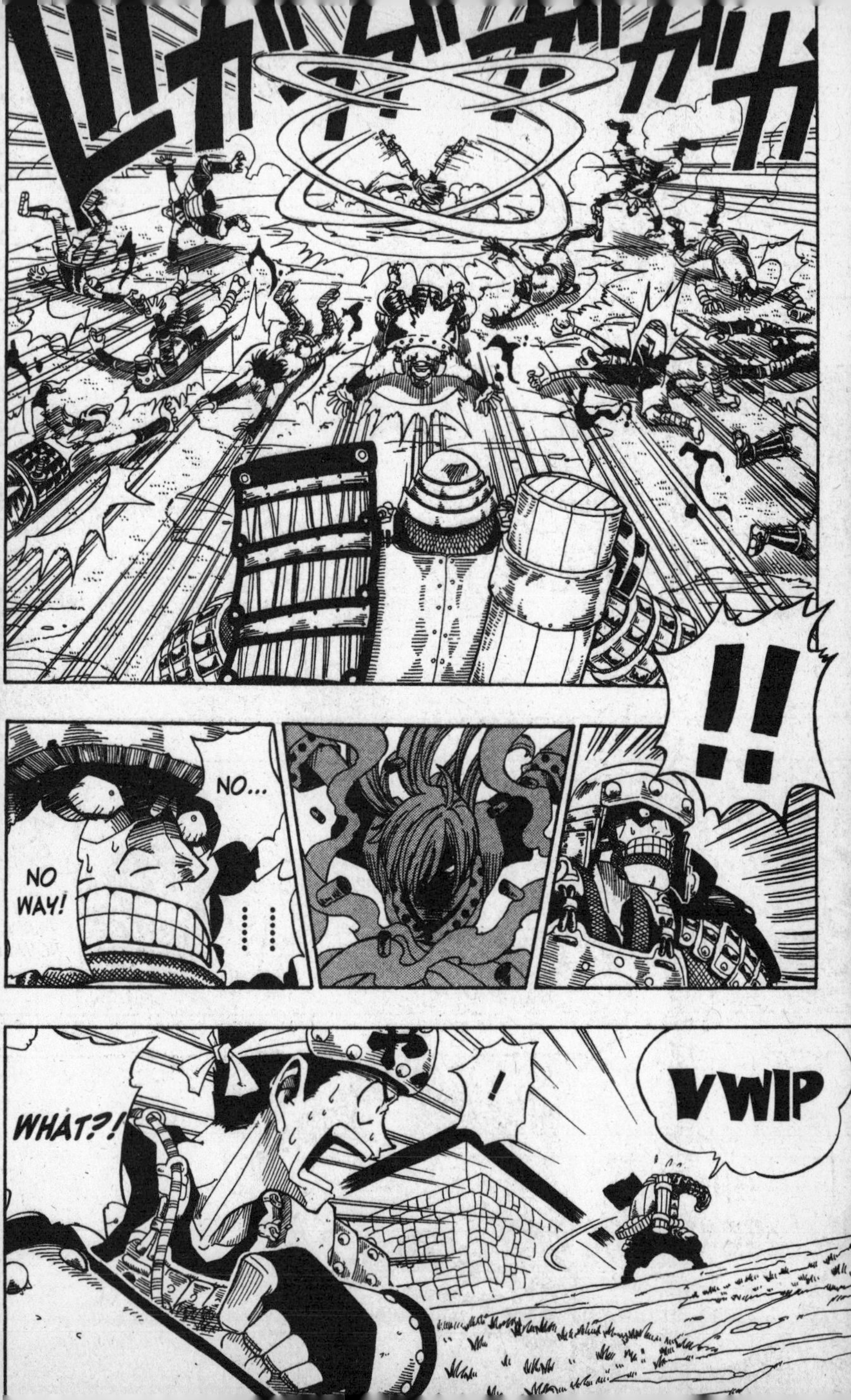
!!
......
NO...
NO WAY!
VWIP
!
WHAT?!

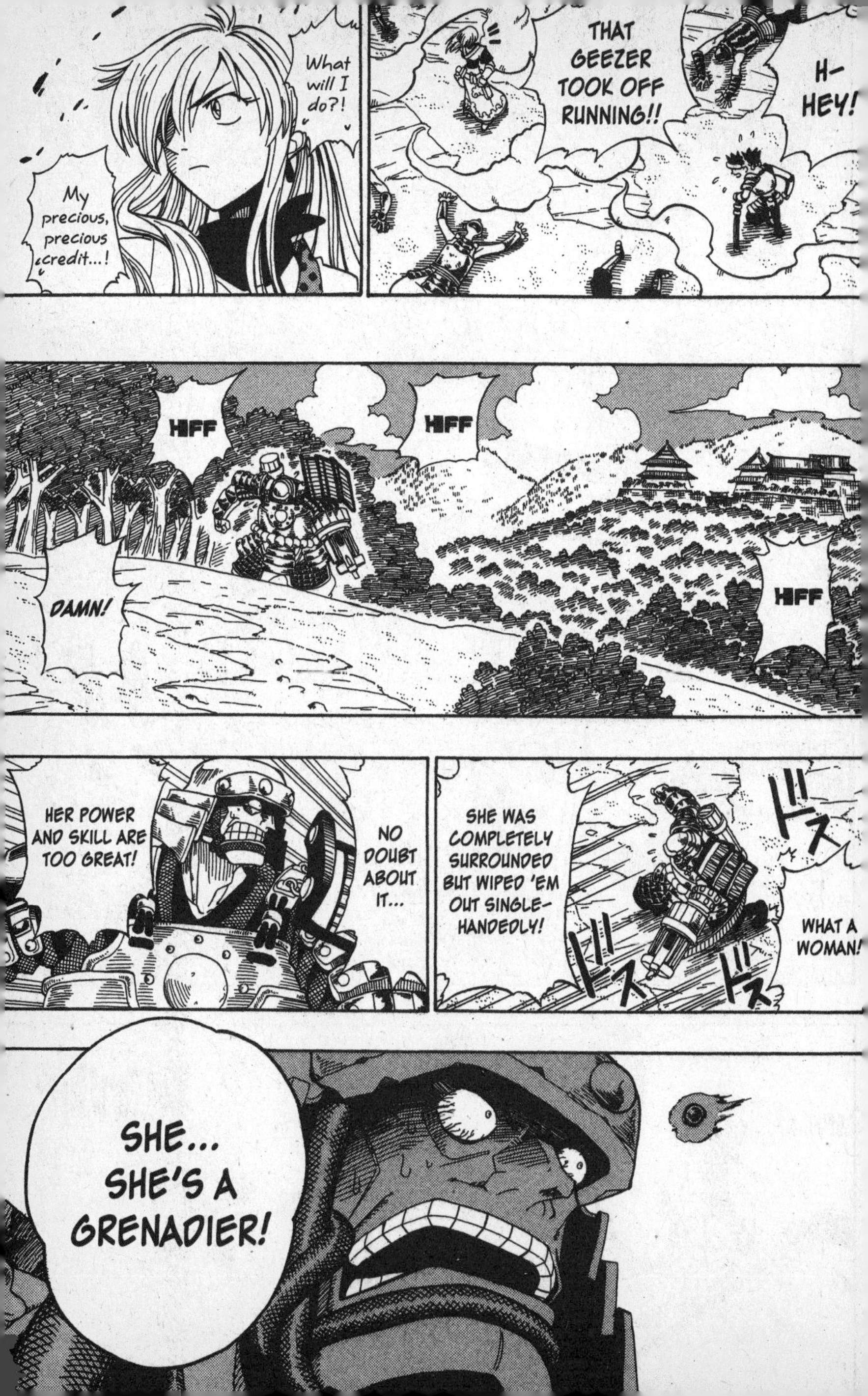
H-HEY!
THAT GEEZER TOOK OFF RUNNING!!
What will I do?!
My precious, precious credit...!
HIFF
HIFF
HIFF
DAMN!
ドス
WHAT A WOMAN!
SHE WAS COMPLETELY SURROUNDED BUT WIPED 'EM OUT SINGLE-HANDEDLY!
ドス
ドス
NO DOUBT ABOUT IT...
HER POWER AND SKILL ARE TOO GREAT!
SHE... SHE'S A GRENADIER!

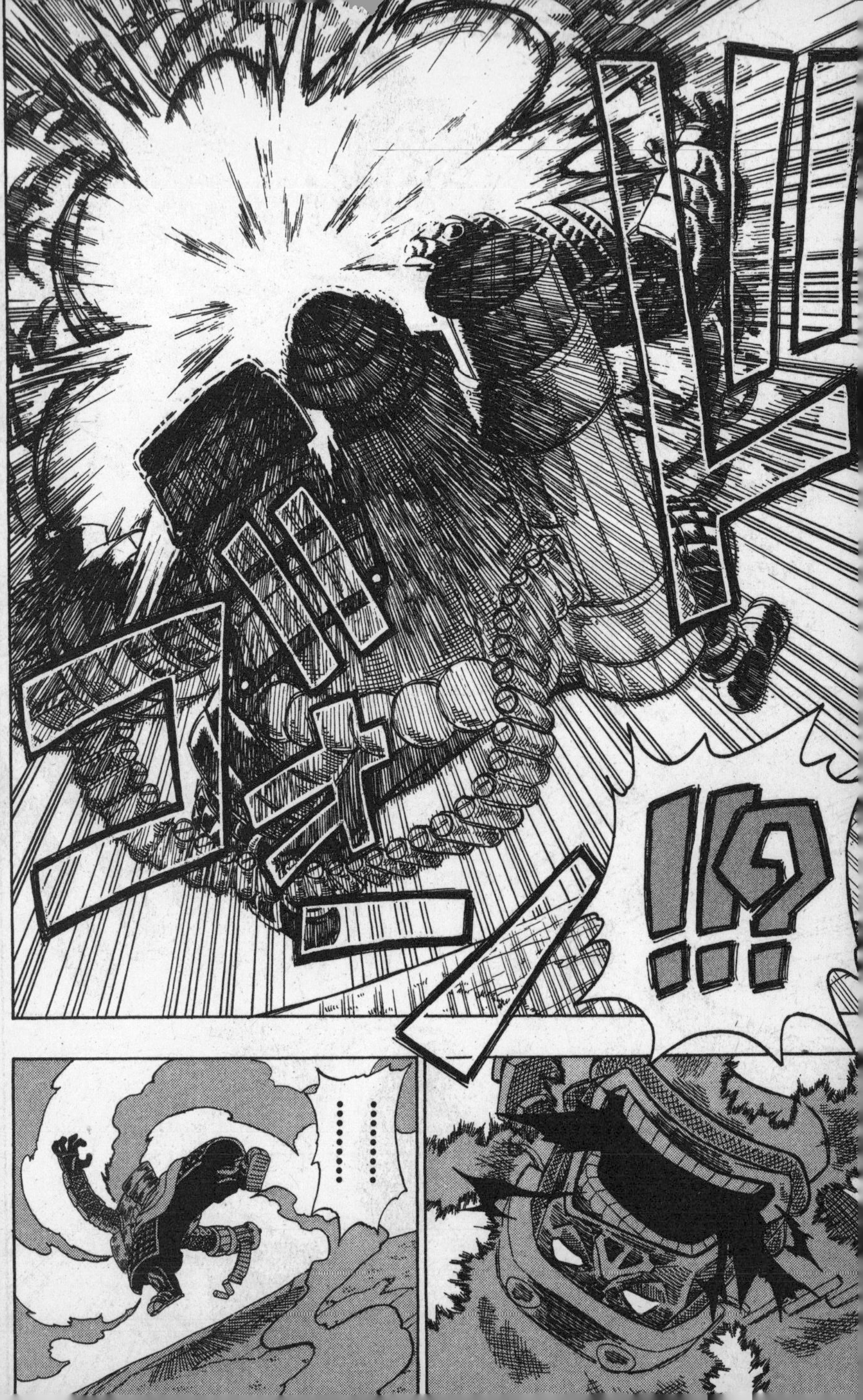
!!?
……

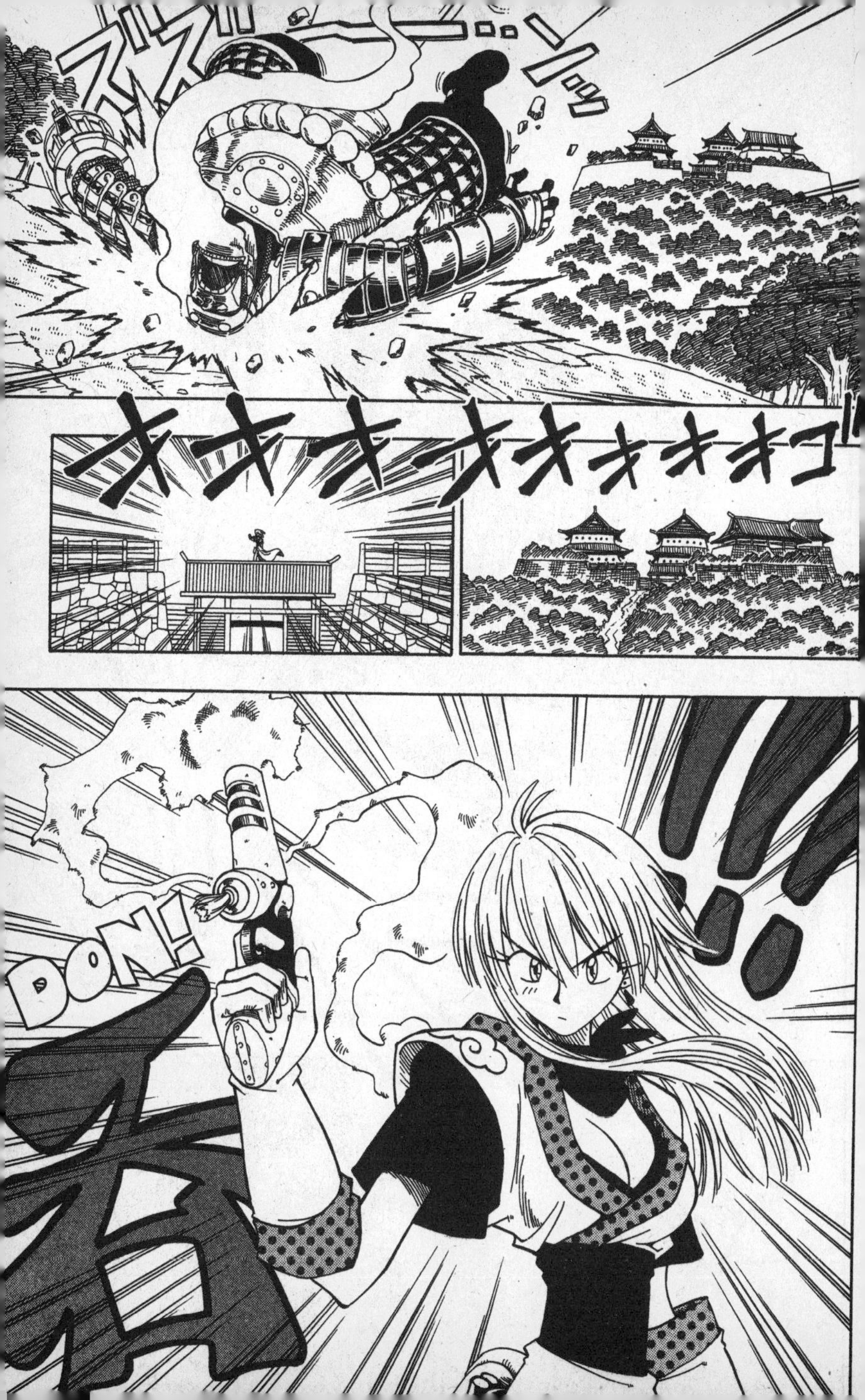
DON!

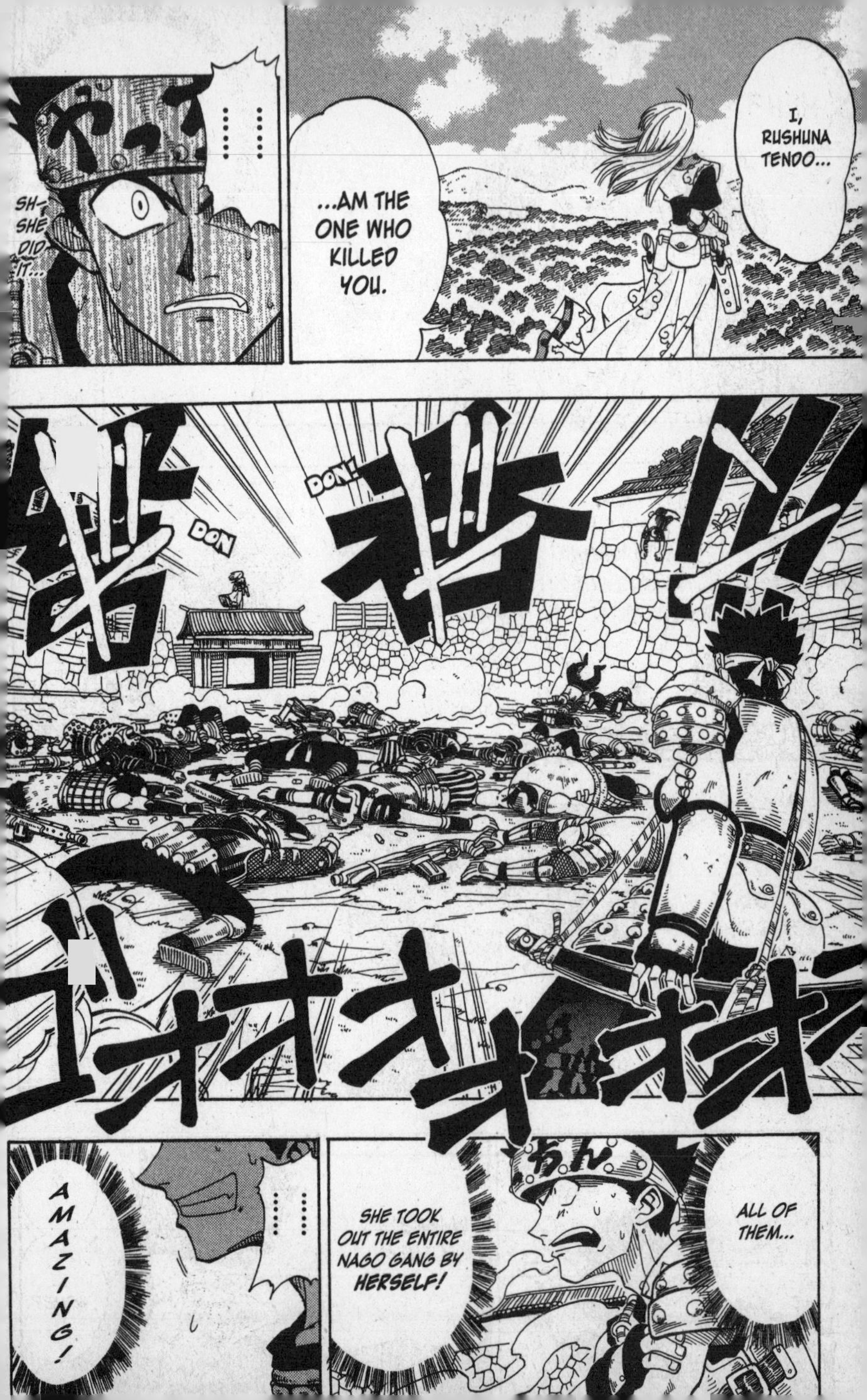
I, RUSHUNA TENDO...
...AM THE ONE WHO KILLED YOU.
......
SH-SHE DID IT...
DON!
DON
ALL OF THEM...
SHE TOOK OUT THE ENTIRE NAGO GANG BY HERSELF!
......
AMAZING!

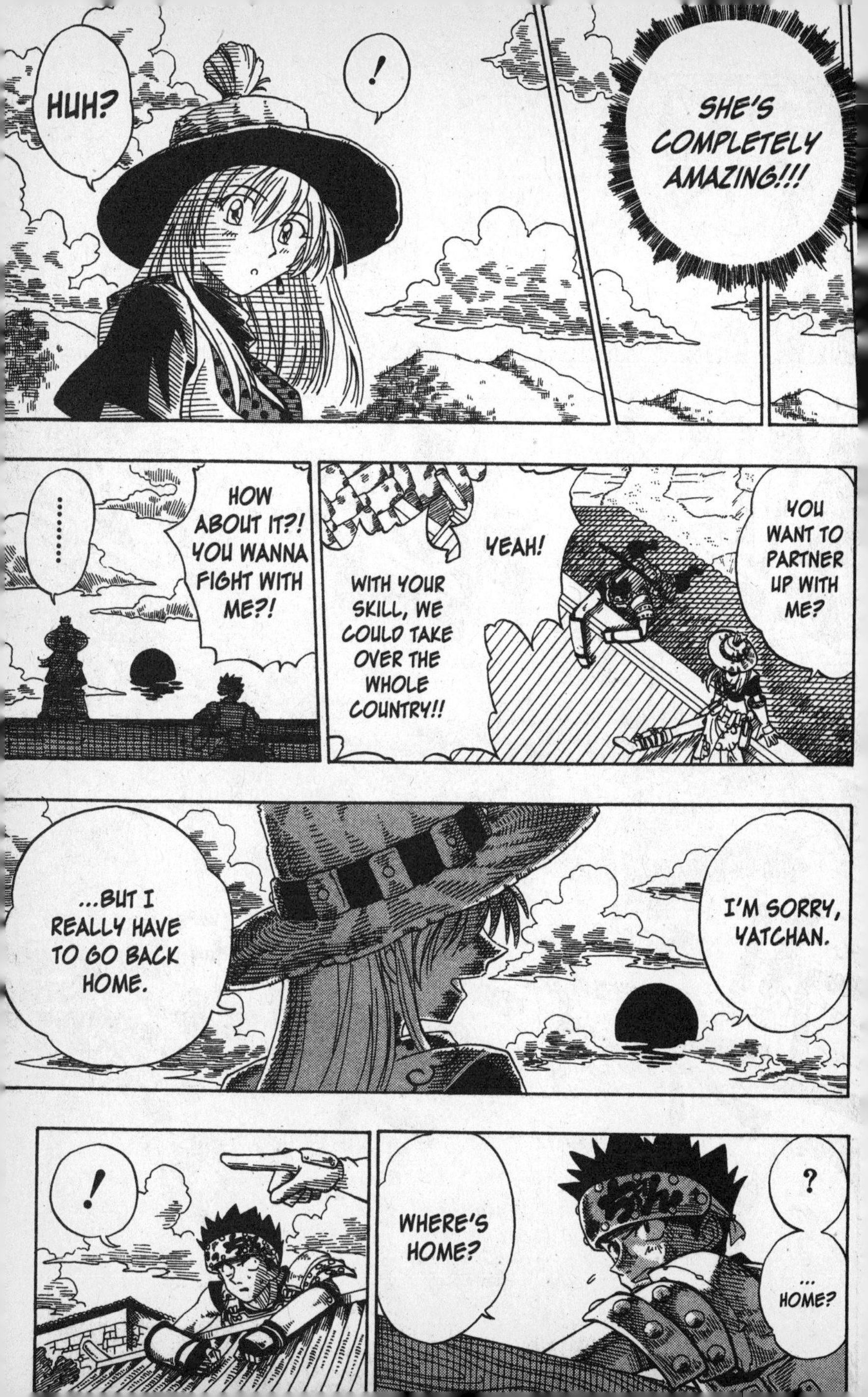
SHE'S COMPLETELY AMAZING!!!
!
HUH?
YOU WANT TO PARTNER UP WITH ME?
YEAH!
WITH YOUR SKILL, WE COULD TAKE OVER THE WHOLE COUNTRY!!
HOW ABOUT IT?! YOU WANNA FIGHT WITH ME?!
......
I'M SORRY, YATCHAN.
...BUT I REALLY HAVE TO GO BACK HOME.
?
... HOME?
WHERE'S HOME?
!

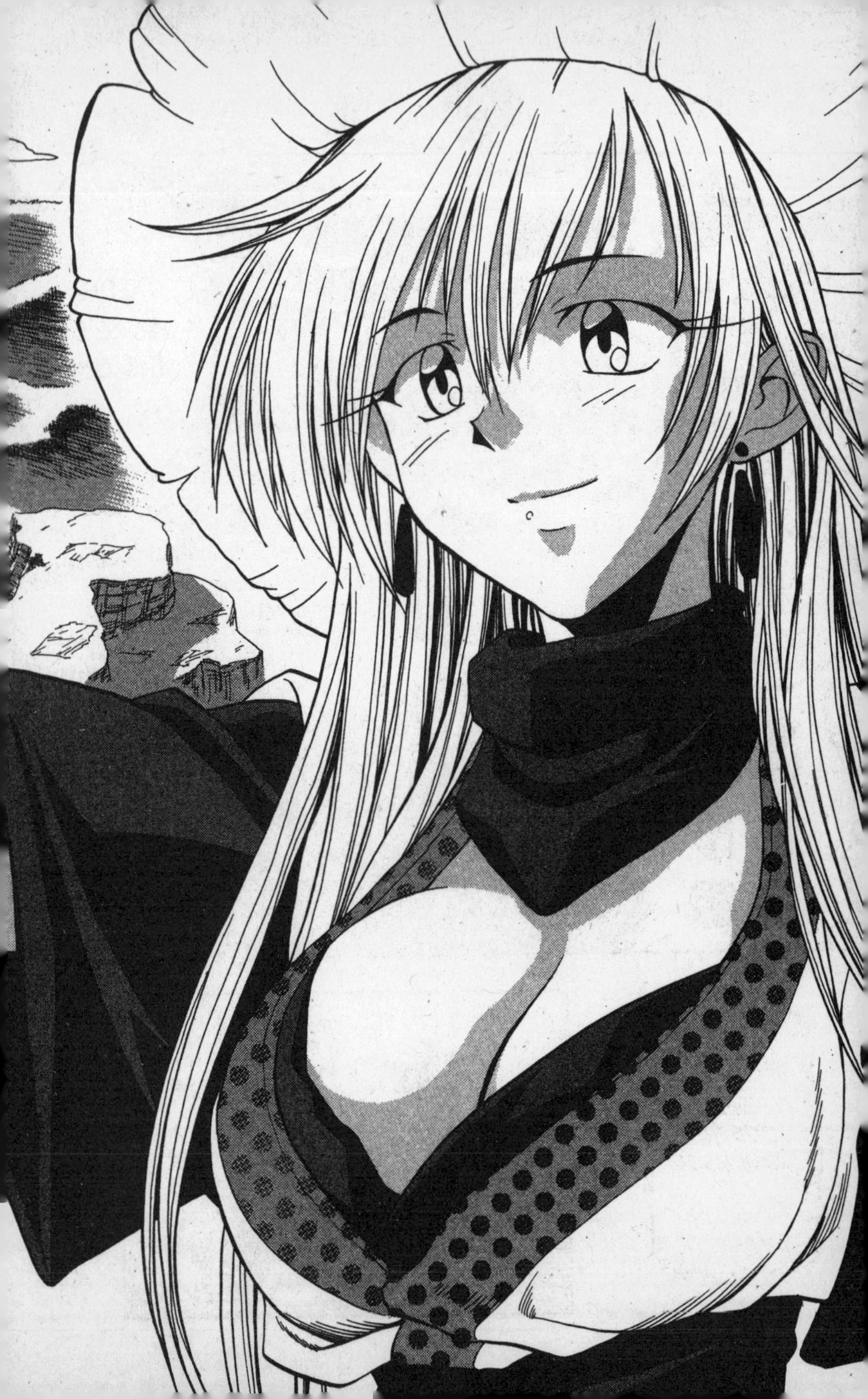

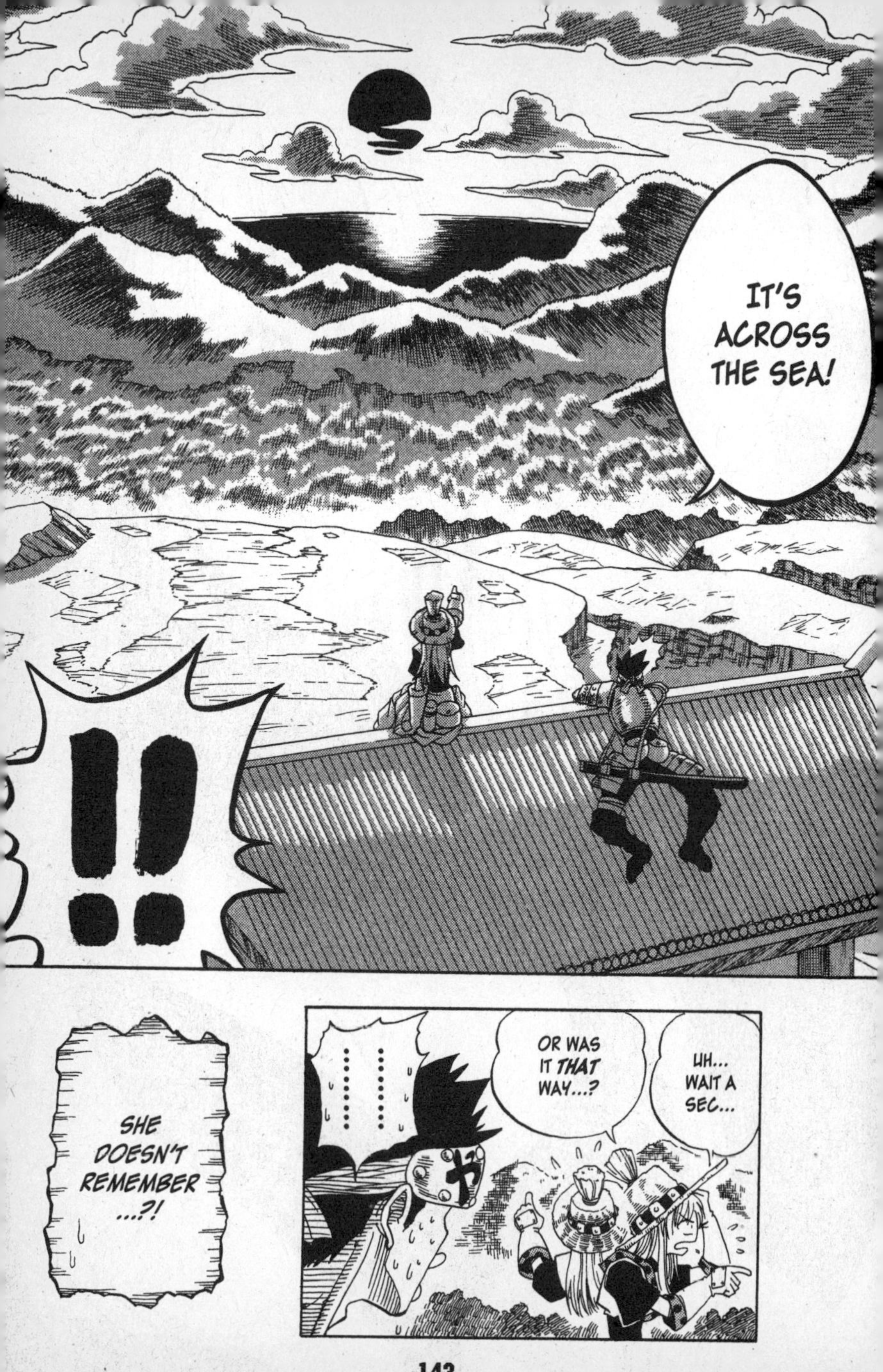
IT'S ACROSS THE SEA!
!!
UH... WAIT A SEC...
OR WAS IT *THAT* WAY...?
......
SHE DOESN'T REMEMBER ...?!

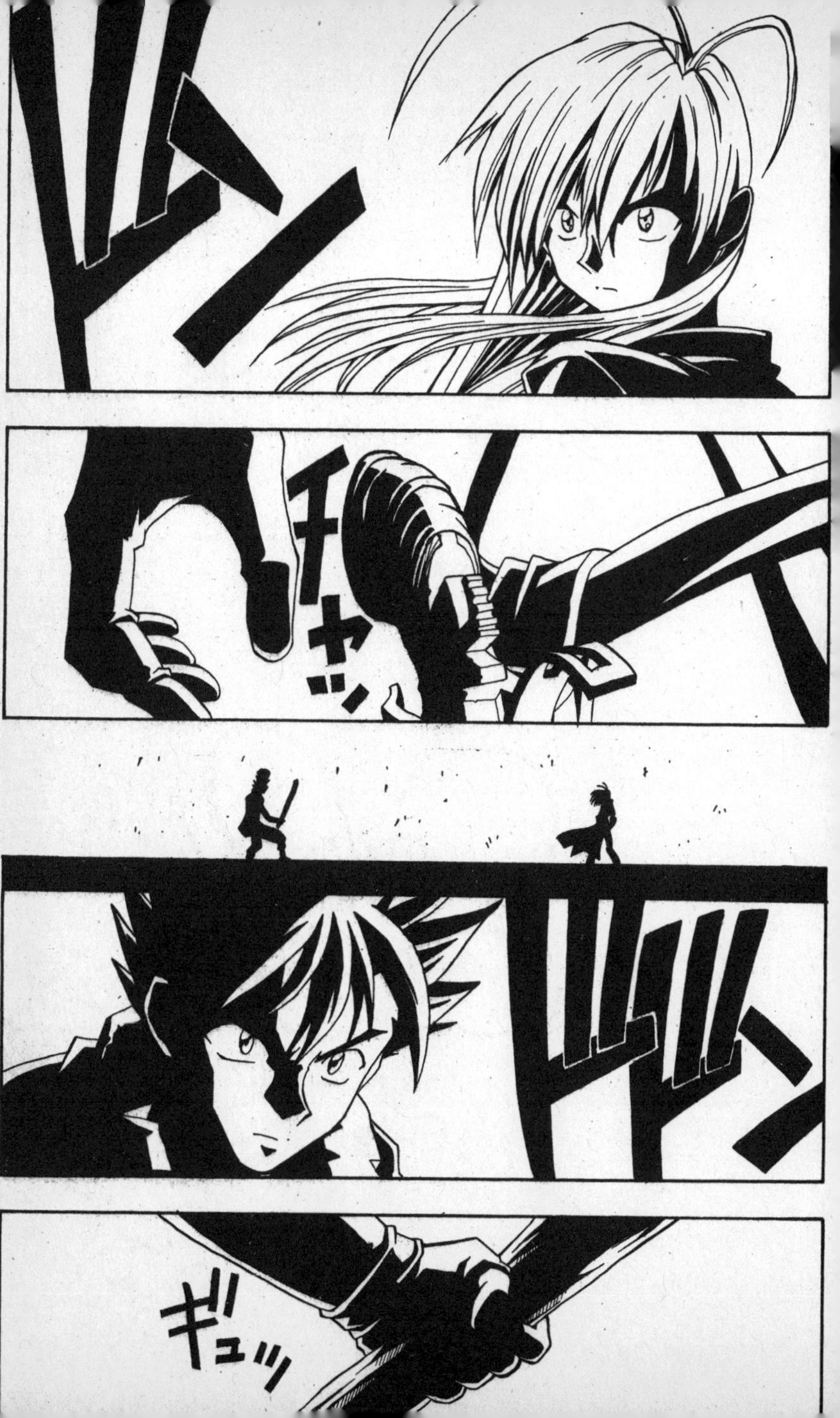
ドン
チャ゛ン
ドン
ギュッ

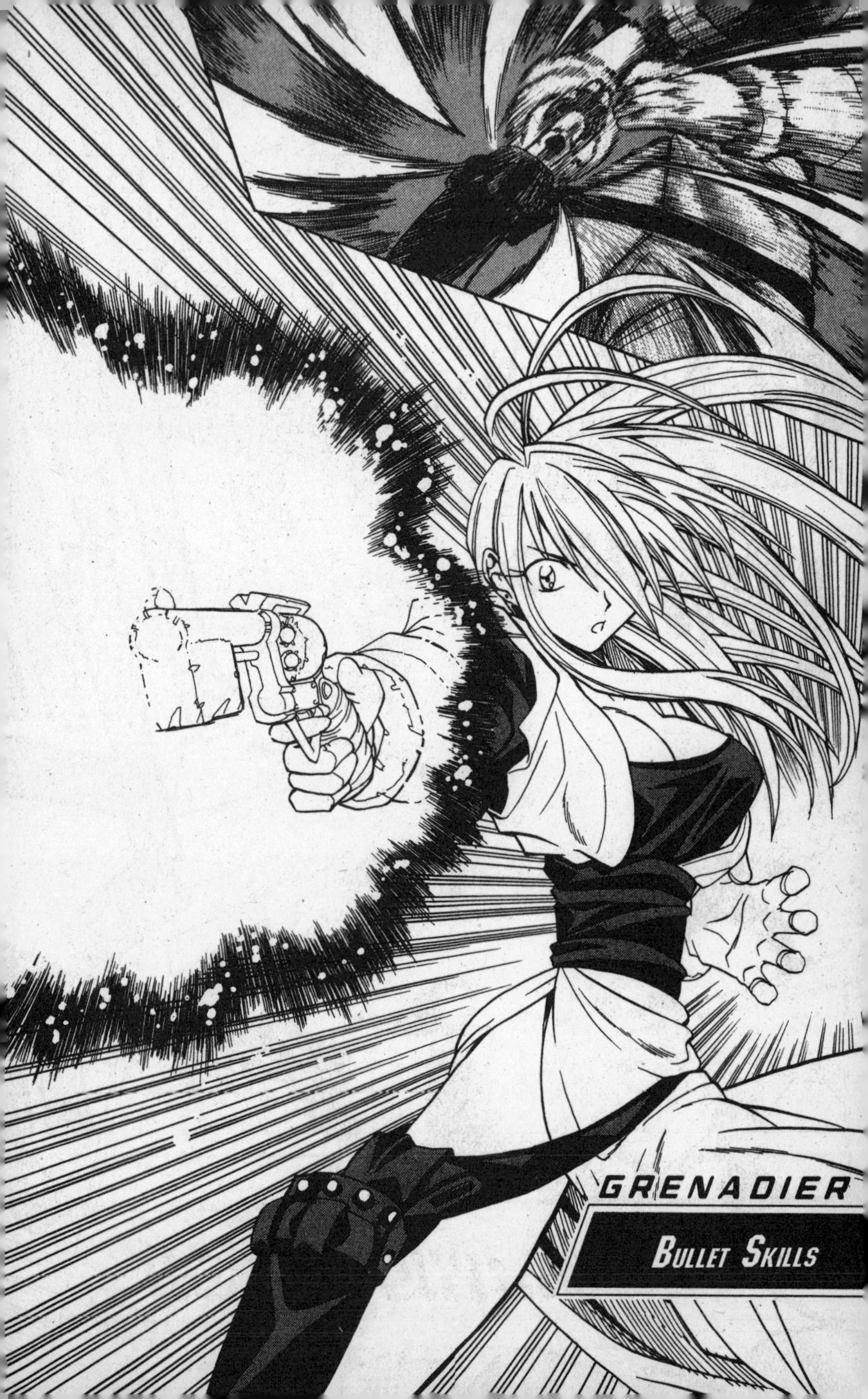
GRENADIER
BULLET SKILLS

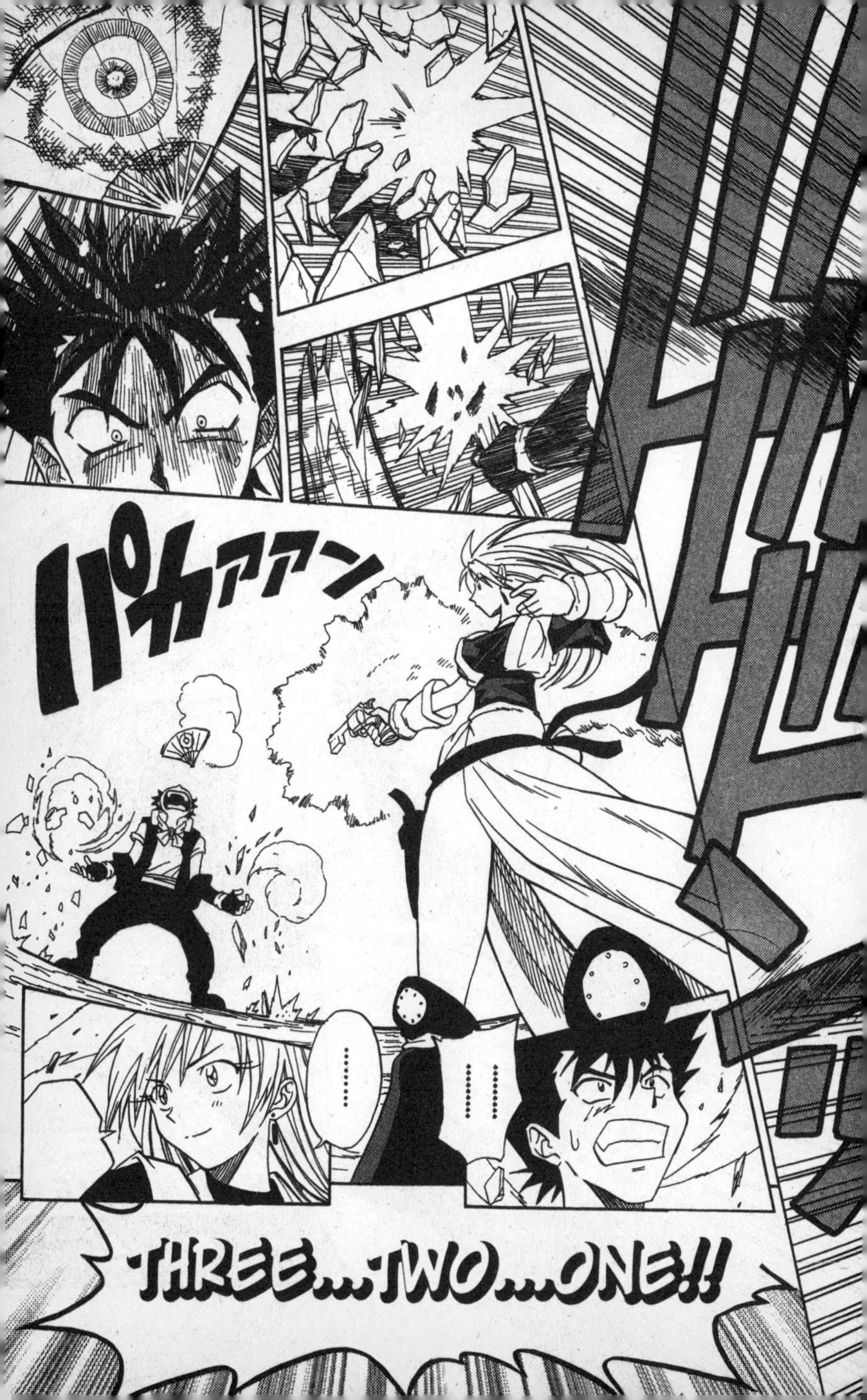
パカアアン
……
……
THREE...TWO...ONE!!

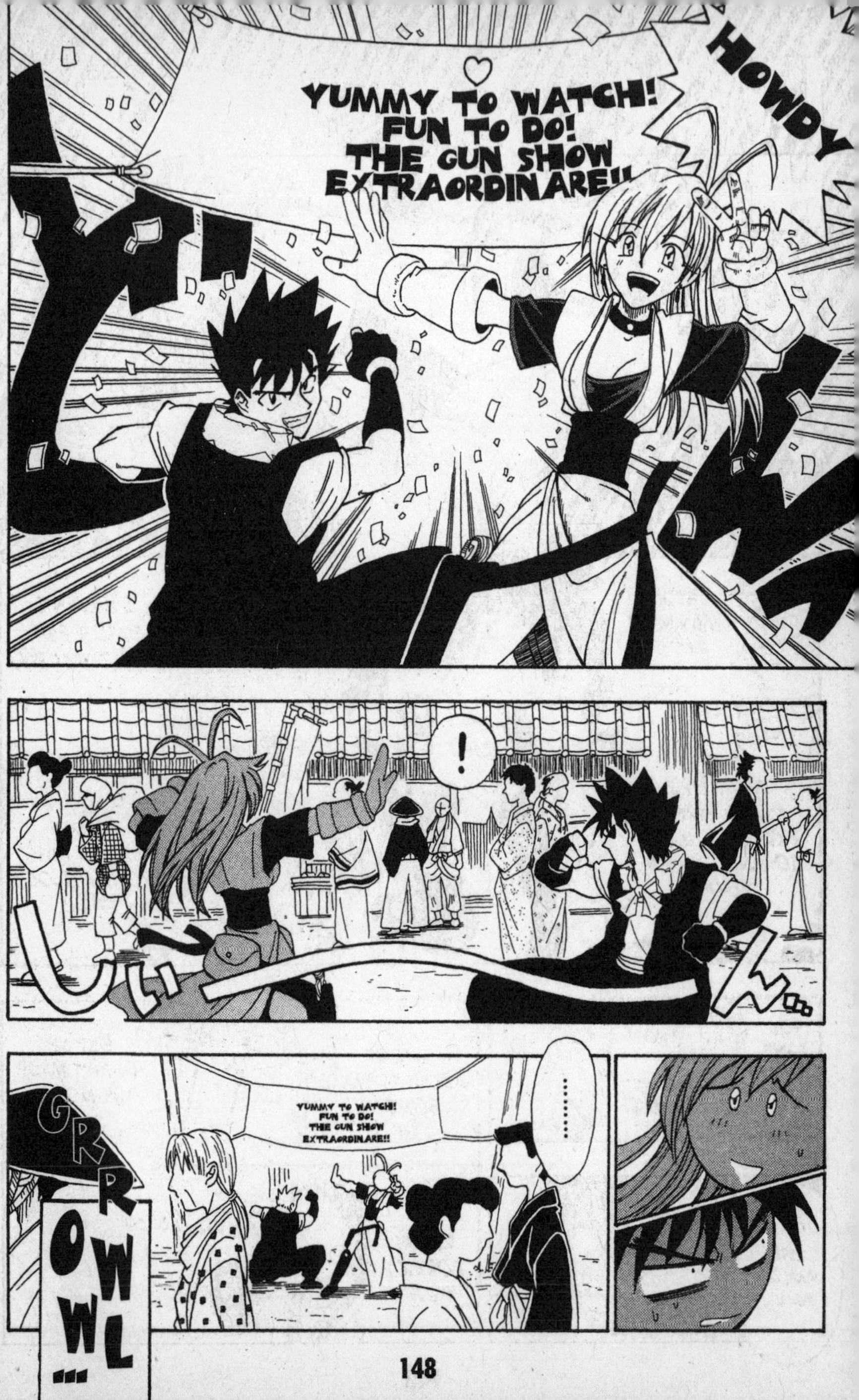
HOWDY
YUMMY TO WATCH! FUN TO DO! THE GUN SHOW EXTRAORDINARE!!
!
......
YUMMY TO WATCH! FUN TO DO! THE GUN SHOW EXTRAORDINARE!!
GRRROWL...

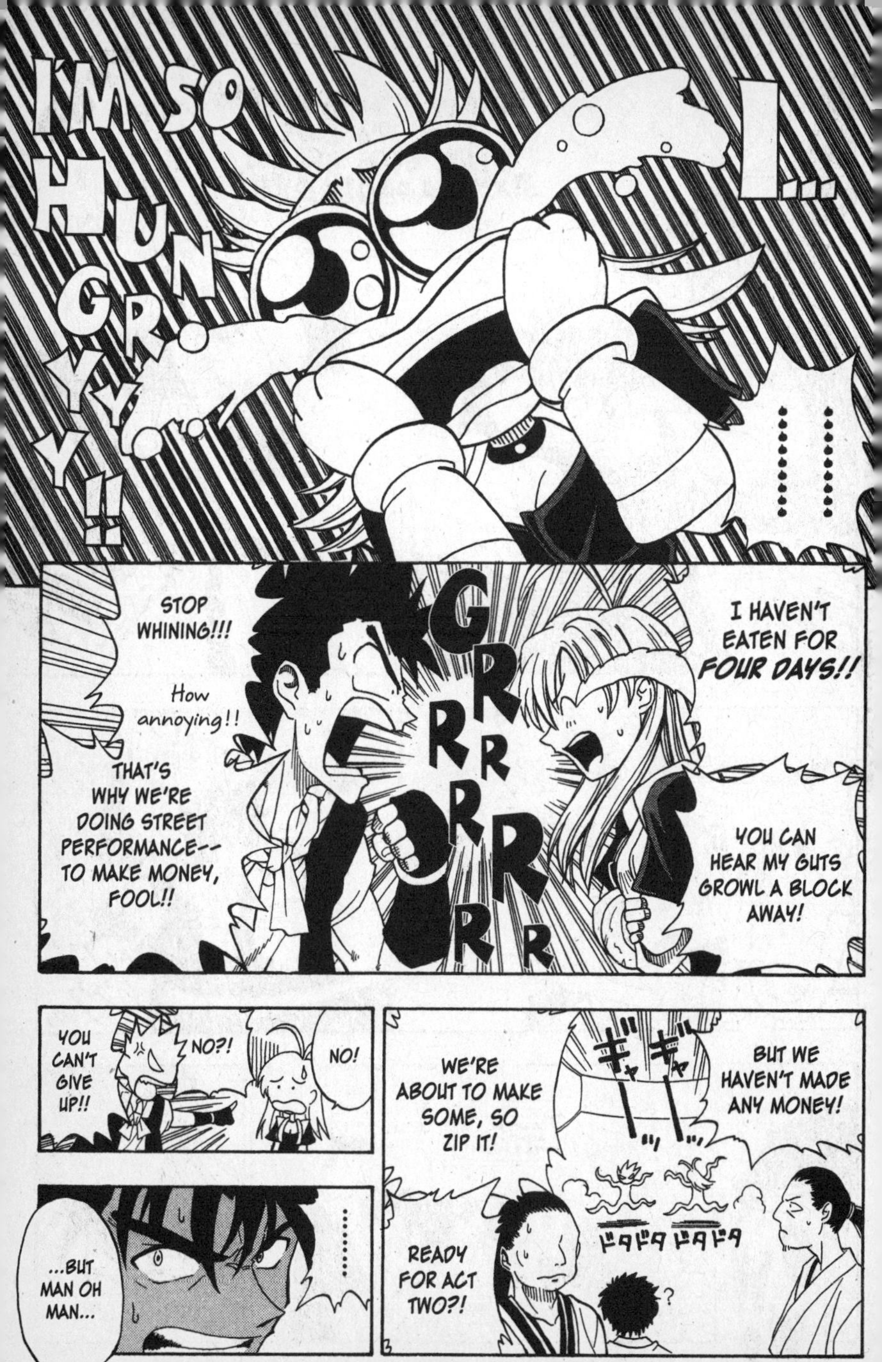
I...
......
I'M SO HUNGRYYY!!
I HAVEN'T EATEN FOR FOUR DAYS!!
YOU CAN HEAR MY GUTS GROWL A BLOCK AWAY!
GRRRRRRRR
STOP WHINING!!!
How annoying!!
THAT'S WHY WE'RE DOING STREET PERFORMANCE--TO MAKE MONEY, FOOL!!
BUT WE HAVEN'T MADE ANY MONEY!
ギャ ギャ
WE'RE ABOUT TO MAKE SOME, SO ZIP IT!
ドタドタ ドタドタ
?
READY FOR ACT TWO?!
NO!
NO?!
YOU CAN'T GIVE UP!!
......
...BUT MAN OH MAN...

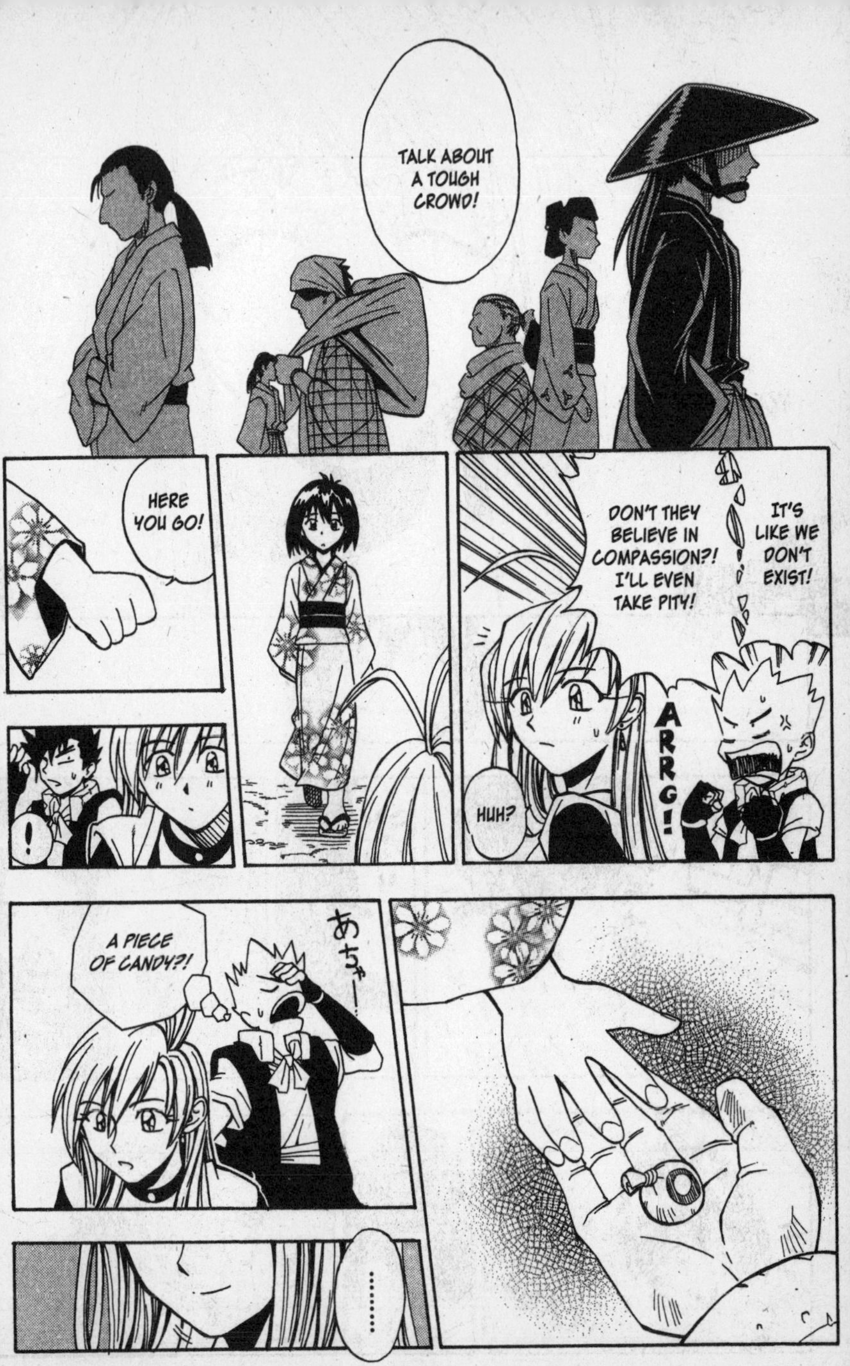
TALK ABOUT A TOUGH CROWD!
IT'S LIKE WE DON'T EXIST!
DON'T THEY BELIEVE IN COMPASSION?! I'LL EVEN TAKE PITY!
ARRG!
HUH?
HERE YOU GO!
!
A PIECE OF CANDY?!
あちゃ――……
……

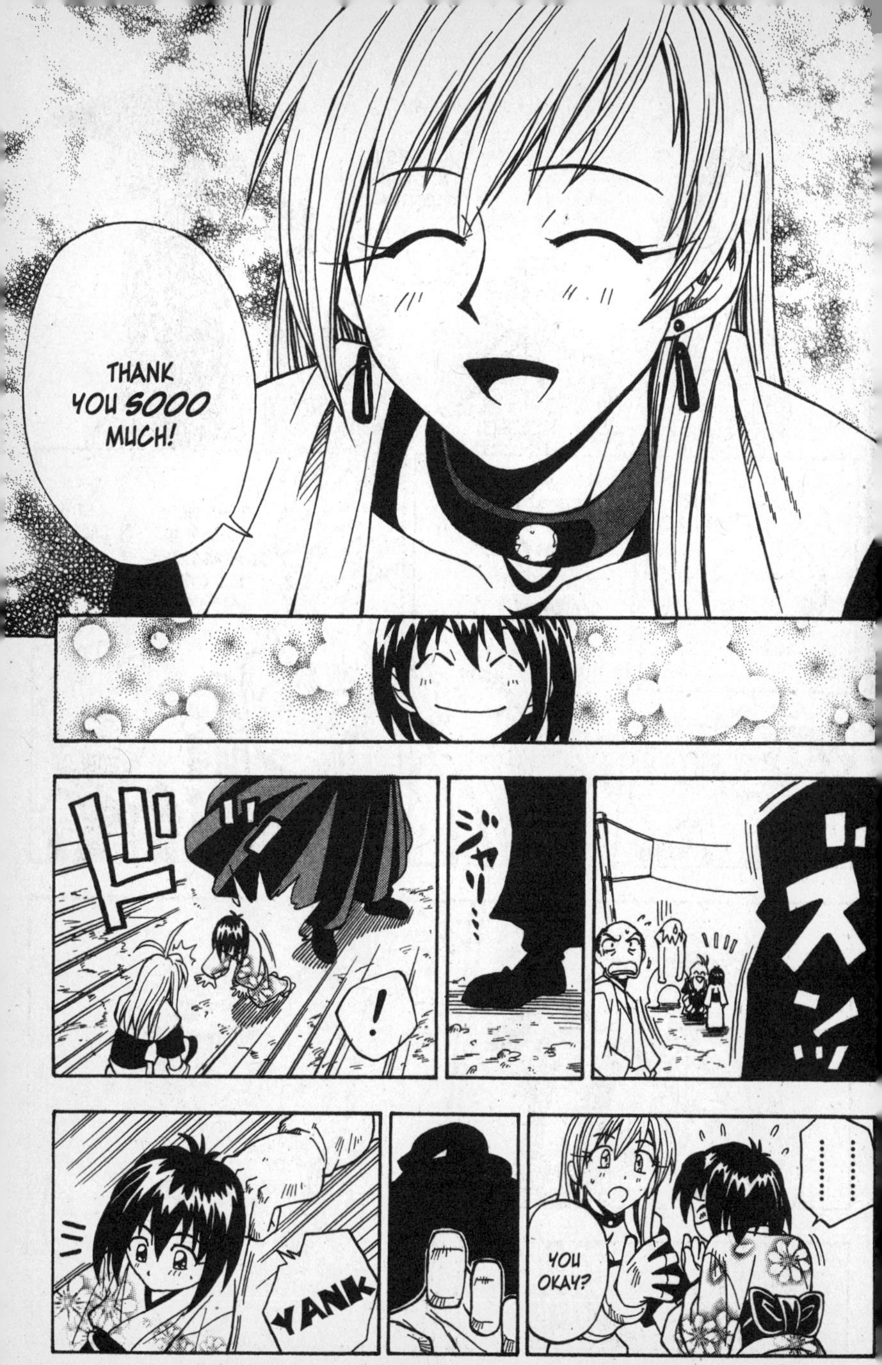
THANK YOU SOOO MUCH!
ズン!!
ジャリ…
ド
!
……
YOU OKAY?
YANK

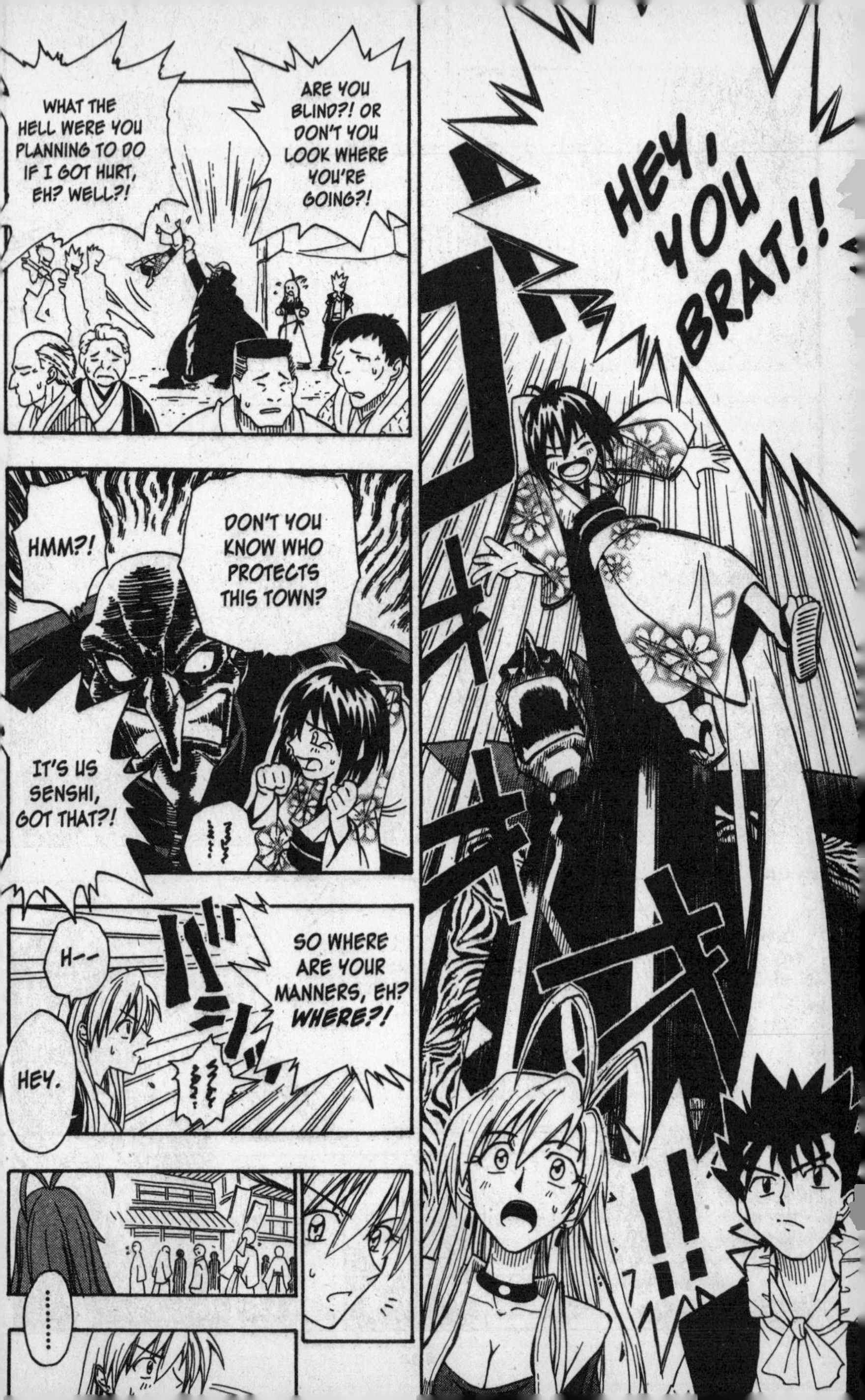
HEY, YOU BRAT!!
!!
ARE YOU BLIND?! OR DON'T YOU LOOK WHERE YOU'RE GOING?!
WHAT THE HELL WERE YOU PLANNING TO DO IF I GOT HURT, EH? WELL?!
DON'T YOU KNOW WHO PROTECTS THIS TOWN?
HMM?!
IT'S US SENSHI, GOT THAT?!
SO WHERE ARE YOUR MANNERS, EH? WHERE?!
H--
HEY.
....

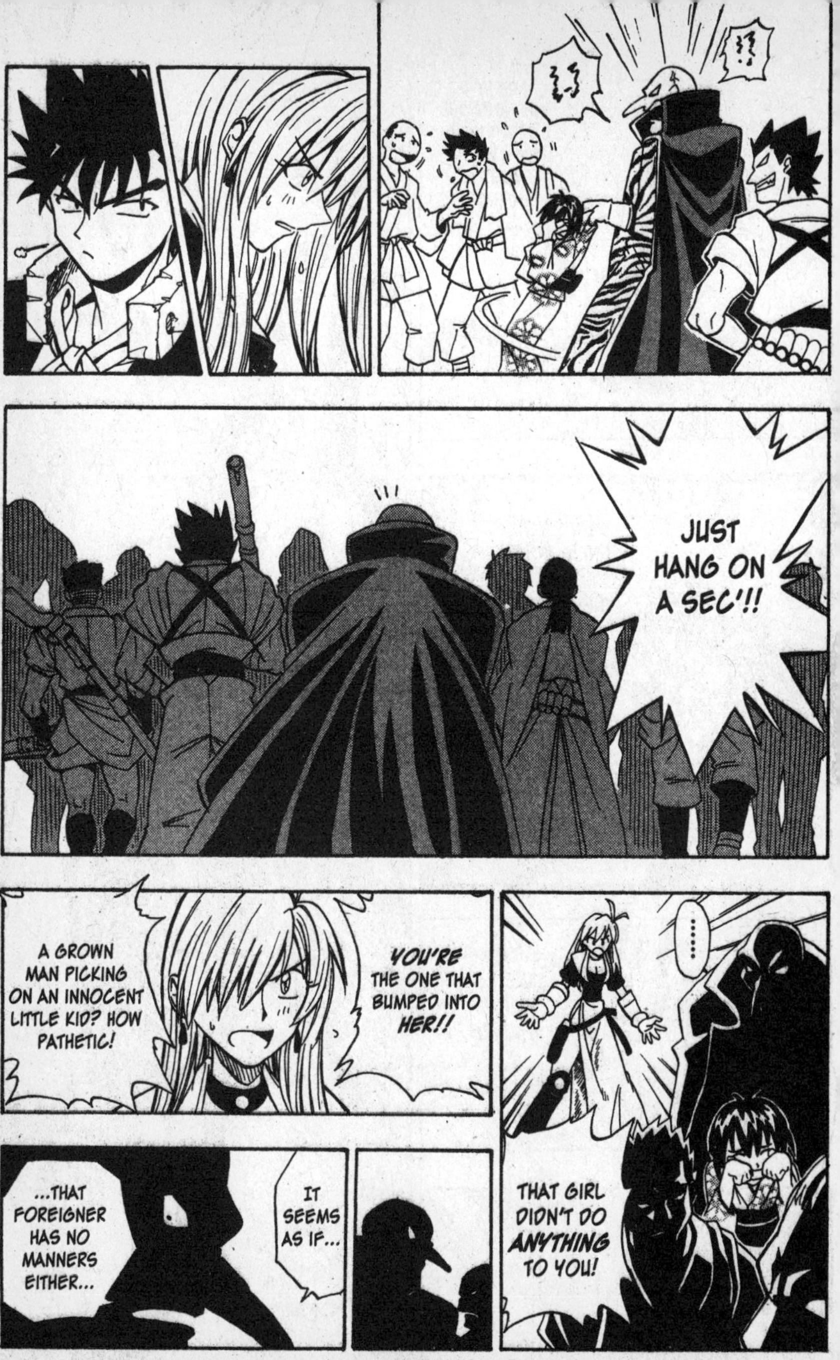
JUST HANG ON A SEC'!!
......
THAT GIRL DIDN'T DO ANYTHING TO YOU!
YOU'RE THE ONE THAT BUMPED INTO HER!!
A GROWN MAN PICKING ON AN INNOCENT LITTLE KID? HOW PATHETIC!
IT SEEMS AS IF...
...THAT FOREIGNER HAS NO MANNERS EITHER...

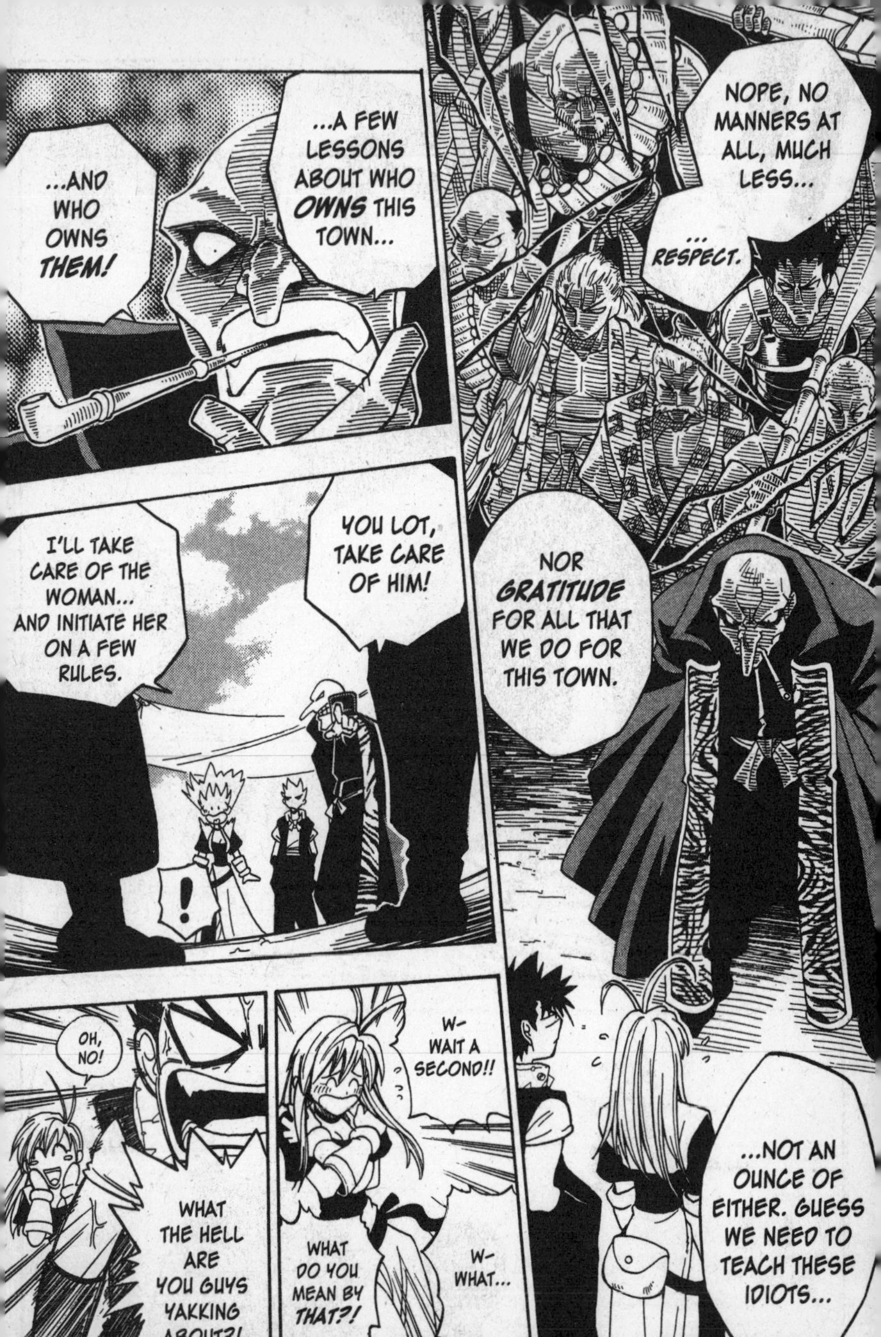
NOPE, NO MANNERS AT ALL, MUCH LESS...
... RESPECT.
NOR GRATITUDE FOR ALL THAT WE DO FOR THIS TOWN.
...NOT AN OUNCE OF EITHER. GUESS WE NEED TO TEACH THESE IDIOTS...
...A FEW LESSONS ABOUT WHO OWNS THIS TOWN...
...AND WHO OWNS THEM!
YOU LOT, TAKE CARE OF HIM!
I'LL TAKE CARE OF THE WOMAN... AND INITIATE HER ON A FEW RULES.
!
W- WAIT A SECOND!!
W- WHAT...
WHAT DO YOU MEAN BY THAT?!
OH, NO!
WHAT THE HELL ARE YOU GUYS YAKKING ABOUT?!

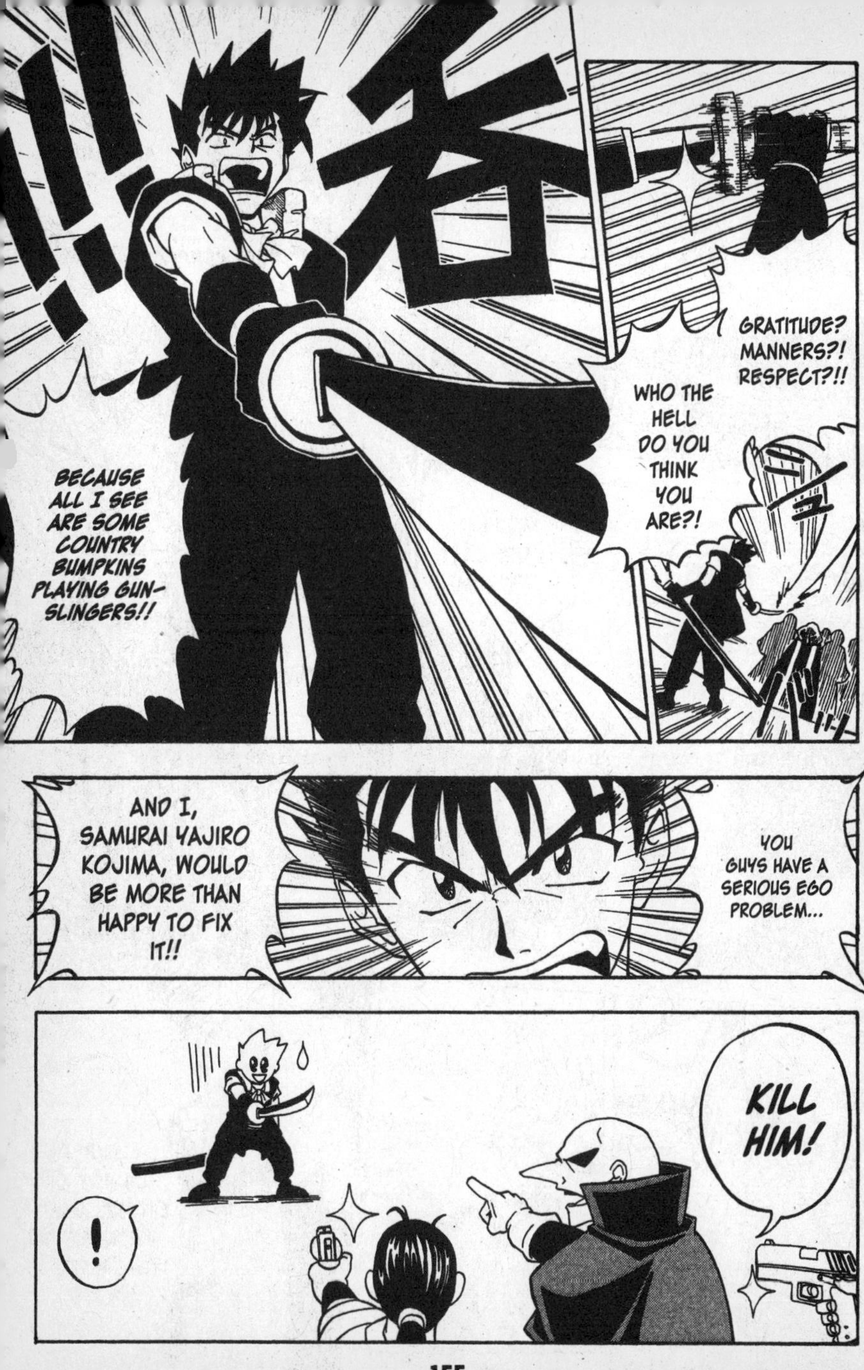
GRATITUDE? MANNERS?! RESPECT?!!
WHO THE HELL DO YOU THINK YOU ARE?!
BECAUSE ALL I SEE ARE SOME COUNTRY BUMPKINS PLAYING GUN-SLINGERS!!
YOU GUYS HAVE A SERIOUS EGO PROBLEM...
AND I, SAMURAI YAJIRO KOJIMA, WOULD BE MORE THAN HAPPY TO FIX IT!!
KILL HIM!
!

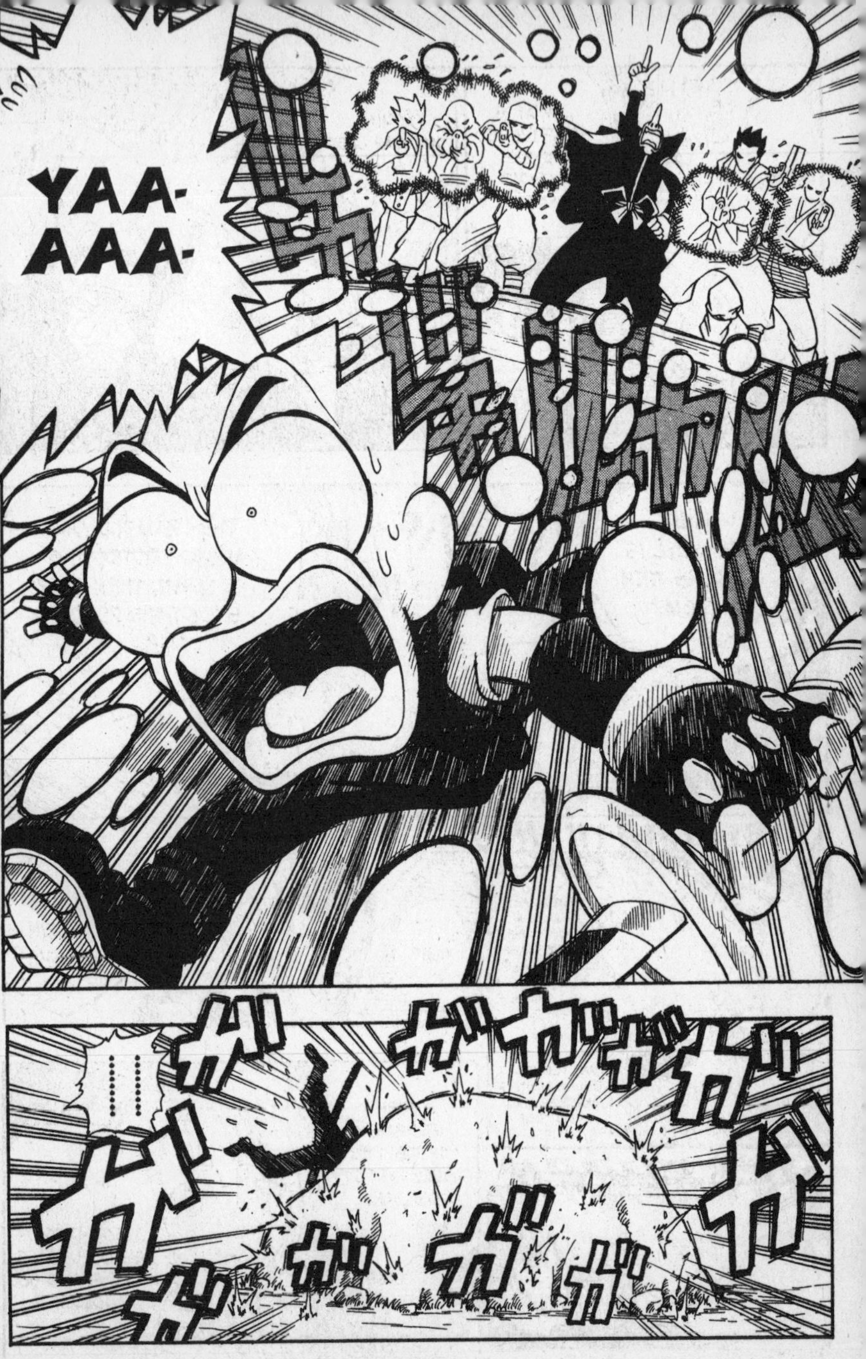
YAAA-
AAA-
!!
ガガガガガガガガガガガ

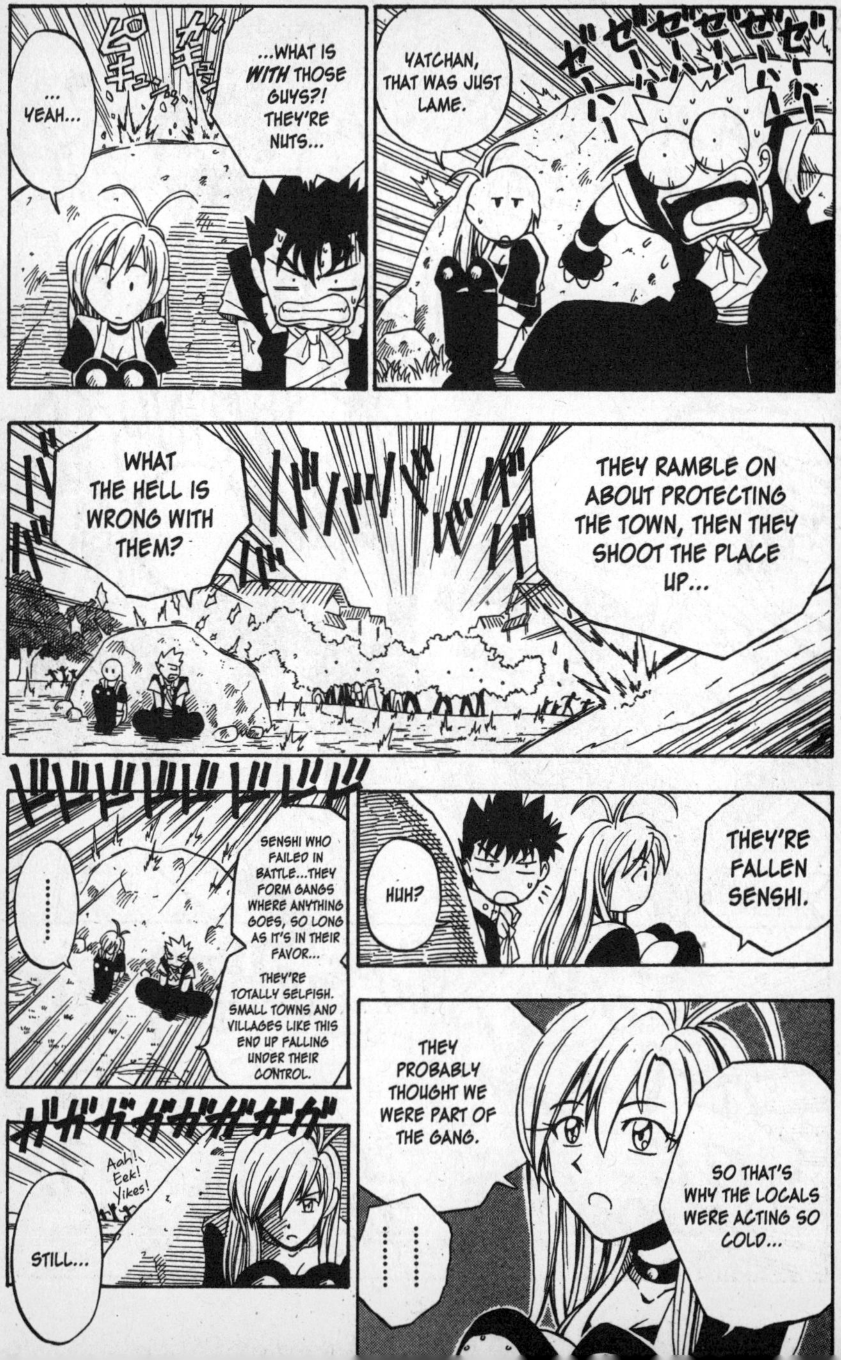
YATCHAN, THAT WAS JUST LAME.
...WHAT IS *WITH* THOSE GUYS?! THEY'RE NUTS...
... YEAH...
THEY RAMBLE ON ABOUT PROTECTING THE TOWN, THEN THEY SHOOT THE PLACE UP...
WHAT THE HELL IS WRONG WITH THEM?
THEY'RE FALLEN SENSHI.
HUH?
THEY PROBABLY THOUGHT WE WERE PART OF THE GANG.
SO THAT'S WHY THE LOCALS WERE ACTING SO COLD...
......
SENSHI WHO FAILED IN BATTLE...THEY FORM GANGS WHERE ANYTHING GOES, SO LONG AS IT'S IN THEIR FAVOR...
THEY'RE TOTALLY SELFISH. SMALL TOWNS AND VILLAGES LIKE THIS END UP FALLING UNDER THEIR CONTROL.
......
Aah! Eek! Yikes!
STILL...

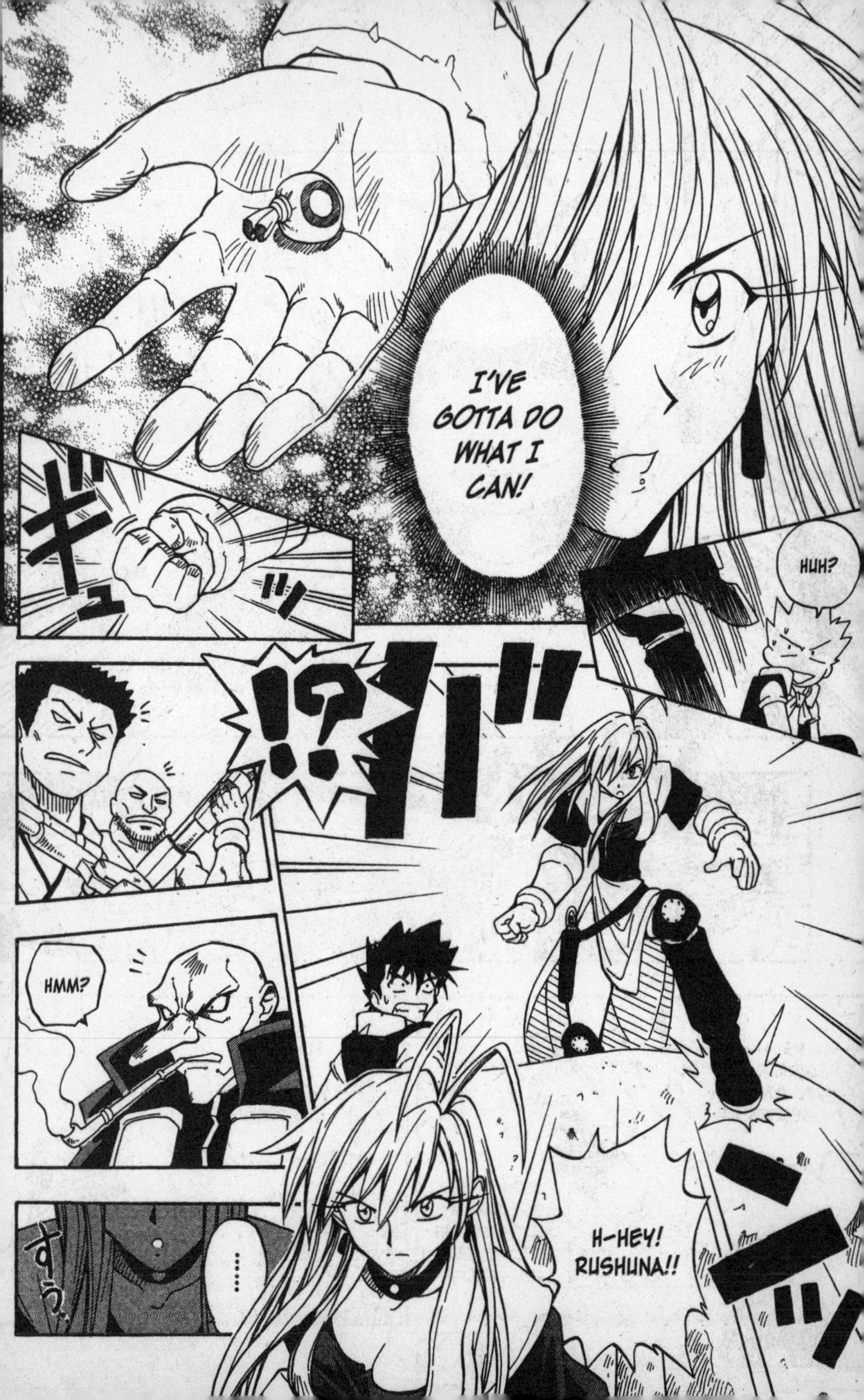
I'VE GOTTA DO WHAT I CAN!
ギュッ
HUH?
!?
HMM?
H-HEY! RUSHUNA!!
......
すぅ...

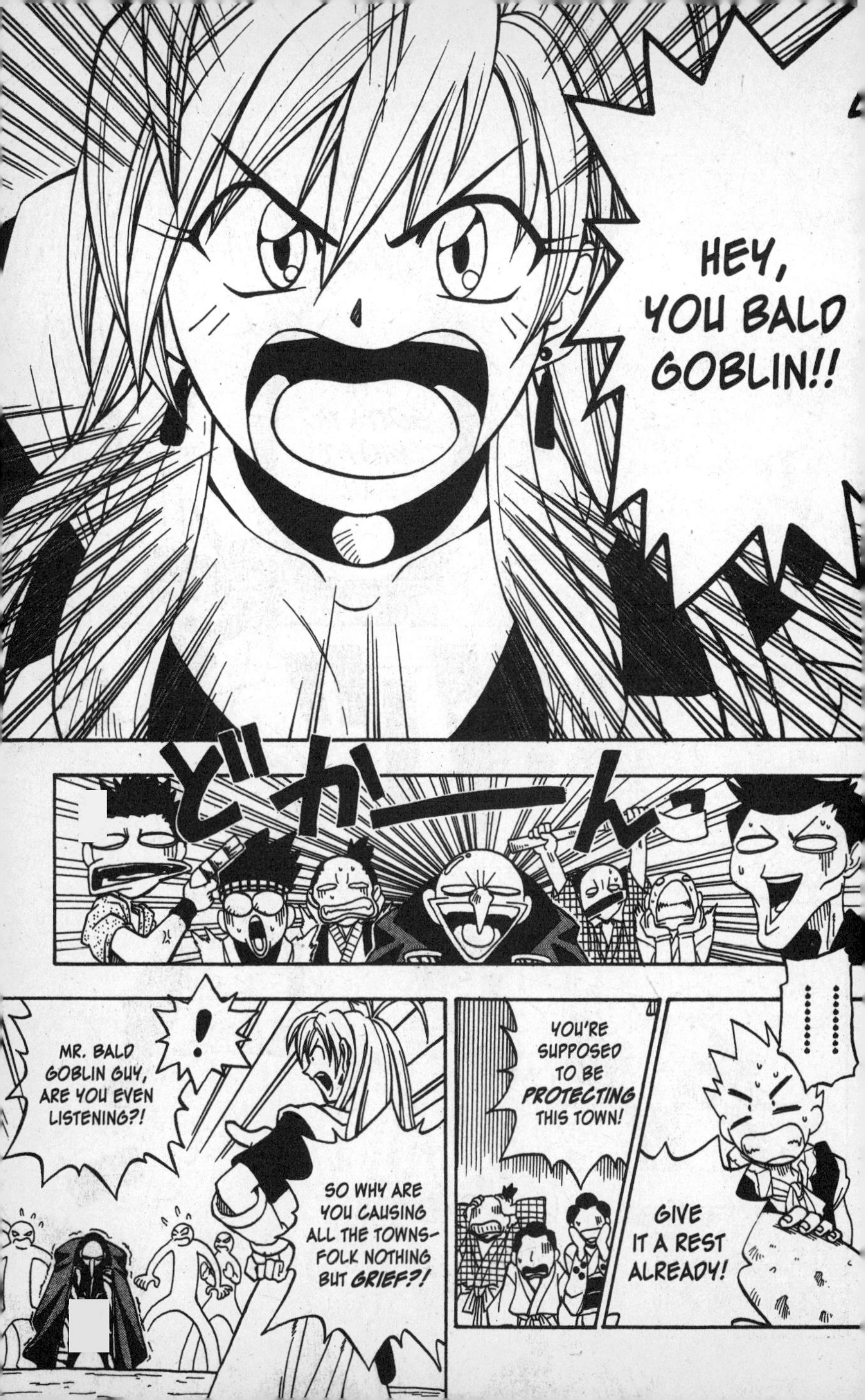

HEY, YOU BALD GOBLIN!!
どかーん
......
YOU'RE SUPPOSED TO BE PROTECTING THIS TOWN!
GIVE IT A REST ALREADY!
!
MR. BALD GOBLIN GUY, ARE YOU EVEN LISTENING?!
SO WHY ARE YOU CAUSING ALL THE TOWNS-FOLK NOTHING BUT GRIEF?!

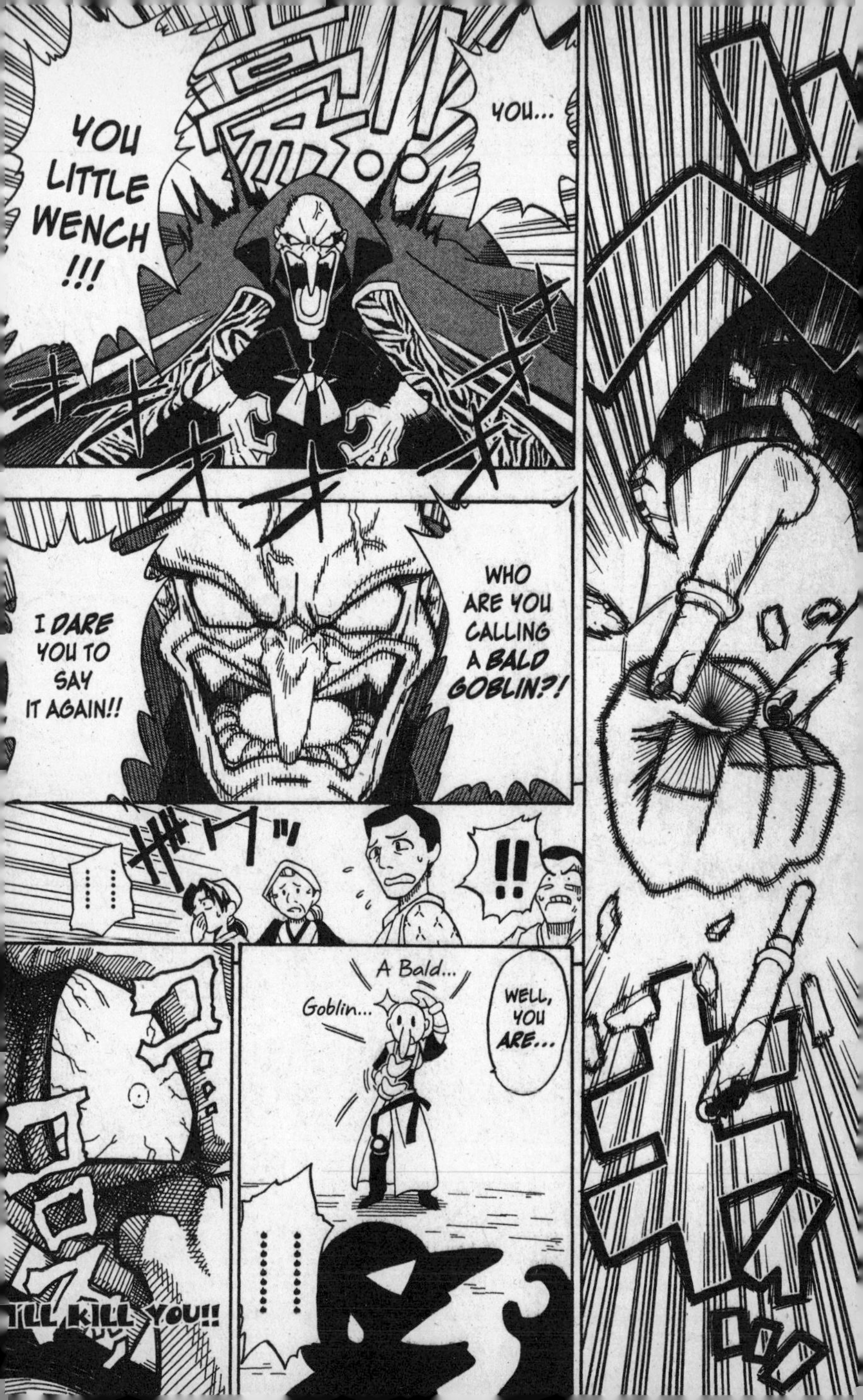
YOU...
YOU LITTLE WENCH!!!
WHO ARE YOU CALLING A BALD GOBLIN?!
I DARE YOU TO SAY IT AGAIN!!
!!
......
WELL, YOU ARE...
A Bald...
Goblin...
......
I'LL KILL YOU!!

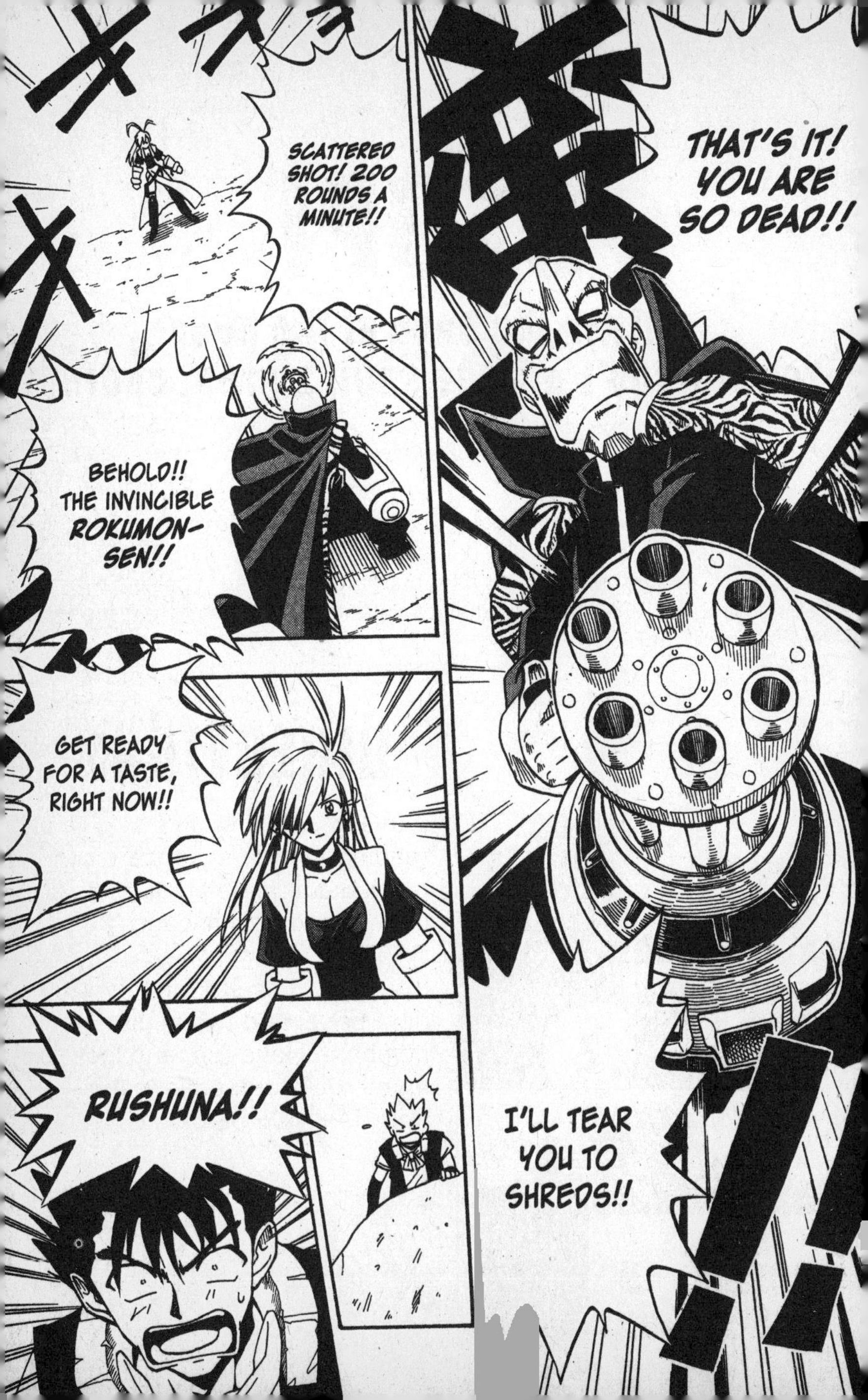
THAT'S IT! YOU ARE SO DEAD!!
I'LL TEAR YOU TO SHREDS!!
SCATTERED SHOT! 200 ROUNDS A MINUTE!!
BEHOLD!! THE INVINCIBLE ROKUMON-SEN!!
GET READY FOR A TASTE, RIGHT NOW!!
RUSHUNA!!

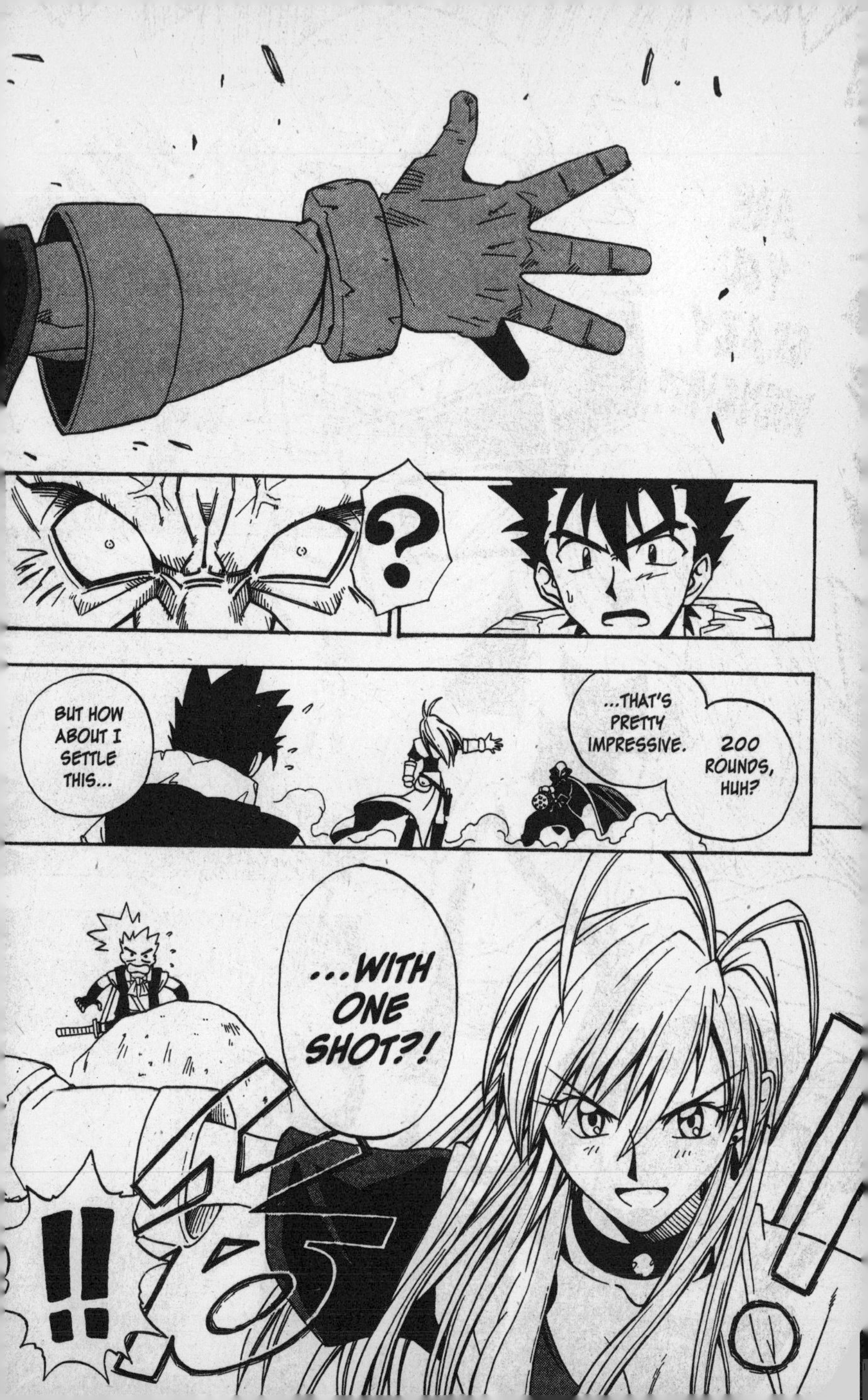
?
200 ROUNDS, HUH?
...THAT'S PRETTY IMPRESSIVE.
BUT HOW ABOUT I SETTLE THIS...
...WITH ONE SHOT?!
!!

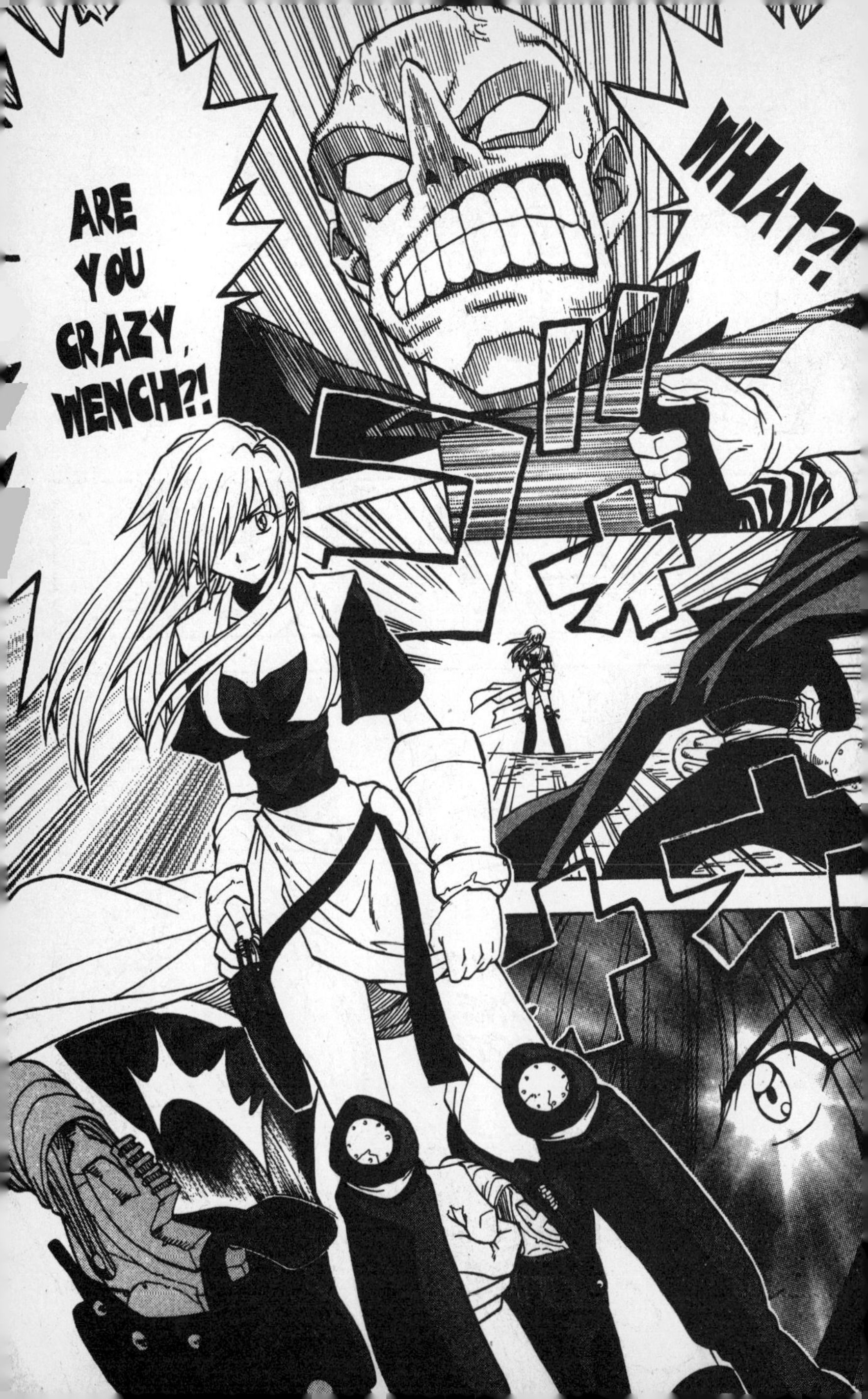
WHAT?!
ARE YOU CRAZY, WENCH?!

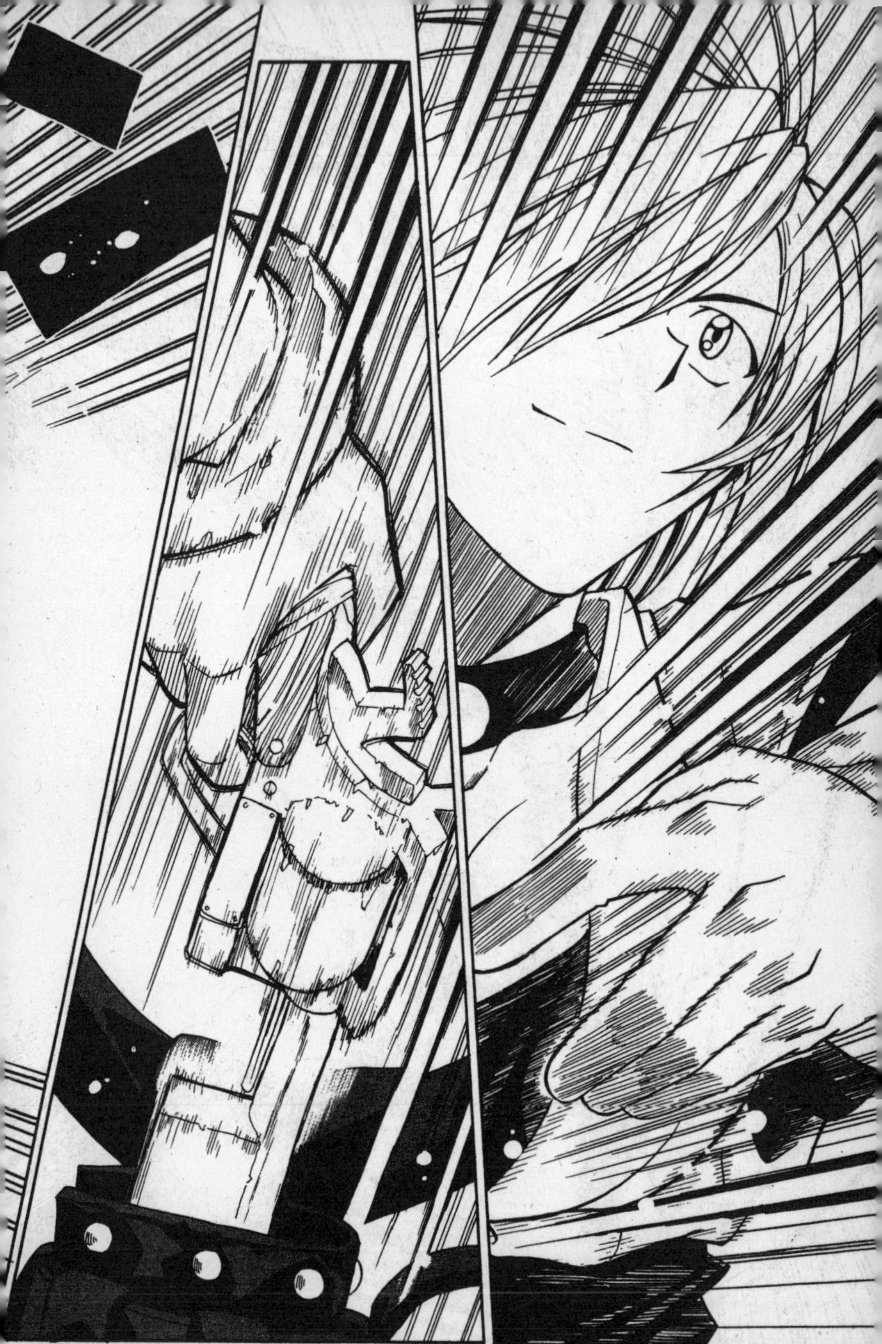

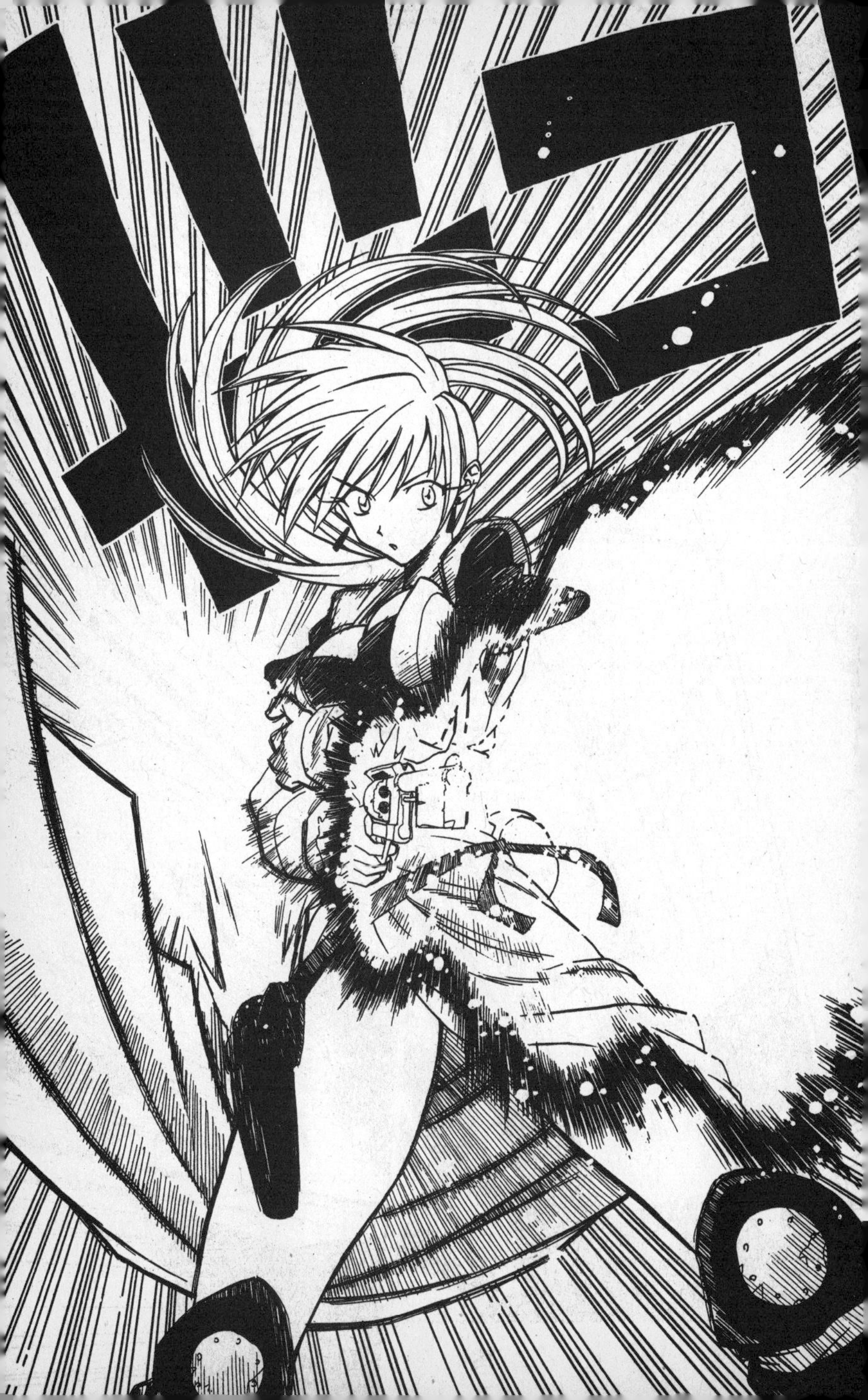

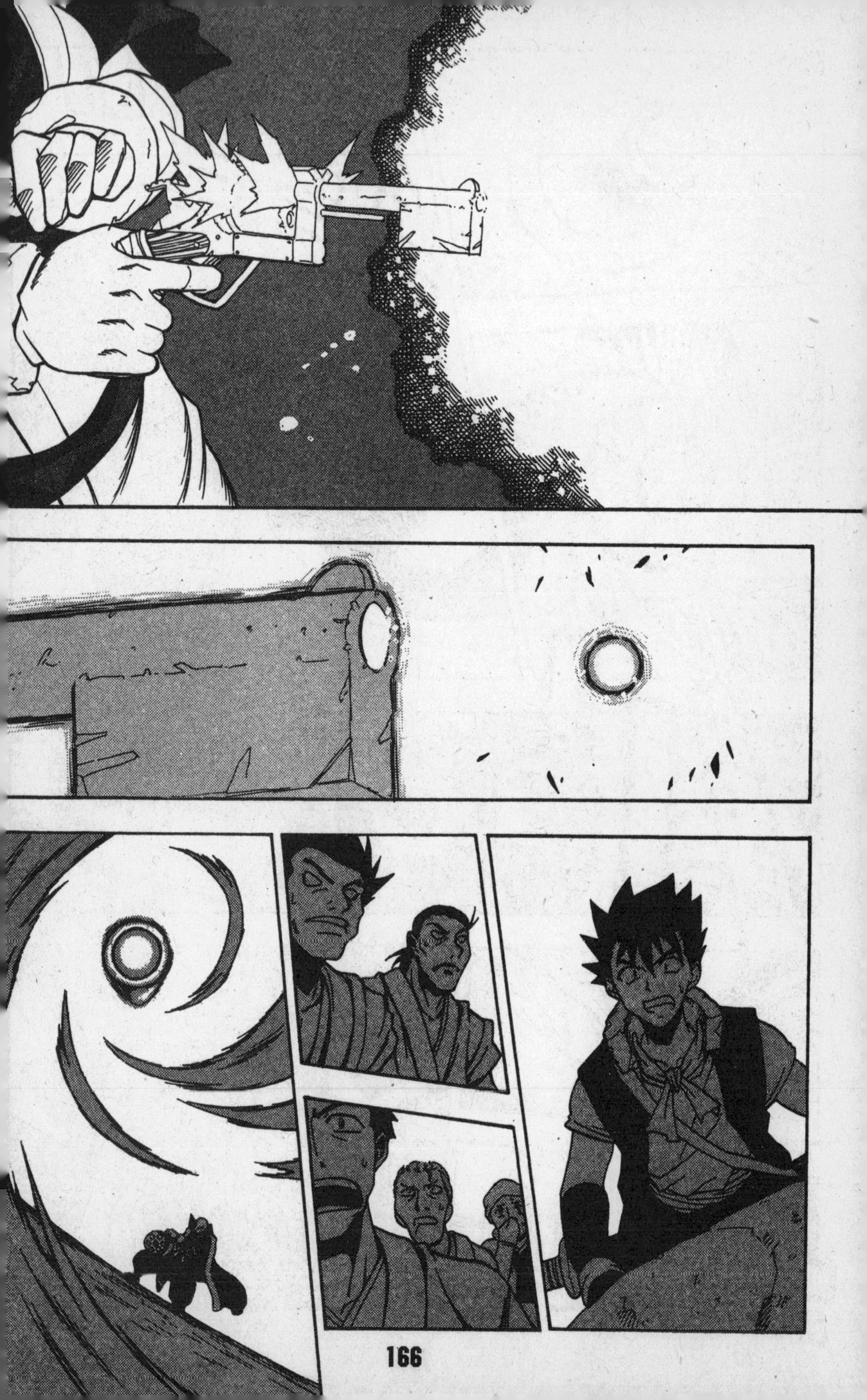

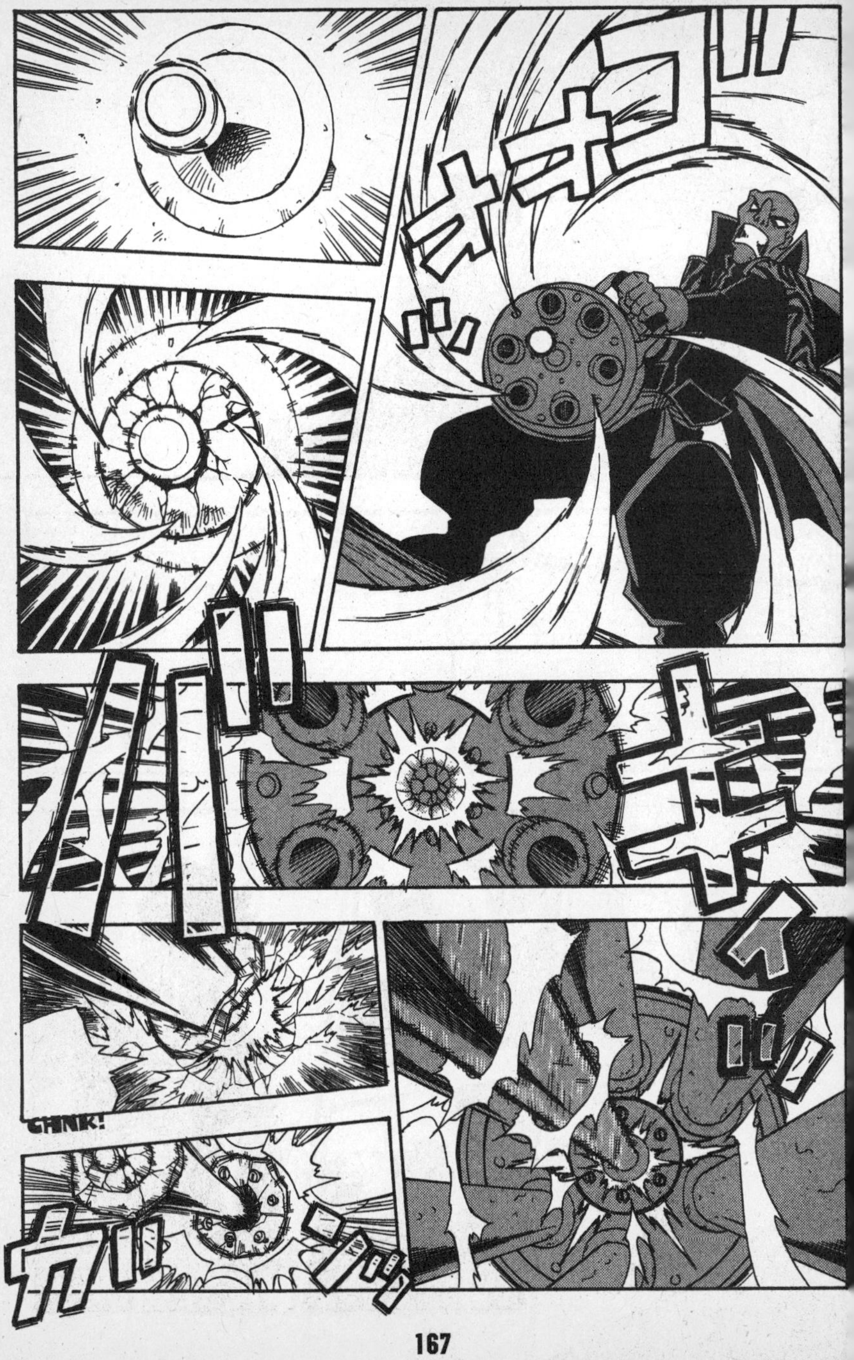
CHNK!

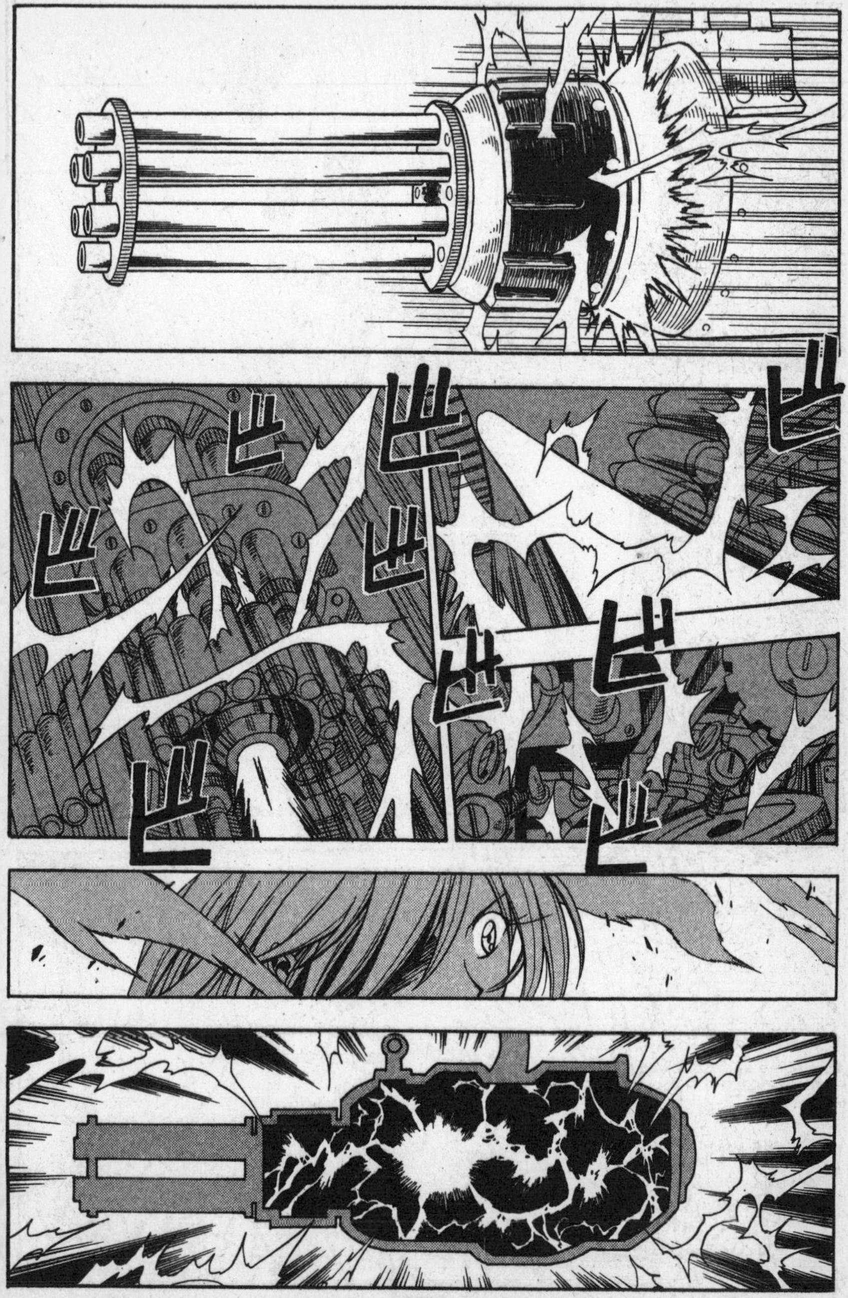
ビ
ビ
ビ
ビ
ビ
ビ
ビ
ビ
ビ

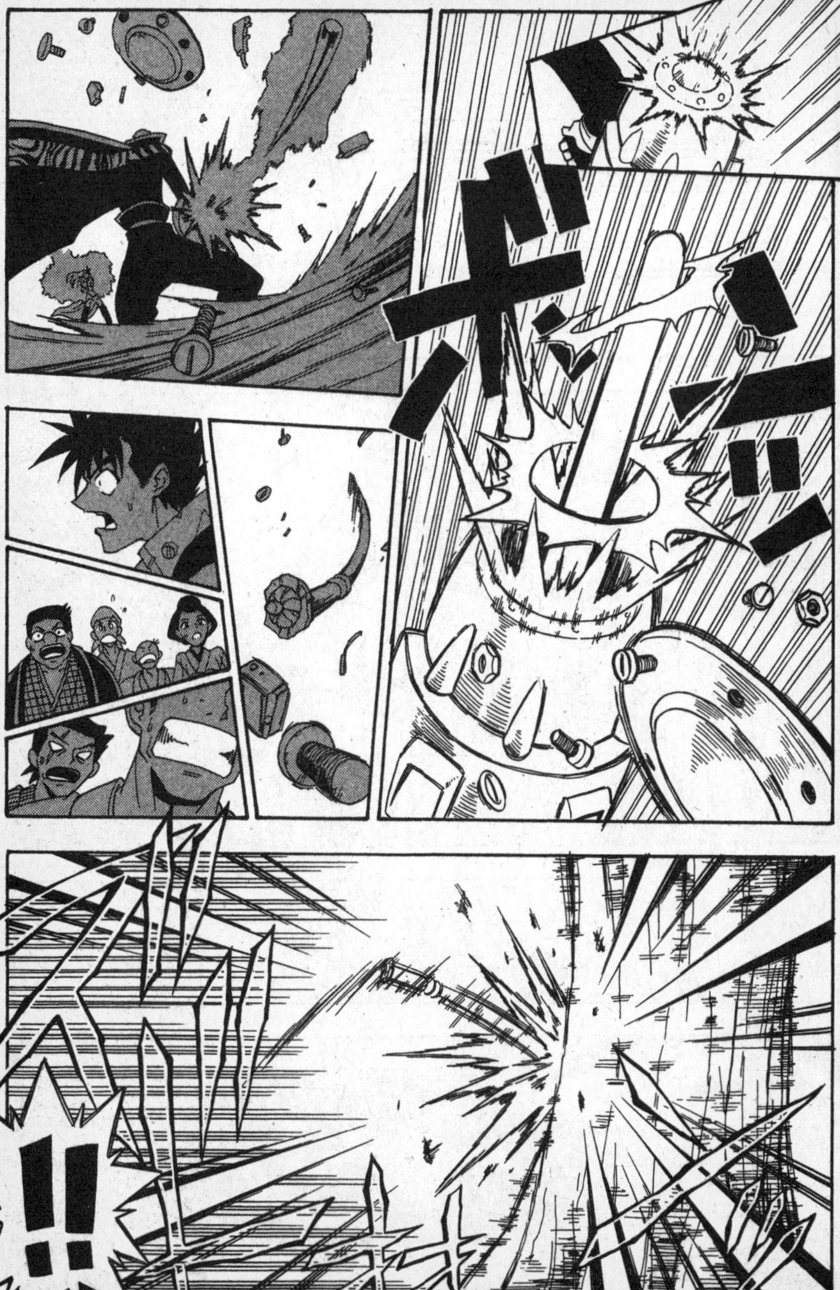
!!

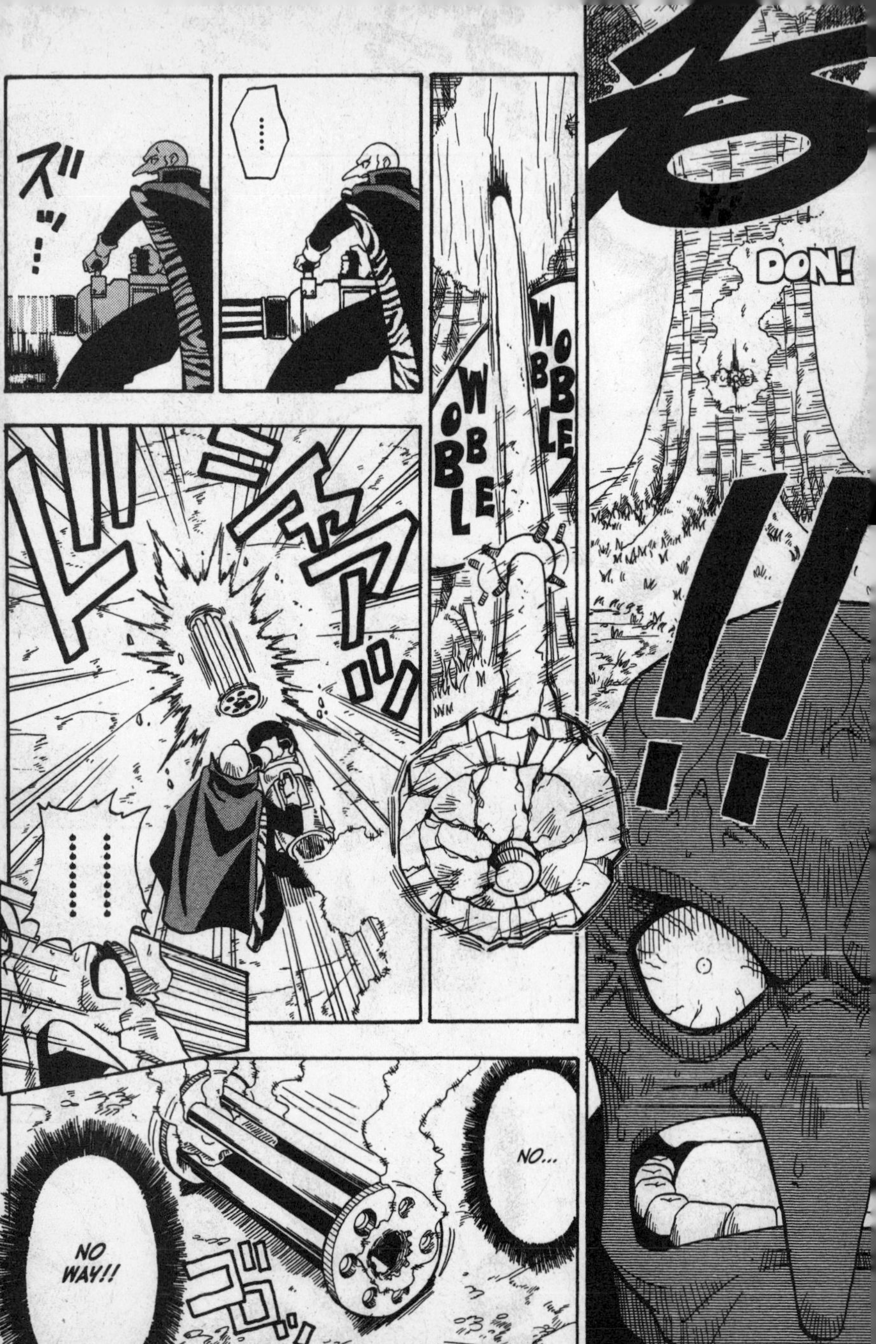
DON!
WOBBLE WOBBLE
WOBBLE
......
ズッ…
ドシャア
......
NO...
NO WAY!!

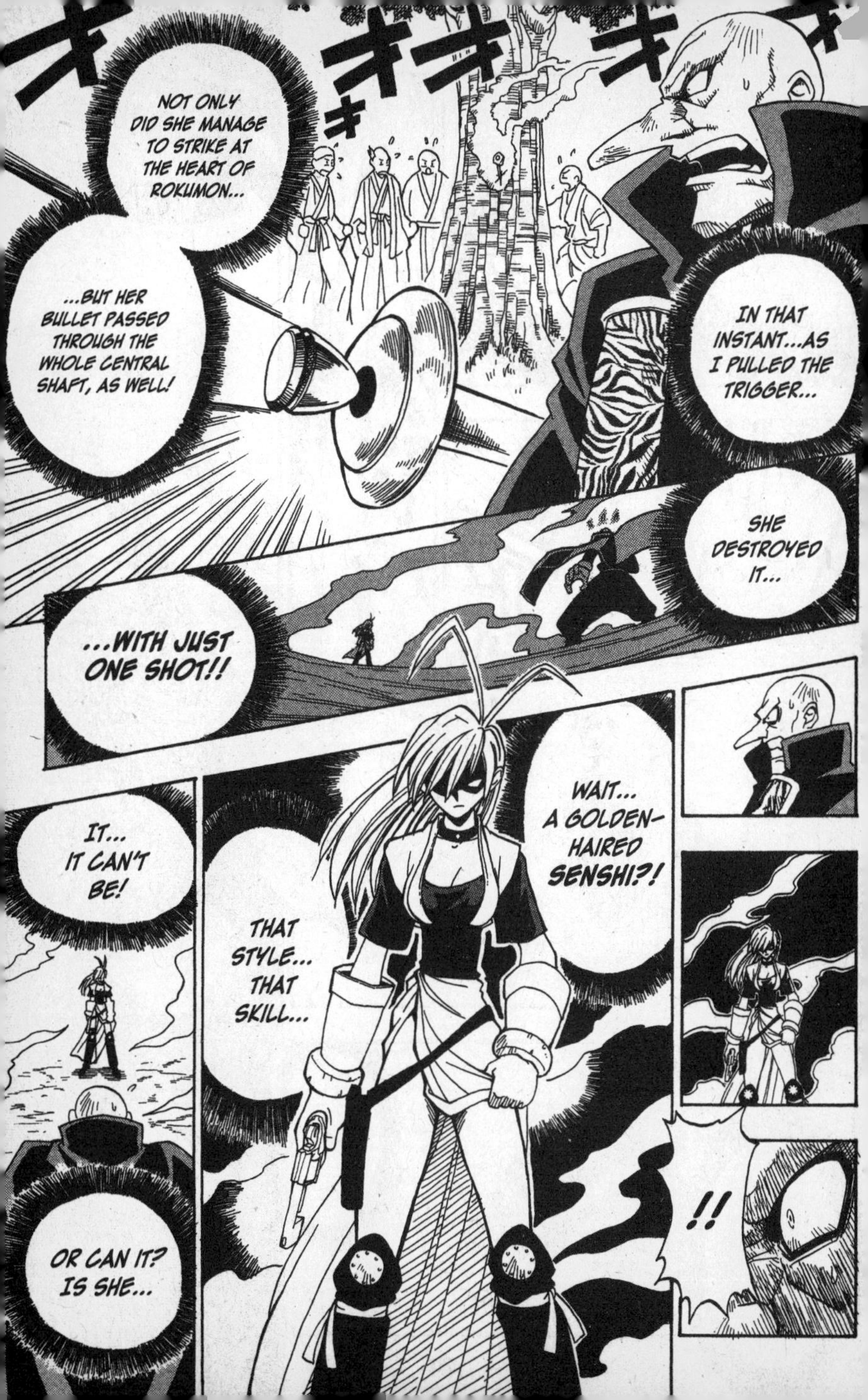
NOT ONLY DID SHE MANAGE TO STRIKE AT THE HEART OF ROKUMON...
...BUT HER BULLET PASSED THROUGH THE WHOLE CENTRAL SHAFT, AS WELL!
IN THAT INSTANT...AS I PULLED THE TRIGGER...
SHE DESTROYED IT...
...WITH JUST ONE SHOT!!
!!
WAIT... A GOLDEN-HAIRED SENSHI?!
THAT STYLE... THAT SKILL...
IT... IT CAN'T BE!
OR CAN IT? IS SHE...

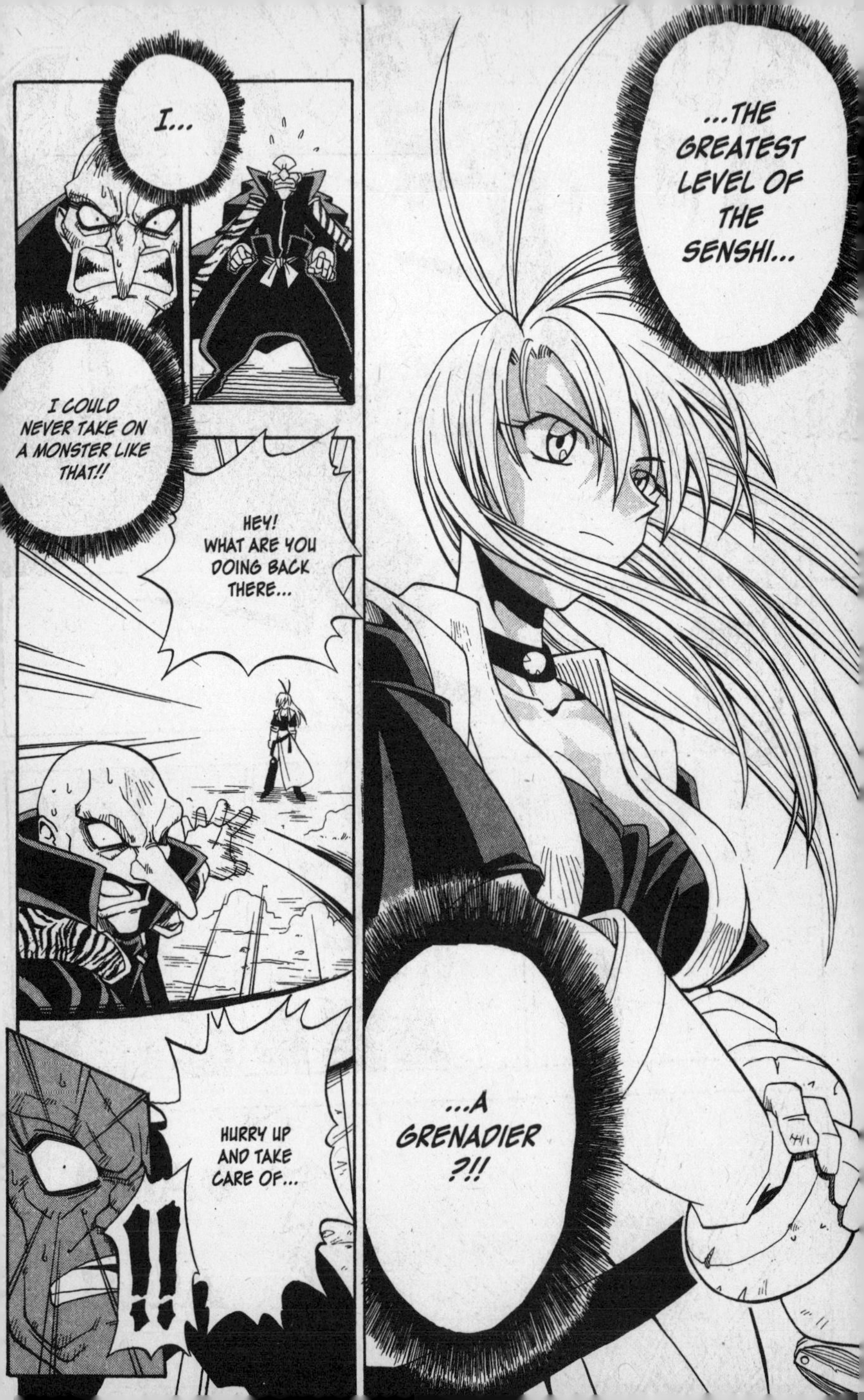
...THE GREATEST LEVEL OF THE SENSHI...
...A GRENADIER ?!!
I...
I COULD NEVER TAKE ON A MONSTER LIKE THAT!!
HEY! WHAT ARE YOU DOING BACK THERE...
HURRY UP AND TAKE CARE OF...
!!

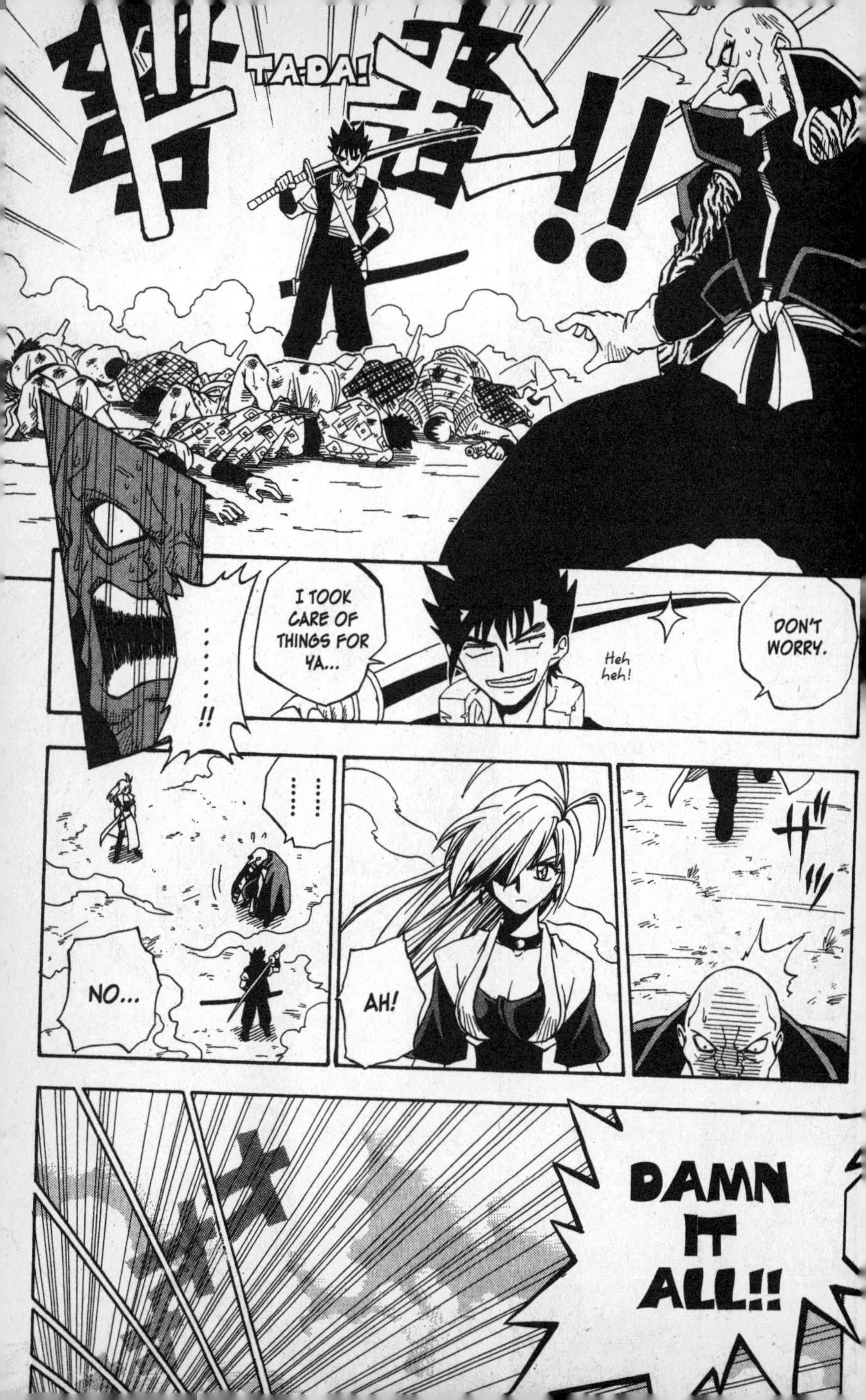

TA-DA!
DON'T WORRY.
Heh heh!
I TOOK CARE OF THINGS FOR YA...
......!!
AH!
......
NO...
DAMN IT ALL!!

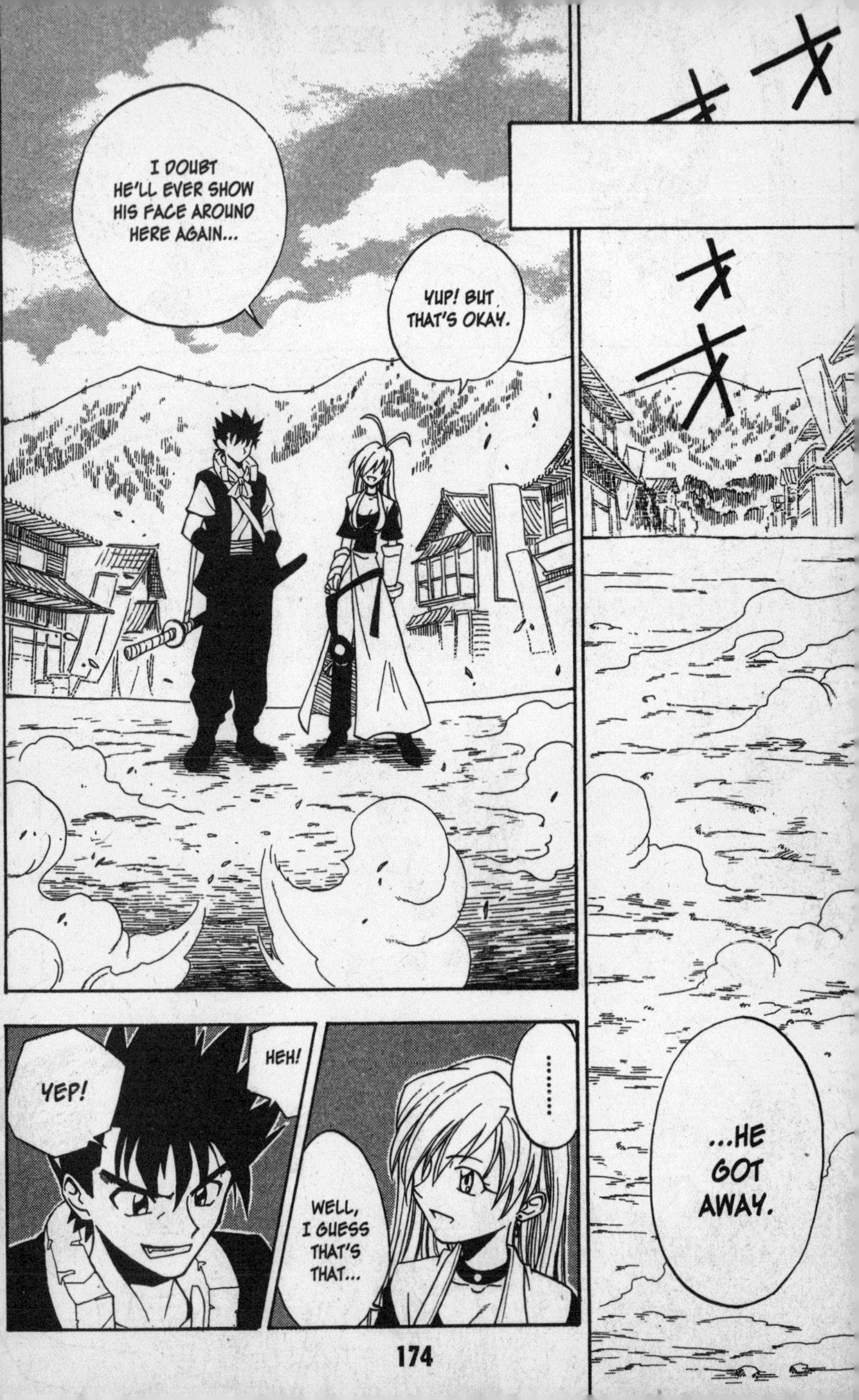
...HE GOT AWAY.
I DOUBT HE'LL EVER SHOW HIS FACE AROUND HERE AGAIN...
YUP! BUT THAT'S OKAY.
....
WELL, I GUESS THAT'S THAT...
HEH!
YEP!

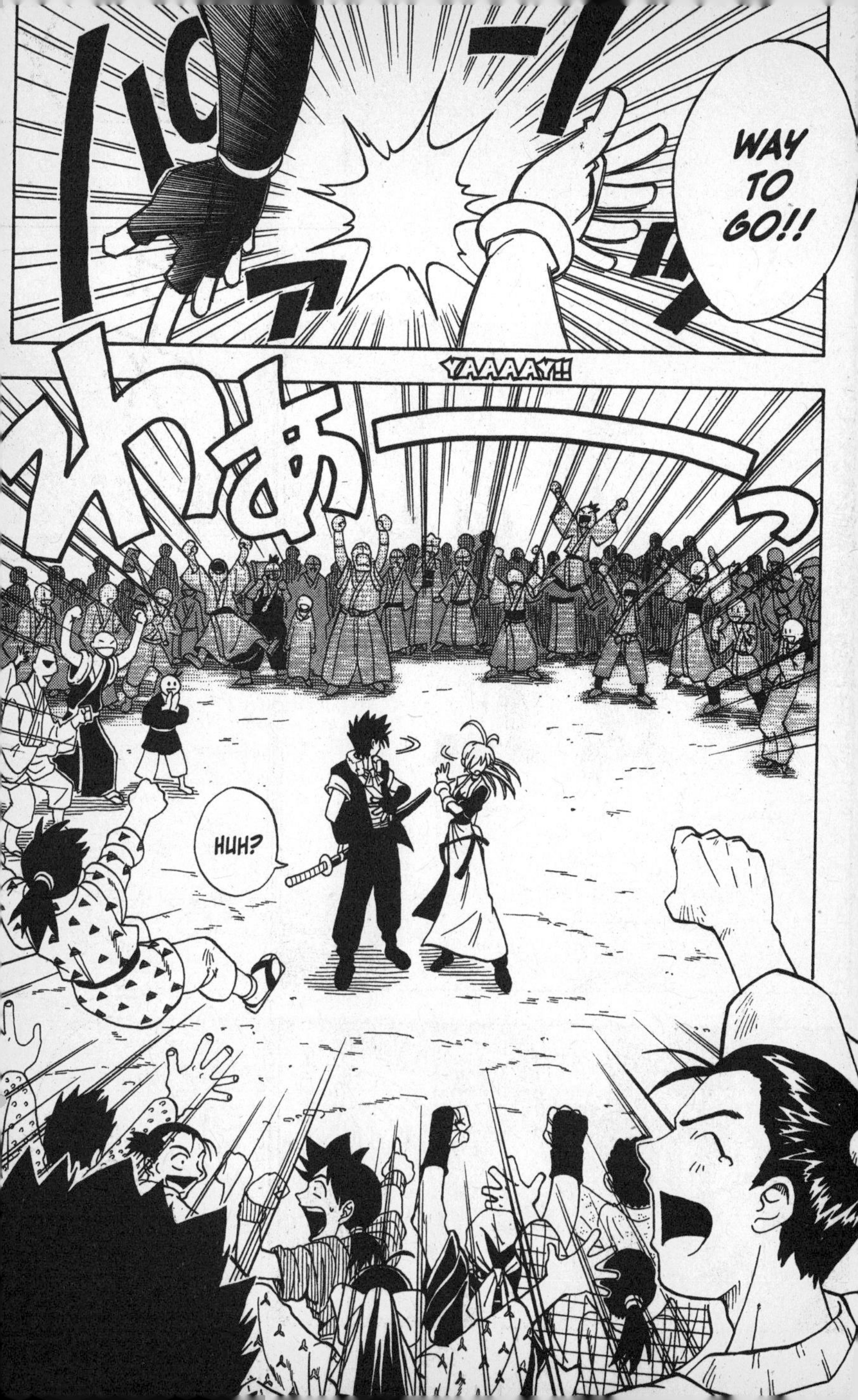
WAY TO GO!!
YAAAAY!!
わあーっ
HUH?

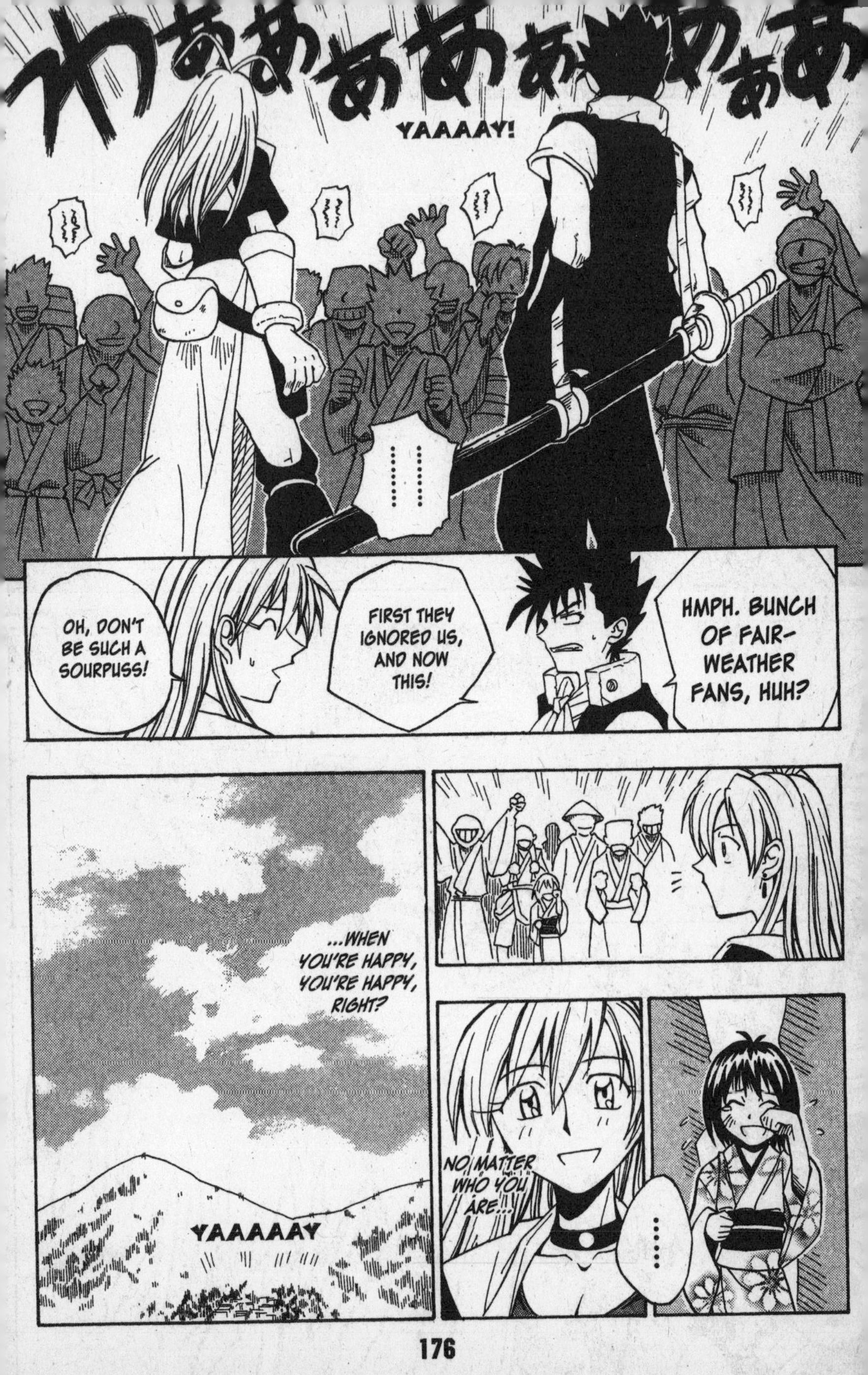
YAAAAY!
......
HMPH. BUNCH OF FAIR-WEATHER FANS, HUH?
FIRST THEY IGNORED US, AND NOW THIS!
OH, DON'T BE SUCH A SOURPUSS!
......
NO MATTER WHO YOU ARE...
...WHEN YOU'RE HAPPY, YOU'RE HAPPY, RIGHT?
YAAAAAY

Prelude to the Next Battle

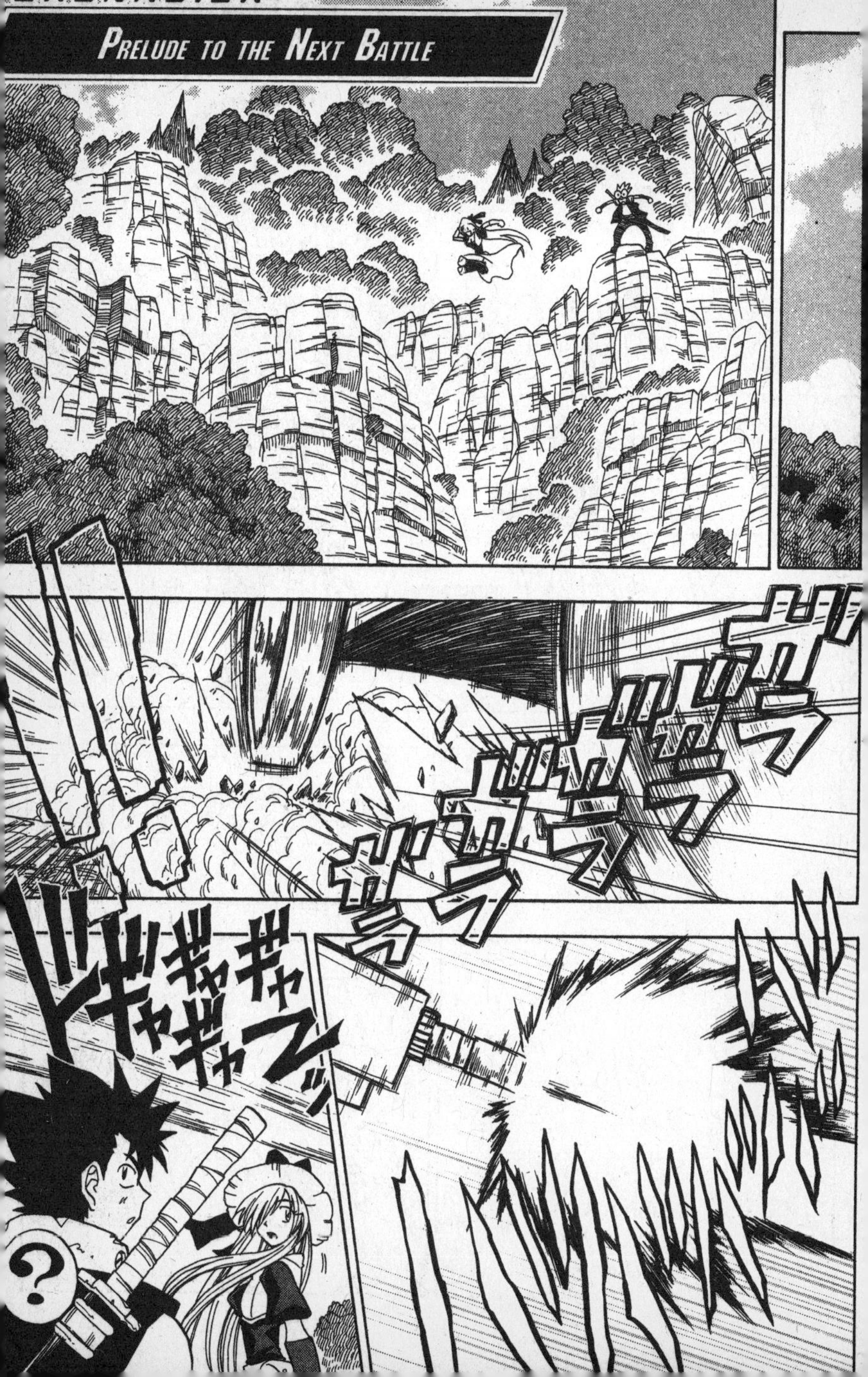
?

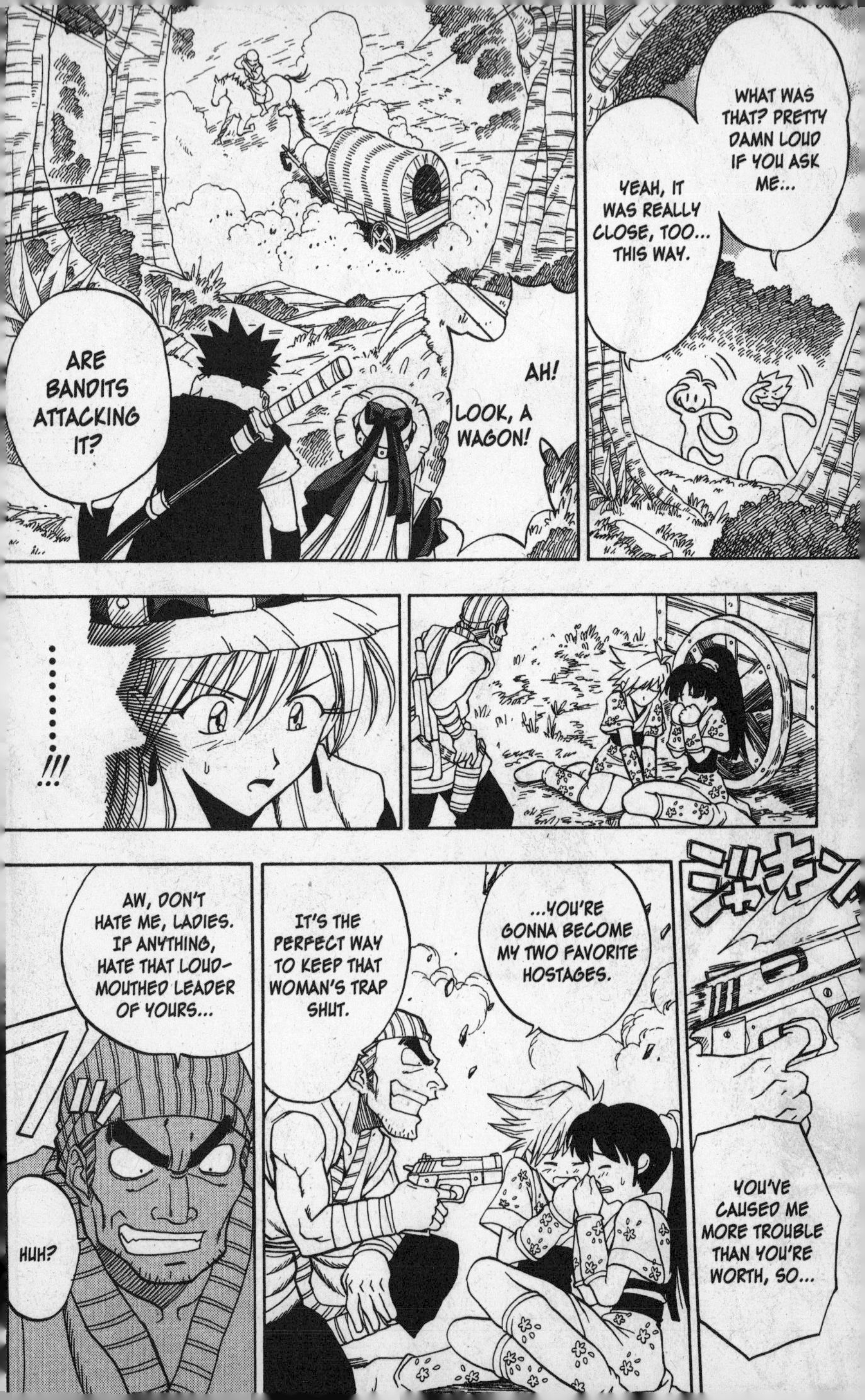
WHAT WAS THAT? PRETTY DAMN LOUD IF YOU ASK ME...
YEAH, IT WAS REALLY CLOSE, TOO... THIS WAY.
AH!
LOOK, A WAGON!
ARE BANDITS ATTACKING IT?
......!!!
ジャキン
YOU'VE CAUSED ME MORE TROUBLE THAN YOU'RE WORTH, SO...
...YOU'RE GONNA BECOME MY TWO FAVORITE HOSTAGES.
IT'S THE PERFECT WAY TO KEEP THAT WOMAN'S TRAP SHUT.
AW, DON'T HATE ME, LADIES. IF ANYTHING, HATE THAT LOUD-MOUTHED LEADER OF YOURS...
HUH?

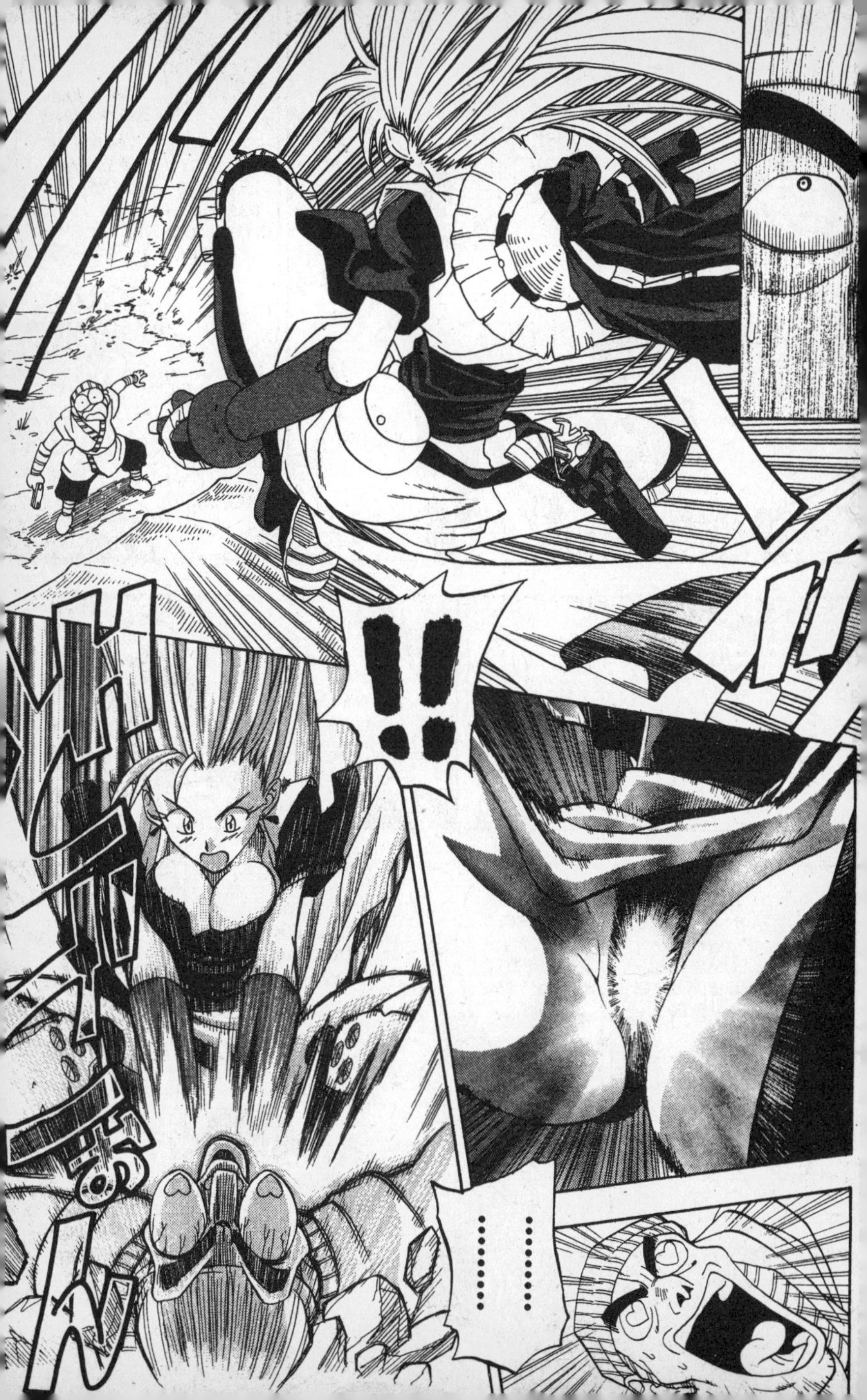
!!
......

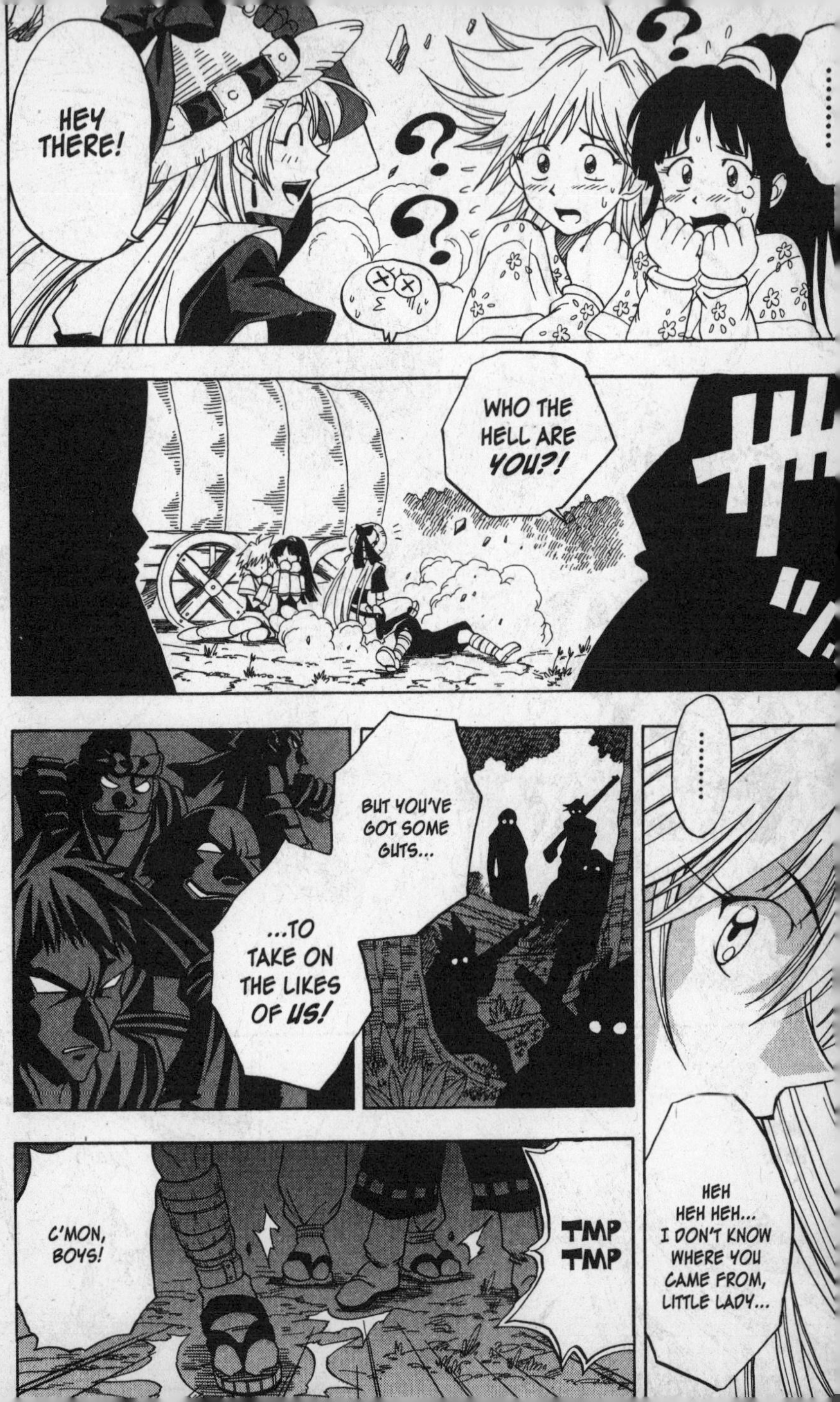
HEY THERE!
WHO THE HELL ARE YOU?!
......
HEH HEH HEH... I DON'T KNOW WHERE YOU CAME FROM, LITTLE LADY...
BUT YOU'VE GOT SOME GUTS...
...TO TAKE ON THE LIKES OF US!
TMP TMP
C'MON, BOYS!

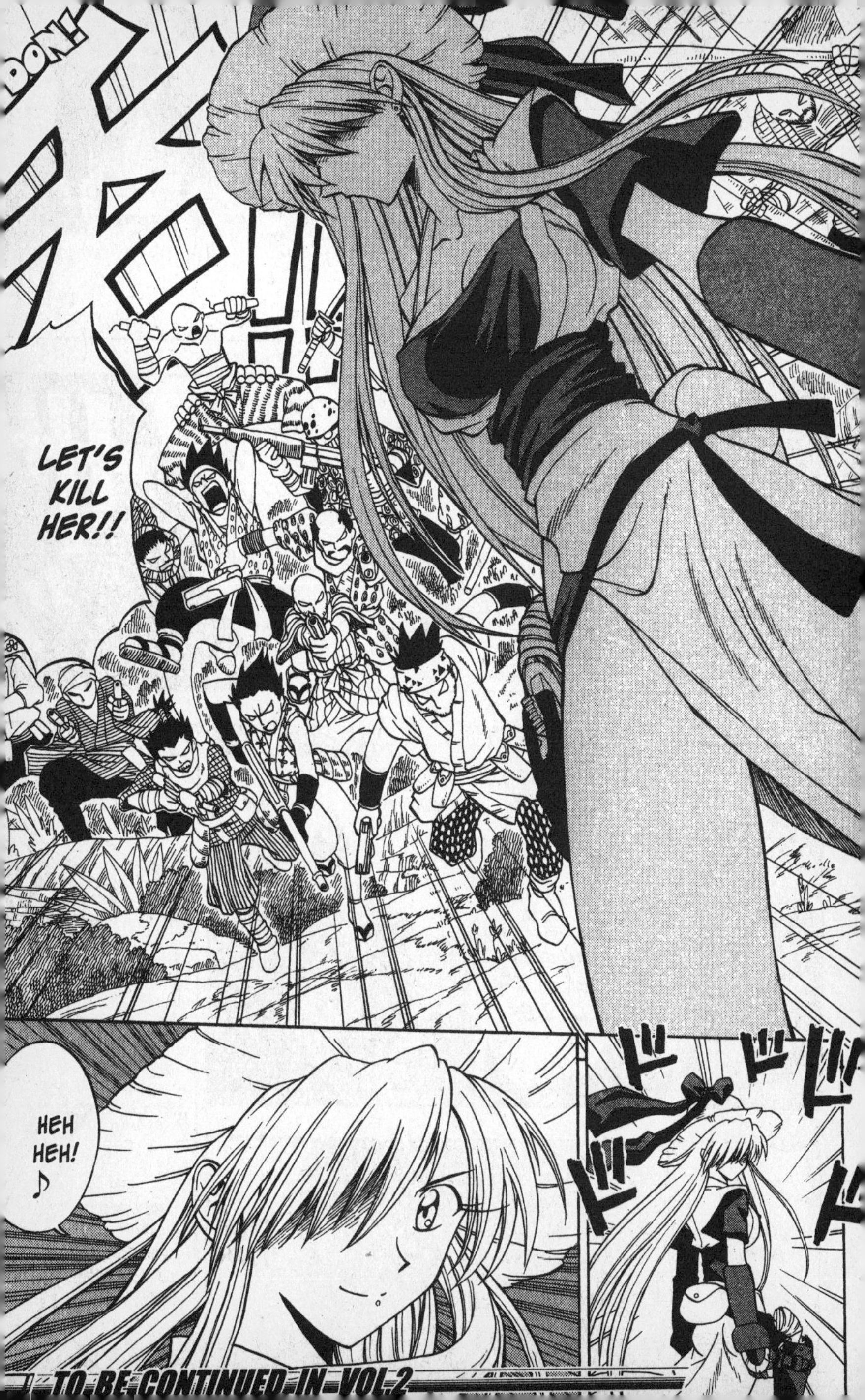
DON!
LET'S KILL HER!!
ドドドドド
HEH HEH! ♪
TO BE CONTINUED IN VOL.2

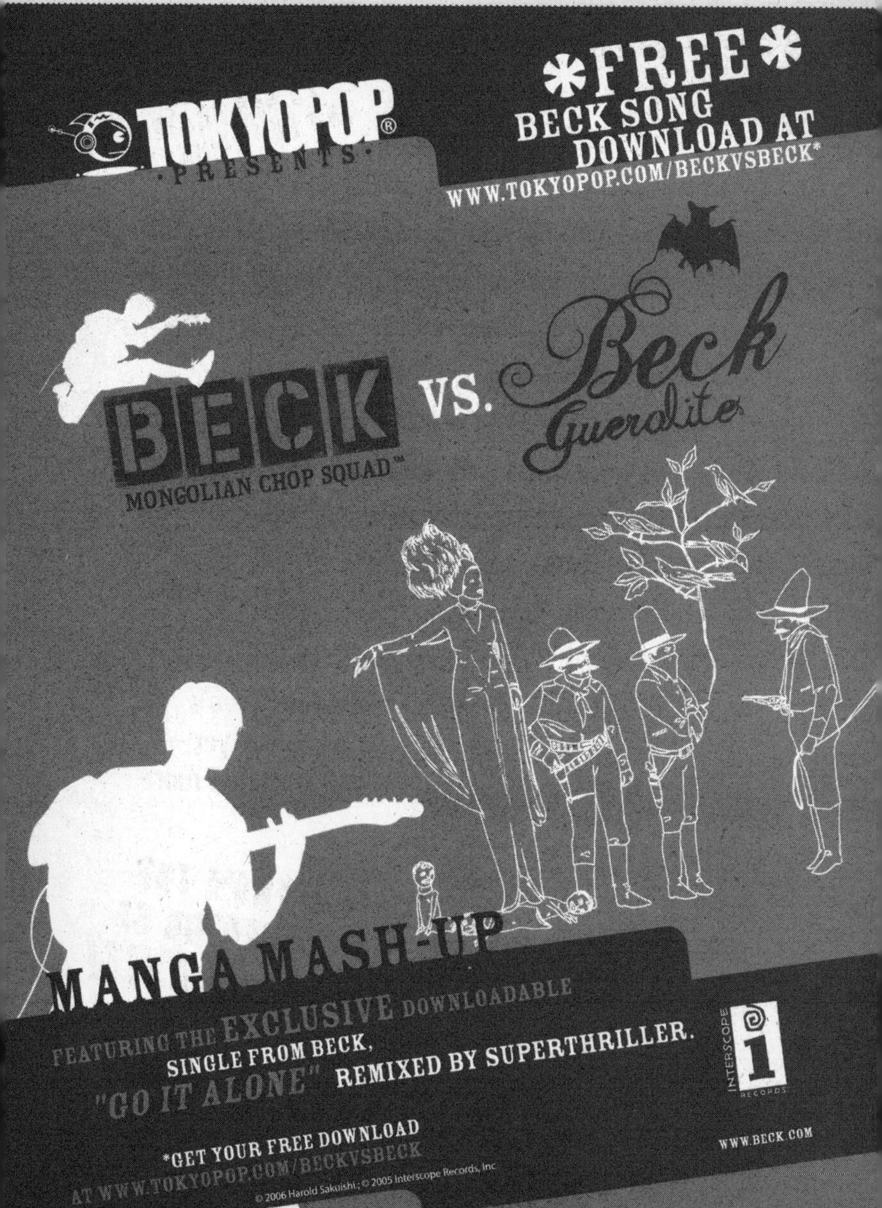
TOKYOPOP® PRESENTS
FREE
BECK SONG
DOWNLOAD AT
WWW.TOKYOPOP.COM/BECKVSBECK*
BECK
MONGOLIAN CHOP SQUAD™
VS.
Beck
Guerolito
MANGA MASH-UP
FEATURING THE EXCLUSIVE DOWNLOADABLE
SINGLE FROM BECK,
"GO IT ALONE" REMIXED BY SUPERTHRILLER.
*GET YOUR FREE DOWNLOAD
AT WWW.TOKYOPOP.COM/BECKVSBECK
© 2006 Harold Sakuishi; © 2005 Interscope Records, Inc.
INTERSCOPE RECORDS
WWW.BECK.COM

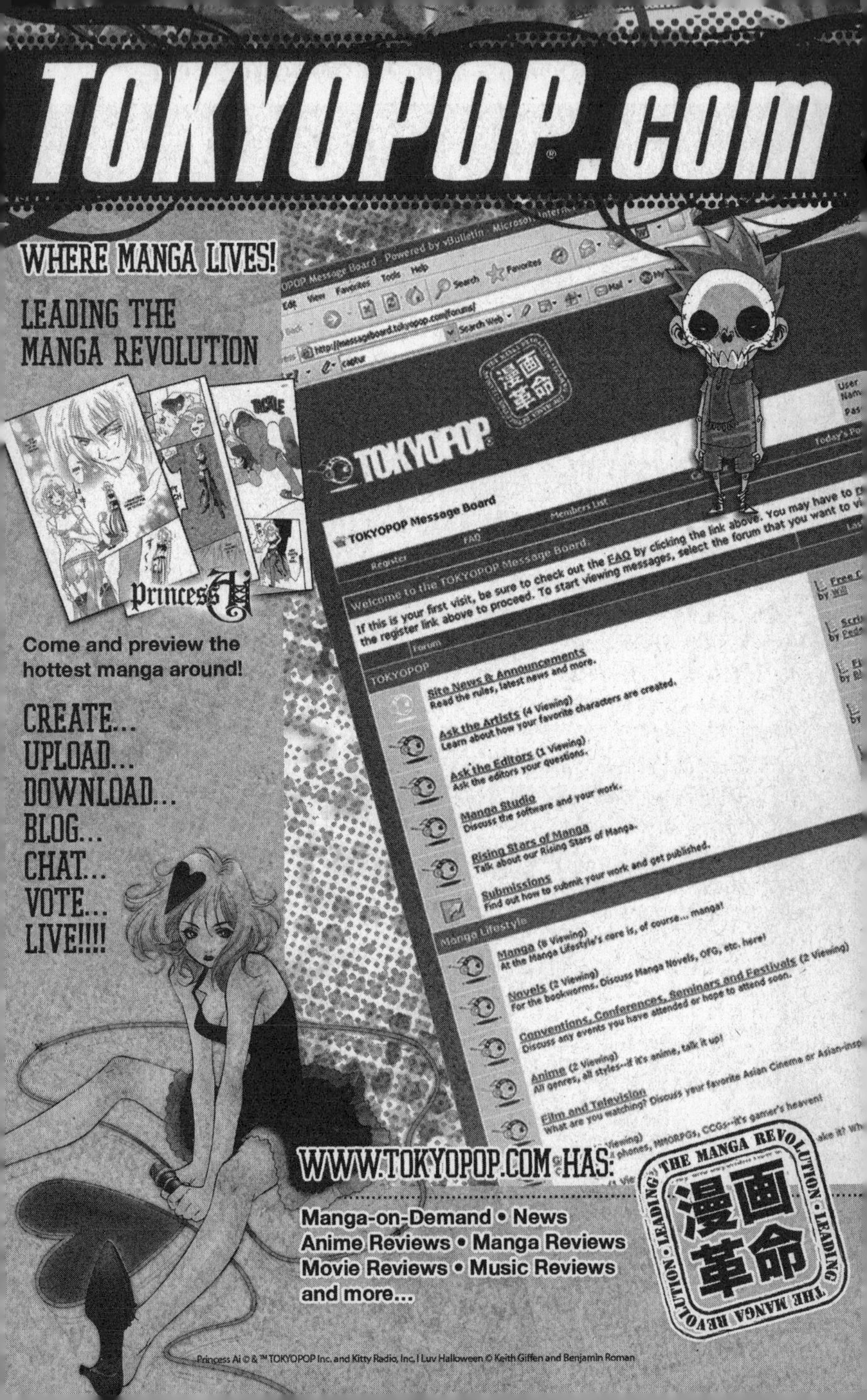
TOKYOPOP®.com
WHERE MANGA LIVES!
LEADING THE MANGA REVOLUTION
Princess Ai
Come and preview the hottest manga around!
CREATE...
UPLOAD...
DOWNLOAD...
BLOG...
CHAT...
VOTE...
LIVE!!!!
WWW.TOKYOPOP.COM HAS:
Manga-on-Demand • News
Anime Reviews • Manga Reviews
Movie Reviews • Music Reviews
and more...
THE MANGA REVOLUTION • LEADING • THE MANGA REVOLUTION • LEADING
漫画革命
Princess Ai © & ™ TOKYOPOP Inc. and Kitty Radio, Inc. I Luv Halloween © Keith Giffen and Benjamin Roman

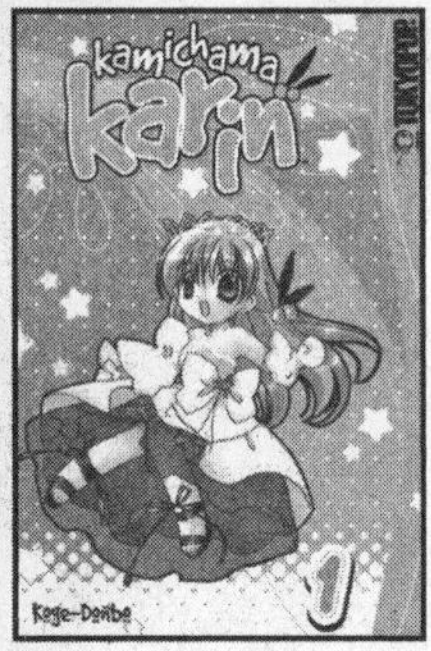
kamichama
karin
TOKYOPOP
1
Koge-Donbo

ROMANCE

Y
YOUTH AGE 10+

KAMICHAMA KARIN

BY KOGE-DONBO

This one was a surprise. I mean, I knew Koge-Donbo drew insanely cute characters, but I had no idea a magical girl story could be so darn clever. *Kamichama Karin* manages to lampoon everything about the genre, from plushie-like mascots to character archetypes to weapons that appear from the blue! And you gotta love Karin, the airheaded heroine who takes guff from no one and screams "I AM GOD!" as her battle cry. In short, if you are looking for a shiny new manga with a knack for hilarity and a penchant for accessories, I say look no further.

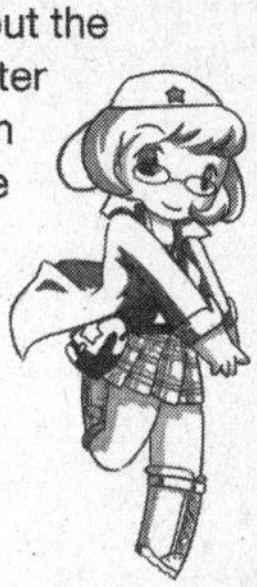

~Carol Fox, Editor

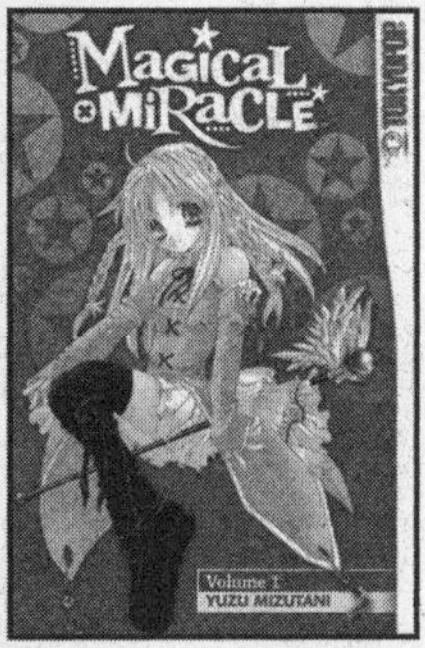
Magical
×Miracle
TOKYOPOP
Volume 1
YUZU MIZUTANI

FANTASY

T
TEEN AGE 13+

MAGICAL X MIRACLE

BY YUZU MIZUTANI

Magical X Miracle is a quirky—yet uplifting—tale of gender-bending mistaken identity! When a young girl must masquerade as a great wizard, she not only finds the strength to save an entire kingdom...but, ironically, she just might just find herself, too. Yuzu Mizutani's art is remarkably adorable, but it also has a dark, sophisticated edge.

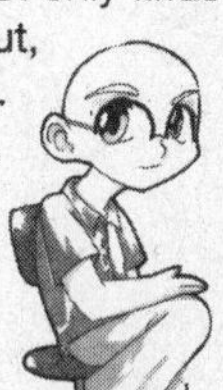

~Paul Morrissey, Editor

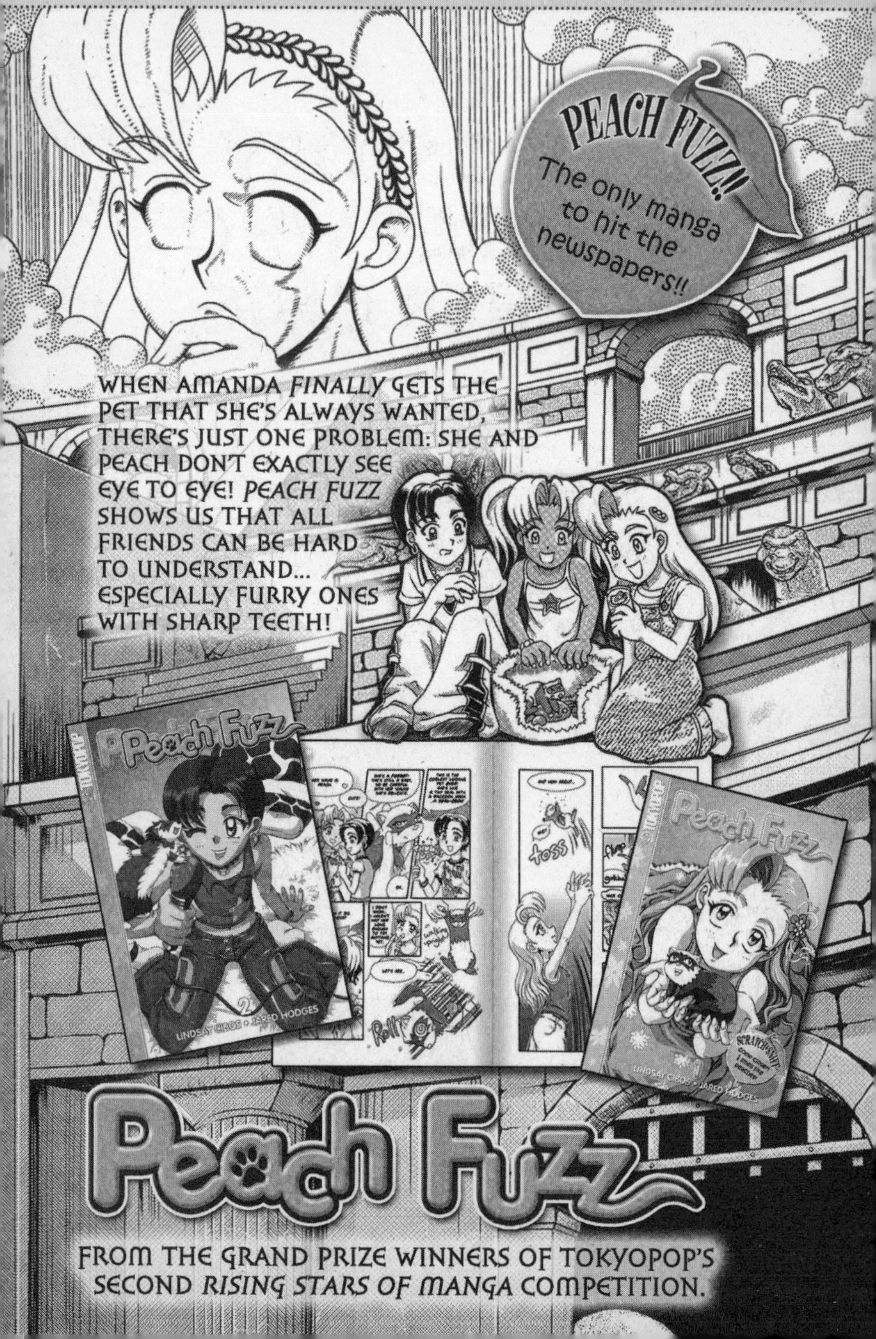
PEACH FUZZ!!
The only manga to hit the newspapers!!
WHEN AMANDA FINALLY GETS THE PET THAT SHE'S ALWAYS WANTED, THERE'S JUST ONE PROBLEM: SHE AND PEACH DON'T EXACTLY SEE EYE TO EYE! PEACH FUZZ SHOWS US THAT ALL FRIENDS CAN BE HARD TO UNDERSTAND... ESPECIALLY FURRY ONES WITH SHARP TEETH!
Peach Fuzz
TOKYOPOP
2
LINDSAY CIBOS • JARED HODGES
toss
Roll
Peach Fuzz
TOKYOPOP
LINDSAY CIBOS • JARED HODGES
Peach Fuzz
FROM THE GRAND PRIZE WINNERS OF TOKYOPOP'S SECOND RISING STARS OF MANGA COMPETITION.

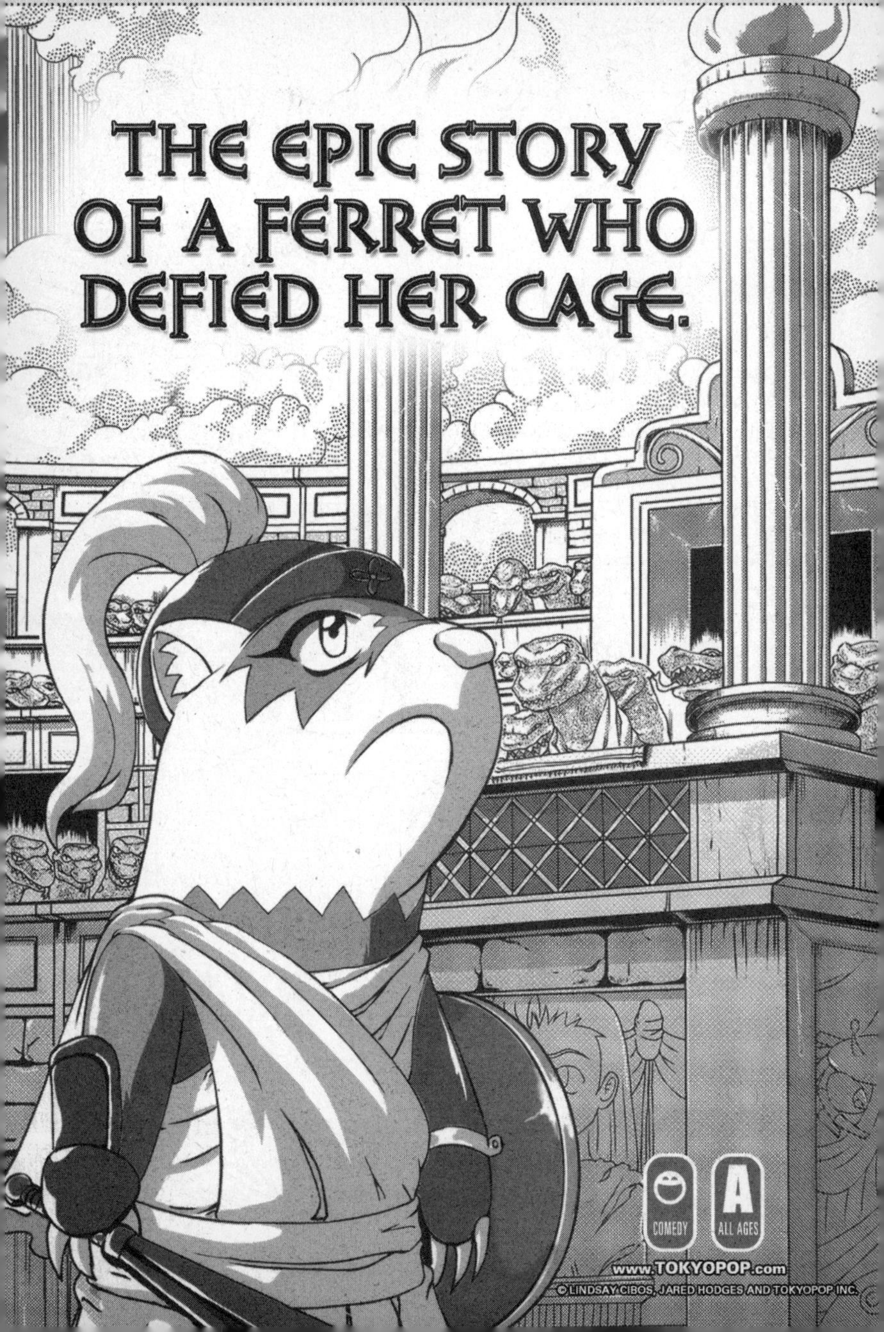
THE EPIC STORY OF A FERRET WHO DEFIED HER CAGE.
COMEDY
A
ALL AGES
www.TOKYOPOP.com
© LINDSAY CIBOS, JARED HODGES AND TOKYOPOP INC.

STOP!

This is the back of the book.
You wouldn't want to spoil a great ending!

This book is printed "manga-style," in the authentic Japanese right-to-left format. Since none of the artwork has been flipped or altered, readers get to experience the story just as the creator intended. You've been asking for it, so TOKYOPOP® delivered: authentic, hot-off-the-press, and far more fun!

DIRECTIONS

If this is your first time reading manga-style, here's a quick guide to help you understand how it works.

It's easy... just start in the top right panel and follow the numbers. Have fun, and look for more 100% authentic manga from TOKYOPOP®!